MICROPATTERNS

BOOKS BY DARREL MARTIN

FLY-TYING METHODS

MICROPATTERNS
Tying and Fishing the Small Fly

MICROPATTERNS

TYING AND FISHING
THE SMALL FLY

DARREL MARTIN

FOREWORD BY
JOHN GODDARD

PREFACE BY
TED LEESON

SWAN·HILL
PRESS

First published in the United States of America
by Lyons and Burford
First published in the UK in 1994
by Swan Hill Press
an imprint of Airlife Publishing Ltd

Portions of this text previously appeared in *Fly Rod & Reel* and
Fly Fishing & Fly Tying. I am pleased to acknowledge the
permission of these magazines to use material that originally
appeared in their pages.

British Library Cataloguing in Publication Data
A catalogue record for this book
is available from the British Library

ISBN 1 85310 542 2

Printed in the United States of America

Designed by M.R.P. Design

Swan Hill Press

an imprint of Airlife Publishing Ltd.
101 Longden Road, Shrewsbury SY3 9EB, England

For MIKE, whose field work greatly contributed to the text and with whom I never fish enough

For MICHELLE, who also loves all things small

For my wife and companion, SANDRA, who cleared the springs to make the words flow

And, once again, to the master of us all, Salmo trutta, whose shy shadow is the ring giver.

Contents

Acknowledgments

A sincere effort was made to credit original methods and patterns and to assure the accuracy of all statements made. With the legions of experimenting tyers, however, similar methods and patterns can evolve from different vises and credit errors can occur. Where a method or pattern has been attributed to several tyers and its origin is obscure, no credit has been granted.

Thanks must go to those tyers who submitted patterns that were not included due to space limitations; I appreciate their silent contribution. The following people and companies have been most generous with their time and talents. I wish to thank Ron Abby (Dyna-King), Paul D. Betters (Angler Sport Group), Alan Bramley (Partridge of Redditch), Marc Bale (Sage), William Black (Spirit River, Inc.), Leif Dorffel (O. Mustad & Son), Marty Downey (Cortland Line Co.), Luis Antunez Espada (Salmo), Kenneth Ferguson (Spirit River, Inc.), Peter Fisher, Don Green (Sage), Christopher Helm, Henry Hoffman (Whiting Farms-Hoffman Hackle), Ron Holloway, David Hughes, Stephen Kennerk (Rocky Mountain Dubbing), Bruce Kirschner (Sage), Lefty Kreh, Mel Krieger (G. Loomis), Wayne Luallen, Jamie Lyle (Sage), Frank Matarelli (Matarelli Tools), Thomas W. McCullough (Cortland Line Company), Craig Mathews (Blue Ribbon Flies), Ken Menard (Umpqua Feather Merchants), John Mingus, Skip Mortensen (O. Mustad & Son, USA), Sylvester Nemes, Deems Okamoto, Lars Ake Olsson, Jean-Paul Pequegnot, Datus C. Proper, Harry F. Ranger, Andy Renzetti (Renzetti, Inc.), Bruce Richards (Scientific Anglers/3M), Tom Rosenbauer (Orvis), Garry Sandstrom (The Morning Hatch), Tom Schmuecker (Wapsi Fly, Inc.), Shane Stalcup, Andrija Urban, Bas Verschoor, Bob Weet (Angler Sport Group), Dr. Thomas Whiting (Whiting Farms-Hoffman Hackle), Jeff Wieringa (J. W. Outfitters), Davy Wotton, Miloš Zeman (Bohemian Fly Fishers).

I would like to express a special appreciation to the following people whose friendship and scholarship added immensely to this text.

Marjan Fratnik: who introduced me to the river Unec.

John Goddard: who shared water and wisdom.

Rick Hafele: aquatic biologist, a river companion whose extensive entomological field data forms part of this text.

Ron J. Holloway: for presenting the challenge of the Martyr Worthy waters.

Dr. Gerald F. Kraft: Professor of Biology, Western Washington University, for the invaluable information on the chironomids.

Ted Leeson: for "stream rehabilitation," making glides out of this river of words. All the backpools and rapids are mine.

Dr. J. Stewart Lowther: a scholar of all things small, and the University of Puget Sound for the microscopy.

Nick Lyons: whose friendship and encouragement make books like this possible, and who cherishes "the very difficult business of fishing a small dry fly on glass-flat water."

Norman E. Norlander: a friend who translated the ideas into brass and steel.

Dr. Sherman B. Nornes: Professor of Physics, Emeritus, Pacific Lutheran University, the gentle piscator and scholar whose passionate study of hook and line made a significant contribution to this book.

Joze Ocvirk: a friend who shared the remarkable charm and challenge of Slovenian streams.

Edgar Pitzenbauer: a friend who spoke his wisdom beneath the tower.

Dr. Milan Pohunek: who shared his passion of patterns.

Dr. Bozidar Voljc: whose friendship and discussions became treasures.

Ron Wilton: a friend whose waters helped to write this book.

Taff and Madeleine Price: angling companions, with whom, as Chaucer would say, I have "crossed many a strange stream."

Foreword

I have known and fished with Darrel Martin for over twenty years and have come to know him very well. I first thought of him as a very quiet and unassuming person, but eventually realized that beneath his apparently gentle exterior lies a very different personality—the proper metaphor would surely be, "Slow water runs deep." In matters piscatorial, this sums up Darrel extremely well, for his depth of knowledge really is quite exceptional. He is not only an excellent fisherman but he has traveled extensively throughout Europe in recent years and is consequently on first-name terms with many of the leading fly fishers and fly dressers in England and the Continent. He has a very inquiring and inventive mind, and he delights in trying out new ideas or techniques pertaining to both fly fishing and fly tying. You can rest assured, however, that whenever he writes about these matters, his conclusions are always based on practical trials that he has undertaken himself rather than on theories, as so many writers seem to base their opinions today.

Although *Micropatterns*, as its title suggests, is basically about tying and fishing small flies, it also covers many subjects of general interest to all fly fishers and fly tiers. Some of the areas covered—for example, hooks—have never been analyzed in such depth before, and although some of this information is extremely technical, it will doubtless prove very valuable to those who may be interested in increasing their knowledge of the subjects covered. In addition, *Micropatterns* promotes many new and often radical ideas and techniques, some of which are fascinating. Dressing and fishing small flies— particularly those smaller than size #20—requires very special techniques. Many of these methods have only been perfected in recent years, and few fly fishers have a better knowledge of this subject than the author of this book. This subject has never been covered in any depth before, so I feel certain that *Micropatterns* will provide a major step forward in angling literature.

Apart from being a very knowledgeable and experienced fly fisher, Darrel Martin is also a supreme fly dresser; so any book written by him must be taken very seriously indeed, since within its covers will be found a wealth of sound advice and information that will help all of us—even the most experienced fly fishers—to become more adept.

—JOHN GODDARD
Cobham, Surrey
England

Preface

From an historical standpoint, there may in fact be no such thing at all as "fly fishing," for no fixed body of principles or practices has consistently defined the sport over time. The history of fishing artificial flies is nothing if not a chronicle of change, and the "tradition" of fly fishing, much as we might envision it as something uniform or static, has never stood still. In this perhaps paradoxical regard, modern fly fishing is remarkably traditional, for it perpetuates the oldest impulse in the sport—the propensity to adapt and transform itself.

Some of these changes are obvious—we travel to destinations and fish for species that would have astounded Izaak Walton. Other innovations are subtler, though more pervasive. In my fly-fishing lifetime, I have seen the evolution of two pivotal developments in modern trout angling. The first came with the widespread acceptance and use of nymphs, and a substantial volume of literature surrounding both natural insects and their imitations. The second, and more recent, innovation is the trout fisherman's growing reliance on small flies—what Darrel Martin calls "micropatterns."

A diverse set of forces has conspired to expand the popularity and use of small flies. Now, for instance, more than at any time in the past, it is technically feasible to do so. Fly-tying hooks in sizes 18 to 26 are readily available. Strong, fine tippet material has made fishing these tiny flies significantly more practical. We have rods and reels designed to cushion and protect these delicate tippets, and we have better lines for delivering the flies.

More has changed, however, than simply the tackle. We have changed many of our rivers as well, and so, altered their fish and fishing. In the United States, there are an estimated 80,000 dams. A lamentable number of these have destroyed salmonid habitat, but the tailwaters below some of these dams have created trout streams where there were none before, or improved existing river conditions, or at the very least, transformed their ecological characters. And above many of these same dams, vast impoundments of water have come into being and formed stillwater trout fisheries that are completely new.

Despite their obvious differences, the tailwaters and lakes do share some noteworthy characteristics—they are currently among the most popular domestic destinations; their trout grow at a staggering rate; and enormous numbers of small flies—*Chironomids*, *Tricos*, *Caenis*, *Baetis*, and micro-caddis—flourish in these newly created habitats. Tiny insects are becoming more important to today's fishermen because in many ways they are more important to today's fish.

Even on free-flowing rivers and natural lakes, micropatterns are playing an increasingly significant role. Decades of catch-and-release fishing have "educated" generations of trout. The fish have grown warier and cannier, less susceptible to ordinary patterns and methods. Catching them often requires fishing on a smaller and more careful scale, using tiny flies, longer leaders, more accurate casting, and a more studied approach.

Nowhere are these demands more pressing than on spring creeks, where the most discriminating of trout inhabit the most exacting of waters. Over two decades ago, Vince Marinaro's pioneering article, "The Hidden Hatch," explored the angling opportunities afforded by the hatches of tiny *Tricos* and *Caenis*, and since then spring-creek fishermen have routinely turned to micropatterns and small-fly techniques to take difficult fish under challenging conditions.

As a result, fishing small flies is no longer a technique of last resort or the province of the specialist. It has become essential to the versatile and successful fly fisherman.

Until now, however, the use of small flies has generally been little more than a footnote in the literature of fly fishing, examined, when it has been examined at all, primarily as a scaled-down version of tying and fishing larger flies. The publication of *Micropatterns* marks the first comprehensive treatment of small-fly fishing as a world of its own, an acknowledgment and exploration of the fact that tying and using tiny patterns make special demands on fishermen and tackle, require particular techniques and approaches, and, of course, involve special satisfactions.

Part of the real achievement of *Micropatterns* lies in the way that it explores two directions simultaneously. The book works inward to examine the details and minutiae of insects, trout streams, trout, fly patterns and materials, and fishing. At the same time it pushes outward, arranging these details in more comprehensive contexts of understanding, finally building a complete picture of small flies and small-fly fishing. This is not a reductive, algorithmic, "system" book. Rather, it is a "pattern" book—articulating patterns of imitations and fly tying, patterns of fishing, and patterns of problem solving on those waters where big, wise trout sip the tiniest of bugs.

Much here is superbly original. The results of computer-analyzed stress tests on small hooks, for instance, have never before been published, and they provide fascinating and surprising data that will prove invaluable to tyers. Internationally known as a fly tyer and fisherman, Darrel Martin presents a number of important ideas drawn from European fly fishing and emphatically dispels the notion that American anglers have nothing to learn from the Old World. From specific fly patterns and tying materials to the building and use of the ultra-supple "furled leader," *Micropatterns* offers useful information from across the Atlantic that is little known here. This book is as broad as it is deep, and it is monumentally both.

I've had the pleasure of watching Darrel Martin tie flies, of fishing with him, and of learning from him in many wonderful hours of conversation about angling. He is eclectic, iconoclastic, and in the very best sense of the term, a relentless reinventer of wheels. No fly-fishing practice or precept is too basic to escape questioning and testing, and in the process he sometimes discovers that conventional fly-fishing wisdom has got it all wrong. But what has always come through most clearly to me about Darrel Martin, even beyond the detail and scope of his knowledge, is his restless and overwhelming curiosity about anything that impinges on the life of a trout stream. And whether the medium is feathers and fur, pen and ink, photographic film, or words, his effort to understand what he sees invariably sheds a fascinating and instructive light.

Micropatterns was born from the same spirit of inquisitiveness. Its observations are keen, its insights revealing, and its advice enormously useful. And throughout, the book is suffused with its author's passion for the world of tying and fishing small flies, a world whose special density and texture make it a distinct "sport within a sport."

—**TED LEESON**
Corvallis, Oregon

*I*ntroduction

Viator: This is a very little hook.
Piscator: That may serve to inform you, that it is for a very little flie, and you must make your wings accordingly; for as the case stands it must be a little flie, and a very little one too, that must do your business.

> —*The Compleat Angler*
> Sir Izaak Walton and Charles Cotton
> (Part II, Chapter VI)

Heraclitus, the ancient Greek philosopher, once claimed that "You cannot step into the same river twice for new waters are ever flowing upon you." So it seems with rivers and books and angling. Both admired and abused for his philosophy, Heraclitus found comfort in change and saw the rushing water as a sensual symbol of eternal flux. Heraclitus recognized the moving water in all things.

It was J. C. Mottram, in *Fly Fishing*, who wrote that the angler, wading those moving waters, "wanders from experiment to experiment. Flies, guts, rods, are all tested in this way, and yet the solution, instead of coming nearer, seems, like the mirage, to keep receding before him as time passes by, until at last he must leave the problems unsolved, fortunately for the everlasting pleasure of those who follow."

Just when you understand something about tying and fishing the micro-pattern, the currents change. Much of the pleasure of the small fly comes from this change, this continual rediscovery. And there are some waters that are willing to teach us.

The chalkstream "mirror" at East Lodge flows slowly, its glazed surface obscuring the currents. Not long ago, I was granted three days on the mirror. The days became a three-act play in which I, a poor player, would strut and, eventually, fret my hours on the stage. The first day, fish rose here and there, the odd banker or cruiser. The evening finally brought rising trout to the mirror. A casual cast hooked a remarkably large and attractive trout. I brought him close, but my poor net could never capture him. He fought well, and the hook, bent in the struggle, came away. It was a grand fish with a corner lie on the far bank.

The next day, I bought a larger net and fished for that elusive trout. After my failure, I had an interest in him. I hunted him, taking now and then the odd trout. And then I saw him, sulking on the bottom of the bend, a proud creature that eluded me. He owned that river, moving neither to dry nor nymph. Perhaps you cannot fish for the same trout twice. That day, he only allowed me the honor of visiting his wildness. He would not rise.

On the final day, the mirror was bright and clear. As I caught and released other trout, I thought about my trout. Ron Wilton, the riverkeeper, was the first to find him rising rhythmically to midges. Now was the time to take a grand trout. I checked the camera and extra film. I tied on a fresh tippet and a midge tied on a small, strong hook. This would take him. I positioned myself to present the fly with minimal disturbance and drag. Extending the handle of the net, I laid it ready. I wanted to be certain that I could land him. A trout like that makes a summer's angling. And it would make me feel as though I had some answers.

I cautiously measured a cast over my bank, rather than the water, so as not to disturb him. I did not want to overcast and spook him. Then I pushed a soft cast to him. Too short. Another careful cast and my pattern drifted over him. But he took another, more tempting offering. Here was a trout that could convince an angler that exact, minute imitation was essential. Yet, he sometimes rose indiscriminately to a variety of insects—duns, spinners, midges. He rose regularly, hour after hour. No amount of casting, unless heavily done, put him down. He rejected patterns and tippets that would hold him. He rose to naturals next to artificials, time after time. He continually rose to naturals next to my empty drifts.

Another cast. The leader drove out, turned over, and dropped the fly a foot in front. He looked, rose, and took. I struck and recovered slack line. I would fight him from the reel. Why he took remains a mystery. There are times when trout take us more than we take them. Such a lovely, lithe, and muscled creature took my fly. A bent rod united me to a powerful, square-tailed, brightly rosetted and stippled brown. I desperately wanted to capture him forever on film and return him to the water. I wanted him as a memory of a summer's day.

With deliberate power, my trout entered the central stream and slowly worked upriver. I gave side pressure to bring him home. But he wouldn't come. I grabbed my net and, with arched rod and tense tippet, escorted him upstream. *When he comes close to the bank*, I thought, *I will put my net under and lift.* He drove, with determined calm, midstream and upstream. Then, with a wild shake of his head, the leader and fly snapped back, limp and defeated. He was a better trout than I was an angler.

Later, when the winter rains rose false trout rings on my window, Ron Wilton called to say that *my* trout was spawning. Perhaps, my trout would produce others, that other anglers would come to regret.

This book is a product of failure—of large trout that take naturals only, of seemingly perfect presentations gone awry, of riseless matched hatches, of faults in tackle and technique. Failure teaches more than success. Success teaches small things; failure teaches everything else. If our intention is to catch fish, we should use the appropriate tackle. Small flies are attractive. But to present a small fly to all trout under all conditions is affectation. I want to land and release trout, so I use the most appropriate patterns and the strongest tippets I can. Breaking off fish is not sport. Instead of *far and fine* angling, I want short and thick. But often enough, trout are insensitive to my desires, insisting instead on the delicate and the diminutive. Is the problem in the pattern or the presentation? Perhaps the problem is too complex for a simple answer. Yet difficult trout, rising everywhere but to my fly, disturb and challenge me. They make few mistakes. If I cast often enough over a rising trout, mere time may result in a take, but that isn't an answer, just an accident, a temporary tactic. All the original questions remain. The trout know, but they are born to it. I am still learning.

This book is an attempt to solve some of the difficulties associated with small flies, large trout, and slow water. Perhaps written more for the author than for the reader, it presents my own struggles of designing and dressing small flies, of selecting tackle, of casting and presenting the small fly, and of landing the large trout that rise to them.

Naturally, what makes a fly *small* is contingent and relative. To the pocket-water angler in the West, a size 18 may be small. To the tail-water devotee who routinely fishes size 20 midges, 24s and 26s are small. For the purpose here, the small fly begins at 18, and the dividing line is not entirely arbitrary nor without historic precedent. The average fly used in the American Rockies is about a size 14. Each year the fly seems to shrink. Standard patterns that were 14, 16, and 18 are now tied in 18, 20, and 22. Thus a size 18 will correspond to the average angler's notion of the *start* of the small fly. More experienced anglers, however, will tie a 20 or 22 to their tippets. More importantly, aquatic insects seem to observe the magic number 18 as well. A hook of this size measures about 6 millimeters (about a quarter of an inch) and an enormous number of insects will be this length and smaller. Furthermore, as we shall see, there is also an historic precedent for 18 as the beginning of the small.

Finally, though this is probably more perception than truth, size 18 constitutes a threshold at which the problems of dressing and angling "multiply like villainy." Size 16 patterns are relatively easy to dress, to track on the water: They allow the use of relatively strong tippets and offer the trout a good gap. But the drop to 18 seems beyond the pale, the beginning of a different sport for the fisherman and, sometimes, for the trout.

There are various reasons why small patterns may work better than larger ones. Many of the reasons may be traced directly to the insects themselves. Looking at the head waters of streams, the insects are larger. As you move into the lower sections of river, you find slower water, finer substrate, and a change in insect community: They are smaller. In the head waters, the substrata and interstitial niches are larger; large insects can hide. But in the lower, slower river, in the smaller substrata, large insects lack security. There are exceptions, of course. The larger *Hexagenia* solves the problem by burrowing. One characteristic of a spring creek is the slower water, finer drift and preponderance of smaller insects. The river continuum theory professes that the insect community correlates to the size of the substrata. Dragonflies, hellgrammites, and stoneflies are the larger herbivores and carnivores. They consume the richest foods and grow large. In "the peanut butter and bread theory," the decomposed leaves are the bread while the organic slime, the periphyton, fungi, and bacteria, is the peanut butter smeared on the leaves. In the lower water, the larger particles are sieved out so the drift is finer. The small net-spinning caddis, with narrow head and consequently narrower mandibles, weaves a delicate and diminutive net for fine particles. Slow, "fine water" makes small insects. Alfred Ronald notes that ". . . a small fly is usually employed when the water is fine, because the fish is then better enabled to detect an imitation and because a small fly is more easily imitated. The resemblance of each particular colour, etc., is not required to be so exact as in the case of a large fly."

At any one time in a stream, insects 18 and smaller will be more plentiful. Stream studies indicate that nearly one-half of the available insects are midges. Small insects are more prevalent in the drift and, consequently, more available to trout. Large insects, heavier and stronger, are more able to stay on the bottom. And most insects, size 18 and larger, were, at one time, smaller. In brief, most macroinsects were, at one time, microinsects. It seems that the smaller the insect, the more abundant it is.

As trout receive greater angling pressure and achieve greater selectivity, they often require smaller and smaller patterns. Conventional wisdom affirms that the smaller and more realistic the pattern, the better the angler must be. It seems at times, however, that the more generic the pattern, the more likely the take. There are other times when a trout can be remarkably selective to size, shape, and even color. Some waters demand that their large, muscular trout be taken on tender tippets and fine hooks. Selective trout seem less threatened by a small pattern. Often anglers have confidence in receiving more takes (even if they are not confident in hooking and landing large trout) with smaller patterns.

Last, small flies are often successful due to the particular requirements of tying and trouting. As patterns become smaller, so do the defects in color, proportion, and silhouette. Instead of creating more realistic imitations for fastidious fish, a tyer merely ties small. Micropatterns simply reduce, minimize the inherent deficiencies of imitative tying. Pattern errors shrink, making shy, streamwise trout less wary.

Moreover, the micropattern reverberates through the equipment we use. It demands finer, stronger, less conspicuous tippets, longer and more pliant leaders, lighter and more delicate fly lines—all that fosters less surface disturbance and more natural drifts.

Fly fishing, of course, is more than trout taken; it is how they are taken. Trout are not the only ones who may develop a taste for small flies. For the angler, tying and casting the small fly is pleasant in itself. Paul Schullery credits Vincent Marinaro's *A Modern Dry-Fly Code* as the "the symbolic beginning of American fly fisher's fascination with what Marinaro called *minutiae*, those hordes of tiny insects that had always interested a few fisherman but were ignored by most." Ed Shenk, Charles Fox, Bill Pfeiffer, Ed Koch, and Bing Lempke all pioneered patterns that were "next to nothing."

A twenty-inch trout on a size-20 pattern is success in the highest degree. There is pleasure in the bone flats, pleasure in wild steelhead, but as angling becomes smaller, it becomes richer. The reduced scale challenges the tying and the trouting, revealing a new world of complexities, textures, and density of details. This is as true for the waters as it is for the tying and fishing.

Tying is a creative process where even scraps of ideas may have value. T. R. Henn, in *Practical Fly-Tying*, describes the pleasured pain of tying. "This, then, is the joy of what I have tried to describe: an art not without frustration; easy, but difficult to carry out supremely well (as Clausewitz wrote of war); perpetually filled with excitement and interest, because it remains an art, being only partially a craft, and somewhat remotely a science; touching all sorts of stray activities outside itself: and, above all, forcing the fisherman . . . to extend his mental investigations ever further and further, and yet force his physical skills to keep pace with them." Sometimes I think that tying the micropattern is akin to Zen archery, where hitting the target is irrelevant. The essence is the process. *Ligo, ergo sum.* "I tie, therefore I am." And, at other times, I think that tying the small fly is nothing more than wrapping scraps around bent steel. I don't think I will ever be able to tell the difference.

There is some of the past in this book. Although I own few, I love old tying books. They seem to possess a wealth of information that is best shared. G. P. R. Pulman's *Vade-Mecum of Fly Fishing for Trout* (1851) has "plain and copious instructions for the manufacture of artificial flies" and insightful comments on imitation, materials, and "humouring the fly" upon the water. H. G. McClelland's *The Trout Fly Dresser's Cabinet of Devices* (first published in 1898) is replete with backward patterns, detached bodies, and theories on ribbing, hook penetration, and dyeing. A *Companion to Alfred Ronalds' Fly Fishing Entomology*, a canvas wallet with extracts from Ronalds' work and actual patterns, matches the season's hatches. "Flies for April: The Golden Dun Midge, The Grannom, The Iron Blue Dun. . . ." Most are specks, some emaciated by time. A few parchment pockets are vacant, left only with a penciled inscription: "This beautiful fly is on the water generally from ten o'clock until three, and is one of our best flies." On blank pockets, meant to be filled by the angler, are scribbled notations: "Hare's Ear" and "Greenwell's Glory." But the hare is fled and the glory gone. What faith, what assurance there was in pattern and nature so long ago. With that handsome wallet, an angler might approach a long season with confidence. I would like to capture some of that ancient charm in my vise. That too is part of the pleasure of fly fishing. That too is part of the truth in the adage: *Piscator non solum piscatur.* "There is more to fishing than fish."

At the end of my copy of Roger Woolley's *Modern Trout Fly Dressing* (1932) there is an inked comment: "Grayling Pattern—Size 0 long hook, body of soft otter underpelt, dyed blaze orange in picric acid and red ink. Eight or nine turns bright ginger hackle, wound centrally, dividing thorax from abdomen, from the neck of the wild jungle fowl, ribbing none, hot-orange tying silk." Whose pen scribbled that, what skills tied it, and what waters welcomed it?

Then we cast our patterns upon the waters. They are usually the slower waters, the pooled backwaters and rippling eddies of large' rivers, the silent stillwaters, the gliding chalk streams, and the spring creeks. In a tactical sense, these are the most difficult waters with the most difficult fish. These are waters where late-summer browns cruise the shallows, where rainbows tip to tricos in the backpools. Such angling requires light lines, long rods and, usually, small flies. This is the world of weed-choked channels, muscular trout, luxurious hatches, and water woven into corduroy currents. Such places, of course, have their rewards—revealed fish, restricted wading, short casts, abundant insects, and frequent rises. But these are often necessities, given the difficulties of selective trout, refused patterns, and the numerous hatches that require close matching. Here is the world of emergers, of fine tippets, of sparse patterns, of problems and solutions. But no matter how much we know, our pattern and drift may be refused.

An angler does not go to these waters to display talent. Anglers don't fish them to swagger their skills. These are waters where one rise is success, where hooking and releasing two or three trout is an exquisite day. As we duel trout, they parry with refusals. Our thrusts of line only make wiser adversaries. These are silent, enigmatic waters that challenge us with their perplexing and endless possibilities. Dwelling in such waters, the wise and poetic Water Rat from *The Wind in the Willows* perhaps understood them best: "It's my world and I don't want any other. What it hasn't got is not worth having, and what it doesn't know is not worth knowing."

This book is about tying and fishing the small fly as taught by the waters and fish, albeit imperfectly and incompletely. Though there is much said here about fly dressing, this is not merely a tying book. It is about methods and materials, history and hooks, rods and reels, trout and water. For complex and unconventional patterns, illustrations clarify the particular methods. Some patterns require extended discussion and illustration, others do not. Nevertheless, most methods and patterns pass beyond standard fare. Many traditional patterns may be tied on small hooks, but there are enough books that describe the Adams, whether size 12 or 20. I have attempted to present less conventional, more creative patterns and a greater latitude in approaches, if for no other reason than to acknowledge the Heraclitan inevitability that today's water may not necessarily be tomorrow's water. Water transforms everything it touches with abiding change, imbuing all with its own fluid nature. Fishing the small fly has something of the river's paradox. It is complex and simple, frustrating and fascinating.

This book is my modest attempt to understand and solve some of the problems of the sport within the sport, tying and fishing the small fly. Although today's river may never flow tomorrow, we still want to wade and cast.

—**Darrel Martin**
Tacoma,
Washington

A NOTE ON THE LINE DRAWINGS AND PHOTOGRAPHS

Line drawings generally present a clearer picture of the tying process than photographs. The material that is mounted first is drawn closest to the hook shank. The tying thread is purposely enlarged to show its placement. Not all thread wraps are illustrated, nor do the drawings always depict the correct diameter or number of fibers. Miscellaneous and obvious wraps are omitted for procedural clarity—complete drawings would only clutter and obscure the tying process. The text should clarify all requirements of materials and methods. Only procedures that are complex or unique have been illustrated. It is expected that the reader has adequate tying skills. To preserve detail, some photographic tying sequences within the text show hooks larger than size 18.

$\mathcal{T}$he Insects

The following insects often create those hidden, but significant, hatches. Identifying the small insect poses special problems. Some have furtive habits. Some are rendered inconspicuous by camouflaging themselves with silt or debris. Some are completely enclosed in silk or rock cases. Some are so small that magnification is required for identification. Few small insects have conspicuous features. They often look alike. Their sheer size reduces their differences.

It is claimed that three-fourths to nine-tenths of all insects are less than 6.5 millimeters long. Their size alone makes them numerous and significant. Perhaps there is truth in the assertion that the smaller it is, the more numerous it is and the more significant it is. Many of these small insects inhabit the clear, slow, selective waters—the spring creeks, lakes, and rivers.

The small mayflies, such as the *Caenis*, the *Tricorythodes*, and the *Baetis*, are likely to be familiar to most fly fishers. Fly fishing has always been disproportionately concerned with mayflies, hence even the smaller species fall within the purview of most anglers. The particular profile of small mayflies makes them visible on the water. Furthermore, the patterns used to imitate them are often merely shrunken versions of larger, standard patterns. Other small insects, however, may not be as familiar to the angler—the Dance Fly, the Reed Smuts, and the Microcaddis. Even the common Chironomid deserves greater understanding and more effective imitations.

An angler identifies an insect for various reasons. A captured dun may give a clue to nymph behavior and later to spinner fall. Most of us capture insects to match them at the vise. Size, color and silhouette, the imitative trinity, are the strongest links to our patterns. Sometimes all elements of the trinity are critical, other times, one or two. Yet nothing is lost by such imitation, and much may be gained. The ensuing discussion of insect morphology and behavior enables an angler to identify and match the important small insects encountered.

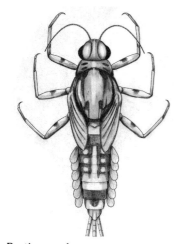

Baetis *nymph*

Pseudocloeon *nymph*

BAETIDAE

The baetidae, including the genus *Baetis*, *Pseudocloeon*, *Cloeon*, *Callibaetis*, and *Centroptilum*, are widespread and adaptable to various waters. They commonly hatch from March to November, but may sporadically appear throughout the year. Except for the nymphs of the *callibaetis*, which may be as large as 12 millimeters, these darting swimmers generally range from 3 to 9 millimeters, averaging approximately 5 millimeters. The nymphs are typically small and cylindrical. The adults vary in size, but generally are small with reduced venation, and some genera lack hind wings. Although found throughout North America, they thrive in rich, alkaline spring creeks. *Baetis* live in a variety of static and moving waters, including mountain streams, meandering rivers, and spring creeks. They may constitute a major population of bottom dwellers in a system. *Baetis* are among the most common insects taken in drift samples. In North America, the genus *Baetis* may be the only mayflies present in high mountain streams. Sometimes called "minnow mayflies," these streamlined, swimming nymphs have long antennae, usually two or three times head width. The hind wing pads are usually minute. Plate-like gills are present on abdominal segments 1–7, 1–5, or 2–7. Posterior abdominal segments 8 and 9 rarely have posterolateral spines. The slender, streamlined nymphs dart about in subaquatic vegetation. They perch and forage among the subaquatic foliage with long, slender legs.

THE NYMPH

Although the *baetis* nymphs emerge rapidly, they often float lengthy distances before the duns struggle free. The duns accumulate along banks and back eddies where trout "smut" the hapless, drowned duns. In slow, clear water, trout often take time to study the emerger or the exactness of the imitation.

The Baetidae produce the majority of significant small mayfly hatches, ranging from size 18 to 24. Some species, such as the *Callibaetis* (6 to 12 millimeters), are longer. The Little Quills from the Baetidae family often preempt the more important hatches of larger mayflies. The Baetidae are multibrooded, emerging several times during the season. The duns can carpet the waters, making these small quills important to all anglers. Selectivity often depends on the abundance and availability of the insect.

THE ADULT

The eyes of the male are stalked and turbinate (somewhat similar to an inverted cone); the eyes of the female, small and undivided. The hind wings are reduced, veinless, or absent. Two tails are present. Marginal veinlets of the forewing are paired and costal cross veins at the base are entirely lacking. Adults characteristically wag their abdomen from side to side. Spinners swarm at eye level over stream and lake banks. They are multigenerational, and a species that emerges in April, for example, may also emerge in July and later in October. Such proliferation makes the Baetis an ubiquitous and significant pattern.

The Blue-Winged Olive is a title granted to several small *Baetis* and *Pseudocloeon* duns. However, not all *Baetis* are olive. The dusty gray *Callibaetis* is important in the West, especially the *Callibaetis coloradensis* and *Callibaetis pacificus*.

Frank Sawyer's Pheasant Tail Nymph, an olive nymph, and the Gray Goose, a pale watery nymph, imitate the *Baetis'* slender, cylindrical body and prominent tail. Sawyer notes, in *Nymphs and the Trout*, that "none of my patterns has anything included in the dressing to suggest legs. When swimming nymphs are indeed swimming, they do so with the legs tucked in closely to the body, to, in fact, bring about a streamlined effect. The tail is the propulsion unit with these insects, which acts to propel, and also to steer." Sawyer believed that a prominent tail is desirable in the nymph patterns. *Baetis* nymphs dart through the water by rapidly flicking their abdomen and tail up and down. Some have a propensity to drift in the current. Nymph patterns should be fished with short and swift, nervous darting twitches near weedbeds, boulders, and weed channels. As some *Baetis* are highly adapted to rapid currents, where they cling to the top of stones, nymph patterns may be especially effective in riffles and rapids.

Most small patterns lack weight and proper water entry; they do not sink or swim well. Sawyer's Pheasant Tail Nymph tied traditionally with fine wire is an excellent solution. When tying nymphal imitations, incorporate the principal features: a slender, cylindrical, minnow-like body; a prominent tail (from one-half to full body length), and small wing pads (contrasting dark wing pads may make the pattern more enticing).

FAMILY CAENIDAE

The smallest of the mayflies, the cosmopolitan Caenidae—the Snowflake Mayflies or Angler's Curse—occurs in a variety of waters, usually waters warmer and slower than Trico waters. A mature nymph is a minuscule 2 to 8 millimeters excluding tails. The *Caenis*, the *Tricorythodes*, and the *Brachycercus* all have enlarged second gills. Their respiratory systems allow them to tolerate silt and sluggish currents. Unlike the triangular gills of the *Tricorythodes*, the *Caenis* and *Brachycercus* have squared or rectangular gill plates. Furthermore, the *Brachycercus* is further distinguished by the three prominent tubercles on its head. Mature Caenidae nymphs usually have minute hairs and conspicuous black wing pads. Their size and silty camouflage protect them from predators as they cling to plants or clamber along the bottom. Collected in scoops of silt or marl, they are nearly invisible until they move.

Genus *Caenis*

The Nymph

Smaller than the *Tricos*, the *Caenis* nymphs have an enlarged (operculate), rectangular second gill. The three-tailed, robust nymph has no hind wing pads. The forelegs are nearly as long as the middle and hind legs, whereas

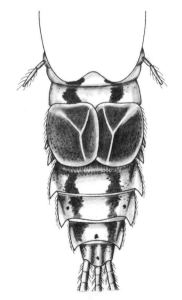

Caenis *nymph: operculate gill*

prominent posterolateral spines appear on the middle abdominal segments. Coloration tends toward light brown or tan. They usually inhabit the slower, silty waters and back pools. According to Fred L. Arbona, the *simulans* is the most common species found in North American trout waters. Caenidae commonly occur in still waters.

THE ADULT

The adults have a single pair of oval, clear, wide wings with few cross veins. Wing width is usually two-thirds their length. The only other insects of value to the angler lacking hind wings are the *Pseudocloeon* and *Cloeon*. The male has three long tails; the female, three short tails. Body colors tend toward buff, tan or yellow. They are sporadic evening emergers, often with remarkable density. Emergence usually occurs in late afternoon or at night. The nymph floats to the surface in shallow water. The subimago promptly ruptures the nymphal shuck and takes wing. Within five or six minutes after emergence, the subimago molts to imago. Hatches occur in June and July with erratic and sporadic hatching in May and September. Dusk hatches may be dense with ovipositing at night. Some *Caenis* appear to have positive phototropism; I have observed *Caenis* gathering around camp lamps at dusk and during dark on the shallow alkaline lakes of Eastern Washington. Idaho's Silver Creek, near Sun Valley, has heroic hatches of Caenidae.

Genus *Brachycercus*

THE NYMPH

The genus *Brachycercus* nymph displays its tail in a scorpion-like stance when captured. The body is somewhat flattened with short forelegs. The small (3 to 8 millimeters long) *Brachycercus* nymph has a nearly imperceptible, sluggish crawl. More slender than the *Tricorythodes* or *Caenis* nymph, the *Brachycercus* nymph has rounded gill covers and three cone tubercles (knoblike projections) on the head. Unlike the surface tapestry of the *Trico* duns and spinners, the *Brachycercus* produce only minor hatches. Stream nymphs, covered by a fine silt coat, inhabit the shallow waters (often only three or four inches deep) near the banks. Generally they do not form major Western hatches.

THE ADULT

The adult stage is very brief, lasting just a few hours. Depending on the species, the subimagoes emerge either at dawn or dusk. When duns or spinners are taken, the imitative problems lie principally in hook size, usually 24, and hook strength. Tying and fishing the Caenidae is often regarded as the definitive micropattern experience.

Imitation of the Caenidae has always proven a problem. The patterns usually require a hook smaller than size 20, predominantly sizes 24 to 28. Due to the small size, a hook with heavy wire and adequate gap should be selected.

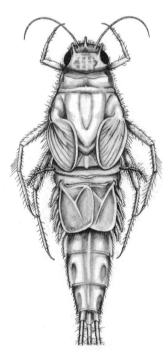

Brachycercus *nymph*

Dun and spinners patterns often include a synthetic wing, a split tail of barbs or Microfibetts, a thread body, a minute mole-fur thorax, and appropriate hackle. Such patterns, despite their size, are readily tied if materials and wraps are minimal. Thread patterns, such as Datus Proper's Hackle Wing and Tatsuhiro Saido's Trimmed Hackle Dun, may prove effective.

THE CHIRONOMIDAE

The *Chironomids*, or nonbiting midges, have one or more generations per year and are the most prolific and widespread of all aquatic insects. It is claimed that Chironomidae inhabit half the available waters and, when present, there will be 50 or more species. There are over 100 genera and over 2,500 species in North America. Larval density of 50,000 per square meter is not unusual and may be exceeded. Super-rich water can contain 100,000 per square meter. The larval stage, with four instars, usually lasts from two weeks to six months, dependent upon species, temperature, and food. Those that inhabit the deep, Northern lakes may require up to seven years to develop. The Chironomidae (Greek: chironom,—us, "one who moves the hands") take their name either from the plumose or palmated, hand-like male antennae or "one who gestures with the hands, referring to the upraised waving forelegs" of the adult. Anglers call the Chironomidae midges or gnats, the Scottish, "blae and Black," and the English, "buzzers." Other species of *Diptera* are often confused with midges: the Reed Smut or Black Fly (*Simulium spp.*) and the Black Gnat, a most ubiquitous title to a myriad of insects including the Black Dance fly (*Hilara femorata*) and Dixa Midge (*Dixa minuta*).

Although capable of inhabiting a variety of substrata, *Chironomids* often exhibit a distinct preference for a particular substratum—rock and gravel (the Orthocladiinae and the Diamesinae), silt and sand (the Chironominae and the Tanypodinae), or plants or submerged wood (some Orthocladiinae and Chironominae). The marginally rooted stream vegetation provides large areas suitable for the development of expansive and dense populations of midges. Larval coloration is often associated with a particular habitat:

1. Olive and browns (high alkalinity and high oxygen)
2. Red and purple (high acid and low oxygen)

The angler may base pattern color on habitat alone. In general, olives are most common in moderate or high-oxygenated waters, whereas the red larvae are usually in low-oxygenated waters. The Reds, sometimes called "blood worms," live in lake mud, in oxygen-poor bogs, or lake depths (the profundal), as well as rivers and streams. Some species tolerate a wide range of salinity. Larval development may be rapid, dependent on temperature and food quantity. Studies support the view that increased temperatures increase development (5.2 days as opposed to 20 days, about five times faster). Higher temperatures appear to increase the rate of maturation, but apparently have no effect on size. Larvae reared in lower temperatures do increase length. Overwintering Chironomids frequently construct cocoons and show a tolerance to freezing.

Midges may be classified according to their feeding strategies: scrapers, strainers, predators, and combination feeders. The varied diet includes finely particulate detritus, diatoms, bacteria, periphyton, and algae. The number peak of larvae in the English chalk streams appears to correspond to the spring diatom bloom, but the bacteria associated with the algae may constitute the main source of energy. Diet changes often appear based by developmental stage of the larvae. Although they may not require food, some adult chironomids take in carbohydrate solutions, such as honeydew and nectar. The adults may live from a few days to two weeks for reproduction and dispersal.

The Chironomidae are one of the few insects to emerge in abundance from the deepest areas of a lake. When so doing, it makes a soft, slow rise known as a smut rise. Most Chironomidae emerge at dusk—a few at dawn. In *Biology of Freshwater* Chironomidae, L. C. Pindar notes that "Fish that feed on chironomids show a high degree of selectivity," and "Such selectivity is likely to be caused, at least in part, by differences in behavior that make certain species or life stages more, or less, available. Sometimes, however, it also appears to be related to size of larvae." Trout, dragonfly nymphs, and birds all feed on the larvae. An English study claims that in the summer months as much as 80% of the species found in stomach contents of fish may be chironomid larvae and pupae.

Aquatic chironomids usually lay eggs in a gelatinous string that is either free or attached. Chironomid populations in rivers undergo great fluctuations. Rivers may rapidly be repopulated from a small residual colony. Five or six weeks generally suffices for the Orthocladiinae larvae to build up to around 60,000 per square meter in summer.

THE LARVAE

The larvae typically have well-developed, nonretractile head capsules with biting mouth parts. The segmented, maggot-like body has no distinctive thorax or abdomen. There may be, however, a distinct, sclerotized (hardened, plate-like) head capsule. Some species have fine, scattered body hair, tufts, or fringes. Small, fleshy projections—called tubercles—may be present on one or more body parts. In many species, the tubercles form prolegs with small, curved hooks or crotchets. Both predacious and herbaceous larvae have conspicuous hair tufts on the dorsal apex. Usually, there are 12 segments behind the head with a pair of pseudopods on the prothoracic and anal segments. The dorsal anal segment bears a pair of pedestals mounted with a tuft of setae. Some larvae are free-living, either naked or cased, whereas others are sedentary under a silk net or in a fixed tube. Larva cases may appear as small tubes with extended arms that support nets. The active larvae, ranging from 2 millimeters to 30 millimeters, are usually white, brown, green, or red. Some species, the tube-dwellers that possess hemoglobin and live in low-oxygen waters, are red. Other species, especially those that live among vegetation, are colorless or green. The blood worm, a phrase granted to all red larvae, may be prolific and may constitute the principal food for certain fish.

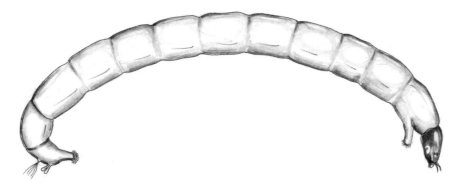

Chironomid *larva*

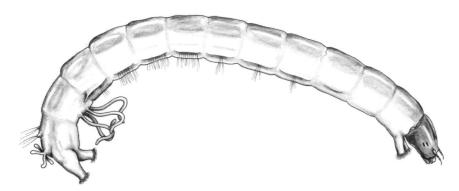

Chironomid *larva*

THE PUPAE

The pupae are obtect (the appendages are sealed to the body surface) or coarctate (the pupal state is passed in the puparium or last larval skin). The head, thorax, and wings are clustered together. There may be filamentous gills on top of the thorax. The pupal stage begins with apolysis (the separation, but not shedding, of the larval integument from the pupal integument). Pupation occurs in the last larval skin, although some species pupate in a silk cocoon or gelatinous purse. Prior to emergence, the pupa, provided with respiratory horns, may hang vertically in the surface film. After ecdysis (the actual shedding of the larval integument), the pupa hides in debris until emergence. The developed adult in the pupal case is called the pharate adult. The pupae—either free swimming or partly enclosed within a larval tube—are provided with respiratory filaments or horns. According to Bryce and Hobart, although fish may actively seek out chironomid larvae on the bottom, devouring both larva and case, they feed principally on the pharate adult. Pupation generally occurs on the bottom and the pharate adult secretes gas into the intercuticular space, causing the insect to rise to the surface. The pupa has tufts on the head instead of respiratory trumpets; these wave in the water and absorb dissolved oxygen. During emergence, the tracheal system contains

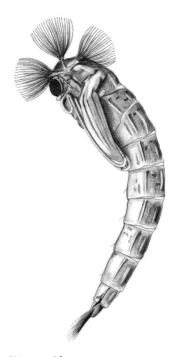

Chironomid *pupa*

enough air to enable the pupa to ascend to the surface aided by a few wiggles. When the pupa arrives at the surface, it stretches out along the surface and pumps blood into its thorax to split the pupal case. As the insect emerges from the pupal case, *the thorax and wings are orange-red*. The thorax, pumped full of blood to split the case, inflates the wings with blood to expand them. Once the insect is free from the pupal case, muscular contractions return the blood to the abdomen. The wings gray as the blood drains. Some patterns take advantage of the unique and seductive *red* emergence phase.

Emergence, although fairly rapid, is the most vulnerable stage in the life cycle and fish often gorge themselves at such times. Due to the length of hatch activity, most temperate waters will have midge activity throughout the year. Due to the fact that the adults fly low over the water and seldom land on it, the pupae are, perhaps, the most common pattern stage. However, my own late-season midging is done with adult patterns. Size appears more important to trout than color for midge patterns.

THE ADULT

The male is identified by a distinctive plumose or feather-like antenna, often longer than the head. Emergence differs in species; there is usually a spring and summer maxima, the period of greatest hatching, in March or April and later about July. Otherwise, they emerge sporadically throughout the year. Winter midging can be excellent due to the multibrooded midge and the lack of competing hatches. The gnat-like adults, with sucking mouth parts, have scaleless, simply venationed, flat-lying wings, usually shorter than the body. Neither sex has tails, and the male has mating forceps. The wings are either dun or clear, whereas the body is often greenish gray, green, or black. They have minute balancing knobs or haltere (halters) in place of the rear wings, a thickened mesothorax, and long, slender legs. The forelegs are the longest.

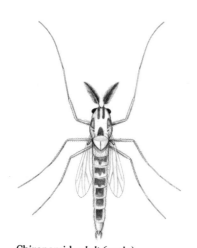

Chironomid *adult (male)*

CLASSIFICATION

The identification of Chironomidae is difficult for the layman angler and seldom significant. Taxonomy is based on the male adult. The larval level relies on head features and body structures. A simplified classification may take only the broader, diagnostic elements such as wing venation, the tarsal–tibia ratios, the absence or degree of macrotrichia (long hair) on the wing membrane, and the tibial spurs and combs. Chironomidae may be divided into seven subfamilies—Tanypodinae, Podonominae, Diamesinae, Corynoneurinae, Orthocladiinae, Clunioninae, and Chironominae. Two basic larval head types may be distinguished—predacious (such as the Tanypodinae) and nonpredacious (such as the Orthocladiinae). The Chironominae are typical blood worms.

Subfamily Tanypodinae: The larval head capsule, pliant and supple for swallowing whole prey, is adapted for small invertebrate predation. They have pincer mandibles for capturing and holding prey, retractile antennae creating a streamlined head, and stilt-like prolegs that produce jerky movement. Most are free swimmers that vary in color, but are often red because of hemoglobin. Bryce and Hobart note that "In many genera of Chironominae the functional significance of haemoglobin seems to be associated with the maintenance of normal feeding activity at reduced oxygen tensions, whereas the ability to respire anaerobically seems to be associated with survival during periods of oxygen lack." The genus *Chironomus* can respire anaerobically, enabling it to survive periods of oxygen deprivation.

Although there are exceptions, the other subfamilies have a scraper tooth plate for scraping algae and detritus off surfaces and an armature for dispersing silk strands. Although silk is primarily used for case or tube building, some species produce nets or webs for filter-feeding. A few of the nontanypodinae chironomidae are predacious. Some families have little significance for angling. The subfamilies Podonominae and Diamesinae appear adapted to cold water of mossy mountain springs. The Clunioninae, a small subfamily, inhabits the marine, coastal "holdfast" areas such as barnacle beds and rock pools where salmon fry feed upon them.

Subfamily Orthocladiinae: The Orthocladiinae scrape algae off stones and plants, and typically live under a loose silk tent. A few construct mucilaginous cases. Absence of hemoglobin in the larvae restricts them to oxygenated waters. Many are camouflaged in green.

Subfamily Chironominae: The Chironominae are typically red due to the presence of hemoglobin. The subfamily Chironominae is subdivided into two tribes—the small Tanytarsini (detritus and filtration feeders with tubes or mobile cases like caddis) and the larger Chironomini (detritus, filter feeders, and predators). Some Chironomini are burrowers, such as the *Chironomus*, that take in detritus directly from the water, whereas others, such as the *Glyptotendipes*, trap detritus in conical nets. The tube dwellers construct their cases with silk cement and mud particles, sand, or debris. The larva clings to the tube with its false legs while undulating its body to maintain a flow of oxygen. Many tube dwellers graze on the organic matter trapped in the mud.

If there are adults on the water, pupa will commonly be active in the water column. Midge larvae are bottom feeders and, consequently, will be available to trout on the bottom among the tangled roots of aquatic plants. Periodically, tube dwellers leave their tubes and swim about with whipping action, *often going to the surface*. Such ramblings are probably done in response to a lack of oxygen. The angler, with draw-and-sink retrieves, imitates this ascent-descent behavior. After such excursions, the larva quickly constructs a new tube. All stages of the midge, which may be effectively imitated, are taken by trout—the larva, the pupa, and the adult. Although the pharate adult is often the main trout food, larvae and pupa can be invaluable. The typical hook size of chironominae larvae ranges from about size 16 to 20, the pupa about 18 to 20, and adult about 18 to 24.

THE DANCE FLY (FAMILY EMPIDIDAE)

The dance flies, so named for their up-and-down or circling swarms over streams, are common, minute insects. Most Empididae larvae are terrestrial;

Empidid *adult*

a few, however, are aquatic and live on the rocky substrata of swift streams. The aquatic larvae, mature length 2 to 7 millimeters, are typically predacious, feeding especially upon Simuliidae (black fly) larvae and pupae. Consequently, dance fly frequently share black fly zones, just as the *simulids*, *empidids* often inhabit running water and moss tracts.

Mating is highly ritualized with dance flies. The males of some genera create a frothy or silken balloon that sometimes contains a small insect and offer it to the female as a mating stimulus. Adults, which feed on nectar, pollen, or smaller insects, are commonly found on vegetation in moist places. The adults control pests by consuming mosquitos and black fly. Although there are many exceptions, most *empidids* have bulky eyes, long legs, large thoraxes and slender, tapering abdomens. Terminal bristles emerge from the antennae. The male genitalia are often distinct.

Tying *empidid* patterns may be supreme affectation. Trout take dance flies as they waltz above the surface or drift through the riffles, but it is doubtful whether they distinguish the differences among empidids, midges and microcaddis. All are small, dark and down-winged. Adult empidids appear on the water as tiny (2 to 6 millimeters), dark diptera and are best matched with smut or midge imitations. Minute midge larval patterns may also match empidid larvae.

THE MICROCADDIS AND THE SADDLECASE CADDIS (FAMILY HYDROPTILIDAE AND FAMILY GLOSSOSOMATIDAE)

The Purse-Case *Hydroptilids*

Hydroptila *case with larva*
(Hydroptilidae)

The true microcaddis, the hydroptilidae, are found in diverse habitats—the smooth glides of weeded spring creeks, the pools of wide, free-stone rivers and small ponds and lakes. The genus *Hydroptila* is common in most trout waters. Throughout North America, the *hydroptilids* are an abundant and highly diverse group. They graze on filamentous algae and periphytic diatoms. Although the larvae have various body shapes, antennae lengths and proleg

Hairy Hydroptila *(adult)*

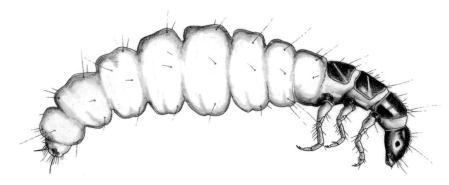

Hydroptila *larva (Hydroptilidae)*

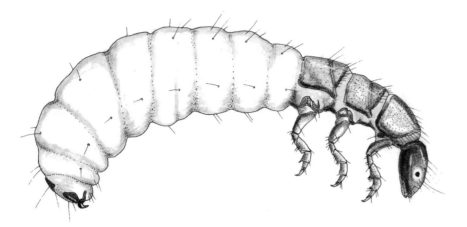

Ochrotrichia *case (Hydroptilidae)*

Ochrotrichia *larva (Hydroptilidae)*

patterns, they do share some common characteristics: sclerotized (hardened) plates on all three thoracic segments and the general absence of abdominal gills. Because of size and structure, though, it is difficult to confuse the microcaddis with other caddis. The hydroptilids are unusual because the first four instars are spent caseless.

Case-making does not occur until the final instar. At this time, the cased abdomen becomes grotesquely enlarged. The family, generally known as *purse-case caddis*, construct portable, bivalve silk-cases of sand. They continually enlarge the purse-cases to accommodate the growing abdomen. Those with a bivalve case merely slit the seam, add more silk and "sew" it closed again. Some larvae spin silk "bottles" or, like the *Neotrichia*, spin cylindrical tube-cases similar to common caddis. Other hydroptilidae, with more cryptic habits, are firmly attached to the stone substrata or embedded in crevices. Many microcaddis overwinter during the final instar. The term pharate pupa (Greek: *pharos*, "garment") refers to the period when the developing pupa is enclosed, but separated from the larval cuticle. When a caddis leaves the pupal case and rises to the surface, it is functionally an adult.

After hatching, microcaddis drift and struggle great distances. In slow currents, trout will drift with them before the take. They may produce, at times, the same "smut" rise often attributed to chironomids and simulids. And, although they are small, local concentrations may produce prodigious hatches. The cased larvae, about 5 millimeters long, drift freely in the current and are found in drift samples. Dr. Norman Anderson of Oregon has recorded their association with ranunculus and their high-drift rate on the Metolius River.

These motley, minuscule caddis are so diverse as to deny a comprehensive description. There are, however, some generalities. Many prefer slow water. Many have olive-gray bodies, rusty-gray legs and mottled wings. Antennae are shorter than the forewings. They range from 3 to 6 millimeters long (hook sizes 22 to 24). Most adults are hairy and about 4 millimeters long. The wings, usually narrow with long fringe hairs, are a solid or mottled black, brown or, sometimes, tan. The wings may appear flatter, more midge-like, than

Leucotrichia *larva (Hydroptilidae)*

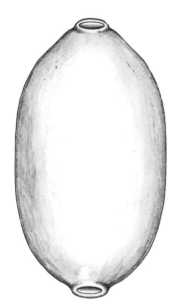

Leucotrichia *case (Hydroptilidae): dorsal view*

Leucotrichia *case: lateral view*

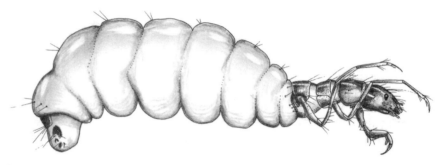

Oxyethira *larva*

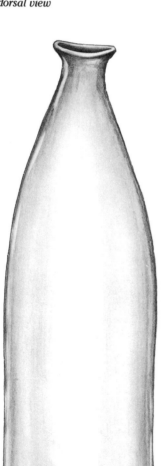

Oxyethira *case*

the tented wings of larger caddis. A realistic wing imitation is the distinctly fringed hen-hackle tips, tied, cupped, and oval, as delta overwings. The furry halo of CDC barbs also creates realistic microcaddis wings.

The most thorough discussion of the microcaddis appears in LaFontaine's *Caddisflies*. Little has been written about them and it is arguable whether or not the genus level is important. When feeding on microcaddis, trout also take midges. Both are small, dark and overwinged. According to Gary LaFontaine the microcaddis are productive during two periods—during emergence and during ovipositing.

For imitations, LaFontaine suggests an 18–22 copper Brassie for the drifting larvae of the *Hydroptila*. H. B. N. Hynes' *The Ecology of Running Water* refers to a study by Cianficconi and Riatti that contends that the *Hydroptila* do not colonize the upstream face of stones. Hynes presents extensive data on the correlation between specific caddis and their preferred zones. Microcaddis prefer the downstream side of boulders. LaFontaine's black-diving-caddis fished *behind* midstream boulders proved successful on the Madison. The ovipositing females return to lay eggs by descending the downstream side of boulders. As LaFontaine points out, a slack, dead-drift imitation fished in the slack water behind boulders can be effective.

The Brambridge Caddis, which may be tied in micro-sizes, has a mole fur body and pheasant tail barbs mounted *forward*. The barbs are then folded back to create the thoracic swell. The Brambridge is whip-finished immediately behind the thorax. The Mole Microcaddis, another dry pattern, wears a black Voljc overwing and a dark brown or black mole fur body and thorax.

The Saddle-Case Glossosomatids

Although not true microcaddis, the Glossosomatids are small, widespread, and abundant. The larvae, found only in flowing water, have restricted pastures: the upper and exposed surfaces of rocks where they browse, with their scraper mandibles, on algae and diatoms. The genus *glossosoma* appear only where fine sand does not clog their specialized scrapers. The larvae, which lack abdominal gills, have dark pronotum plates and equal-length legs. A mature larva commonly ranges from 3 to 7 millimeters long, and occasionally beyond 9 millimeters.

Glossosoma *case (Glossosomatidae): ventro-lateral view*

The oval, flat-bottomed domed case, often likened to a saddle case or a tortoise case, is made of tiny rock fragments. Unlike common cased caddis, the saddle-case caddis builds a new case after each molt. Ernest Schwiebert, in *Nymphs*, describes the case as a pebbled igloo. For water circulation, the cases have openings at each end and between the stones. The caddis readily reverse themselves in the case so there is no distinction between the front and rear openings. However, some have unusual case architecture; they construct a spring "door-stone" that automatically seals shut when the larva retreats. Exposed as they are on rock surfaces, larvae feed beneath the case for concealment. The larval cases of the *Agapetus* and *Protoptila* have relatively large stones on each side. The adults, 6 to 10 millimeters, are twice the size of the adult microcaddis.

Agapetus *case (Glossosomatidae): ventro-lateral view*

The sporadic hatches throughout the season make these insects important to the angler. Schwiebert lists a pupal imitation, size 16, of the Little Sepia Sedge (*Glossosoma califica*) with a medium brown body and pale-chocolate thread ribbing. Scant information is available concerning emergence. The *Glossosoma*, which prefer medium-sized stones, apparently move into faster water for pupation. Consequently, hatching may occur in the riffles throughout the season. Before drifting a small sedge, whether Hydroptilid or Glossosomatid, behind boulders and through the swirling trough, advance as close as possible. Place the pattern so that it hesitates, with gentle tension, through the turbulence for the short drift. A larva, pupa or adult pattern, sized

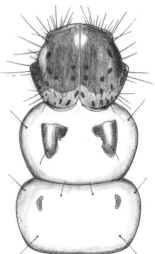

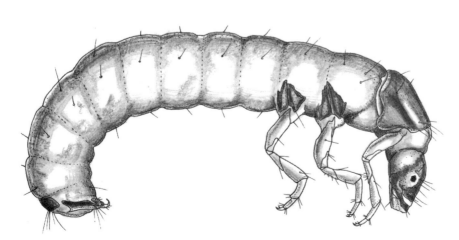

Glossosoma *larva (Glossosomatidae)*

Agapetus *larva*

18 or 22, fished in the backwash or the gathering seams beyond boulders may tempt a reluctant trout.

THE PALE MORNING DUN

The *Ephemerella*, the only genus of the family Ephemerellidae found in North America, is a large, diverse genus, with more than thirty-five species recorded from the Rocky Mountains to the Pacific Ocean, from New Mexico to Canada. It furnishes extended and prominent Western hatches, including the Pale Morning Dun (*E. inermis* and *E. infrequens*). Doug Swisher and Carl Richards, in *Selective Trout*, conferred the title Pale Morning Dun to the small *Ephemerella* with a pale yellow body and gray wings. The Pale Morning Dun or PMD is especially important on Western spring creeks and may constitute, as it does on Idaho's Silver Creek, the principal hatch. The duration and manner of emergence makes it the perfect insect for the fly fisher. Peak emergence usually occurs during July and August, but sporadic activity appears throughout the angling season. "During hot spells," according to Fred Arbona, in *Mayflies, the Angler and the Trout*, "the hatch will begin at nine, last for about an hour, and will emerge again for a short while late in the afternoon." Some subimagoes emerge from the nymphal husk some distance below the surface, others at or just beneath the surface. Once on the surface, they may require extended "flutter time" before flight. On Western spring creeks, I have watched *E. infrequens* float several yards into the mouths of waiting trout. Such extended floats on slow, smooth water require seductive patterns and exemplary drifts.

THE NYMPHS

Arbona notes that "No reliable characteristics are known to separate the nymphs of *E. inermis* from those of *E. infrequens*; however, the latter species is markedly larger in size (8.5 to 9.5 millimeters) and lacks the pale medial stripe usually exhibited by the *E. inermis* nymphs." The smaller *inermis* (7 millimeters) is more abundant and widespread than the larger *infrequens* (9 millimeters). The nymphs have banded, pale amber legs and may be smooth, hairy, or have conspicuous lateral spines. The robust nymphs have three equal tails that are retained as imagoes. Unlike the interlocking hairs of the paddle-tail Baetis, the PMD has sparse hair whorls. The gills have a distinct sequential undulation and the nymphs swim with a vertical whipping wiggle. The nymphs have small gills, located dorsally on segments 3 through 7, or 4 through 7 only. The gills on segment 4 may be operculate, covering other gills. *Ephemerella* nymphs have diverse body shapes and three equal tails with spines, hair whorls or both. The variable body color generally tends toward the olive-browns. The larger *infrequens* usually emerges earlier in June than the *inermis*, its "sister species."

Due to diversity, this cosmopolitan genus is found in all running water types, some species occurring in lakes with prominent wave action. The

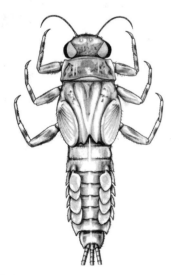

Ephemerella inermis *nymph*

nymphs inhabit the slow, silty pools and backwaters, especially the idle water near banks and at the base of plants. They are feeble swimmers; when dislodged they move with erratic, up-and-down undulations of the abdomen. Nymph imitations should be fished dead-drift with slight tension. Heavy waters may require weight. Swisher and Richards recommend that the nymph "should be fished near the bottom without action."

THE EMERGERS

The subsurface emergence of the PMD makes emerger patterns effective. The PMD generally hatches in smooth, flat water where drift and drag is most important. Patterns should be sparse, often without hackles. The Caucci and Nastasi's Pale Morning Comparadun, dressed with a deer hair wing and olive-yellow dubbed body, may prove effective. Other patterns, with snowshoe hare fibers or cul de canard feathers, are also effective. Emergers should be fished shallow on light hooks and floating materials such as CDC. Doug Swisher and Carl Richards, in *Emergers*, list a single pattern for the Pale Morning Dun Floating Nymph: The imitation has a brown fur body and yellow-tan duck rump barbs tied on sizes 18 or 20 Tiemco 100. The pattern imitates the stunted, unfurled wings of the emerging dun. Most patterns imitate the PMD in hook sizes 18 to 20. Angling literature places significant importance on the PMD. Daily hatches occur between ten and one. Emerger or dun patterns are usually the most effective stage imitated and presented.

THE DUNS

The adult hind wing has a costal hook, technically termed projection or angulation, and the adults appear, like the *Tricorythodes*, sexually separate on the water. The extended hatch (from May through September) makes the Pale Morning Dun important. The dun wings are slate gray to pale yellow dun. Hind wings have a distinct, slightly rounded costal projection. The three tails are one-half to three-fourths body length. The body color ranges from bright olive-green to yellow amber, pale cream, yellow tan, or sulfur yellow.

THE SPINNERS

Fred Arbona declares that "Spinner falls of *E. inermis* and *E. infrequens* are just as important to the angler as the hatch itself. The spinners appear twice a day, in the morning and again at dusk. The females choose the riffles to oviposit their light olive eggs." The clear winged spinner has three tails and variable body coloration, similar to but often darker than the dun. Angling literature records numerous patterns—nymph, dun, and spinner—for the PMD.

THE PARALEPTOPHLEBIA

Depending on the species, the genus *Paraleptophlebia* is known variously as the Slate-winged Mahogany Dun, the Blue Dun, the Iron Blue Dun, and Jenny Spinner. Several Western species are occasionally called the Dark Blue Quill. The most common Western name, however, is merely *Paraleptophlebia*. Much has been written about the small *Paraleptophlebia*, popularizing the name. The ubiquitous duns, especially prevalent from the West Coast to the Rockies, are recognized by their size, the mahogany body, three equal tails, and pale gray wings. Body color ranges, in fact, from a pale blue dun to a deep reddish-brown, the so-called mahogany. They generate notable early spring hatches that continue through October, becoming part of the autumn insect bloom. Adults have been recorded in Oregon as late as November.

THE NYMPHS

The nymphs are common in shallow, wadable, moderately rapid streams. Similar to the *Baetis* and *Pseudocloeon*, the *Paraleptophlebia* is small (6 to 8 millimeters long) and slender. The nymphs, somewhat flattened, are usually recognized by their squared head, visible mandibles (both when viewed from above) and the distinctly "forked" or "prong" gills. The nymph has three tails as long as or longer than its body. Mayflies, in general, are microhabitat specialists living in specific zones delineated by depth, current, cover, and food. *Paraleptophlebia* nymphs are adapted to faster water than the *Leptophlebia*. Many species creep among the leaf debris in slow to moderate currents. Other species, adapted to current, occur in riffles and rapids, hiding beneath rocks. Nymphs are poor swimmers, moving by lateral undulations. Some species may occupy the substrate cracks and crannies during the day and the substrate surface at night. Their feeble swim makes them, at times, a major ingredient in drift samples. They are often found near rooty banks, wood debris, gravel, and rocks. As they mature, they may migrate, like the *Leptophlebia*, to calmer waters prior to hatching. They usually crawl out on rocks and plants to emerge.

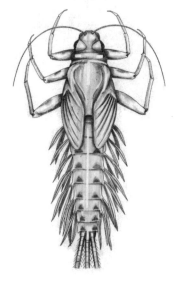

Paraleptophlebia *nymph*

THE DUN

The males usually have whitish midbody segments. The hind wings are broad and without costal projections. They have three tails. Females may be reddish or purplish brown. Northern species require a full year for development. Late morning and early afternoon emergence often occurs near banks or in back eddies. Prior to emergence there may be repeated false emergence to the surface that stimulates trout interest. Once hatched, they may float long distances before flight, thereby producing profound dry fly rises. Duns usually molt within twelve to forty-eight hours.

THE SPINNER

Mating flights usually occur over water during midmorning and midafternoon. Mating flights are described in *Mayflies of North America and Central America* (1976): "The females were seen about thirty minutes after the males began their flight; upon entering the swarm each female was seized by a male. Mating was completed during the time it took the pair to fall about three feet. Immediately after a pair separated, the female dropped to the water surface, released some eggs, then rose to fly a short distance to repeat the performance twice more; the spent female then flew to nearby vegetation."

There are few patterns for the nymph; Sawyer's Pheasant Tail Nymph is perhaps one of the best. The best hatches for the angler occur in moderate, smooth currents. Those species that flee the heavy flow, migrating into the shallows to emerge above water, are less accessible to trout. Imitations for the nymph, dun, and spinner are usually tied on size 18 hooks.

THE REED SMUT (FAMILY SIMULIIDAE)

The female reed smut, known also as black fly, riffle smut, buffalo gnat, or black curse, announces its presence by biting. Although a few species do not feed on blood, many female reed smuts are pests as well as carriers of parasites to man and beast. The males are content to feed on nectars. The label *buffalo gnat* comes from the humpbacked profile of the adult. Reed smuts oviposit in various ways: The female may broadcast eggs by tapping her abdomen on the water surface during flight; the female may deposit eggs on wet surfaces such as plants trailing in the water; or the female may crawl beneath the surface to deposit eggs.

The larvae, usually a dirty yellow, cream, brown, and pale olive, pass through four to seven molts and one or more generations per year. The larval body is cylindrical and swollen, creating a "bowling pin" profile. Both the single, thoracic proleg and body posterior have rings with rows of hooks for securing the larva to the substrata. The larvae cling to weeds and rocks and are harvested by trout and grayling. With the terminal hooks on the abdomen, the larvae attach themselves, sometimes in dense colonies, to vegetation, rocks, and debris in the current. They hang with their head downstream to filter the food suspended in the drift. They trap food particles with their head brushes, "cephalic fans" or "mouth brushes."

Reed smut larva (Simuliidae)

A smut does not swim; rather it uses its proleg hooks and posterior hooks for "looping"—extending the proleg and gripping, releasing the posterior, and bringing it forward just behind the proleg, then repeating the motion. As it advances, it releases a continuous silk strand. When alarmed, the larva releases its hold, drifts away, and remains suspended in the current on a silk strand. The smut leaves the sheltering weeds and rappels into the open water immediately downstream of the weed beds. It may drift downstream on silken threads until a suitable attachment site is found. *Nothing imitates this activity better than a tiny pattern on a fine tippet.* Consequently, the tiny, drifting larval pattern is effectively fished to close, visible trout immediately below weed beds. It is remarkable how large trout will select such small tidbits from their watery table.

My first encounter with the reed smut took place several years ago. A worthy trout rose along the side of an anchored weed-boat, a small paddle-wheeler with cutters. From behind the boat, I could approach very close to the trout. I cast several dries and several dries drifted back to me. Then I noticed that the trout was nosing just beneath the surface. Upstream weed cutting and the current had washed some reed larvae along the side of the boat. I had only one smut larva in my box, a size 22 Spanish pattern. I tied it on, more in fancy than in faith. I did not think that it would take a trout. A trout probably would never see a size 22 in the drift. I cast and waited. When I thought the pattern had passed the trout, I lifted the line, and, instead of coming clear, a startled trout struggled with my smut. The startled trout startled me, but not for long. The tippet quickly broke, but there was time enough for the trout to teach me the power of a tiny, drifting smut larva.

The pharate pupae spin variously shaped cocoons, such as the common "slippercase," that anchor and protect them. The wider or open end faces downstream. The pupal thorax bears a pair of extended "strand" gills, the branched spiracular gills. The pupal stage lasts from four to seven days. During emergence, the wings expand and the adult rises to the surface, buoyed to the surface by an air bubble. The bubbled, emerging adult is difficult to imitate, but sink patterns that incorporate a glass or silver bead aid the deception. The unwetted adult quickly flies off the water to find rest and time for the cuticle to harden.

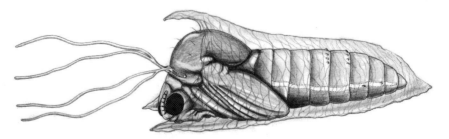

Reed smut pupa in slipper case (Simuliidae)

The adults range from a minuscule 1.5 to 5.5 millimeters long. They are usually black or dark brown, but may be reddish, gray, orange, or yellow. The antennae are short and stout. The thorax is large and arched, mounted with broad, transparent wings. Like the larvae, the adult patterns, those that imitate the ovipositing females, are more productive when fished downstream of weed beds. The females lay eggs on stones or emergent plants, both on and beneath the surface. When a female oviposits beneath the surface, she penetrates the surface, gathering a silver air globule, and crawls down the emerging plant a few centimeters. When ovipositing is completed, she struggles to the surface, though sometimes sent awash in the current to feeding trout. Small wet flies may imitate the sunk, ovipositing females. Reed smuts are important, perhaps sometimes as important as midges, in quick-flowing weedy stretches of moderate-sized streams. In 1915, J. C. Mottram devised an early sinking smut: "On the smallest and lightest of hooks make close to the eye, with black floss silk, a tiny bead: leave the rest of the hook bare; in front of this, wind on half a turn [the companion drawing may depict a full turn] of the tip of a starling's hackle." Mottram believed that it "must be fished like the gnat or midge larva." Preben Torp Jacobsen of Denmark created a novel Reed Smut Nymph of red cow hair over a base of fine copper wire, with four or five turns of fine silver wire fore and aft. When soaked in silicone, the impregnated hairs trap air and the silver wraps create the impression that an emerger is sheathed within. John Goddard, after his encounters with the smutting trout of the weedy Anton, developed an effective and simple pattern: four or five turns of fine, black ostrich for the body and two turns of a short-barbed, black hackle. The stomach contents of rising trout, verified, to Goddard, that trout take both smuts and midges. "The results confirmed that most trout were indeed feeding upon both species at the same time, as on many occasions I found their stomachs packed both with smuts and small brown or green chironomids and in some cases both green and brown." Goddard also compared the rises to the simulid and the chironomid. "I had always associated trout feeding in slow flowing sections of rivers upon chironomids with a slow leisurely head and tail rise, but as this rise form is somewhat similar to the slow sipping rise of trout feeding upon smuts, I idly wondered whether there may be some connection particularly with trout feeding in this manner in faster water where the precise rise form is more difficult to establish." Perhaps a smut rise is a slow rise in fast water. After all, the reed smut is the riffle smut; it normally lives and emerges in riffles or currents. The Bubble Emerger, an emerging smut pattern, unites the air shroud of CDC with the sink of a silver bead. Appropriate midge and microcaddis patterns match the adults.

TRICORYTHIDAE

Kindred to the *Caenis* and *Brachycercus*, the *Tricorythidae*, a microsprawler, has an enlarged second gill. The Trico's second gill, often described as triangular or oval, forms a protective shield that prevents silting of the functional gills on abdominal sections 3–6. The Trico, or White-winged Black, is often prolific in tail waters and spring creeks. Both the *Caenis* and *Brachycercus*, the latter only occasionally of consequence to the angler, inhabit the warmer, more stagnant waters—waters less hospitable to trout.

NYMPHS

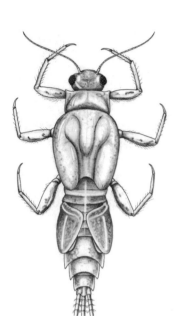

Tricorythodes nymph

The nymphs prefer the marl-rich silt of alkaline waters, the corixa and scud waters, and the slow eddies near a rip flow. They inhabit the substrata feeding on periphyton slime, diatoms, and algae. Nymphs occur in streams with perceptible current and inhabit aquatic vegetation. The *Tricorythodes* nymphs lack hind wing pads. The nymphs, ranging from 3 to 10 millimeters, swim to the surface to emerge. Same generation nymphs may develop at different times, so although there is a midsummer and early fall peak emergence, there are duns emerging continuously after midsummer. They are feeble swimmers, propelled by slow undulations of the body. Otherwise, the nymphs move almost entirely by crawling. Nymphs are regarded as the least important stage for the angler, ranging in size from 20 to 26. The greater challenge, after tying such minuscule nymphs, is fishing them. Fred Arbona, in *Mayflies, the Angler, and the Trout* (1980), indicates that hatching usually takes place from about 4:00 AM to 11:00 AM, from late June through October. He considers nymph fishing of little importance due to the time of emergence, the early morning, rather than their minuscule size. Some Tricos live interstitially in the top few centimeters of silt, where they may be dislodged for collecting. They usually mature rapidly in about five weeks. Such rapid growth allows two generations a summer—first emerging in June-July and later in August, September or October.

ADULT

Emergence occurs in several ways: Some species emerge as duns under water and drift to the surface, while others bob to the surface, where the subimagoes burst into being. Some nymphs crawl up rocks or plants just above the water line. Dave Hughes and Richard Hafele have observed that *minutes* appeared in surface film as well as on rocks just above the water line. Some species evidently cast the nymphal shuck under water, reaching the surface with dun wings trailing above the thorax. According to Ernest Schwiebert, stomach analysis of trout indicate that the hatching dun is the preferred phase. Schwiebert suggests adding marabou or fluff above the nymph pattern to imitate the unfurling wing. Buoyant, cul-de-canard fluff may prove more effective for the emerging nymph. Males emerge throughout the night; females in the early morning. For some species, both male and female emerge in the morning. During emergence, blizzard hatches can produce remarkable trout activity—the duns molt to spinners in two minutes to two hours. Low floating, clipped-hackle duns are fished dead drift. Mating almost immediately, great swarms often hover above water, peaking at midmorning, and falling spent by late morning.

SPINNERS

By midmorning, both are spinners and mating takes place soon thereafter. The spinners occur quickly after the dun emerges from nymphal shuck. Some impatient spinners take wing before shedding the dun coat. The imago may carry the dun coat a distance, hence the so-called "flight-hatch" of the Trico. The adult has three tails that are at least three times as long as the body, a pair of roundish wings, and a blunt pair of tubercles at the rear of the head. The adult is usually about 3 to 6 millimeters long and best imitated in hook sizes 20 to 24. The female adult Trico has short forelegs and a stout body. The wings of both sexes are about 1 millimeter longer than the body. Some anglers consider the spinner fall the classical micropattern event.

After mating, the gravid female either returns to bank foliage to "plump" its fertilized eggs prior to ovipositing, or the female drops immediately to extrude egg packets on the surface. The ova may overwinter with eclosion occurring in spring or early summer. The females follow the male "drop" by approximately half an hour. The males fall first; thus Arbona believes that the spinner patterns should be the size and color of the males.

IDENTIFICATION

Identification of the Trico is relatively simple. The nymph has a dominant triangular or oval second gill not meeting medially and compound eyes similar in size to the ocelli (simple eyes). The nymph has gill lamellae on segments 3–6, simple or bilobed and without fringed margins. They have three tails in all stages and, as adults, lack hind wings. The imago has a heavy thorax. Wing venation includes a turned-down CuP. The IMP and MP extend less than three-fourths the distance of MP. The MA has a symmetrical fork. Their appearance is generally one of a small black insect with white wings.

The *T. minutes*, with light brown femurs, and the *T. fallax*, with red-brown femurs and a purple-brown body, are common western hatches. Some females may have a gray body in contrast to the black-bodied males. In *The Mayflies of North and Central America* (1978), the authors state that *fallax* differ from the *minutes* only in color. "At most, *T. fallax* and *T. minutes* seem worthy of subspecific rank, but we believe that these will best be regarded as mere clinical variants and hereby designate *fallax* as a synonym of *minutes*." They classify them as one species with color differences due to water chemistry and geographical distribution. Most Western hatches are caused by *minutes*, emerging from the Northern Rockies to the Pacific Northwest. McCafferty claims that the three most important species are *atratus* and *stygiatus* in Central and Eastern North America and *minutes* in Western North America.

There are few established Trico patterns in angling literature. Cluster patterns and RFC Hackle Duns often prove effective. Size 20 and 22 hooks usually imitate the duns and spinners. This is demanding tying and demanding presentation, a fragile 22 tossed to close rising trout.

THE COLOR CODE

See the color section for a personal example of a Color Code

In *Floating Flies and How to Dress Them* (1866), Frederic Halford included a plate to indicate the various colors appropriate for dyeing and tying. The color code is a similar system for the angler who wishes to record insect and pattern color. Selective trout are often selective to one or more elements: size, silhouette, drift, and color. In glides and pools, trout often drift with a pattern, perhaps assessing its action and authenticity. No trout or tyer can ignore color. Like size and drift, color may be pivotal to the take. Alfred Ronalds, in *The Fly-Fisher's Entomology* (1844), states that "an exact resemblance of the *shape* does not seem to be quite as essential a requisite as that of colour, since the former varies according to the position of the insect either in or upon the water." Ronalds' preference for color over form may be excessive; nevertheless, an insect has several shapes (i.e., various stances including rough blown or drowned), but only one color at any given time.

Not all angling experiences and conditions require the creation of a personal color system; but it is especially valuable for pattern records, hatch matching, and insect research. It allows the angler, later at the tying table, to create a more accurate imitation. Most tyers are aware of the "dazzle" illusion of movement created by the flecked cree hackle and barred grizzly wing of the Adams. The illusion of motion may also be created by color alone. When placed beside each other, complementary colors, for example, increase the illusion of movement.

There have been various attempts at producing a color system for anglers, notably Al Caucci and Bob Nastasi's *Fly-Tyer's Color Guide* and Gary Borger's *Borger Color System*. Borger notes that it is not necessary "to qualify colors into finer shades" because "all species of food organisms exhibit some variation in color." The natural color variations themselves are further distorted by water refraction. To some extent, all objects mirror or reflect a portion of the colors found in local objects. Nor is color a single entity.

Color has three characteristics: hue, chroma, and value. Hue is that quality that distinguishes one color from another; it is the name of a color, such as red or blue. Hue may be a primary color or a combination of colors. Chroma is the saturation or strength of a hue. For example, red and pink may be the same hue, but red has a high chroma, while pink (which is actually a weak red) has a low chroma. Value or brightness is the relative amount of lightness or darkness in a hue. Hue is the more specific term for color because it includes the color attributes of value (the lightness or darkness) and chroma (the purity or strength). The more often a color is mixed, the less intense or less brilliant it becomes. The noncolors like black and gray lack all chroma.

At times, trout do not appear to discriminate between values. At other times, however, trout do distinguish degrees of value as well as degrees of chroma. A spring creek in Montana once illustrated how color-selective trout may become. Sulphur duns rode the drifts and, try as I may, my sulphur-winged patterns were no match. The trout seemed to prefer a paler sulphur wing. That evening, in the motel room, I crafted sulphur duns only to find, the next day, how far from the natural sulphur color they were. Most humans have poor color retention. The subtle sulphur wing was finally captured with a rapid watercolor wash on the stream. Later, that color helped capture several admirable trout.

According to John Goddard and Brian Clark, trout "have shown that they can not only unerringly distinguish between different colours, but between different shades of the same colour." They may even see these shades in a different way. The slightly triangular shape of the trout's pupil enhances forward vision. There are strong indications that ultraviolet light is visible to salmonids. Trout may also filter nondirectional light, like we do with polaroid glasses. According to *Trout*, "Whatever the extent of these capabilities, the emerging picture suggests that salmonids have polarotaxes and that underwater light is polarized to a considerable degree; that is, it is more directional than diffuse." Further research, hopefully, will complete our understanding of trout vision. Until then, our understanding of color can only enhance our understanding of trout.

A personal color code should be completed with a superior transparent watercolor—Grumbacher, Rowney, Winsor & Newton. The more opaque gouaches, though less brilliant, may be used. Unlike transparent watercolor, it is possible to work from dark to light with gouaches, adding white rather than water to lighten colors. Due to their flat, matt character, neither gouache nor colored pencils have the subtlety and range of transparent watercolor. Watercolor tube paints, due to their fluid blends, are recommended over dry or semidry color cakes. (See Color Code in color section.)

Each color block of the color code illustrates a range, from light to dark, of a particular color. To make a color block, such as iron-blue, blend the color and then paint a value range of the color on a block. Thereafter, when an angler wishes to record a pattern color or an insect color in the field—such as a pale, medium iron blue—he merely writes the notation IB2. Any number of numbers may be used to divide the color value scale. The IB indicates iron-blue and the 2 indicates the value on the IB scale. The postscript number allows a precise reference to a wide value range of each particular color. A notation of IB3.5 may refer to the 3.5 value on the iron-blue scale.

Another method of creating the color code is to paint the color value strips on quality paper, and then cut and mount the strips on color blocks for reference. Hot pressed, 140- to 300-pound paper will accept heavy washes and produce smooth blending. This will prevent blending errors on the page and even allow for color changes by strip replacement. If this method is used, the color abbreviation letters may be written at the top of the strip itself. This is perhaps the best method as it allows for color correction and change. There are some commercial color plates available that may be cut and mounted; however, commercial color chips usually have neither the correct color range nor the value range. Although the color range of insects is not great, the value range is. Even as early as 1939, McClelland in *How to Tie Flies for Trout* claims that "It is often found there is an appreciable difference of colour between the upper and the under sides of the [insect] body. It is fairly objected that the mirror throws upward upon the under side of the fly more light than would be reflected by the bottom of a river or pond; but the surface of the water in sunlight itself reflects no little light upon the insect; and, further, the general tendency of the dresser is to dress rather more darkly than the color and natural luminosity of the fly warrants. The fault induced therefore, if any, is likely to be on the right side." Often tyers match only the color (the hue) with little concern for chroma and value. In any case, here are some color considerations useful for matching the micropatterns.

(1) Color is generally considered important for fly patterns, especially subsurface imitations.

(2) Insect species may exhibit, even in the same riffle, a range of colors. Air temperature may affect color. The colder the day, the darker the color. Coloration may differ dependent upon the habitat and light. Insect coloration, even in the same species, may vary somewhat depending upon food and water chemistry. In many cases, according to Wigglesworth, the body color is synthesized by the insect itself and has no relation to food or water chemistry. Swisher and Richards conclude that "The color of mayflies varies considerably, even in the same hatch on the same riffle. It varies to even how many seconds have elapsed after the actual splitting of the nymphal case. The longer after emergence from the case, the darker the fly." Early and late hatches are usually darker than summer hatches. The male mayfly is usually darker than the female. The older the spinner, the darker the color. *Smaller insects, in general, tend to be darker.* Some species may have greater color latitude than other species. According to John Goddard, "where a colour variation does occur, it is more a lightening or darkening of the basic colour. One notable exception is the Blue-Winged Olive. When this fly first appears in early June the body of the female is sometimes quite a bright olive green, but in October the colour is often quite different, being a distinct shade of rusty brown." Due to such color variations, some anglers postulate that color is not a discriminating criterion for patterns. Such reasoning commits a sin of omission. *Even though a particular insect may hatch with variant colors, this does not dismiss the possibility that trout may key on that paricular color at that particular time.* This may be especially true for selective trout feeding on small insects.

(3) Due to water clarity, water chemistry and light, trout may perceive color differently.

(4) There are times when trout will be attracted to color other than those of the naturals. The most effective imitation may not have a counterpart in nature.

(5) Value (the brightness) may be as significant at times as the color. *Value is the single most important factor in color matching.*

(6) Like all living creatures, insects vary in size, usually smaller rather than larger. Often a few size 28 Tricos will appear in a size 22 Trico hatch. Lack of food, lower temperatures, and water chemistry may reduce insect size. Perhaps this is another rationale for the micropattern: Small is more a typical variation than large. Nothing takes the place of precisely measuring an insect; match the length to the hook shank.

(7) Examine the color when the pattern is wet as most colors darken when wet. Materials for nymphs and wet patterns should be matched to the natural when wet. Dry patterns should be matched when dry.

(8) Use living naturals and view their color in natural light. Artificial lights lack equal distribution of color. Incandescent light is predominately red-yellow and lacking in blue. This type of light makes reds and yellows stronger and blues weaker. Conversely, under a cool-white fluorescent light, which is high in blue-green energy and low in red, the reds are weak and the blues are strong. Small fly tyers may wish to use the color corrected, "full spectrum" lights now available. For accuracy, each shade should be matched under different lights to overcome the problem of metamerism, the phenomenon of an object appearing to be different colors when viewed in different light sources. The spectrophotometric curves in the light from the surface of a natural or artificial that appear as the same color when viewed under one light source may appear as different colors when viewed under a different light source with different color distribution. Remember, too, that from a distance bright colors or advancing colors make a small insect appear larger than the actual insect. Dark colors or receding colors make an insect appear smaller. It is always best to capture and measure, with a millimeter ruler or fly pattern, the natural insect.

(9) Even if color is not critical, a pattern still must have color. If we tie with colors appropriate for naturals, then it makes selecting the imitation easier. Even if our Adams is a variant shade of gray, it is still a more accurate match of the Callibaetis than a Cahill.

(10) Color memory can be erroneous. It is very difficult to remember a particular color because a color is not one thing; it is, at least, three things—hue, chroma, and value. It is best to record the color with the live natural in hand.

Commercial fly tying dyes, such as Veniard dyes, may be used for the color strips; they come in forty colors and may be mixed to produce other colors. If this method is used to create colors, a complete record of blend ratios should be kept for dyeing. This is an excellent method if you wish the pattern color to be based upon standard, commercial dyes. No matter what method is used, the color code should include the following field colors:

a. olive-green (burnt umber and veridian or raw sienna and Winsor green)
b. olive-brown (burnt umber and Hooker's green)
c. olive-dun (Payne's gray, burnt umber and veridian)
d. blue-dun (cerulean blue and Payne's gray)
e. iron blue-dun (cerulean blue, Payne's gray, and cobalt blue)
f. gray (Payne's gray)
g. black (lamp black)
h. Cahill (Chinese white, cadmium yellow, and burnt umber)
i. ginger (light cadmium red and burnt umber)
j. sulphur (cadmium yellow and sap green)
k. dark brown (Vandyke brown)

Other colors—such as golden olive, grannom green, lemon yellow, scarlet, insect green, and cinnamon—should be added to the color code. All the above colors and blends, based upon Winsor & Newton watercolors, are easily attained with modest skill and practice. When color-matching the wing or body of a specific insect, a value scale may not be necessary. Although most tying requires only the color of the body and wing, a complete color code would include the color of the tail, the body, the wings, and the legs. Be certain to identify the color of each insect part.

Remember that every color mixture is at the expense of its brilliance, and that the paper color becomes part of any transparent watercolor. When matching colors, select the nearest to it and modify it, if possible, with only one other color. Every color is degraded or neutralized by the addition of black, brown, and gray or the addition of its complementary color. Each color strip should display a wide value range from light to dark. To achieve this blended contrast, begin the strip with full color saturation. Continue to wash the color down the strip with water dilution until the desired light value is reached. Never darken or lighten a color with black or white. The light value of a color should merely be the dilution of the full saturated color. Watercolors, like all colorants, are not pure primary colors. Alizarin crimson and Payne's gray both contain a touch of blue that they will pass on in mixture. Remember also that the color of the natural insect is seldom the color used in dyeing. The natural color of the tying material and its absorbency will necessarily modify the value and hue of the dye color.

If care is taken in selecting and blending colors, the color code will improve with the seasons. It will permit accuracy and standardization in the fly diary as well as at the tying table. And the angler will come to know the subtle esthetics of the natural world and imitative tying.

FIELD IDENTIFICATION OF THE SMALL INSECT

Identifying small insects is a matter of knowing the field marks, the diagnostic "badges" that distinguish one insect from another. Some anglers reject insect identification as too difficult; there are just too many insects. Others may reject the academic terminology, and a few may believe that identification is not essential. The purpose of this chapter is to illustrate, without recourse to complex terminology, the basic small insects, especially those insects that create selective hatches. Knowing what insect, if only to the family level, that a trout takes is knowing what pattern to select and how to present it.

The identification of an insect is largely a matter of knowing what to look for—what "field marks" distinguish it as a particular insect. Field classification depends upon recognizing the diagnostic badges and upon the process of elimination, by deleting other insects that it may resemble. Shape and size are important, as well as color, habitat, movement, and behavior.

How does a birder identify a large, black bird? From a distance, it may be a crow or a raven. Size alone doesn't work; it could be an immature raven or a mature crow. What are the diagnostic field marks? In flight, the raven has measured, driving wing beats (movement), fondness for open country (habitat), a gruff and throaty "pruk-pruk-pruk" (call), a massive black bill and a wedge tail (shape). A mature crow is one-third the size, rarely far from coniferous or deciduous woods, has frequent wing beats and a square tail. A similar field system may work for the angler. Insects may be identified, with reasonable accuracy, by diagnostic features that include size, shape and color.

There is no universal directory of common names for all the angling insects. Tradition has determined some of the them. Common names may be regional, changing with the locality; this is especially true for some wide-ranging species. The most complete guide to the fly fisher's mayfly names appears in W. Patrick McCafferty's *Aquatic Entomology*.

The following *Field Identification* includes the common name, the scientific name, the habitat, the distribution, the structure, and the behavior of the common microinsects. The following taxonomic synopses are primarily based upon the immature insect at the family or genus level. The section, *Similar Taxa*, lists similar and commonly confused insects. The *Key Behavioral Features* allows the angler to present, in a natural manner, the pattern to the trout. Methodically collect insect encounters. After identifying an insect, study it. Make it part of the angling experience. The microcaddis that you meet today will become a friend on future waters. Field work may require a small millimeter ruler, a 20X hand lens, and a sketch book. A quick sketch of an insect, noting its prominent features, can lead to greater specificity. For further research, consult the entomological references listed in the bibliography. Naturals can be as enchanting as their imitations. Fly tying is imitating the shape, size, and color of the insect; fly fishing, the movement and habits of the insect. It is hoped that the following information and illustrations lessen the burden of field identification and make the object of imitation, the insect, a fascinating feature of fly fishing.

Common Name: Blue-Winged Olive, Little Olive

SCIENTIFIC NAME

> *Order:* Ephemeroptera
>
> *Family:* Baetidae
>
> *Genus: Baetis*
>
> *Species:* Approximately 40 species in North America. The most important species include *Baetis tricaudatus*, *Baetis bicaudatus*, and *Baetis hageni*.

Habitat: Baetis are tiny swimmers in streams and rivers of all sizes. They prefer the moderate to fast waters with gravel or cobble bottoms. They also like slow currents where aquatic plants grow, especially the rich spring creeks.

Status and Distribution: These are the most widespread and abundant mayflies in trout streams across North America. They occur over a wide range of stream types and habitats, and wherever they occur they become part of the trout diet.

Field Identification: It is difficult to distinguish individual species, especially the adults. Features that characterize the nymphs of the three most important species follow.

IMMATURE NYMPH/LARVAE

1. General Features:
   a. Size: 3–12 mm
   b. Number of Tails: 3, center tail ¼ to ½ as long as outer tails.
   c. Color: Tan, brown, gray, and olive
   d. Comments: Antennae at least 3X longer than head width.

2. Diagnostic Features:
   a. Key Physical Features:
      i. Slender, streamlined body
      ii. Three tails with center tail shortened
      iii. Single, oval gills on abdominal segments 1–7

B. bicaudatus	B. tricaudatus	B. hageni
only 2 tails	3 tails, middle tail ½ or less the length of outer tails	3 tails, middle tail ½ or less the length of outer tails
	10th abdominal segment brown	10th abdominal segment white

   b. Key Behavioral Features:
      i. Excellent swimmers. They swim with an up-and-down flipping action of the abdomen.
      ii. Very abundant in stream drift
      iii. Swim to surface for emergence.
      iv. Typically have 2 or 3 generations per year.
   c. Similar Taxa: *Callibaetis* (restricted to slow streams and lakes), *Pseudocloeon*, and small immature *Ameletus*.

MATURE ADULT

1. General Features:
   a. Size: 3–10 mm
   b. Number of Tails: 2
   c. Color: Tan, gray, or olive

2. Diagnostic Features:
   a. Key Physical Features:
      i. 2 tails
      ii. Very small wedge-shaped hind wings. May be difficult to see, but always present on species of the *Baetis* genus.
   b. Key Behavioral Features:
      i. Float long distances (30–100 feet) on surface during emergence
      ii. Spinner falls occur in morning or afternoon over riffle tailouts.
      iii. Excellent hatches occur in summer, fall, and late winter.
   c. Similar Taxa: Same as nymphs

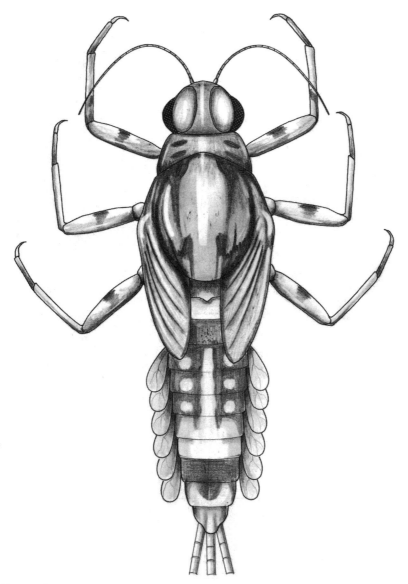

Baetis *nymph*

Common Name: *Caenis*, White-Winged Curse, Angler's Curse, Snowflake Mayfly

<u>Scientific Name</u>

Order: Ephemeroptera
Family: Caenidae
Genus: Caenis, Brachycercus
Species: C. simulans

Habitat: Nymphs prefer warmer, slower, and siltier waters than Tricos, which they closely resemble. Major populations may occur in waters of marginal trout quality.

Status and Distribution: Found across North America.

Field Identification:

IMMATURE NYMPH/LARVAE

1. General Features:
   a. Size: 3–4 mm
   b. Number of Tails: 3
   c. Color: Brown or tan
   d. Lacks hind wing pads

2. Diagnostic Features:
   a. Key Physical Features:

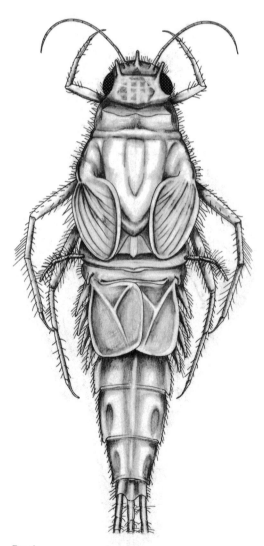

Brachycercus *nymph*

    i. One of the smallest insects that angler will encounter.

    ii. Gills on second abdominal segment large, rectangular and operculate, covering the remaining gills on segments 3–7

  b. Key Behavioral Features:

    i. Evening emergence followed immediately by spinner fall

  c. Similar Taxa: Tricos

MATURE ADULTS

1. General Features:

  a. Size: 3–4 mm

  b. Number of Tails: 3

  c. Lack hind wings

2. Diagnostic Features:

  a. Key Physical Features:

    i. Diminutive

    ii. Lack hind wings

    iii. 3 tails

    iv. Pale brown or tan

  b. Key Behavioral Features:

    i. Sporadic evening emergers, but may hatch with remarkable density.

    ii. The genus *Brachycerus nymph* displays tail in scorpion-like attitude when captured.

  c. Similar Taxa: Tricos

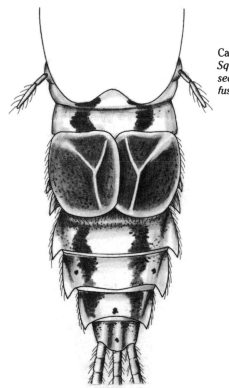

Caenis nymph
Squared, operculate gills on second abdominal segment not fused at midline

Common Name: Chironomids, Midges

Scientific Name

> *Order:* Diptera
>
> *Family:* Chironomidae
>
> *Genus:* Over 1,700 genera in North America
>
> *Species:* Over 1,000 species in North America

Habitat: All aquatic habitats, including such marginal habitats as spring seeps, pitcher plants, and tree holes. All habitats in streams and lakes that support trout and other fish also support numerous species of chironomids or midges. They thrive in all river sections, from fast rocky rapids to slow, silty pools.

Status and Distribution: Midges are widespread across all of North America, existing in a wide range of tolerances of temperature and water quality. Some species are found only in cool, clean water, whereas others are abundant in warm, polluted waters.

Field Identification: The complexity of this family makes it impossible to give field characteristics to distinguish specific genera or species. Consult the section on chironomids.

Immature Nymph/Larvae

1. General Features:
   a. Size: 1–20 mm
   b. Number of Tails: 0
   c. Colors: Green, black, gray, yellow, tan, and red
   d. Comments: The size range above indicates that some species get quite large. The majority of species, however, ranges from 1 to 10 mm, and this is one of the most important insects for the angler to imitate.

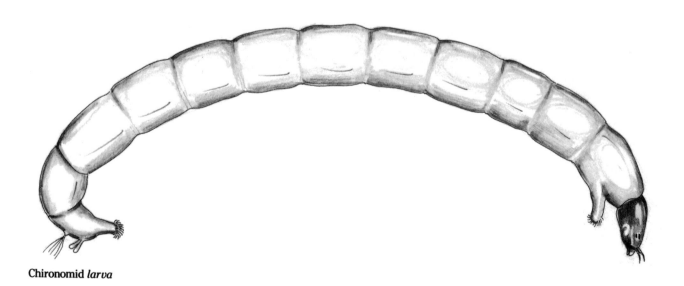

Chironomid *larva*

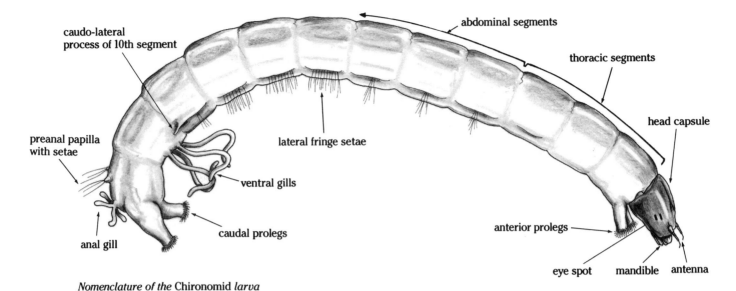

Nomenclature of the Chironomid *larva*

2. Diagnostic Features:
   a. Key Physical Features:
      i. No legs
      ii. Small, round dark head
      iii. First thoracic and last abdominal segments have a pair of short, ventral prolegs.
   b. Key Behavioral Features:
      i. Larvae do not swim
      ii. Larvae common in behavioral drift
      iii. Many species live in slender silk tubes attached to the substrata of the stream or lake bottom.
   c. Similar Taxa: Other small diptera, such as black fly (Simuliidae), No See-Ums (Ceratopogonidae), and small crane flies (Tipulidae).

MATURE PUPAE

1. General Features:
   a. Size: 1–15 mm
   b. Number of Tails: 0
   c. Color: Same as larvae
2. Diagnostic Features:
   a. Key Physical Features:
      i. Last abdominal segment flattened
      ii. Head, thorax, and wing case clustered at front of body.
   b. Key Behavioral Features:
      i. Rise slowly from the stream or lake bottom to the surface during emergence.
      ii. Pupae very common in stream drift.
      iii. Similar Taxa: Same as similar taxa of the larva plus some of the small caddis pupae such as the Hydroptilidae.

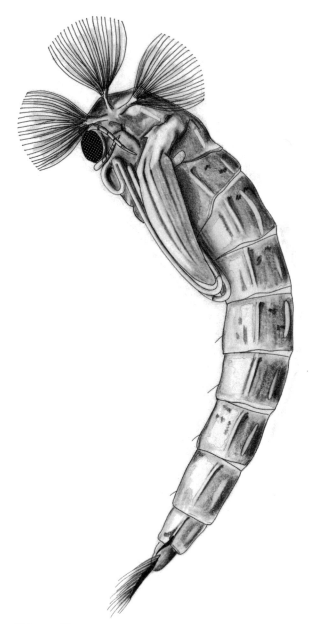

Chironomid *pupa*

MATURE ADULT

1. General Features:
   a. Size: 1–15 mm
   b. Number of Tails: 0
   c. Color: Same as larvae
2. Diagnostic Features:
   a. Key Physical Features:
      i. Only two wings (one pair)
      ii. Slender body and wings

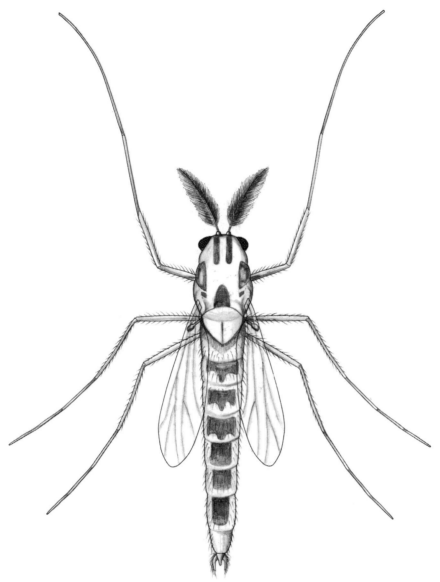

Chironomid *adult (male)*

    iii. Small, nonbiting mouth parts
    iv. Antennae with more than 5 segments, less than ½ body length.
       Males have bushy or hairy antennae (plumose antennae).
  b. Key Behavioral Features:
    i. Adults form large mating swarms from several feet to over 100 feet
      above the bank or water.
    ii. Adults drift on water surface during emergence.
    iii. Adult females oviposit underwater by crawling down rocks or
      aquatic plants.
  c. Similar Taxa: Same as pupae.

Common Name: Dance Fly, Empidids

<u>Scientific Name</u>

Order: Diptera

Family: Empididae

Genus: 19 genera in North America

Species: Approximately 240 species in North America

Habitat: Found in slow to moderately fast streams of all sizes. Most common in depositional areas where organic debris accumulates.

Status and Distribution: Very common insect. Adults frequently fly just above the water in circular or up-and-down patterns, hence the name dance fly. Their importance in angling is not well known, but their abundance suggests that they are an important food.

Field Identification:

Immature Nymph/Larvae

1. General Features:
    a. Size: 2–8 mm
    b. Number of Tails: 0
    c. Color: yellow, brown, tan, or olive
2. Diagnostic Features:
    a. Key Physical Features:
        i. Head not distinguishable, and reduced to a few simple rod-like structures
        ii. Paired prolegs present on abdominal segments
    b. Key Behavioral Features:
        i. Larvae live in bottom sediment and in organic drift, hence not readily available to fish
        ii. Predacious larvae feed on simulid larvae and pupae.
    c. Similar Taxa: Midges (*Chironomidae*) and other small fly larvae, such as the Watersnipe Fly (*Athericidae*).

Mature Pupae

1. General Features:
    a. Size: 2–8 mm
    b. Number of Tails: 0
    c. Colors: Yellow, brown, tan, or olive
2. Diagnostic Features:
    a. Key Physical Features:
        i. Pupa similar to chironomid pupae, but lack bushy gills above the head.
        ii. Some species with distinctive hair-like processes extending from sides of abdomen.
    b. Key Behavioral Feature:
        Pupae develop in damp soil, organic debris, or stream margins.
    c. Similar Taxa: Midges (*Chironomidae*), crane flies (*Tipulidae*) and other small diptera.

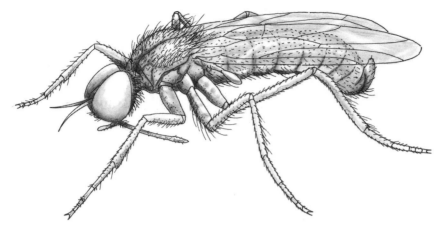

Empidid *adult*

Mature Adults

1. General Features:
   a. Size: 2–6mm
   b. Number of Tails: 0
   c. Color: Black, brown, or gray.
2. Diagnostic Features:
   a. Key Physical Features:
      i. Small, slender, delicate body. Most have enlarged thorax, but slender abdomen, unlike the stocky black fly.
      ii. Short, piercing mouth parts
      iii. 3-Segmented antennae with long, slender filament on last segment
      iv. Male genitalia, which are terminal, may be conspicuous
   b. Key Behavioral Features:
      i. Adults are predacious and feed on other small insects hatching or caught in surface film.
      ii. The dance behavior occurs as adults fly low over the water searching for food.
   c. Similar Taxa: Many small diptera, including midges (*Chironomidae*) and crane flies (*Tipulidae*).

Common Name: Mahogany Dun, Paraleptophlebia

Scientific Name

Order: Ephemeroptera

Family: Leptophlebiidae

Genus: Paraleptophlebia

Species: Approximately 33 species in North America.

Habitat: Found in all size streams and creeks. Prefer slow to moderately fast currents. Junior nymphs occur in faster water and, as they mature, move into slower water. Many nymphs found in organic debris such as leaf packs that provide food and shelter.

Status and Distribution: These are important mayflies in both free-stone streams and spring creeks. Though widely distributed, more species occur in Midwestern and Eastern states.

Field Identification:

IMMATURE NYMPH/LARVAE

1. General Features:
   a. Size: 7–9mm
   b. Number of Tails: 3
   c. Color: light tan, brown, or pale olive
2. Diagnostic Features:
   a. Key Physical Features:
      i. Slender, "tuning fork" gills on abdominal segments 1–7
      ii. All 3 tails of equal length
      iii. Mouth parts directed forward
      iv. Square head, in dorsal outline
   b. Key Behavioral Features:
      i. Nymphs crawl along bottom rocks and debris
      ii. Nymphs are weak swimmers that move with slow undulations of abdomen
      iii. Typically emerge by crawling out of water on rocks or plants near the bank
      iv. Some emerge just below the water surface in moderate to slow currents
   c. Similar Taxa: General body shape similar to the Pale Morning Dun

MATURE ADULTS

1. General Features:
   a. Size 7–9mm
   b. Number of Tails: 3
   c. Color: Duns—dark mahogany body and wings
      Spinners—Females have dark mahogany bodies and pale wings. Males have dark bodies and white abdomens.
2. Diagnostic Features:
   a. Key Physical Features:
      i. 3 tails
      ii. Hind wing evenly rounded without costal angulation
   b. Key Behavioral Features:
      i. Typically emerge in shallow or slow waters.
      ii. Spinner fall, which occurs during afternoon and evening, often important
      iii. Major hatches occur in spring and fall.
   c. Similar Taxa: Pale Morning Dun and *Heptagenia*.

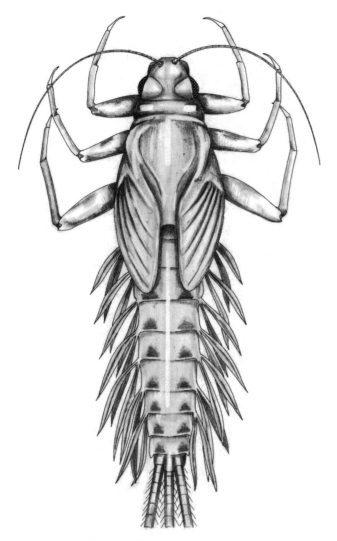

Paraleptophlebia *nymph*
This Paraleptophlebia *is typical of*
many of the species of
Paraleptophlebia.

Common Name: Microcaddis, Purse-Case Caddis

SCIENTIFIC NAME

Order: Trichoptera

Family: Hydroptilidae

Genus: 14 genera in North America. Most important include
Hydroptila, Leucotrichia, Oxyethira, Ochrotrichia

Species: Over 200 species in North America

Habitat: Most species prefer streams and rivers, where the larvae live
on rocks and boulders in fast to moderate currents or on attached algae and
plants in slow water. They feed on diatoms and other algae by scraping the
surface of rocks or piercing and sucking the nutrients from plant cells. Some

species are also common in still water, where they live on aquatic plants and algae.

Status and Distribution: Abundant populations appear throughout North America in nutrient-rich streams and lakes. Most are tolerant of warm water and organic enrichment.

Field Identification:

IMMATURE (NYMPH/LARVAE)

1. General Features:
   a. Size: 3–5 mm
   b. Number of Tails: 0
   c. Color: Yellow, brown, or olive
   d. Comments: Larvae are free-living (they build no case) until they begin their fifth and final instar (final larval stage). They then build a slipper or bottle-shaped case made of fine sand or parchment-like silk.

Hydroptila *case with larva (Hydroptilidae). The final instar of the* Hydroptila *has a laterally flattened case fabricated from two silk valves usually covered with sand, and sometimes with diatoms or algae. The bi-valve case has slit openings at each end.*

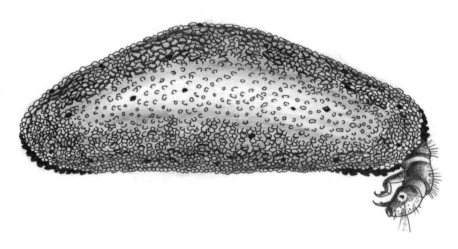

Ochrotrichia *case (Hydroptilidae) The* Ochrotrichia *case, similar to the* Hydroptila *case, is composed of two silk valves sprinkled with sand grains or filamentous algae. Although rare, the Ochrotrichia case may be a single convex valve carried tortoise-like.*

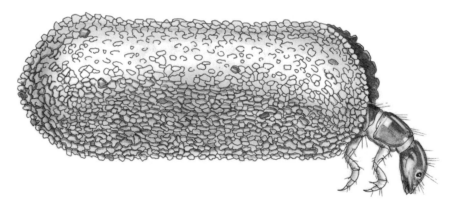

Leucotrichia *case (lateral view)*

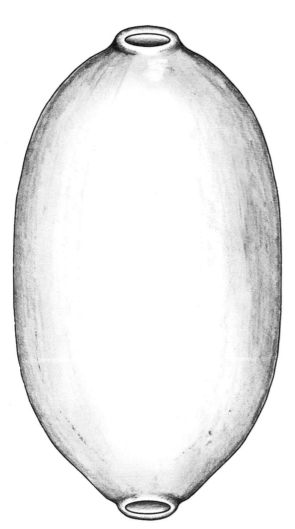

Leucotrichia *case (Hydroptilidae). The flattened case, entirely made of silk and anchored along its borders to a rock, has circular rimmed openings at each end (dorsal view).*

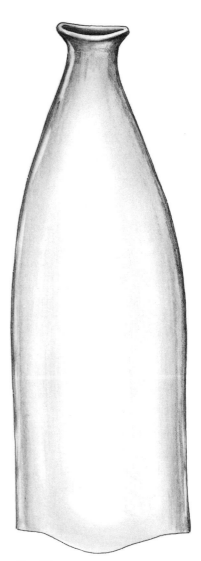

Oxyethira *case*

Glossosoma case (Glossosomatidae) Glossosoma cases, composed of fairly uniform stones, tend to be long (up to 12 millimeters) and usually lack silk around the openings (ventro-lateral view).

Agapetus *Case (Glossosomatidae)* An Agapetus *larval case has relatively large stones on each side and is higher in relation to length than other Glossosomatid cases. Main openings may have silk "gates" for complete closure (ventro-lateral view).*

2. Diagnostic Features:
   a. Key Physical Features:
      i. Diminutive size
      ii. Typically swollen and greatly distended abdomen of mature larvae
      iii. Dorsal plates on all three thoracic segments. Features that characterize the larvae of the four major genera are listed below:

Hydroptila	*Ochrotrichia*
Abdomen only slightly enlarged	Abdomen only slightly enlarged
Laterally compressed purse-like case covered with fine sand	Case similar to *Hydroptila*

Leucotrichia	*Oxyethira*
abdomen greatly enlarged	abdomen greatly enlarged
Flattened elliptical case on the sides of rocks	Bottle-shaped cases made of silk

b. Key Behavioral Features:
   i. Rarely seen. Mature larvae hide in sediments or attach themselves to rocks and plants.
   ii. Larvae are weak swimmers, but common in the stream drift.
c. Similar Taxa: Most likely to be confused with small Diptera larvae, especially chironomids that build tube shelters.

MATURE PUPAE
1. General Features:
   a. Size: 3–5 mm
   b. Number of Tails: 0
   c. Color: Yellow, brown, or orange
   d. Comments: Pupae drift and swim to the surface for emergence.

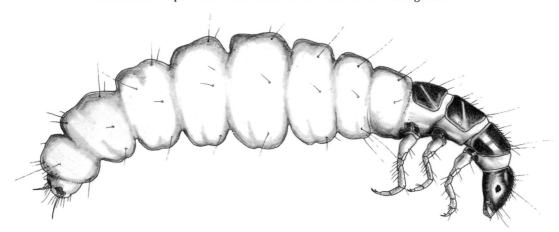

Hydroptila *larva (Hydroptilidae)*
The Hydroptila, *which apparently feed upon filamentous algae, inhabit lakes and streams. Approximately 60 species inhabit North America and are found throughout most of the continent.*

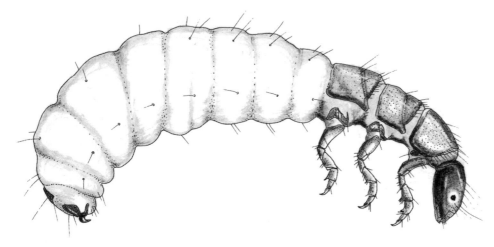

Ochrotrichia *larva (Hydroptilidae)*
Generally similar to the Hydroptila, *the* Ochrotrichia *larvae do lack the apical filamentous gills of the genus. There are slight size differences among the three pairs of legs.*

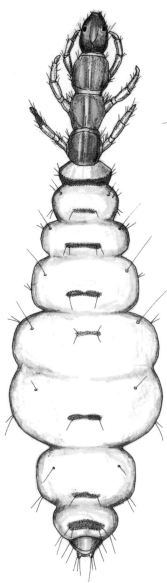

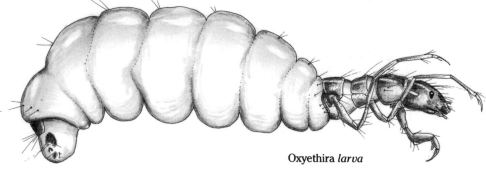

Oxyethira *larva*

2. Diagnostic Features: (Difficult to distinguish the four major genera in the field.)
   a. Key Physical Features: diminutive size
   b. Key Behavioral Features: Swimming and drifting to the surface, where emergence occurs.
   c. Similar Taxa: Small Diptera pupae such as *chironomids*.

MATURE ADULTS

1. General Features:
   a. Size: 3–5 mm
   b. Number of Tails: 0
   c. Color: Body color ranges from yellow to brown to green with tan or black mottled wings.
   d. Comments: Antennae relatively short, about ½ body length, for caddis.

2. Diagnostic Features: (Difficult to distinguish the four major genera in the field.)
   a. Key Physical Features:
      i. Diminutive size
      ii. Hind wing narrow and pointed with posterior fringe of long, fine hairs
   b. Key Behavioral Features:
      i. Most commonly seen scurrying rapidly over rocks and plants along stream banks or lake shores.

Leucotrichia *larva (Hydroptilidae).*
The Leucotrichia *larva has a bright green abdomen with distinct laterally distended abdominal segments. The larvae, which graze on periphyton and particulate detritus, live on rocks in swift currents. Most larvae overwinter in the final instar and emerge as adults from May through August.*

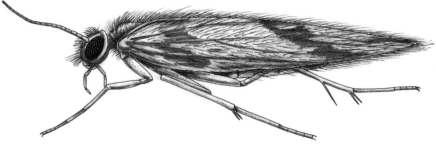

Hairy Hydroptila *(adult)*

ii. Females dive under water to lay eggs.
c. Similar Taxa: Small Diptera adults, especially chironomids and black flies (Simuliidae).

Common Name: Pale Morning Dun, PMD

Order: Ephemeroptera

Family: Ephemerellidae

Genus: Ephemerella

Species: inermis

Habitat: Pale Morning Duns are found in various stream habitats. They are abundant in the rich aquatic weeds of spring creeks, and are often one of the most abundant mayflies in freestone streams. They occur in moderate currents with a gravel substrate. Their broad and varied habitat make them one of the most common mayflies on a trout stream.

Status and Distribution: Abundant on all types of trout streams throughout the West.

Field Identification:

IMMATURE NYMPH/LARVAE

1. General Features:
   a. Size: 7–9 mm
   b. Number of Tails: 3
   c. Color: Dark brown
2. Diagnostic Features:
   a. Key Physical Features:
      i. 3 tails of equal length with lateral fringe of fine hairs
      ii. Rectangular body with head narrower than thorax.
   b. Key Behavioral Features:
      i. Moderately good swimmers. Swim with a slow up-and-down motion of whole body.
      ii. Common in stream drift
   c. Similar Taxa: *Baetis tricaudatus, Ephemerella infrequens, Attenalla margarita*

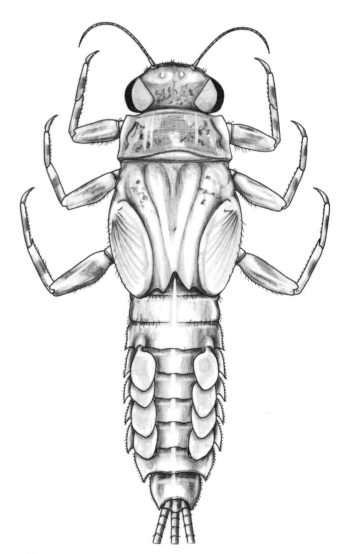

Ephemerella inermis nymph

MATURE ADULT

1. General Features:
   a. Size: 7–9 mm
   b. Number of Tails: 3
   c. Comments: Colors generally vary from pale olive to creamy yellow.
2. Diagnostic Features:
   a. Key Physical Features:
      i. 3 tails
      ii. Hind wing conspicuous and evenly rounded except for slight angulation on front margin.
   b. Key Behavioral Features:
      i. Emerge morning or afternoon
      ii. Spinner falls often heavy, morning and afternoon.
   c. Similar Taxa: *Baetis tricaudatus, Ephemerella infrequens, Attenalla margarita.*

Common Name: Reed Smuts, Black Flies, Buffalo Gnats, Riffle Smuts

SCIENTIFIC NAME

Order: Diptera

Family: Simuliidae

Genus: 10 genera, most common are *Simulium* and *Prosilmulium*

Species: Approximately 143 species in North America

Habitat: Found in various water types, but generally in moderate to fast currents. Can be abundant in spring creeks with ample aquatic plants. Common on both rocky substrata and aquatic plant stems. Larvae and pupae occur in same habitats.

Status and Distribution: Widely distributed in streams throughout North America. In many areas, they are significant pests, as adults have piercing mouth parts and ingest blood.

Field Identification:

IMMATURE NYMPH/LARVAE

1. General Features:
   a. Size: 3–15 mm
   b. Number of Tails: 0
   c. Color: Dirty yellow, pale tan, gray, olive, or black
2. Diagnostic Features:
   a. Key Physical Features:
      i. Body slender, anteriorly enlarged to a bulbous posterior. Bowling pin appearance.
      ii. Distinct pair of cephalic fans extending above the head. Fans designed to filter plankton from the current.

Reed Smut larva (Simuliidae). The Reed Smut or Blackfly larva likes swift currents. The head carries prominent fans that extract fine particulate food matter from passing waters. The posterior of the larva has a disc of hooks that attach the larva to a silk patch spun of the substrata. In the semi-upright feeding position, the larva extends the concave surfaces of the head fans against the current. The fans filter out plankton, detritus, and bacteria as small as one ten-thousandths of a millimeter. The larva may move by spinning a small patch of silk onto the substrata immediately in front of it. It then hooks the finger-like proleg into the patch and releases its attachment. When the posterior hook-disc grips the new silk patch, the proleg releases its grip. The movement is slow and deliberate.

In the northern hemisphere, emergence occurs from spring to autumn. Distinct population surges occur at certain times, such as spring, when trout may feed mostly on Reed Smuts. The emergence, the black body cloaked in a silvery bubble, is highly conspicuous. Smut larvae will be in the drift all year, with increases in spring and during water level changes. Trout mostly take larvae and adults. The hump-backed adult, the "Buffalo Gnat," is vulnerable to dish predation during emergence, when male mating columns fly low to the water and females are sent adrift during ovipositing. Ovipositing varies among species—broadcasting eggs over the surface, depositing eggs on submerged plants, or by laying eggs on partially submerged stones. In submerged ovipositing, females will actually alight on the stones and deposit a patch of white eggs up to 20 centimeters beneath the water surface.

   iii. Subfamilies:

      Subfamily Prosimuliinae: If cephalic fans are present, then terminal antennae segments much darker than paler basal segments (McCafferty).

      Subfamily Simuliinae: All have cephalic fans and lack contrast between the terminal antennae segments and basal segments (McCafferty).

  b. Key Behavioral Features:

    i. Found on top of rocks and aquatic plants exposed to the current

    ii. Common in stream drift

    iii. Larvae will leave substrata attached by a silk thread and hang in the current. A larvae pattern and tippet imitate this behavior.

  c. Similar Taxa: Chironomid larvae and small crane fly larvae (Tipulidae) somewhat similar.

MATURE PUPAE

1. General Features:

  a. Size: 3–5 mm

  b. Number of Tails: 0

  c. Colors: Brown, gray, olive, and black

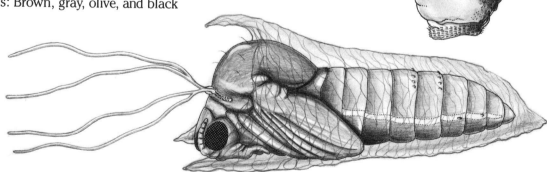

Reed Smut (Simulium) pupa in Slipper Case (Simuliidae)
The final instar larva spins a silk cocoon for pupation. Depending upon the species, the cocoon is either an open-ended "slipper" or a closed-ridge "shoe." Slipper cases are usually found in slower waters than shoe cases. The pupa has body hooklets that firmly imbed it within the pupal sheath. At the head of the pupa are "plastron gills," branched breathing filaments. The shape of these gills provides a simple method for identifying a species.

2. Diagnostic Features:
  a. Key Physical Features:
    i. Triangular silk case, somewhat vase-like, attached firmly to substrata
  b. Key Behavioral Features:
    i. Pupa not found in the drift (firmly attached to substrata)
    ii. Pupation completed in 2–8 days
  c. Similar Taxa: None.

MATURE ADULTS

1. General Features:
  a. Size 3–6 mm
  b. Number of Tails: 0
  c. Other: Short, stocky body
2. Diagnostic Features:
  a. Key Physical Features:
    i. Short, pointed, conical antennae, shorter than thorax, never plumose
    ii. Stocky body with hump-backed thorax
  b. Key Behavioral Features:
    i. Midstream emergence from pupal case
    ii. Adults may swarm and become serious biting pests.
    iii. Eggs deposited on the underside of rocks, aquatic plants, or logs in broken, fast water.
  c. Similar Taxa: Midges (*Chironomidae*), Dance Flies (*Empididae*).

Common Name: Saddle-Case Caddis

SCIENTIFIC NAME

Order: Trichoptera

Family: Glossosomatidae

Genus: 6 genera in North America. Most important are *Glossosoma* and *Agapetus*

Species: About 60 species in North America

Habitat: Found only in flowing water. Prefer the tops and sides of grapefruit- to bowling-ball-sized rocks in medium to fast currents.

Status and Distribution: Widespread and abundant across North America. Particularly abundant in free-stone streams in mountainous regions. Require cool, clean water and are sensitive to pollution.

Field Identification: Distinguishing the different genera of adult glossosomatids requires detailed keys and microscope. Features of the larvae of the two most important genera are described below:

IMMATURE (NYMPH/LARVAE)

1. General Features:
  a. Size: 5–8 mm

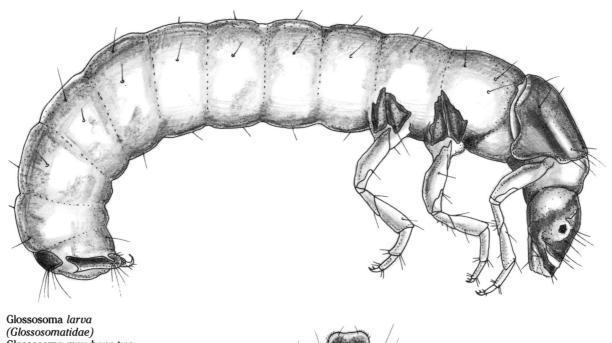

Glossosoma *larva*
(Glossosomatidae)
Glossosoma *may have two*
generations a year and feed largely
upon algae and detritus. They may
be the dominant saddle-case
caddis in cold, swift streams.

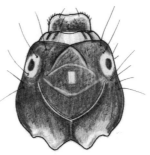

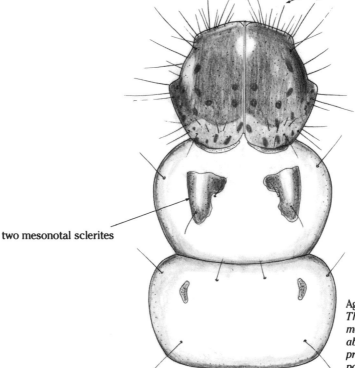

dense pronotal setae

two mesonotal sclerites

Agapetus *larva (Glossosomatidae)*
The Agapetus *larva has two*
mesonotal plates (sclerites) and
abundant hairs (setae) on the
pronotum, especially near the
posterior margin.

  b. Number of Tails: 0
  c. Color: Brown to dirty yellow-orange
2. Diagnostic Features:
  a. Key Physical Feature(s):
    i. Larvae lack gills
    ii. Dome- or igloo-shaped case made of sand or fine gravel.
    iii. Case completely covers larvae so neither head nor rear can be seen from above.
  b. Key Behavioral Features:
    i. Larval cases are attached on the top and sides of rocks, where they are easily seen.
    ii. Larvae move very slowly, scraping diatoms off the rock surface.

Glossosoma	*Agapetus*
Thoracic sclerites (plates) present only on first thoracic segment	Thoracic sclerites (plates) present on all thoracic segments
Case made of evenly sized pieces of small gravel	Case with a large, oversized stone on each side

  c. Similar Taxa: Aquatic moth larvae (Family: Pyralidae)

MATURE PUPAE

1. General Features:
  a. Size: 5–8mm
  b. Number of Tails: 0
  c. Color: Brown, pale yellow or pale orange
  d. Comments: Wingpads are dark brown or black
2. Diagnostic Features:
  a. Key Physical Feature: Hind legs are flattened, forming a paddle for swimming.
  b. Key Behavioral Features:
    i. Very active swimmers when emerging
    ii. Swim with erratic kicks of the hind legs
  c. Similar Taxa: Other microcaddis such as the *Hydroptilidae*.

MATURE ADULTS

1. General Features:
  a. Size: 6–10 mm
  b. Number of Tails: 0
  c. Color: Dark brown or tan body with black wings
2. Diagnostic Features:
  a. Key Physical Features:
    i. 3 ocelli
    ii. No fringe on margins of hind wings
    iii. 5th segment of maxillary palpi similar in shape and length to 4th segment.

b. Key Behavioral Features:
  i. Adults common on streamside vegetation, where they remain quiet until disturbed.
  ii. Adult females dive underwater to lay eggs.
c. Similar Taxa: Other small caddis, especially *Hydroptilidae* and some *Brachycentridae*.

Common Name: Tiny Blue-Winged Olive, *Pseudocloeon*

SCIENTIFIC NAME

Order: Ephemeroptera

Family: Baetidae

Genus: Pseudocloeon

Species: Approximately 20 North American species

Habitat: Streams with moderate to slow currents. *Pseudocloeons* seem to prefer sections with small gravel or aquatic plants. Some of the best populations occur in spring creeks, but many freestone streams also contain *Pseudocloeons*.

Status and Distribution: Pseudocloeons occur across North America, and have their greatest distribution and diversity in Eastern and Midwestern streams. Apparently only two species occur in Western waters: *P. edmundsi* and *P. turbidum*. *P. edmundsi* is the most common and abundant of the two.

Field Identification:

IMMATURE NYMPH/LARVAE

1. General Features:
  a. Size: 3–9 mm
  b. Number of Tails: 2
  c. Color: Pale olive
  d. Lacks hind wing pads
2. Diagnostic Features:
  a. Key Physical Features:
    i. Only 2 tails. One other *Baetis*, *B. bicaudatus*, has 2. All other *Baetis* have 3 tails.
    ii. Lacks hind wing pads
    iii. Body is stouter, squatter than typical *Baetis*.
  b. Key Behavioral Features:
    i. Active swimmer
    ii. Common in stream drift
    iii. Nymphs swim to surface during emergence.
  c. Similar Taxa: *Baetis bicaudatus.*

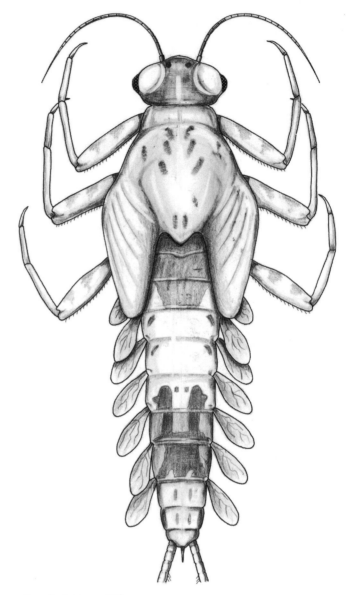

Pseudocloeon *nymph*

<small>Mature Adults</small>

1. General Features:
   a. Size: 3–9 mm
   b. Number of Tails: 3
   c. Comment: Lacks hind wing

2. Diagnostic Features:
   a. Key Physical Features:
      i. No hind wing. The only other mayflies with two wings are *Tricos*, *Caenis*, and *Cloeon*.
      ii. Small size
      iii. Two tails

b. Key Behavioral Features:
  i. Typically emerges late afternoon
  ii. Spinner falls in the morning.
c. Similar Taxa: *B. bicaudatus*, *Tricos*, *Caenis*, and *Cloeon*.

Common Name: Trico, Black and White

Order: Ephemeroptera

Family: Tricorythodidae

Genus: Tricorythodes

Species: T. minutus

Habitat: This tiny crawler mayfly prefers slow to moderate currents in freestone or spring creeks. They are often most abundant in rich spring creeks with heavy aquatic plant growth. These nymphs can tolerate silt and fine sediment more than most mayfly species.

Status and Distribution: Tricos are found across North America from small to large streams and rivers. As indicated above, major populations usually occur in spring creeks. Because of their small size, most anglers may not notice their presence unless they encounter a heavy hatch.

Field Identification:

IMMATURE NYMPH/LARVAE

1. General Features:
   a. Size: 3–5 mm
   b. Number of Tails: 3
   c. Color: Dark brown to black
2. Diagnostic Features:
   a. Key Physical Features:
      i. Small size
      ii. First pair of gills (segment 2) are large, triangular, and operculate (cover), shielding the remaining gills on segments 3–7.
      iii. Gills on segments 3–7 are without fringed margins.

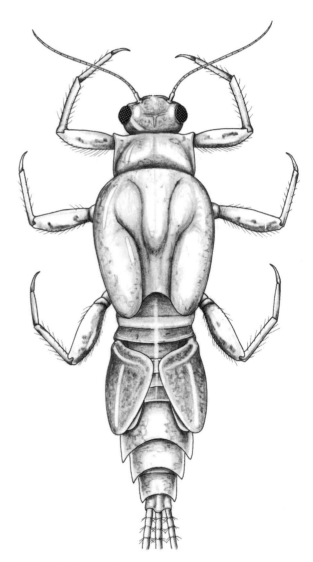

Tricorythodes nymph

   b. Key Behavioral Features:
      i. Found in siltier and warmer stream sections than most mayflies.
      ii. Nymphs are weak swimmers, often abundant in the drift.
   c. Similar Taxa: Family Caenidae, genus *Caenis*

MATURE ADULT

1. General Features:
   a. Size: 3–5 mm
   b. Number of Tails: 3
   c. No hind wings
2. Diagnostic Features:
   a. Key Physical Features:
      i. Small
      ii. Lack hind wings
      iii. Three tails two to three times body length
   b. Key Behavioral Features:
      i. Large spinner swarms common early to midmorning.
      ii. Duns molt to spinners in only a few hours.
   c. Similar Taxa: Species of families Baetidae and Caenidae.

*T*he *Tools*

Tying the small fly does not require many tools. Tools will not compensate for poor methods or materials; however, some tools do make tying simpler and patterns better. Here are some tools especially appropriate for tying small.

The Hair Stacker

Standard hair stackers may not work well for micropatterns. Owing to the short hairs used in tying small patterns, the free- bore (the space between the male end and the female end) should be short, about 3.5 millimeters. This allows minimal extension of the fibers for extracting. Some standard stackers have a long free-bore that allows the fibers to drop before they are withdrawn. The wall must be thick enough so that the fiber tips do not scrape the cup wall when the tube is withdrawn. If they touch, the fibers will pull askew. The bore diameter should be small, about 6 millimeters to "parallel" and bundle the fibers. To facilitate removal of fibers, a slight cutaway may help; but then the stacker would have to be oriented correctly during drumming and before removal of hairs. When stacking, a few vertical taps separate and loosen the fibers, allowing natural adjustments. Continued vertical stacking spreads the hair tips so that they are misaligned when withdrawn. Next, gently drum the stacker barrel at 45° to bundle and align the fibers in the "gutter" of the stacker. Violent, vertical raps will only misalign and displace the small fibers. For a faster, more accurate stack, clip the longer hairs to the length of the shorter ones to prevent their ends from hanging up on the shorter fibers. Make certain that the fibers are withdrawn from the tube already in position for tying. Avoid passing the stacked fibers between hands. When flaring fibers, rather than wrapping with a flat thread, spin the bobbin to tightly twist the thread so that it "knifes" into the fibers to spread them. It is this attention to detail that produces a more delicate, durable, and thoughtful pattern. The Renzetti Midge stacker has two different sized tubes, one at each end, for patterns size 16 and smaller.

The API "Pin Holder" converted for extended-body patterns

API Pin Holder

Although originally designed to hold special pins for tying tube flies, the Tube Fly Tying Tool from Angling Products, Incorporated, also holds needles for tying extended body patterns. Unlike a vise jaw, the V-block design, which holds any pin up to ⁵⁄₃₂ diameter, prevents all needle movement. This is especially critical when holding fine needles for extended-body micropatterns. The Tube Fly Tying Tool clamps into the jaws of any fly-tying vise.

Scissors

Nothing makes tying a pleasure like sharp, finely pointed scissors. Micropatterns require scissors that cut at the tip. Selection and care of scissors are important. Serious scissors should be free of casting pits. The blades should be sharpened at a uniform bevel and depth down the blade. The standard bevel is approximately 25°, but scissors designed for specific materials may be ground down as far as 40°. To snip a fine barb or thread, scissors must be acutely pointed; no flat surface should appear at the top of the blade tips. Double- or single-ground ultrafine points, approximately 10°, are preferred. When worked, quality scissors have a solid, swishing sound without stuttering. Some tyers find that curved blades increase visibility and reduce arm movement. The blades of scissors touch at only two points—the pivot point and the cut point. The cut point, much like the center of a cross, moves along the edges of the shear bars, as both blades wrap around each other when closing. Thus, a single cut or shear point passes down the blades when closing. This traveling cut point should never hesitate. The finger loops or rings should be large and comfortable. The curved, inner frame notch of some scissors can cut tying wires. Otherwise, small, finely pointed side-cutters should be used. Some tyers magnetize the tips for selecting and handling small hooks. The Orvis' Micro Scissors and Iris Scissors and Umpqua Feather Merchant's Micro-fine Squizzers have remarkably fine points for precise trimming. Such fine and delicate points should not be used for cutting coarse materials.

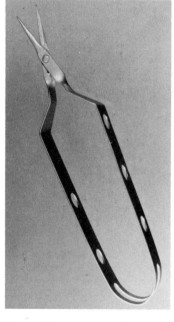

Umpqua's stainless-steel Squizzers are squeezable scissors. Manufactured by a surgical instrument company, these blades, with dramatic overlap, are remarkably sharp and fine. The comfortable and substantial handle makes them easy to pick up and prevents them from twisting while cutting. Such fine tips are appropriate for tying micropatterns.

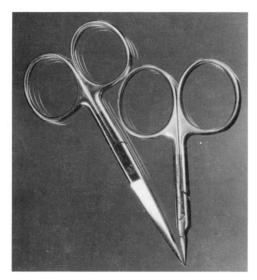

Micro-pointed scissors

The Tying Vise

The vise is the center piece of tying the micropatterns. The modern tying vise—with its spinning jaws, spring jaws, canted jaws, and interchangeable jaws—is a wonder. Specialized vises bite down on anything from midges to muddlers. Although most vises will hold small hooks, some do it better than others. A good vise should hold a hook firmly with minimal adjustment while allowing access to the hook. It should be simple and reliable. A popular and simple system is a spring-lever that exerts continuous pressure on the jaws. The Regal vise jaws, although not as slender and delicate as other jaws, require no adjustments. They are merely wedged open by a lever to accept the hook.

The draw-cam system, as seen on a modern Thompson A, has a rotating lever with an increasing radius cam or wiper cam that draws the tapered rear of the jaws into a sleeve or collet, thereby closing the jaws. A reverse system, the push cam, appears on a few vises. The push-cam system levers the jaws through a collet that compresses and closes the jaws. In this system, the jaw that exits the collet is correspondingly smaller in diameter, making the push-cam vises superior for small patterns. The push-cam system appears on various vises, including those from Dyna-king and Renzetti. A smooth cam closes the short-radius jaws of the Dyna-King. The blunt, bullet jaw of the Dyna-King has a short radius that accommodates small hooks.

Perhaps the most popular push-cam vise that midwifes micropatterns is the Renzetti Presentation vise. Made of stainless steel, brass and aluminum, the Renzetti Presentation vise employs the push-cam, the "reverse" jaw system. Various jaws, including the RVJ-1 jaw for sizes 18 to 28 hooks, are quickly changed by turning the jaw actuator knob, dropping the jaw out, and inserting the desired one. The most important feature for the small-fly tyer is the extended and angled jaw head that offers excellent tying clearance around the hook.

The Dyna-King Prince vise with adjustable moon

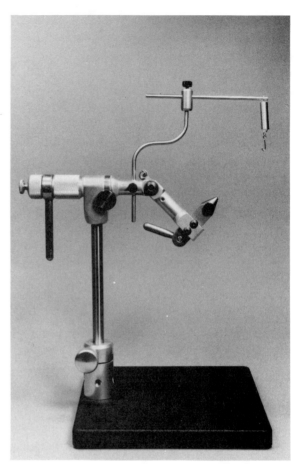

The Renzetti master vise and gallows

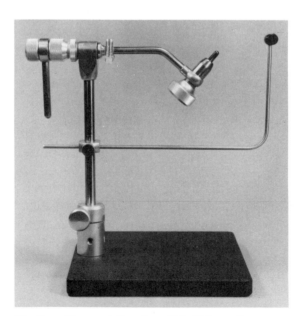

The Renzetti presentation vise with bobbin cradle

The smooth, angled head prevents fine thread from becoming entangled (out of thread's harm) while tying. The vise comes complete with a material spring and bobbin cradle. The bobbin cradle, replete with an O-ring embedded in the slip-clamp, maintains adjustment and supports the thread or bobbin when required. The finger space beneath and behind the hook makes this a superior vise for small patterns. The angled head, often considered the most remarkable advancement in tying vises during the first quarter of the twentieth century, allows tying space. The Renzetti increases that tying space due to the extended head and small jaw.

Most rotary vises pivot on the jaw axis; however, due to Renzetti's offset jaw, the hook is in line with the rotary shaft, allowing the hook shank to twirl on its own axis. This permits viewing the pattern while tying. Furthermore, rather than orbiting the hand around the shank when applying materials, the hook itself twirls on the materials. When tying small, "precision" patterns, the rotating vise allows the tyer to roll the fly for observation. When winding ribbing or palmer hackles, rotation promotes uniform spacing and controlled tension. Flies are three-dimensional, and thread tension often pushes our mistakes to the far side of the hook, out of sight. A rotating vise shows the tyer the complete pattern. Look at the left side of a right-hand tied fly; that's where errors often live. To avoid off-side errors, Oliver Edwards of England wraps the thread in the opposite direction so that errors are pulled toward him, where they may be seen and corrected. Steve Brocco, a master salmon fly tyer of Seattle, makes ribbing spirals progressively wider, for a pleasant aesthetic touch. Much can be learned from the thread and material manipulation of master salmon fly tyers. Like the Parthenon, the harmony of a fly comes not from monotonous and methodical arrangement, but from harmony of parts and subtle refinements. The outer columns of the Parthenon lean inward to correct the optical illusion that they lean outward. If ribbing is perfectly uniform, the pattern may appear static and dead. The rotary vise allows the tyer to see the ribbing mount at every point on the body. A palmer hackle should go immediately *behind* the rib. If it's in front, the rib will kick the body hackle out. The Palmer will slip on the rib. Furthermore, the hackle is held at the same angle throughout mounting so that the barbs are uniformly canted. When working with a dubbing loop, rotate the hook shank a quarter turn (counterclockwise when viewed from the hook eye) to move the point out of the way of the dangling and spinning loop. Posting wings is simpler when viewed from the top. And when applying cement, rotation produces a smoother finish. Simply stated, a rotary vise encourages careful tying. It allows more precise and natural placement of various materials. A rotary vise promotes three-dimensional tying.

In small-fly tying, various accoutrements (gallows hook, thread keeper, or tool cradle) are sometimes employed. A universal slip-clamp that could be left on the vise stem to hold a variety of attachments, such as gallows tool, tying moon, or bobbin cradle would be beneficial. Grooved or serrated jaws, no matter how finely etched, are not recommended for small, fine hooks. Some jaws may not expose enough hook heel for tying small or sloped-shank patterns. Although grooved jaws may hold a small hook, they may damage it,

Hand carders for blending and aligning dubbing

or prevent it from being correctly positioned. Smooth jaws are safer when tying on fine-wire hooks. Most quality vises have interchangeable jaws with special jaws for small hooks.

Carders and Grinders

Micropatterns commonly require finely chopped and blended dubbing. Small electric mills with sharp propellers quickly blend and mince dubbing for micropatterns. The electric mills are excellent for producing CDC dubbing. Small wool carders, wire brushes used for disentangling fibers or raising a nap, also blend small amounts of dubbing easily. Furthermore, carders can align the fibers for particular dubbing applications.

The Belgium Dubbing Rake

The Belgium dubbing rake, when stroked in the direction of fur growth, cuts and separates the underfur from the guard hairs. The guard hairs may be then

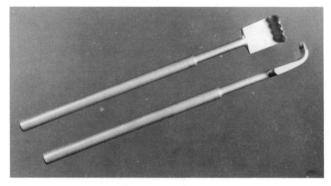

Belgian dubbing rakes made by Lawrence Waldron

plucked from the dubbing. Furthermore, it slashes the fur to various lengths, facilitating dubbing. The toothed cutter has sharp and beveled inside edges that shear and scrape. With light strokes, the beveled cutters will remove the underfur with minimal guard hairs. When greater pressure is applied to the stroke, the dubbing rake crops the guard hairs as well. It is a superior method for extracting fine fur from hides.

The Yorkshire Moon

Beyond adequate and proper lighting is the problem of contrast. Trying to match split tails on a size 24 against the background clutter of most tying tables is agony. As Emerson said, "A foolish consistency is the hobgoblin of little minds." Perhaps there is a way of having a messy desk *and* a neat fly. The Moon—created by Mike Mee of Yorkshire, England—is an adjustable shield placed behind the fly for contrast, making viewing and tying easier. For small-pattern tying, the Mee Moon may improve detail and lessen eye fatigue.

Some moons offer interchangeable neutral gray or pale cream shields, a color on each side, for contrast. Shields may connect with a Velcro patch to vary the angle and position. Adjustable moons are positioned to prevent glare while allowing a clear view of fine barbs and thread work. Some moons connect to the vise stem with an angled shaft and slip-clamp, and have complete articulation. Like a real moon, it "orbits" the vise shaft to offer an adjustable backdrop for tying.

Magnetic Hook Dish

A useful tool for holding small hooks is the Clipwell Magnetic Dish. Shallow and stable, the dish readily offers the tyer a size 24 hook. It also sweeps the floor to pick up dropped and hidden hooks. Select a dish color, such as cream, that readily displays hooks without undue glare. If hooks linger in the dish, they will become magnetic. Mild magnetism, however, usually is no problem in tying.

The magnetic hook dish

The Dubbing Whirl

The Dubbing whirl is excellent for dubbing bodies, fur collars, or legs for small nymphs. The mere weight of the whirl, when "on the dangle," should close the supple hooks to trap any material placed in the thread loop. Short strips of squirrel or mole, with the hide line attached, are placed in the thread loop. The hide line is then trimmed, leaving the fibers trapped between the threads. Twirl the whirl to create a fur brush. To produce fine microdubbing, hang the whirl on a thread loop. On one thread, apply wax and dust dubbing. When whirled, the dubbing, mounted on a single strand, creates a fine haze around the twisted, double threads.

The Dubbing whirl

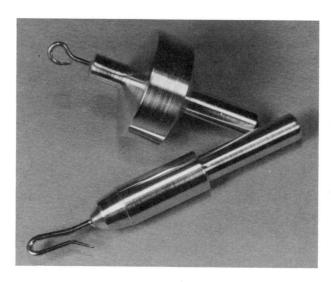

Single-hook whirls made by Frank Matarelli

Matarelli's Ultra-light Single-Hook Spinner for whirling dubbing loops and fine-wire dubbing brushes

The Single-Hook Whirl

A weighted, single-hook whirl allows a tyer to form wire-core dubbing brushes. Unlike the larger dubbing brush spinner, a single-hook whirl is portable. Heavier, single-hook whirls can make furled leaders.

Dubbing Wax

For small patterns, a hyper-adhesive wax facilitates tying. Although there are excellent high-tack waxes available, some tyers still search for the perfect formula. Marjan Fratnik of Milan uses Avenarius Baumwachs, an adhesive grafting wax, mixed with beeswax. Patterns tied with beeswax and a softening agent will stay pliable for years. Marvin Nolte makes a tacky finger wax that is designed for dubbing fur. A finger wax, applied to the thumb and index finger, allows the tyer to twirl on dubbing with greater ease. It gives the fingers increased traction. Some of the wax is transferred to the dubbing, thereby matting it during twirling. The better finger waxes will be without toxins, will replace finger moisture, and will have the correct amount of soft tack. A finger wax should always stay soft. Due to low flame point, melt the beeswax in a double boiler. Then slowly add the rosin and softening agent. Use extremely low heat; the mixture is flammable. And use a pan dedicated to wax making—it is virtually impossible to clean the container. Nolte makes both finger and thread wax.

Finger Wax Formula
Rosin, 3 parts
Beeswax, 6 parts
Castor oil, 1 part
Paste fly flotant, 10 parts

High-Tack Thread Wax Formula
Rosin, 7 parts
Beeswax, 2 parts
Castor oil, 1 part

Pine pitch produces an excellent rosin. It is merely a matter of melting and mixing the ingredients. Any ingredient should be filtered if it contains particles. John Newbury of Chewelah uses a recipe that comes from the late

Everett Caryl. He gathers Ponderosa pitch balls, *gently* heats them in the microwave, and then filters them through cheese cloth to sift out debris. Next, he mixes the pitch with an equal volume of beeswax—perhaps a pinch more of pitch. A touch of turpentine or castor oil keeps it pliable. Finally, he *gently* reheats the wax and pours it into twist-up containers. The container keeps the fingers clean while using the wax. When heating, attentive care must be taken to avoid an open flame or overheating. Use low heat only; pitch and wax will quickly ignite.

Frank Matarelli, manufacturer of fine fly-tying tools, uses H600, a pressure-sensitive hyper-adhesive. Matarelli places a smear of the glue between a folded plastic strip that is stapled at the bend. The strip keeps the glue clean and allows the thread, when drawn between the plastic leaves, to capture the proper amount of adhesive. Only a haze or mist of glue, nearly invisible on the thread, is required.

Andy Friesch, producer of H600 and president of Hartland Adhesives and Coatings in Wisconsin, states that H600 is an inert, hydrophobic rubber-base adhesive that will not deteriorate in water. When an optimal, tenacious tack is required for dubbing or dubbing brushes, H600 excels.

Light

According to Genesis, light is the first element of creation. If light is important to tying, is color? Some tyers think so; others think that silhouette, size, and presentation are more important. To most tyers, though, color has some significance and, as you must tie with color anyway, why not make it the "correct color" if possible? Perhaps the dedicated tyer matches the hatch in natural light. Artificial lights lack equal distribution of color. Incandescent lighting is predominantly red-yellow and lacking in blue. This type of light makes reds and yellows stronger and blues weaker. Conversely, under a cool-white fluorescent light, which is high in blue-green energy and low in red, the reds are weak and the blues are strong. For color accuracy (if there is such a thing), each insect color should be matched under natural light to overcome the problem of metamerism, the phenomenon of an object appearing to be different colors when viewed under different light sources. In other words, the pattern at the tying table may be one color and another color when tied on to match the hatch. Our own color selections, especially with dyed materials, are generally grosser and darker than the delicate shades of an insect. Even as early as 1939, McClelland, in *How to Tie Flies for Trout* claims that "the general tendency of the dresser is to dress rather more darkly than the color and natural luminosity of the fly warrants."

Let us assume, for a moment, that light, and its attending colors, is important to tying. Light is visual radiant energy, and this "visual radiant energy" has advanced significantly of late. There are now special lights that are "color corrected" to emit light with a more realistic, natural distribution of color. Total color accuracy would require shade matching under more than one light source, even if the lamps were color corrected. But tying is simpler than this.

Each wave length of light is associated with a certain color. A simple, high school science experiment uses a prism to demonstrate this principle by dividing white light into its various wave-length colors. Understanding that light is made up of various colors explains why a fly may appear one color under the tying lamp and another on the stream. To really see the confusion of color, use outdoor film under fluorescent lights.

The Illuminating Engineering Society of North America publishes tables that provide recommended footcandle levels (the quantity of light that falls on a surface) for various tasks. Fly tying would fall somewhere between 500 to 1000 FC ("prolonged performance of exacting visual tasks") or 1000 to 2000 ("special visual tasks of extremely low contrast and small size"). Typical visual tasks that include high contrast and large size require a mere 50 FC. Tying requires strong lighting.

Low, red-orange light (under 3200K) is considered warm. Conversely, a high color temperature (blue-white) is considered cool. These divisions are sometimes confused by tyers because of the fact that high temperatures are usually associated with warm and low temperatures with cool. Although the color temperature scale describes the actual appearance of the light being produced, it gives no indication of how the color will affect the appearance of the pattern.

Another rating, the Color Rendering Index or CRI (from 1 to 100), describes how a lamp will affect the appearance of an object. A higher CRI rating generally indicates that the lamp will render colors more accurately than a lamp with a lower CRI value. A 100 CRI rating, for example, would render a color much as a person would expect the color to appear under natural light. The CRI scale is based on the average of eight different color shifts, but still provides no insight into how a light will affect a specific color. The CRI is useful, yet there are inherent limitations in the scale. In general, tyers concerned with color matching should select lamps with a high CRI rating. Unfortunately, the CRI information is usually not readily available for some lamps.

For many years I have used a 120-watt engineering flood lamp for tying. It brightened my table and warmed my tying. But now there is something different, the "full spectrum lamp." These incandescent lamps, developed in Finland (the land with little light) and color corrected with the rare earth element neodymium, match "the Northern sky in summer." The Chromalux lamp, made by the Lumiram Electric Corporation of France, makes a 100-watt, 3500-hour "full spectrum lamp" that "closely simulates natural daylight." Supposedly, it would make color matching more accurate. "By increasing the black and white contrast," Chromalux claims to reduce eye strain and "restore purity and freshness to colors." The light seems to cast a violet tinge to the tying table. Some tyers may find the violet tinge somewhat unnatural. It does make the primary colors appear more intense.

To prevent eye fatigue, the light source should be behind and to the side of the tyer. However, in tying, this is normally not the case. Often the tyer places the light in front and to one side. This positioning may cause glare and strain. We all admire the polished brass bases and burnished steel vises. But these tools, like others, may reflect light back to the tyer. Eye strain can result from these reflective surfaces.

Tying Lamps

Some desirable features of a tying lamp might include:

1. A lamp that accommodates a 100-watt bulb
2. An interior reflector for concentrating the light
3. An aluminum heat-sink for maintaining a cool head
4. A gooseneck or arm that rotates away when not needed, yet resumes position when rotated back. This is especially practical for a magnifier.
5. A rimless magnifier. It is claimed that rimless magnifiers reduce eyestrain by as much as 90%. Some magnifiers always seem in the way of seeing and tying. A rimless magnifier (2X to 4X), which eliminates the need to refocus the eye, could pivot out of the way when not needed.
6. Multiple, lock-down mounting systems for the lamp and magnifier

$\mathcal{T}$he Materials

A micropattern is not merely a large pattern wrought small. Often the feather, the fur, the hair used for a size 12 cannot be used for a size 24 pattern. The markings, structure, proportions, and bulk may not be suitable for the smaller pattern. Be fastidious when it comes to details: Clean furs and feathers not only look better, they tie better. They are softer, more pliable, and stack straighter. Wash hairs in Ivory or Woolite to relax the fibers, allowing them to reclaim their natural contours. When tying, work with, rather than counter to, the natural curves. Comb body and tail hairs to loosen, align, and fluff the fibers. Plump peacock herls by steaming.

Soapy, hard water often combines with the water minerals (such as iron salts, calcium, and magnesium), leaving a scum that lessens the luster. When washing natural or protein fibers, this problem may be averted by adding a tablespoon of vinegar per quart of water in the next-to-last rinse. The weak vinegar acid neutralizes the alkaline residue.

Various synthetic yarns—such as Antron, Z-lon, Krystal Flash, and Sparkle Wing—add shine and seduction to wings and shucks. Glassy coq de Leon barbs and ultra-fine Microfibetts produce tails for micropatterns.

The crescent cross-section of the Coq de Leon barb

Beaver guard hairs and underfur

Antron filaments

In general, fibers with *static cling* are less absorbent, producing excellent dry fly materials. Amorphous areas in the molecular structure partly determine absorbency and architecture of a fiber. Although synthetics do not readily absorb moisture, they may absorb oils into the molecular structure. At 95% humidity, polyester has 2% moisture content, nylon has 6.5%, silk 25%, and wool as high as 29% moisture. Acrylics (Acrilan, Creslan, and Orlon) and olefin (polypropylene) all have relatively low absorption.

Some natural fibers may resist moisture absorption. Because of the fine, crinkled, and scaled fibers, mole and beaver furs, sans guard hairs, dub readily. Both are naturally water resistant, making superior bodies for diminutive dry patterns.

New materials continually appear on the market: there are several ultra-fine dubbings, both natural and synthetic, for small flies—Davy Watton's Finesse, L & L Product's Ultra-Dub and K-Dub (kapok), Spirit River's Fine & Dry Dubbing, and Mad River's Beaver Dubbings. The following materials are especially appropriate for tying micropatterns.

Angora Rabbit

The angora rabbit yields, either clipped or plucked, about 12 ounces of fine (averaging about 14 microns), silky fibers per year. Colors range from white, blue dun, brown-gray, and black. When dubbing Angora, keep as little twist as possible to produce an airy, fuzzy body. Do not place in a fabric softener as this removes the static electricity that makes it fluffy.

Antron

The smooth, faceted fibers of DuPont's Antron reflect light. The flash may imitate the "dazzle sheath" or air cloak worn by some insects. Antron's spark and shine may also mimic the bubbles trapped beneath a spinner's wing. Antron is usually described as trilobal with lateral channels that catch and scatter light. Rabbit fur, when blended with fifteen to twenty percent clear

Antron, preserves its color and dubbing quality. Antron yarn also produces tails and trailing shucks for small patterns.

Craig Mathews and John Juracek, in *Fly Patterns of Yellowstone*, popularized Z-lon, another trilobal synthetic similar to Antron. Like Antron, it also snares and scatters light. Z-lon, available in varius colors and fine diameters, create shucks, wings, and tails especially appropriate for micropatterns.

Trilobal Z-lon filaments

Beads

Across America, from the Deschutes to the Battenkill, tackle shops sell countless bead patterns, traditional and original. The bead heads sell well because they are effective; they have weight and flash. The weight puts it down among trout, and the flash or sparkle imitates, perhaps, the air shroud of emerging insects. They take trout.

The origin of the bead head is obscure. Beads have appeared on gutted patterns from the turn of the century. For decades, the Northern Italian-Austrian border has produced early patterns. Brass head nymphs have also been popular in the mountain river Saalach on the border of Bavaria-Austria. Roman Moser of Austria has promoted the bead heads with his Golden Kopf pattern, a simple and effective tie with Antron dubbing, a wrap of hackle and a brass bead. Edgar Pitzenbauer of Bavaria traces the bead heads to the coregonae, a small-mouthed fish somewhat like grayling. Coregonae live deep in the high, cold mountain lakes of the Bavarian, Austrian, and Swiss Alps. Small weighted nymphs, three to five on a line, catch coregonae as deep as 150 feet. Anglers slowly jig the "lures" inches off the bottom. Perhaps this is the origin of the bead head.

Water tension alone will support a small hook. Small patterns may require weight to achieve quick water entry and deep drift. The want of weight has been a traditional problem with small nymph and shrimp micropatterns. Some companies, however, are resolving this problem. Spirit River markets double-drilled brass beads, expressly designed for the fly tyer, as small as .100 for size 18 and smaller hooks. The double-drill design should accommodate the modern, barbless and minibarb hooks. The double diameter hole allows

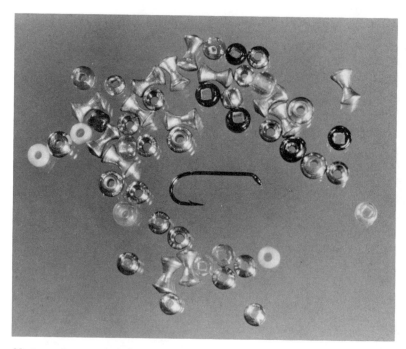

*Miniature brass and glass
beads and eyes*

the bead to thread over the barb and around the bend of most hooks, yet not pass over the eye. Clear-coating prevents tarnish. The beads, in brass and silver finish, are available in four sizes: the mini (under ⅛″), ⅛″, ⁵⁄₃₂″, and ³⁄₁₆″ diameters.

A variety of beads is available from different suppliers: brass, aluminum, silver, and colored glass in a diversity of designs, including solid, open shell, and closed shell. Obviously, the hollow, shell beads (made from flat metal), do not have the weight of the solid beads. Most hollow, split heads are European. Some tyers see a need for a solid, split bead, with a small hole and slightly opened, split radius. This would allow the bead to be placed directly on any hook shank and squeezed shut. The tyer would not have to be bothered whether a particular hook accommodates a particular bead. The split-shot image, however, may bother some tyers.

One technique for mounting beads to a small hook is to slowly compress the bead with smooth-jaw pliers to "oval" the hole, allowing a forged hook and barb to slip through. The bead may then be crimped on the shank or reformed and secured with thread. One advantage to this method is that the flattened bead may be rotated to diminish the bead's obstruction of the gap. This is particularly important with small hooks.

Camel Down

Camel down, actually an underfur, comes from the two-humped Bactrian camel. The double coat—a soft down beneath a thick hair—is gathered rather than shorn. Fallen clumps are placed in a basket on the last camel in the

Camel underfur

caravan and sold in towns along the way. Each fiber consists of a double wall for thermostatic insulation. The down, similar to and sometimes mistaken for cashmere, measures from 17 to 22 microns. Combined with other fibers, camel down makes excellent dubbing for small patterns, often creating a halo effect around the dubbed body. Natural colors range within the ruddy tans. Camel down is finer and shorter than camel top; however, both are excellent for small body dubbing. Camel top is more expensive than camel down.

Cape Hackle

Grading capes is usually done by "web ratio" based on a dry hackle. The superior number 1 saddle should have less than 20% webbing of the total hackle length. A number 2 should have 30% or less, and a number 3, less than 50% in webbing. Due to genetic breeding, a grade 1 of one year may be a grade 2 the next year. A quality number 1 cape 15.5 cm long, 9 cm wide, and 23 mm deep yielded a total of 1261 hackles, with 561 hackles size 18 and smaller. Each centimeter band may contain more than one hackle size. The hook sizes were calculated on *¾ shank length as barb length* based on the standard Mustad 94840 dry fly hook. Other hooks may require different barb lengths. The horn or crest (the 1, 2, and 3 cm bands in the drawing), possess the shortest hackles; most horn hackles may be too short, under 2 cm (¾), for tying.

The more preferred colors for small patterns include grizzly, cree, barred ginger, badger, black, and dun variants such as honey dun and rusty dun. Barred Plymouth Rock produces grizzly. Brown Leghorn provides furnace, and Silver Laced Wyandotte, badger. Personally, I favor those variant capes that combine colors with flecks, bars, and speckles. Insects are seldom one color.

Cashmere Goat

Cashmere is the soft, underdown of the kashmir goat found on the high plateaus of Mongolia, China, and India. This slippery and silky down comes from the goats at the highest altitude, up to 15,000 feet. The Kashmir goat, like the camel, yields two distinct fibers—the slippery silky down and the coarse guard hairs.

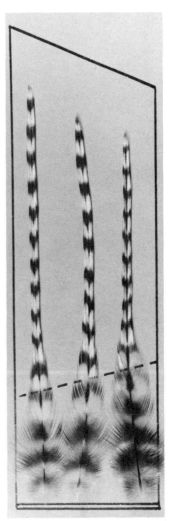

Hackle grades

From the left, hackle grade one, grade two, and grade three. As illustrated, a grade-one genetic hackle should have minimal webbing with maximum length.

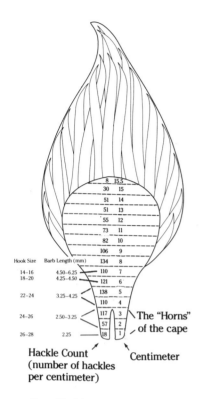

Hook Size	Barb Length (mm)		
		8	15.5
		30	15
		51	14
		51	13
		55	12
		73	11
		82	10
		106	9
		134	8
14–16	4.50–6.25	110	7
18–20	4.25–4.50	121	6
22–24	3.25–4.25	138	5
		110	4
24–26	2.50–3.25	117	3
		57	2
26–28	2.25	18	1

The "Horns" of the cape

Hackle Count (number of hackles per centimeter)   Centimeter

Cape Hackle

Cul de Canard

The Moustique series of cul-de-canard flies, made from the preen feathers of ducks, has been used for over 100 years in the Jura region of Switzerland. The preen feathers, which cap and circle the uropygium gland at the base of the upper tail feathers, aid in transferring oil to the duck's bill by capillary action. Although they appear as down feathers, even when dry these preen feathers are not as fluffy as other down or plumose feathers. The cul-de-canard feathers form a "wick" that transfers oil to the duck's bill during preening. Preening is essential in maintaining the flight feathers and, due to their delicate structures, insulating and regulating body temperatures. Preen oil also keeps the feathers flexible and waterproof while inhibiting fungi and bacterial growth. Most aquatic birds, such as ducks, swans, and geese, have preen feathers. In Europe the feathers are sometimes plucked (they return after molting) from live birds. Although the CDC appears somewhat like a down feather, it is unique, remarkably water-repellent (hydrofuge) and buoyant. CDC patterns require no flotant; they already have naturally embedded oils. According to Jean-Paul Pequegnot's *French Fishing Flies* (1984), which was the first book in America to appraise the CDC, the CDC pattern originated at Vallorbe in the Swiss Jura. In the Franche-Comté, where the CDC pattern was popularized, it was sometimes called the *Mouche de Vallorbe*. Pequegnot also notes some variations on CDC design: Aimé Devaux's bracing gray hackle behind a CDC collar, Henri Bresson's bent-back CDC fibers, and Pequegnot's own gray-palmer body and CDC head hackle.

For over a hundred years in Europe, the preen feather and the pallid-yellow or pinkish gland oil have been used to float flies. Adding a flotant to a CDC pattern will only nullify some of its natural attributes listed below. CDC patterns will sink, but they are usually renewed with brisk backcasts. Truly, this unique feather deserves special attention and a place in pattern architecture. CDC patterns may dispel some mythology of tying: they are simple and effective. The CDC feather is especially appropriate for shallow floating patterns—patterns that imitate emergers or spent insects caught in the surface film. The CDC may also be used for standard dries and drifting wets as well. The fine, filamentous barbs duplicate the breathing gills of midge or mayfly nymphs; however, the long barbs are best used according to their special property: the ability to *float* a pattern. About 100 CDC feathers (over 4 mm) are harvested from each mature, wild duck. My winter count of wild mallards yielded 98 to 108 CDC feathers over 4 millimeters, including the 22 to 27 short, stylet feathers (the nipple plumes) that cap the gland (approximately 15 mm). Six other birds yielded:

Wild Drake: 99 CDC feathers, longest 44 mm
Wild Drake: 105 CDC feathers, longest 39 mm
Wild Drake: 108 CDC feathers, longest 43 mm
Wild Hen: 98 CDC feathers, longest 41 mm
Wild Hen: 97 CDC feathers, longest 33 mm
Wild Hen: 83 CDC feathers, longest 31 mm

Approximately 6 to 12 CDC feathers on each bird were too small for tying.

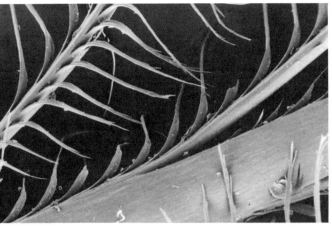

Cul de Canard feather   *Cul de Canard feather barb*

The small, downy CDC feathers have kinked and twisted microscopic barbules that trap a "sheath" of air and, owing to embedded oils, are remarkably water repellent and buoyant. As noted, cul-de-canard flies require no flotants or dressings—if submerged, the trapped air bobs the pattern to the surface. A brisk backcast strips water from the pattern for another fluffy float. The CDC feathers may be "soft-hackle" wrapped for emergers, tied as over-wings on microcaddis and midges, or figure-eighted for spinner wings. Like diminutive marabou barbs, CDC fibers can imitate mayfly shucks, midge pupa gills, and scud appendages. CDC is particularly effective for those numerous, minuscule insects trapped in the surface film: microcaddis, midge, Trico, and Caenis emergers. Sparsity and frugality are the keys for flush-floating spinners and emergers. CDC may also be used *wet*. In fact, the CDC gills for sunken midge pupa can appropriately slow the sink for effective trout taking. CDC barbs range from approximately ¼ inch to 1¾ inch. Barb length can exceed one inch. Colors range from white to beige ("Havana"), brown, dun, and black. Colors should be altered with a cold alkaline dye, rather than a hot acid dye, to preserve the oils and unique structure of the feathers. The oil from the uropygium gland has been used as a fly flotant for decades. Although the Moustique series, using the CDC feather as a dry hackle, produce excellent floaters, they are rather fragile. However, most patterns are simple, fast, and durable.

With the expanding interest in CDC patterns, many tyers are exploring the design possibilities of CDC feathers. The various attributes of the CDC feathers, listed below, should be considered when designing an effective pattern.

THE ATTRIBUTES OF CDC FEATHERS

1. Unlike most barbs, those of CDC may be cut or broken for a nearly natural tip.
2. The barbs, which absorb minimal water, are impregnated with natural oils for superior flotation. The more feather surface exposed to the

water, the greater the flotation. CDCs will sink, but they revive with remarkable rapidity. A paste flotant will only mat CDC barbs, thereby decreasing some of their attributes.

3. The natural CDC gray imitates the wing color of many insects, particularly mayfly duns. The white and Havana CDC feathers may be dyed for a variety of colors.

4. If the CDC feather is mounted in such a manner that the barbs are free, then they are easily stripped of water during the backcast.

5. The CDC feather has a fast-tapered stem with a coarse base and a fragile tip. The major disadvantage to a heavy, thick stem and the weak tip is that the feather is awkward to tie as a hackle. Consequently, various methods have been developed to use the barbs *without* the stem.

6. The small, fluffy CDC feathers have kinked and twisted microscopic barbules that trap a sheath of air. If submerged, the trapped air bobs the fly to the surface. Hence, it is important that as many barbs as possible are exposed to the water surface to aid flotation. The more exposed the barbs, the greater the float. Generally speaking, to increase flotation, slightly space the CDC wraps. Some CDC feathers, especially those smaller than 1½ centimeters, are plumy, totally without stem. These stemless CDC feathers make excellent midge and microcaddis overwings.

7. Another characteristic of the CDC is the sparsity of barbs. A typical 3-centimeter CDC feather has fewer barbs than a quality, genetic dry fly hackle. A typical CDC feather has about 10 barbs per centimeter on each side of the stem. A genetic hackle has two and a half times that amount, about 26 barbs per centimeter. Although the CDC barbs are not tightly spaced, each barb has dense barbules (about 80 on each side for a total of 160 per centimeter) that create flotation. To increase barb density, CDC barbs may be plucked from the stem before mounting. This eliminates the thick stem while controlling

CDC feather, diminutive nipple plume, and CDC dubbing

and increasing barb density.

8. CDC fibers are soft, like many natural insects. The barbs compress when a trout takes, thereby exposing the hook point.

9. There are various CDC feathers: the smaller, stemless nipple plumes and the more abundant surrounding stemmed plumes. There are also two types of stemmed plumes: those with barbs nearly as long as the feather and those with short barbs. Nipple plumes create excellent trailing shucks, microcaddis wings, Caenis, and Trico spinner wings.

Keep in mind the special attributes of the CDC feather so as to take advantage of its properties. Notice too that the appropriate hooks must be used; they should be standard or light. Do not try to float a carriage bolt with CDC. Hooks 1X or 2X fine are appropriate. The ultra-fine hook wires—3X and 4X fine—may not hold wild, muscular fish. Use then the lighter, dry hooks from Tiemco (especially numbers 100, 101, 102, 5230, 5210, 2312); Mustad (AC80000BR, AC80250BR, 3399D, 94836, 94833, 94859); Partridge (E6A, E1A, E3AY, K1A, L3AY), and Daiichi (1180, 1190, 1270, 1480, 1640). Also bear in mind that materials that absorb water (such as floss and chenille) should not be incorporated into CDC patterns that are deliberately designed to float.

Deer Mask

The deer mask—whether whitetail, blacktail, or mule—offers a variety of hair length, colors, tapers, and textures for small fly tying. The deer mask offers short and solid (unchambered), distinctly marked hairs. Mule deer (*Odocoileus hemionus*) are reddish-brown in summer, blue-gray in winter. Face masks range from light to dark. Large ears and black-tipped or black-topped tail identify the mule deer. The smaller Pacific coast black-tail, a subspecies of the mule deer, has a black-tipped tail in winter and a black summer tail—intermediate tails with black center. Whitetail deer (*Odocoileus virginianus*) has body coloring (grey, brown, or red) on top of a large tail with a white underside. The tail serves to identify the three deer. Although dependent on size, the whitetail deer has the longest tail, about 12 inches from the rump to the hair tips. The top surface is brown (sometimes with minor black hair tips), and a white underside. The ventral hairs always extend for a white border. The mule deer's tail, approximately 7 to 8 inches long, tapers rapidly, ending with a black, dorsal tip and white underside. The blacktail deer tail, averaging about 9 inches long, has brown-black dorsal hair extending to the tail tip. Blacktail-mule hybrids have a variable-width black strip running the length of the tail.

The common whitetail mask has various body hairs that service various patterns. Generally, the closer to the area beneath the eye socket, the better the marked hairs for small fly patterns. Some experienced tyers, like Tom Rosenbauer, use the patch beneath the eyes for Comparadun tails. These hairs, however, are not chambered; they do not compress or flare readily. Neither are they buoyant or soft. The softer and longer hairs found on the body should be used for Comparadun wings. The cheek patch yields cream tail hair for Pale Morning Duns and Sulphurs. The brow patch between the eye grants tail hairs for *Paraleptophlebias*. The tract between and forward of the ears has darker, coarser hairs for March Browns and Caddis.

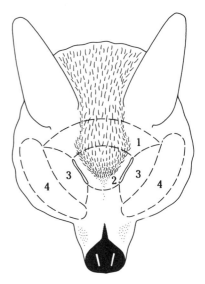

Deer Mask
(1) Coarse, dark hair for March Brown tails and wings

(2) *Paraleptophlebia* tails and wings

(3) Comparadun tails and wings. Note text comments concerning wings.

(4) Fine, cream hair for tails and wings of Pale Morning Duns and Sulphurs.

Duck-wing cross-section of inner panel

Duck-wing cross-section. Note Chambered Quill Panels.

Feathers

Some wings—jackdaw, moorhen, starling, woodcock—have miniature coverts that produce excellent nymph legs, soft hackles, and other fibers for the diminutive patterns. The goose cosset—a short, partially fringed and somewhat rounded shoulder feather—has fine, soft barbs serviceable for tail fibers and wing cases. The finer turkey flats create wings for traditional patterns and, when posted, for parachute patterns.

When mounted, the chambered quill panels should stack on top of each other.

Feather Barbs

Feather barbs—from primary and secondary wing feathers of crow, goose and turkey—make excellent bodies when wound like floss. Tie in the tapered tip (you may have to snip the tender tip so that it will not break) and spiral forward tightly against the previous wrap. The result is a minute, fuzzy body. This is an excellent alternative to dubbing small patterns. Natural and dyed colors

Feather barb (crow). Note fringed margin.

produce a variety of bodies. Any barb from a large primary or secondary wing feather may be used. Oak turkey wing barbs produce a natural, mottled body when wound.

When wrapped, the fringed or frazzled edge of the barb should distend and flare like dubbing.

Fox Mask

Traditionally, the fox pelt offers a variety of hairs and underfurs for tying. The long, black-tipped guard hairs make spinner tails. The tan, beige, and cream underfur, as well as the urine-burned belly fur, create various historic patterns. Both gray and red fox masks offer a pale fur for sundry tuft-wing duns, whereas the soft, peppered hair of the gray fox mask produces excellent Callibaetis wings.

The gray fox has a salt-and-pepper coat with beige underfur. Its bushy, black-tipped tail has a black, medial band. The gray also has rusty-yellow patches on the neck, ears, legs, and feet.

The more widely ranging red fox has a bush-tail tipped with white. The red's coat is normally reddish-yellow with a dark saddle and cream underbelly. The black or silver phase exhibits black body hairs with white tips.

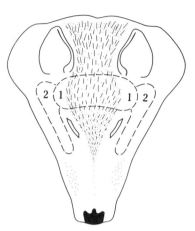

Gray fox mask
(1) Long, black-tipped guard hairs for spinner tails

(2) Pale dun hair for sundry tuft-wing duns. Soft, peppered hair for *Callibaetis* wings (remove guard hairs).

Hen Cape

Available in a variety of colors, the hen cape or patch produces soft, webbed feathers especially appropriate for nymph legs and dun wings. Hen hackle—particularly the wide, round-tipped hackles—forms superior burnt dun wings for small mayfly patterns. The smaller, shorter hackles make soft-hackles and nymph legs.

Hen Patch

Turkey flat wings, bundled and flattened for dun wings, may not be suitable for the smaller micropatterns. Instead, select hen patches or saddles with large, webby, and finely stemmed feathers. Hen patch feathers are softer and finer than turkey flats. The natural colors, especially tans, duns, and flecked duns, produce excellent dun wings. *The broad body feathers provide excellent rolled dun and spinner wings. They also create superior Comparadun wings for micropatterns.* Far easier to fashion than the deer hair Comparadun wings, the hen patch wing mounts in the same manner. When rolled and compressed, the wing, arcing 180°, supports the pattern on the outrigger barbs.

Hare Mask

The hare mask mixes pale yellow with brown, cream, tan, gray, and black. The moderately translucent hair has a gray or pale cream base. The mask fur has a variety of diameters and a ribbon-like appearance and "felts" readily. Black and cream pepper the ear base fur. The cheeks may be a rich tan or pale cream; the

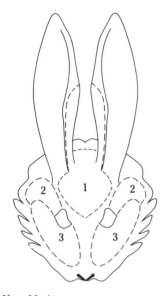

Hare Mask
(1) Gold-Ribbed Hare's Ear nymph body hair (black hair tinged with ginger underfur)

(2) Dark hair for tuft dun wings (remove guard hairs). Dark hair for Gold-Rivved Hare's Ear nymph tail.

(3) Pale ginger hair for tuft dry wings (remove guard hairs). Pale hair for Gold-Ribbed Hare's Ear nymph tail. The short, dark hair is for nymph and spinner tails.

patch from nose to ear, dark brown or black. The mask is a combination of soft and stiff, short and long hairs. The short, spiky fibers from the base of the ears create the shaggy and ubiquitous Gold Ribbed Hare's Ear Nymph.

Kapok

Kapok, a buoyant seedpod fiber, comes from the kapok or silk-cotton tree, related to the baobab and balsa. The light and lustrous creamy fibers, which dub willingly, repel water. Kapok is excellent for micropatterns.

Mole Fur

The short, fine, velvet mole fur is ideal for micropatterns, nymphs, and dries. Mixed and blended with finely chopped Antron, mole fur has sparkle and spike. The smokey-hued fur was popular in the past for English North country spiders. Sylvester Nemes advocates the use of mole for several soft-hackle patterns. Dust dubbing, merely dusting chopped fur along a high-tack waxed thread, produces a fine strand for bodies. Although there is a limited natural color range (from the pale gold phase of the Eastern Mole to the blackish-brown Townsend mole and the jet black Shrew Mole), mole may be bleached or dyed for a full color range. The Eastern Mole has a slate-color phase. Due to the shortness of the fur, remove the fur with a razor blade rather than scissors. A characteristic of mole fur is its ability to relax in any direction: a necessity when a mole must back out of a tight tunnel. The supple fibers are naturally waterproof and translucent. Waterproofing is particularly useful for those moles—such as the Star-Nose Mole and the Shrew Mole—that live in the low, wet ground near streams and lakes. Mole fur should be carefully cleaned and washed. Although detergents nullify some of the natural waterproofing, mole is more easily worked when washed with a detergent. Drying will restore its natural softness and translucency. Working with washed and dyed mole is easier. If waterproofing is required in the pattern, merely soak the fur in clear water to loosen any soil. This fine, flexible fur was used for Alfred Ronalds' Iron Blue Dun and G. E. M. Skues' Iron Blue Nymph. G. P. R. Pulman regarded

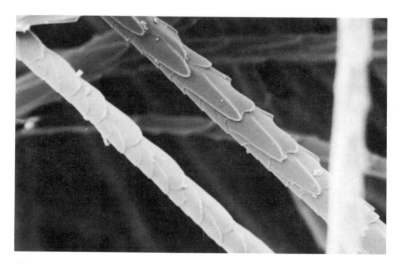

Mole fur

mole as a "valuable fur." Mole fur is scaled and exceptionally fine, ranging from about 19 to 24 microns. *Mole is, perhaps, the choice dubbing for micropatterns.*

Mongoose Guard Hairs

The multicolored guard hairs from the tail of the mongoose make excellent natural-fiber mayfly tails or banded bodies for mosquitoes and midges. Two hairs should be used for size 18 bodies. The hairs are five centimeters long with a remarkably fine .06-millimeter diameter. The tapered hair is tan with two black bands and a brown tip.

Musk Ox

Musk Ox live in the Arctic of North America and Greenland. Closely related to goats, they grow a thick, long coat of brownish-black hair with a fine, downy underfur that is shed in spring. The underfur—varying from off-white, cream, gray, and brown, to dark brown—has properties similar to cashmere. The average diameter is approximately 15 microns, the same range as camel down, cashmere, vicuna, and angora. The easily dubbed underfur from the domesticated musk ox is called "qiviut." Qiviut is usually available from spinning shops.

Nutria

This large South American rodent, spread throughout the United States, is particularly numerous in the marshes of Louisiana and Oregon. The gray-brown fur contains guard hairs, approximately 7 centimeters long and .10 millimeters wide at the shield, that make superior mayfly tails. The guard hairs range from cream and tan to black. Nutria inhabits the marshes, ponds, lakes, and streams, and competes for aquatic foods with the more valuable muskrat.

Siberian squirrel tail (top), nutria patch (lower left), and red squirrel patch (lower right).

Mongoose guard hairs

Peacock Sword

Feather specialist Victor Swalef points out that the peacock sword, when it has herls over 8 inches long, yields the finest "quills" or herls for small patterns. A wax bath waterproofs and simplifies stripping the long, thin herls.

Saddle Hackle

In 1886, Frederic Halford wrote, "Of all feathers required for fly dressing, the *hackle* is the one to be placed first on the list, as being the most important, and, unfortunately, at the same time, the most difficult to procure." Such is not the case now. The quality and quantity of modern dry fly hackles are exceptional. Nothing is better for the small fly than a quality saddle hackle. Dr. Thomas Whiting, at Whiting-Hoffman Farms, believes that there is more "genetic potential" in the saddle than in the cape. The cape hackle is more specialized: It is used for display. A few birds, with "excessive genetic momentum," produce dry-fly hackle down along the legs.

Once, while on a long flight, Henry Hoffman counted 201 hackles on a size 16–14 half saddle. Assuming a symmetrical saddle, that would make 402 total hackles. It's possible to tie six flies from a single 9½-inch saddle hackle with some left over. If you tied only five flies per hackle, that would be 2,010 flies from a single saddle, about five times more than a good cape could produce. The count took place several years ago; saddles are much better now. Long, dry hackles now push into the schlappens—the soft, webby feathers between the saddle and the tail. A few birds even display dry-fly hackles, "web-free to the skin," across the complete saddle. Henry Hoffman has produced saddle hackles up to 16 inches long. The length is only limited by the height of the bird. A rooster treads on long hackles. The standard Whiting-Hoffman saddle has a two-hook range, with modest feathering over and under.

On a typical grade 1, 9½-inch Hoffman-Whiting saddle, there are 68 barbs per centimeter, counting both sides. The stem diameter (measured one-third down from the tip) is approximately eight-thousandths of an inch. These are remarkably long, fine, dense hackles. Some saddles have 30-centimeter hackles with 4-millimeter barbs; others, for smaller patterns, are 17 centimeters long with 2.5-millimeter barbs. Nothing makes tying the micropattern as effortless as the genetic saddle hackle.

Dr. Whiting demonstrates the elasticity of a saddle hackle by stretching it half an inch. Saddles are usually graded 1 (superior), 2, 3, and commercial. There is often a greater difference between 2 and 3 than between 1 and 2. For this reason, a 2 is often considered the best buy. In any case, the best saddles will be relatively web free, have adequate length, and have high color contrast.

Recently, I counted the linear feet of useable hackle on a standard, across-the-counter, grade 1 Hoffman saddle. I excluded from measurement all webbing. The Hoffman saddle—predominantly size 18 to 14, with a sprinkling of 20 and 12 hackles—produced 332 useable feathers, mostly from 8 to 10½ inches long. My count, like Henry's, was based on one side and assumed a symmetrical saddle. The longest single feather was 11¼ inches. Many hackles

The Materials • 81

Saddle hackle webbing

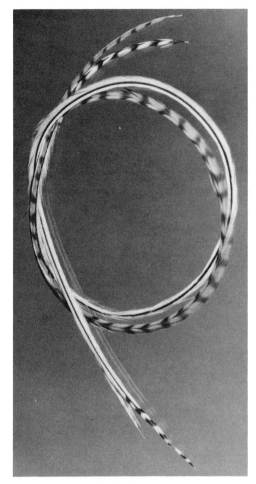

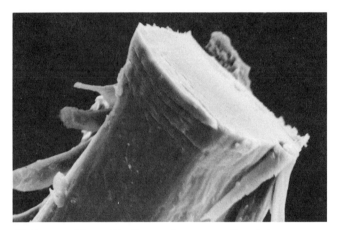

Micropattern saddle hackle

Hoffman saddle hackle. Rectangular cross-section of stem

clustered at 9½ and again at 5 inches long. Based on web-free inches, a dozen schlappens were omitted in this measurement. A dozen feathers were over 10 inches long. *The total length of useable web-free hackle was 169 feet and 4 inches.* At a conservative five flies per hackle, a tyer should produce a minimum of 1660 flies from that saddle.

The rectangular cross-section facilitates tying; triangular, oval, or round cross-sections may frustrate proper hackle placement.

Siberian Squirrel

Siberian or Russian squirrel, a native squirrel, has a bushy tail with reddish brown or black guard hairs. These long, soft hairs create nymph, dun, and spinner tails.

Silk

There are two common types of silk—bombyx and tussah. The bombyx comes from cultivated silkworms fed on mulberry leaves. It is white and very fine, about 12 microns. The tussah comes from the wild silkworm that feeds on oak and other leaves. The tannin in the leaves produces the off-white, ivory, gray, to brown silk. A filament of tussah is flatter, stronger, and about three times coarser than bombyx. If the sericin (the glue of raw silk) is completely removed, the fiber will be lighter, softer, and more lustrous. Spinning shops often sell silk blends, such as Baby camel top and tussah silk top. This long-fibered blend is a streaky tan and easily dubbed. Bleached tussah top is silky and a brilliant, bright white, easily dyed. Silk has high elasticity, absorbency, and strength. Each strand is twisted and fluted longitudinally, producing the reflected sheen of silk. As you twist, the fine, crinkly fibers seem to devour the dubbing in your hand.

Snowshoe Hare Foot

The pad hair on the large hind feet of the Snowshoe Hare (*Lepus Americanus*) makes rough dubbing that promotes flotation. This large-footed hare—which inhabits the entire transcontinental coniferous forest, including Alaska, Canada, the Northern states, the Olympics, the Cascades, and the Rocky Mountains—turns white in winter and dark brown in summer. The winter white is only on the tips of the hair; beneath is a yellowish band followed by a dun base, unlike the tundra hare, whose fur is white down to the skin. The soft, crinkly hairs on the pad of the rear feet are tan, ruddy tan or cream. It looks a little like tiny, tan, calf-tail hair. The hairs, which compress easily while tying, are hydrophobic, float higher and longer than most hairs, are very translucent, and tie with little bulk.

The Orvis CDC Rabbit's Foot Emerger takes advantage of these special properties. The "Usual Series" of flies was the first to use the snowshoe pad hair. Although the hair does not dye readily, the natural colors fit various applications. It is excellent for spinner wings, upright wings and overwings for caddis. It flares well when spun for hackle or wings. The broad "snowshoe" hind-foot does not accrue snow; that would be detrimental to the animal. This hydrophobic hair seems to repel moisture and prevent matting, making it one of the most buoyant natural fibers available. Although availability is limited

*Snowshoe rabbit rear-foot pad hair (*Lepus americanus*)*

(hunted stock only), the material has potential for emergent or floating patterns. Used in a spinning loop, the fibers make excellent faux-hackle for dries.

Squirrel

The short, soft hair of various squirrels, especially the Western gray (*Sciurus griseus*) and Eastern fox squirrels (*Sciurus niger*), makes dubbing and dubbing-brushes for micropatterns. Tail hairs furnish mayfly and nymph tails. The gun-metal underfur is easily dubbed. Body hair, sans guard hairs, can be chopped and blended for dubbing. The Eastern fox squirrel, an important small-game mammal, is rusty yellow with a pale yellow to orange belly and a bushy tail fringed with tawny-tipped hairs. In the Southeast, the body may be sprinkled with yellow, white, and black. Elsewhere the fur may be steel-gray, lacking the tawny. The Western gray squirrel, another popular game animal, has a white or pale cream belly and dusky feet.

Turkey Flats

Turkey flats, a saddle body-feather, make excellent wings for small patterns. Wing slips from the fine, soft barbed turkey flats are more easily controlled than traditional quill wings. Due to the symmetry, a single feather produces both wing sections. A single puff of Grumbacher's Tuffilm Fixative (matte) on the back of the turkey flat will maintain the shape and allow removal of the paired wing sections. Place the wing slips back-to-back to form a single wing. For parachute patterns, post wrap (base wrap) both wings to consolidate and position.

Whitetail Deer

Deer hair quality is determined by various factors: heredity, location, diet, season, sex, and age. According to the deer-hair connoisseur, Chris Helm, the deer inhabiting southern Michigan and northern Ohio, which feed on acorns, apples, corn, soybeans, and other agricultural products, usually produce the best hair. The deer that inhabit the Upper Peninsula of Michigan live in forested areas and swamp lands. Their diet is primarily acorns, spruce trees, and other forest foliage. These deer tend to have much finer and darker hair, black or brown-black. Some parts of the hide, particularly toward the neck area, provide hair for micropatterns, such as caddis, Comparaduns, and humpies. Chris Helm suggests that the best tying hair comes from deer harvested during the second and third week of October. At this time, some hides may still show traces of the summer coat, or "red coat," a color similar to red cedar. The winter coat, or "blue coat," has a bluish-gray cast, but may vary from light to very dark on some parts of the hide. The Northern woodland whitetail is one of the largest deer.

Vicuna

The rare and scarce hair of the vicuna—a rich cinnamon brown to pale brown—is remarkably fine and soft with a diameter of only 13–14 microns.

Production of vicuna, after the near decimation of herds in the 1950s, furnishes only enough for Peruvian spinners and weavers.

Wool

Fine wool fibers have a microcrimp and are covered with irregular, pointed scales that make the fibers cling together during dubbing. The scaled wool fibers—unlike the scaleless strands of cotton, silk, and polyester—interlock into irreversible tangles that augment dubbing. A protective film called yok, an oily mixture of lanolin (wool wax) and suint (dried perspiration) covers raw wool. The elasticity of the fiber (it can stretch up to thirty percent of original dry length) facilitates dubbing. The elasticity keeps the fibers apart, thereby creating maximum air space for flotation. The wool keratin, the most hydrophilic of all natural fibers, is able to absorb up to thirty percent of its weight in water. Although the wool surface is water resistant, its interior is absorbent. When dubbed tightly and siliconed, it forms an excellent dry body; when dubbed loosely, it absorbs water for wets and nymphs. Cotton absorbs about eight percent, whereas synthetics absorb less than five percent moisture. These properties of air space and water absorption make wool ideal for dry and wet patterns. John Veniard, in *Fly Dressing Materials* (1977), lists the disadvantages of wool as bulkiness and the tendency to change color when wet. With 60,000 wool follicles per square inch, the merino sheep fibers are so fine that five strands equal the width of a human hair. Fine wool is also available from the mohair-producing Angora rabbit and the Cashmere goat. The soft "underwools," devoid of the kemps (the bristly overhairs), make exceptional dubbing for micropatterns, especially for small wets and nymphs. Frank Sawyer's Grayling Lure or Killer Bug, originally made from Chadwick 477 wool to imitate shrimp, promptly penetrates the surface and sinks rapidly.

*T*he *Hooks*

The small hook gives frame and function to a fly. Fur and feather flesh the wire spine to produce patterns. It seems that each year the hook shrivels. And, until recently, small hooks, hooks that capture and hold, have been as scarce as winter caddis. To understand the small hook is to understand its origins. After all, "no scale is a standard if it is not public."

Hook Nomenclature

Though there is no universal terminology for hook parts, the following drawing illustrates the most common nomenclature and the terms used throughout this book.

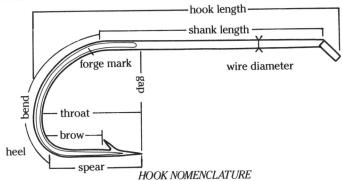

HOOK NOMENCLATURE

Historical Scaling

In George Scotcher's *The Fly Fisher's Legacy*, Jack Heddon's *Explanatory Notes* discuss in detail the sizing problem. In the beginning, a scale was developed when hooks had no eyes. That is why the modern shank measurement excludes the eye. Heddon, who dates the first hook scale from about 1740, notes that "blind hooks were often made rather long in the shank so that the fly-dresser could clip off the end to obtain the required shank length—a facility we have lost with eyed hooks." Consequently, early hooks were scaled by the consistent gap width rather than the variable shank length. Heddon's research, from samples and early illustrations, indicates that some of the early nineteenth-century hooks (pre-1830 and a few pre-1820) were as small as a modern 16 or 17. Most hooks made before 1840 have a finer wire diameter than the modern eyed hook. Hooks had to be fine, Heddon believed, owing to the fact that rods were soft and the hair or gut "casting lines" fragile.

The smallest earliest hooks were generally short of the modern 18 and measured by the gap, not the shank. Heddon lists the known early nineteenth-century smaller hook sizes: Williamson (1808), size 1 (large) to size 10 (small); T. F. Salter (1815), size 1 (large) to size 13 (small); Daniel (1807, hook plates dated 1801), size 1 (large) to size 10 (small). Heddon quotes W. C. Stewart, "Bartlett [Bartleet] numbers his hooks from 1½, the largest size, to 17, the smallest. Addlington's [Adlington's] numbers are from the largest trouting size to 00, the smallest." Salter's size 13 measured, according to Heddon, approximately the size of a "Modern Redditch size 17. The old Number 13 measured approximately 1/16th in gape, Number 11 about 1/8th, and the Number 9 about 3/16th. These sizes would now be approximately Redditch Numbers 17, 15, and 12."

The traditional Redditch Scale measures the length of the hook from the outside curve of the bend to the rear of the eye. The Redditch Scale, then called the "old scale," was developed for eyeless, tapered shanks. In the 1930s, to further confuse the scene, a "New Scale" was developed for the eyed trout hook. The New Scale ran from 9 (the Redditch 7) to 000 (the Redditch 18). On the New Scale, a Redditch size 24 would have the absurd notation of 000000000. If 9/0 had been used, then confusion would result with the Farlow scale and Redditch salmon scale, where a 9/0 was a 3-inch salmon iron.

Part of the problem is the fact that there are several Redditch scales. The Redditch scale bottomed out at size 18 or 000 on the new scale. But beyond 18, and in some cases 17, a problem developed. For these historic reasons, I have begun the small hook at size 18. If a tyer believes that a size 18 is too large for a small hook, then the tyer should select smaller sizes. All size 18s, regardless of length and shape, have been added to the text for completeness.

The Traditional Redditch Scale

Hook Size	Dimension
18	7/32
20	13/64
22	6/32

Extrapolation of the Traditional Redditch Scale

Hook Size	Dimension	The obsolete "New Scale"	
18	28/128	(.2187)	0000
19	27/128	(.2109)	00000
20	26/128	(.2031)	000000
21	25/128	(.1953)	0000000
22	24/128	(.1875)	00000000
23	23/128	(.1796)	
24	22/128	(.1718)	
25	21/128	(.1640)	
26	20/128	(.1562)	
27	19/128	(.1484)	
28	18/128	(.1406)	

The Redditch scale used by J. Edson Leonard and referred to by Datus Proper places a size 18 at 7/32, a size 20 at 5/32, and a size 22 at 3/32. Extrapolation of this scale makes a size 24 a ludicrous 1/32 (.03125), slightly short of 1 millimeter. A size 20 on Leonard's Redditch scale equals a size 26 on the Traditional Redditch scale. Consider, if possible, what a size 28 would measure on Leonard's Redditch scale. Clearly, this early scale prohibited hooks smaller than 22. As hooks become smaller, they become confused. What happens under size 18 is the mystery. This makes a size 28 approximately 3.57 millimeters total length.

Another approach is to produce different scales for different hook models. The following is the Mustad scale for popular hook models. Some tyers still consider the Mustad 94840 as a standard. However, Japanese hook makers have produced some popular hook models that may challenge that standard. A Mustad 94840 size 20 is .2830. On the Traditional Redditch Scale, the Mustad 20 would be an unbelievable size 10 at .2812. Needless to say, hook scales are capricious and erratic.

The Mustad Scale (millimeter)

Model	Size	Total Length	Wire Diameter
3906B	18	8.7	.43
	19	7.9	.40
	20	7.2	.38
94833	18	8.7	.35
	19	7.9	.35
	20	7.2	.35
	21	6.7	.35
	22	6.4	.32
	23	6.0	.32
	24	5.6	.32

(continued)

(continued)

The Mustad Scale (millimeter)

Model	Size	Total Length	Wire Diameter
94840	18	8.7	.38
	19	7.9	.38
	20	7.2	.35
	21	6.7	.35
	22	6.4	.35
	23	6.0	.35
	24	5.6	.32
	25	5.3	.32
	26	5.0	.32
	28	4.7	.30
94845	18	8.7	.38
	19	7.9	.38
	20	7.2	.35
	21	6.7	.35
	22	6.4	.35

Historically, the small hook has undergone redefinition. G. P. R. Pulman's *Vade-Mecum* (1851) notes that "The different sizes of the Kendal hook are indicated by figures, commencing at 00 (the smallest trout size) and ending at 12. The Redditch hooks number conversely, from number 12, the smallest, to number 1, the largest size." Pulman writes, "We never use smaller than number 1 Kendal, from the idea that their little bend is insufficient to retain its hold in the mouth of a strong and struggling fish."

In Roger Woolley's *Modern Trout Fly Dressing* (1932), a frontispiece shows size 000 hook, the "Old Number 17," as the smallest hook. Limerick sizing was even more complex; according to Pulman, "the Limericks are denoted by letters of the alphabet, beginning with the smallest midge with fe, f, ff, fff, c, cc, b, and bb; after which, for the larger, or 'out sizes,' figures are used, commencing with 9-0 (nine out, corresponding with No. 1 Redditch, or 12 Kendal), and going downward for the still larger sizes."

Traditionally, in the trout range, sizes 3 to 13 are measured in 1/16s. In sizes 14 to 18, the divisions are 1/32s. And from sizes 19 to 22, the steps are 1/64s. Notice that the smaller the hooks, the less differential between them. Small hook sizes are often confused because the manufacturing process itself may make different sizes. Even the manner in which the size is read can change the size. Some manufacturers produced different scales for each hook model. We have inherited this historical confusion.

Eric Taverner's *Trout Fishing from all Angles* (1929) lists the smallest hook at size 000 or 18. David Foster's *The Scientific Angler* (1904) goes down to 17 or 000. Roger Woolley's *Modern Trout Fly Dressing* (1932) illustrates hook sizes to 000 new numbers (17 old numbers). H. Cholmondeley-Pennell's *Fishing* (1886) illustrates Pennell snecks and Hall's eyed hooks down to 000. Hence, there is some historic precedent for making a size 18, or thereabout, the beginning of the small hook.

In William Sturgis and Eric Taverner's *New Lines for Fly-Fishers*, hook stress was determined by the average between a barb test and a bend test. For the barb test, the point of the hook was imbedded in leather (from which the load was hung) to the exact depth of the barb.

"The maximum load capacity was determined when the point of the hook had sprung out to a position approximately 30 above horizontal." The average strength represented "the approximate fishing-strength of a hook." After removing the load, the hooks had a permanent set, from 10 to 15. Allcock's Model Perfect 04991, Size 14 Down Eye tolerated an average of 3.8 pounds. Allcock's Sproat 1810, Size 14 Down Eye held to 4.75 pounds. No hooks smaller than size 14 were tested.

A few historic hooks were tested. For a fuller understanding of the following hook graphs and hook performance, consult the discussion on graph analysis.

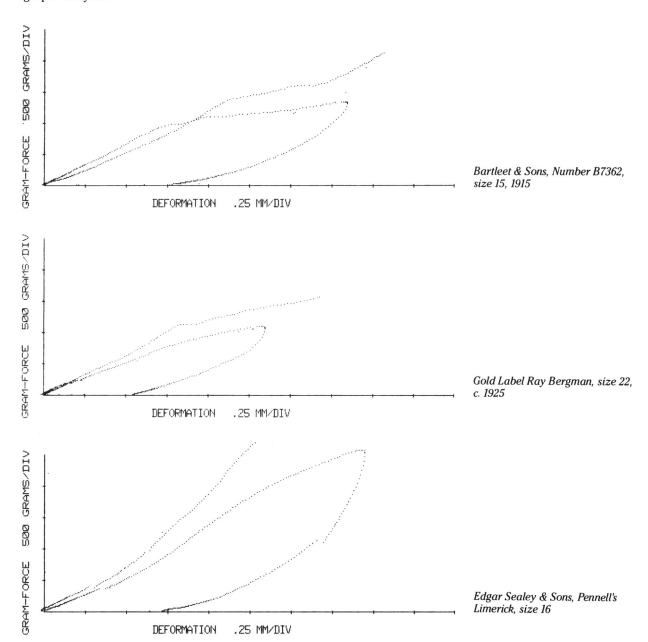

Bartleet & Sons, Number B7362, size 15, 1915

Gold Label Ray Bergman, size 22, c. 1925

Edgar Sealey & Sons, Pennell's Limerick, size 16

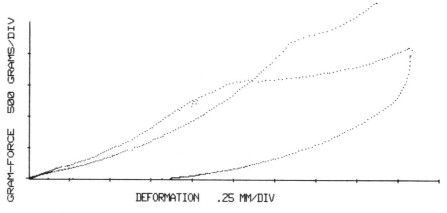

Redditch Offset Sneck, size 0

In general, these historic hooks proved extremely soft. The return trace of each hook, cycled to 45°, exhibited excessive to severe deformation when compared to modern hooks. Time cannot account for this marked difference in overall performance. The hooks also revealed a low stiffness coefficient. At the onset of the force, they showed permanent deformation expressed by a near-zero elastic limit. Both the Bartleet size 15 and the Redditch Sneck, size 0, exhibited excessive metallurgical failure, indicated by the second trace traveling beneath the first trace. The size 16 Seeley, which suffered little metallurgical damage, underwent work-hardening, resulting in a stiffer and tougher hook. The Redditch Sneck was soft out of the gate, damaged by metallurgical failure. The modern hook, when compared to these historic hooks, is a small marvel of metallurgy.

The Hook Dimension Table

Hooks vary, even from the same box. They vary in making and they vary in assessment. Rogue hooks, which exhibit one or more abnormalities, were discarded and not included in any measurements or tests. *The Hook Dimension Table* (see Appendix) allows comparison among the small hooks from various manufacturers.

Mass. Ten hooks of each size and model were weighed and divided to determine the average weight of a single hook.

Length. Length, the *total* length of the hook, extends from the extremity of the bend to the extremity of the eye. Length may vary due to the degree of a turned eye. Ring-eyed hooks (straight-eyed hooks) should have no or limited variance.

Gap. Gap, due to the degree of forming, may vary. The gap was measured from the extremity of the hook point to a point, directly above it, on the inside of the shank.

Shank Length. Shank length is the straight section of the shank, excluding the eye. Traditionally, the shank length extends from a point directly behind the eye to a point on the shank directly above the rear of the barb.

On many hooks, the straight shank does not end at a point on the shank directly over the rear of the barb. The shank length on curved or sloped hooks may vary significantly. Some patterns may carry the body (along with the shank) down, often halfway down, the bend itself. Thus the body length on a curved or slope-shanked hook is an interpretation. Shank length, which matches the natural, is an important consideration in hook selection. We do not measure the gap nor the bend of an insect. *Wire Diameter.* Wire diameter may vary according to the type and depth of finish as well as the point of measurement. Wire diameters, in *The Hook Dimension Table*, were measured at mid-shank, beyond any flat-forging.

No attempt has been made to fault a manufacturer. Ordinarily, every strength of a particular hook has an equal and reciprocal weakness. A single hook cannot serve all patterns. It is still true that hook design is based on hook purpose. And, once the purpose is established, three principles of hook design come under consideration. 1. For every design gain there is an equal, corresponding design loss; 2. Compromise must be made between two opposite and equal design merits that best accommodate the purpose; 3. Compromise must be made between two opposite and equal defects that detract from the purpose. A hook is only "ideal" for the particular purpose and compromises that we accept. No hook can be everything to every situation. Therefore, discretion must be used in interpreting the hook data. Hook curves and specific decimal notations are not significant unless compared to identical hooks (wire diameter, bend, tempering) from a different manufacturer. The requirements of a small hook—adequate gape to shank ratio, adequate wire diameter, adequate strength, and effective design—are still judgments.

The object of angling is landing fish. If a size 14 hook can be used, then it should be used. Always use the most effective hook possible; it is more sporting. I advocate the use of the small hooks when trout select small patterns. If a size 14 knotted midge is as effective as a size 26 midge, then the knotted midge should be used. We use small patterns because, sometimes, trout will only take small patterns. To fish all situations and all fish with small hooks is affectation and, perhaps, unsporting. However, waters and trout may demand that we use the small hook.

READING THE HOOK GRAPHS

Fly fishing requires tools: rods, reels, lines, tippets, and hooks. All have evolved. None has escaped the new technologies. Although we have new bends and points, the hook, perhaps, is the most conservative component, having the least latitude for variance. A hook must be bent to catch a fish and strong enough to hold it. When compared to rod, line, and even tippet, the small hook may be the weakest link. The strength of a small hook is limited by wire diameter, temper, and design. With these intrinsic limitations comes the difficulty of accurately assessing hooks, involving, as it does, metallurgy and dynamic mechanics. Hook stress may not be isolated and studied by itself. It is

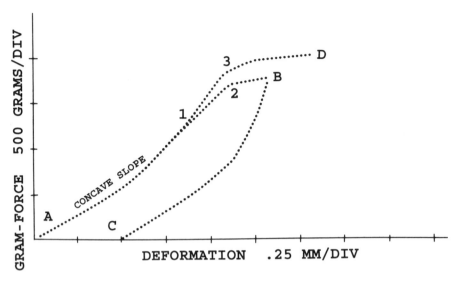

Legend
A–B First Force-Deformation Slope

A–D Second Force-Deformation Slope

B–C Hook Return (Gram-Force withdrawn)

B 45 Hook Deformation Mark

C Permanent Hook Deformation at 45

1 Second slope resistance increase (work hardening)

2 The limit of linear performance

3 Operative

READING THE GRAPHS

based on a theoretically perfect metal, as well as the varying shape of that metal undergoing the stress. Each increment of force creates a new geometry for the hook tested. It is hoped that the following discussion and graphs will lead to greater understanding of the dynamics of hook stress.

The graphs describe a hook's performance, i.e., how a hook responds to an applied force. The graphs measure, with great precision, such features as strength, deformation, plastic flow, work hardening, memory, and brittleness. Hooks are subjected to a steadily increasing force applied along a "floating" draw line.

The graphs show the applied gram-force and the resulting hook deformation. These "ramp charts" indicate the useful forces that can be applied to a hook, the relative amount of plastic flow and permanent bending. Some hook charts illustrate microscopic features, such as fractures, that cause a hook to deteriorate rapidly and break (catastrophic failure). A hook may be perfect until it fails.

The bend of the hook is held by a draw pin (the bend pin). The eye of the hook is attached to another pin (the eye pin). The tester applies continuous and increasing force on the hook. The bend pin engages the bend of the hook and pulls the hook along a "floating" draw line. The hook is stressed, as a trout would stress it, against the bend rather than against the point. The tests assume full penetration of the hook in trout tissue Less penetration or lack of penetration would also result in reduced force readings. In other words, the graphs depict the strongest hook-stress scenario.

The path of a hook expresses its character under stress, its ability to remember and perform. It is not my intent to proclaim some hooks inferior and others superior based on strength alone. A graph reveals much more than the strength of a hook; it records how a hook tolerates the stress. A hook may pass beyond the elastic limit without destroying its integrity. The elastic limit does not indicate hook failure; it indicates that the hook will no longer return to its original shape. Although a hook taken from a trophy trout may be deformed, it has, in the process, performed. A graph illustrates the *dynamic* performance of a hook. Caution, therefore, should be used when interpreting the graphs and judging the hooks.

The force exerted on the hook is plotted on the vertical y-axis and the corresponding deformation on the horizontal x-axis. To illustrate the meaning of the coordinates, the following graph shows that when a 1000 gram-force was applied to the hook, the hook deformed to .35 millimeters on the deformation scale.

The vertical line (y-axis) measures the gram force applied to the hook. The unit of gram force is indicated in each graph. For example, if each division was 500 grams (1.1 pound), then two divisions (2 × 500 grams) would equal one kilogram (1000 grams or 2.2 pounds). The appropriate scale and units are indicated along each axis. Notice that the "ramped" gram-force scale may change from graph to graph, dependent upon hook strength. The graphs illustrate the magnitude of the slowly applied gram-force.

The horizontal line (x-axis) measures the hook deformation in constant .25-millimeter divisions. Four divisions (4 × .25) equal one millimeter (.03937 inch). Hook deformation measures the linear distance increase between the eye pin and the bend pin. Even minor deformation and movement, such as hook slippage and rotation, are indicated in the graphs. The hook graphs appear in two formats, noncycled graphs and cycled graphs.

The Noncycled Graph

The following graph illustrates the typical noncycled hook test. From 1000 gram-force (two divisions on the vertical axis), trace an imaginary horizontal line until it intersects the track of the hook. Project another imaginary line from this point, downward and parallel to the y-axis, until it intersects the *deformation* axis. Read the corresponding deformation at 1000 gram-force. In this graph, it is approximately .66 millimeters deformation. At 1000 gram-force (2.2 pounds), this particular hook yielded .66 millimeters. Would a three-pound trout escape this hook? That may depend, to some extent, upon the skill of the angler and the strength of the trout.

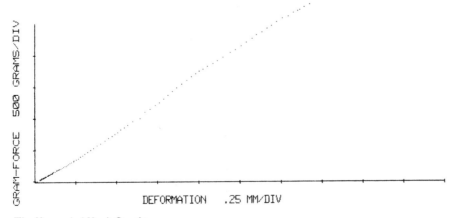

The Noncycled Hook Graph

The Cycled Graph

The unique characteristics of metals result from their atomic arrangement. Not only does the atomic arrangement determine the melting point of the metal, but also the strength, the ductility, the brittleness, and the shine. The position of individual atoms and the relative motion of individual atoms under stress determine the curves. The sundry atomic arrangements provide the properties of each metal.

When the metal melts, order disappears. When it solidifies, order returns. Atoms move and, sometimes, rearrange themselves under stress. The atomic arrangements are not perfect. In the process of building an atomic lattice (atomic arrangement), atoms may have been left out (a vacancy) or an extra atom may have been trapped in the lattice (an interstitial). Atoms could be missing across an entire plane in the third dimension (a plane dislocation). Other defects taking different forms may alter the crystal structure. When a force is applied to the metal crystal, the bonds between adjacent atoms are stretched. If the force is released, the wire will return to its original shape. No atoms have changed positions; the wire has perfect memory. As greater force is applied, however, there is a point at which the atoms are "racheted" beyond their bonds and will not return. Removal of the force will not return the atoms to their original position. These atoms are permanently placed elsewhere. This same process is repeated in countless other positions in the hook wire. The net result is that the hook opens. This is described as *plastic flow*. The point of the hook curve where this plastic flow begins is called the "elastic limit." The hook wire has been stretched and will not return to its original shape.

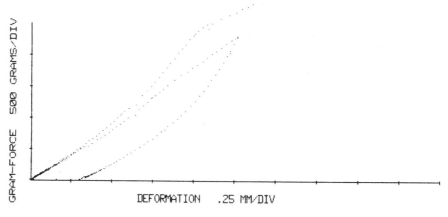

The Cycled Hook Graph

In cycled graphs, the hook is rezeroed after the first track. The force is reapplied and the curve follows, for a brief time, the same path as the initial stress. There is no plastic flow. Elongation results from stretching the atom-atom bonds. These are the same atoms, the same distance apart as before. They are without dislocation; hence they must follow the same stress-strain curve as before.

When the hook reaches its *elastic limit*, the point at which plastic flow began on the first ramping, the hook may actually become *stronger*. When the second hook track diverges and steepens, the hook has become stronger (*work hardened*). The hook now tolerates a greater force than before without further deformation.

Work hardening can be accomplished by other processes. The metal can be heated to temperatures that dislocate the atoms, making them mobile, then rapidly cooled (a process called quenching), thereby freezing in a new configuration of atoms. Various recipes may be used to give hooks various degrees of strength and brittleness. Hooks may be also work hardened by a process called "forging," cold stamping the hook bend. And the same hook may be made soft and pliable by heating and slowly cooling, a process called annealing.

In the noncycled graph, the force is ramped steadily over the entire range of forces until the hook fails, plotting continuously the applied force and the resulting deformation. The point at which the hook spear is bent 45° to the draw line is indicated for each graph in the Hook Graph Table. This arbitrary reference describes the limit of usefulness of a hook. It provides a reference point of force and deformation when comparing hooks.

In the cycled graph, the tester is rezeroed after the first ramp and the hook is reramped. Notice that the two curves coincide for moderate forces but diverge at higher forces. As explained, the point of divergence indicates when plastic flow commenced. In the cycled graph shown, the divergence appears at about 500 gram-force. At this point and force, the hook began to deform permanently. The curve of second stressing demonstrates that the hook will support a greater force with less deformation after the plastic flow occurred in the first ramping. The hook has been work hardened. Continuing to increase the force will eventually cause the hook to bend and finally fail. Hook failure in the depicted cycled graph appears at approximately 2,500 grams-force. Failure probably occurs by virtue of the formation of stress fractures along the curve of the shank and bend. These cracks greatly reduce the effective diameter of the hook wire, causing the hook to fail rapidly under high stress.

THE HOOK TEST TABLE AND HOOK GRAPH

It is the hook that connects the angler to the fish. Yet, nothing may be more problematic than determining the strength and effectiveness of this connection. A hook graph, perhaps, describes this connection best; it illustrates the behavior of a hook under stress. The comprehensive performance of a hook may be obtained by graphing the relationship between the force applied to a hook and the resulting deformation of that hook. The hook trace, the slope, expresses every nuance of design, including metallurgic processing, annealing, hardening, wire diameter, bend radius, bend shape, gap width, eye orientation, and shank length. The hook graphs express the complex interaction of mechanics and metallurgy. Like the DNA analysis of a living organism, the graph is a unique expression of an individual hook. With this complete characterization of a hook, the angler may assess and select a hook that best meets particular angling needs. Unlike larger hooks, a small hook requires only a minor variation to create a major variation in performance. It should be added, nonetheless, that *most small hooks are adequate if fished within their designed parameters*.

The hook graphs follow force-elongation through the entire useful range from zero to absolute failure. In the early stages of stress, the hook curve, characteristically, *"concaves"* upward. The slope increases as the force increases. A simple linear relationship between force and elongation might be expected, but the complex interrelationship of metal and geometry conspire to complicate the behavior. This, of course, is positive behavior: A greater force is required to produce a specific deformation. As the force increases, there is a region where the slope remains essentially constant. In this linear region, an increment of deformation is proportional to an increment of force. The hook may be considered to perform to expectations through the linear region. There is, at least, no significant metallurgical failure. Hook deterioration begins when the slope decreases. Now, the slope *"convexes."* An increment of force produces a greater increment of deformation and strongly suggests that the holding power of the hook is diminishing.

Scale

The scale indicates the gram-force per division. Most scales are 500 gram-force per division; however, a few hooks, due to their strength, require a higher scale for more complete assessment, covering the complete range of hook performance.

Elastic Limit

When stressed, a hook bends in order to provide a resisting force. Ideally, a hook should return to its original shape when the force is removed. For small forces, this is indeed the case; however, there is a force above which the hook no longer returns to its original shape. The force at which this occurs is called the elastic limit. The elastic limit marks the point at which the hook will no longer return to its original shape after being stressed. When force is applied to a hook initially, the hook deforms elastically. In the elastic region, the hook will return to its original shape once the force is removed. There is no permanent deformation. As the force increases, there is a point beyond which the hook will no longer behave elastically: It will suffer plastic flow, the deformation that occurs after exceeding the elastic limit. When strained beyond the elastic limit, the hook will not return to its original shape once the force is removed. There is permanent bending. The total deformation of a hook is a combination of the elastic deformation and plastic flow. The elastic limit and the plastic deformation are both determined from the cycled graphs. After a conventional force-deformation trace, the force is then rezeroed. At zero force, the curve will intersect the deformation axis at a point that corresponds to the total plastic deformation during the first trace. A new trace is begun from the zero–zero point. The two traces will coincide where deformation was due to elastic stretching. Since the hook was work hardened due to plastic flow during the first trace, the maximum force at which pure elastic stretching occurs will be higher, and the two traces, at some point, will diverge. The point of divergence is the point where plastic flow began in the first trace. This point is the elastic limit and is designated by the force at which it occurs. The plastic flow number records the percent of total deformation that is due to plastic flow at 1500 grams-force. By analyzing the cycled graphs, this number may be calculated for other grams-forces. Generally speaking, for hooks of similar size and shape, the lower the number, the stiffer the hook.

Plastic Flow

The percent of plastic flow is calculated by comparing the elongation of the two curves for the same force. The plastic flow, which begins at the elastic limit, indicates the *percentage* of deformation that is due to plastic flow rather than to elastic deformation. The lower the number (the less the percent of plastic flow), the "stronger" or more elastic the hook. Plastic flow is calculated at 1500 grams-force unless otherwise indicated. A few hooks, either extremely soft or extremely brittle, may fail prior to 1500 grams-force and, consequently, must be calculated at a lower force.

Gram Force at 45°

The gram-force at 45° records the amount of gram-force necessary to open the bend and spear at a 45° angle to the shank. The greater the gram-force, the stiffer the hook. The spear bent at 45° to the shank was chosen because it is significant distortion and the paradigm used by Datus Proper in *What the Trout Said*. It should be noted that this measurement point is a value judgment, especially as the hook point passes through the degree index with motion. Interestingly enough, it is a region beyond which most small hooks have already failed in some manner, such as metal fatigue and cracking.

Generally, it should be difficult to bend the spear to 45°. Alan Bramley, of Partridge of Redditch, points out that it is difficult to bend the spear because 1. it is shorter; 2. the spear is bent (as part of hook curve) and, perhaps more importantly; 3. the bend and spear are often cold forged (flattened to increase metal on the shank plane).

The 45° deformation is readily visualized and a basis for some intuitive inferences about the quality of the hook. It is not, unfortunately, an appropriate basis for judging the quality of a hook. Some hooks still perform well at this exaggerated extent while many others have undergone catastrophic failure. Certain design features preclude a poor result on the test. A stiff, brittle hook, for example, may likely fare poorly on this test. While it may have supported an impressive force at low deformation, it may break prior to the 45° deformation. Furthermore, stiff, brittle hooks that attain the 45° deformation will have certainly undergone significant stress fracturing and weakening. Such a hook was not designed to bend.

The Limit of Linear Performance

The *limit* of linear performance registers the point at which the slope begins to decrease. At this point, the slope of the curve decreases, indicating that the hook deforms *more* for a given increase in force. It marks the point at which the hook first surrenders to force. Prior to this point, the slope has increased or remained constant. The limit of linear performance indicates that the force required to produce a certain deformation decreases. Hook performance diminishes as the hook deteriorates.

Stretching a rubber band one centimeter requires little force; stretching the rubber band two or three centimeters, however, requires greater force. At the start of a typical hook trace, the amount of force required to produce a certain deformation increases slightly. Then there follows a linear region where the ratio between the force and deformation remains somewhat constant. After this linear sector (which appears as a relatively straight line on the graph), the amount of force required to produce a deformation begins to *decrease*. The hook then concedes to the stress. The greater the number of *the limit of linear performance*, the more resistant the hook and the better the performance.

Stiffness Coefficient

The stiffness coefficient is the total force divided by the total deformation at the point at which the hook stops behaving linearly. In other words, it is the ratio of the force at the limit of linear performance to the total deformation at that force. The greater the number, the stiffer the hook. The stiffness coefficient is not directly related to the hook strength nor to hook failure. The stiffness coefficient is an excellent indicator of hook performance in that it expresses the hook's ability to resist a force without bending. Rigid hooks have high stiffness coefficients; soft, yielding hooks, low coefficients.

Stiffness Coefficient =

$$\frac{\text{The force at the limit of linear performance} \div 100}{\text{The total deformation at this force}}$$

Operative Failure

Operative failure indicates the point at which rapid and unambiguous hook-strength deterioration begins. Operative failure is not absolute failure; the hook may still hold. Yet, while it holds, it suffers permanent and radical decline. The gram-force at which operative failure occurs is sometimes difficult to determine and is, then, more justifiably assigned to a particular region rather than a particular number. For some hook curves, operative failure may be so poorly defined that a number becomes irrelevant and misleading. In such cases, the column in the table remains blank.

All measurements of failure are arbitrary. The measurements included here are based on resistance against the inside of the bend. The draw line establishes the natural position of resistance on the bend. Forces exerted against the hook bend will be higher than forces exerted against a hook point. Forces against the point use a longer "effective leverage arm" (in this case, the hook gap distance) to exert greater force. Point readings, gram-force readings taken at the hook point, will be significantly lower than bend readings.

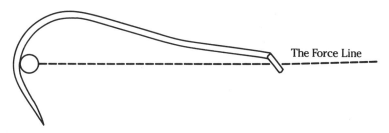

Hook Test on Bend

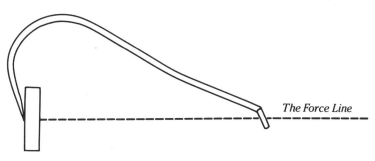

Hook Test on Point

Forces against the point use a longer "effective leverage arm" (the hook gap distance) to exert greater force. Therefore, point readings (gram-force readings taken at the hook point) will be significantly lower than bend readings.

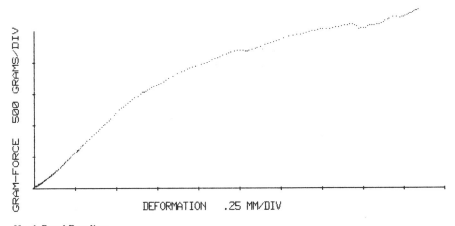

Hook Bend Reading

Standard dry fly, forged, size 18

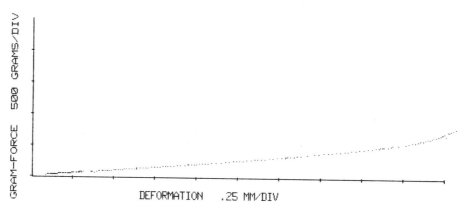

Hook Point Reading

Standard dry fly, forged, size 18

The two graphs—depicting identical size 18 hook models—dramatically illustrate the differences between bend and point readings. The bend sustains 2,000 grams-force for 1 millimeter deformation. The point relents under 250 grams for the same deformation. In other words, the bend supports eight times more gram-force than the point for the same deformation. It is no wonder that a small hook readily yields when encountering bone or cartilage.

The difference is due principally to the extended leverage arm at the hook point as well as the lengthening of the arm during testing as the point rotates away from the shank. A 1-millimeter bend deformation results in greater hook damage than a 1-millimeter point deformation, which distributes the strain over a greater portion of the hook. A 1-millimeter point deformation usually does not exceed the elastic limit. In angling terms, if the hook point encounters a bony structure, only minor force may be required to open the hook. This may account for the sudden or instant release immediately following a strike.

Aberrations and anomalies do occur in testing, and double-digit accuracy is misleading due to the extreme variance of hooks from the same box. The exact failure point varies widely in small, handmade hooks. The point of failure (the exact number of grams required to defeat a hook), while not meaningful in itself, is of comparative value when selecting models, weights, and sizes. Remember that wire diameter, tempering, and hook shape are all involved in hook strength. It may be argued that the difference in small hooks is so slight that no attention need be placed on bend or break resistance. After all, a hook that bends at a few grams force can land a trout of many pounds; much depends upon how the fish is worked. The weakest component may be the hook rather than the tippet. Polymer research has created some remarkably strong and resilient tippets. The 2,500 grams-force graph limit is approximately equal to the breaking strength of a 5X tippet (5.5 pounds). Most small hooks demonstrate significant deformation and failure before the graph limit. Even an 8X tippet (approximately 1.75 pounds) exerts about 795 grams-force on the hook. A 7X tippet (approximately 2.5 pounds) applies 1135 grams-force, while a 6X tippet (approximately 3.5), nearly 1595 grams-force. Nevertheless, a hook should never be rejected merely because it is grams short of perfection. Hook strength may be based as much on how it is used as upon its actual mechanical and metallurgical limitations.

Hooks fail in three different ways: by flexing, by yielding and by breaking. The most effective way to increase hook strength is by changing its shape or increasing its wire diameter.

1. *Flexing* is excessive elastic deformation. The hook momentarily opens, allowing the trout to escape. As the hook has not exceeded the elastic limit, it returns to its original shape. Failure is caused by elastic deformation, the spring of the wire.

2. *Yielding* (or bending) is excessive plastic deformation. The hook opens, thereby allowing the trout to escape. Unlike flexing, the change is permanent. Yielding occurs when the elastic limit of the metal has been exceeded; it produces permanent change in the bend or shape of the hook. Yielding may be gradual or sudden (buckling). Hooks that yield gradually at a constant force undergo "creep." Hook failure may be complicated by the fact that the metallurgical properties (such as work hardening due to plastic flow) and hook shape or "geometry" continuously change during stressing. Each point in time creates a new hook design that reacts to the stress in new and different ways. *Yielding is the most common failure of small hooks*.

3. *Breaking* (or fracture) occurs when crack formation decreases the effective wire diameter, thereby allowing the wire to separate. Simply, the hook breaks. Minute cracks start at a localized point, called a "notch" or "strain concentration," and gradually spread until the hook breaks. Fractures, either delayed or sudden, may occur with no visible signs. Small hooks usually break at the lower, inside bend. A few small hooks, especially those with acutely angled eyes, break immediately behind the eye. The double bend at the eye may weaken the wire. Perhaps this is an appropriate argument for ring-eyes (straight eyes) on small hooks.

Hook Break (below left)

This break appears to have occurred at a point of inhomogeneity in the metal caused by impurities or crystal structure. Notice the diverse texture and the delaminated finish.

Hook Break (below right)

Detail of inhomogeneous metal at hook break

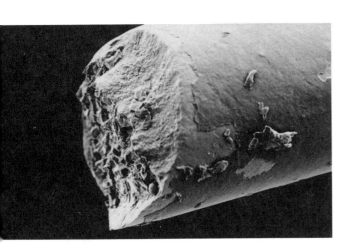

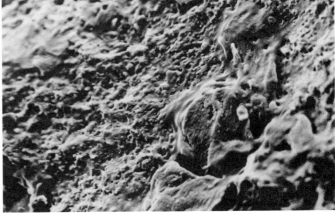

The strength of a hook is determined by several factors: temper, wire diameter, bend, forging, metal composition, and processing. Normally, in tempering, when hardness increases so does brittleness. Some manufacturers add various metals, such as vanadium, to the steel alloy, claiming that such additions decrease brittleness while increasing hardness and elasticity in the wire. Furthermore, different hook sizes and wire diameters react to tempering and cooling disparately. To maintain the carbon content of the steel, a manufacturer may inject a "protection gas" during tempering, arguing that the process produces a tougher, more elastic hook. Most anglers prefer some "stretch" in a hook before it reaches the breaking point. For some small hooks, the take alone may produce profound stress.

HOOK CORRELATION CHARTS

Most hook characteristics are depicted in the hook curves. The curves illustrate the complex blending of variables that dictate hook performance. Information regarding hook selection may be obtained by a careful study of these curves. Through experience and intuition, most anglers acquire an understanding of the design parameters of certain hooks. This understanding, whether rational or intuitive, may be evaluated and tested against the chart data.

A hook, although a remarkably simple device in structure and function, is a complex combination of variables: shape, size, eye orientation, proportion, metallurgy, wire diameter, processing, and others. The number of variables makes the task of analyzing the relative significance of any one variable in terms of hook performance a formidable task.

One important objective of this inquiry is to find some single characteristic of the hook that represents a measure of overall hook performance. Traditionally, the force required to bend the spear to 45° with respect to the shank was used. For many hooks it is a good predictor of performance. However, the hook curves show that many hooks have very serious deterioration of performance before the 45° deformation. As previously noted, some hooks, in fact, experience catastrophic failure before this point is reached.

Two other predictors of hook performance were evaluated: *The Operative Failure* (OF), and *The Limit of Linear Performance* (LLP). Operative Failure marks the force at which serious deterioration in hook performance begins. This is indicated by a steady increase in elongation caused by rapidly diminishing increments in force. For many hooks, unfortunately, this behavior takes place steadily and uniformly over a fairly wide range of forces and hence is difficult to determine with the necessary precision for all hooks.

The other predictor is the Limit of Linear Performance. The typical hook curve almost always shows an easily discernable linear performance followed by an unequivocal decrease in the slope. The LLP is the force at which this linear behavior ends.

Comparisons of both predictors of hook performance, the OF and LLP, are shown in a series of correlation charts: *Linear Performance versus the Force at 45 Degrees* and *Linear Performance versus Operative Failure*.

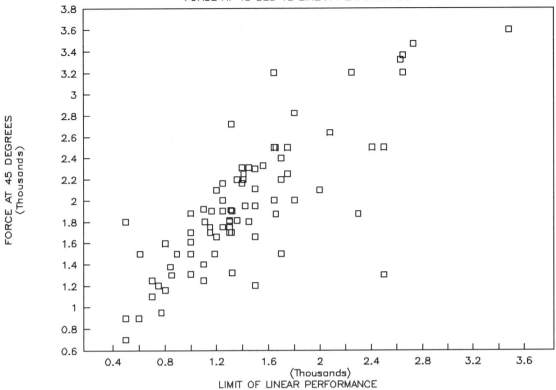

Force at 45° Versus Linear Performance

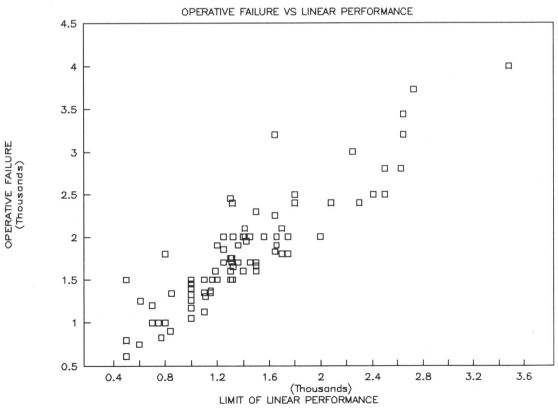

Operative Failure Versus Linear Performance

In the two charts, the performances for the same hooks were plotted against each other. If there is a high correlation, then the plot should lie along an imaginary straight line. A dense spatter along the imaginary line indicates a high degree of correlation. Comparison among these predictors is shown in both charts. Considerable correlation is indicated among all variables. The *Operative Failure versus Linear Performance* chart demonstrates that operative failure has a higher correlation with the limit of linear performance than does the force at 45° with the limit of linear performance. A statistical analysis verifies this conclusion. Given the high correlation, combined with the relative precision of its measurement from the hook curves, *the limit of linear performance is taken to be the most reliable and consistent predictor of comprehensive hook performance.* The objective here is to find parameters that describe the *performance* of a hook rather than merely the *strength* of a hook. Strength, in the vernacular, includes a multitude of meanings and, consequently, lacks quantification and precision. Hook strength, which means so much, means nothing.

Similar correlation studies involving the limit of linear performance reveal a surprising lack of correlation among other design variables. This can be attributed to profuse variables, to the small sample of each variable and to the inability to isolate the effect of any one variable.

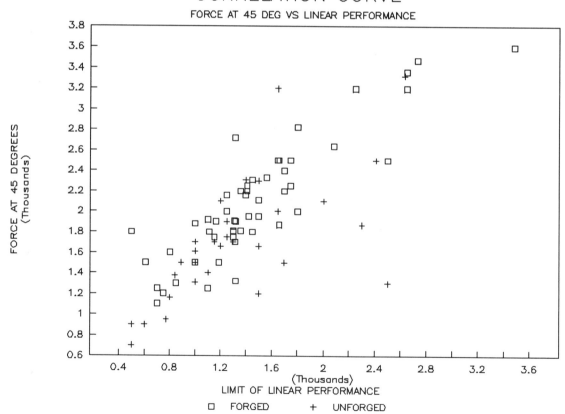

Force at 45° Versus Linear Performance for Forged Hooks and Unforged Hooks

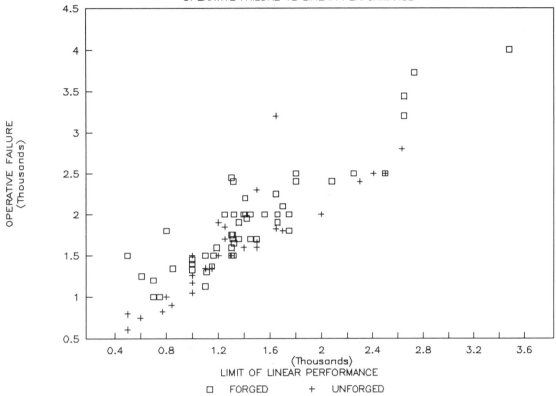

Operative Failure Versus Linear Performance for Forged and Unforged Hooks

In an attempt to reduce the number of variables, the same plots were made for forged and unforged hooks. There were few differences. And when a difference appeared, it was subtle. For example, in *Force at 45 Degrees versus Linear Performance for Forged and Unforged Hooks*, it appears that the scatter is less for forged hooks than for unforged hooks. It may also be significant that there were more forged hooks among the best performers in virtually every comparison. When all hooks are taken as a group, forged and unforged of all sizes, some minimal positive correlation is also found with mass, total length, shank length, and wire diameter. A slight negative correlation is noted in the curve for *Gap versus Linear Performance*, as expected. A longer lever arm requires less force to produce any given deformation. The angler may select a forged or unforged hook based on the variables charted.

Hooks showing superior overall performance are easily identified. In the *Stiffness Coefficient versus the Limit of Linear Performance* chart, any hook that falls in the upper right corner will be stiff, muscular and able to withstand considerable force without metallurgical breakdown.

More detailed analyses show that these same hooks appear in the upper right corner of *The Force at 45 Degrees* and *The Operative Failure* correlation curves as well.

CORRELATION CURVE
STIFFNESS COEF VS LINEAR PERFORMANCE

Stiffness Coefficient Versus Limit of Linear Performance for Forged and Unforged Hooks

The charts demonstrate that particular hooks vary in particular ways. A stiff hook may not be "strong"; a "strong" hook may not be stiff. An excessively stiff hook may sacrifice some linear performance and, consequently, sacrifice overall performance. *The best hook is a blend of stiffness and linear performance*. The *Stiffness Coefficient versus Linear Performance* chart indicates that many hooks sacrifice linear performance for stiffness.

For small hooks, the charts indicate that conventional wisdom—that certain manufacturers produce brittle hooks, whereas others produce soft hooks—is perhaps erroneous. The following chart identifies those manufacturers who market a dozen or more *small* hook models.

Manufacturers produce various hook models for specific reasons. Any chart that identifies a manufacturer must be prudently assessed; strength and stiffness are only two characteristics, and not necessarily the most important characteristics. Significant changes are taking place, confirmed by the fact that many recently designed hooks demonstrated superior performance. Though hook design changes, the procedures of assessment remain constant and may be used for further improvements in hook design. For those interested, the hooks that appear in the correlation charts may be specifically identified in the hook tables by their coordinates. Understanding these principles of hook performance should allow an angler to estimate the practical parameters of other hooks.

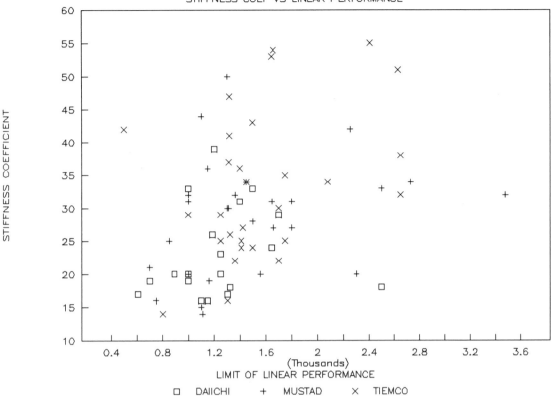

Stiffness Coefficient Versus Linear Performance by Manufacturer

SMALL HOOK CONCLUSIONS

Fundamentally, the hook graphs redefine hook performance, including the merits of some variables. However, hooks with identical weight, wire, temper, size, and shape are required in testing to determine the precise values of such variables as eye orientation, bends, designs, lengths, forging, and tapers. The available small hooks do not include that systematic control. The graphs do suggest, nonetheless, some interesting conclusions concerning the small hook.

Eye Orientation. The down-eye may act like a shock absorber, placing most of the torque on the shank. After the shank is deformed, the stress passes to the bend. Although up-eye and down-eye hooks achieve the 45° at about the same stress, the down-eye hook appears to achieve the 45° sooner. The up-eye pulls more in line with the shank, thereby transferring more stress to the bend than to the shank. The larger the hook and the longer the shank, the more pronounced the effect. In small hooks, the effect is not as dramatic. The integrity of the bend and, consequently, the hold may continue while the shank deforms.

Down-eye hooks tend to be minimally stronger than up-eye hooks. A down-eye hook transfers the strain to the shank, delaying the strain to the bend. Forged hooks may even make the delay more exaggerated.

Wire Diameter and Weight. In small hooks, the wire diameter and weight are critical. The cracks and fissures created by forging and forming (as well as those created by stress) will have less effect on heavier wire. On fine wire, minor defects may produce major faults. It is advisable to select hooks with medium or heavy wire for all patterns under size 20, even dry fly patterns. Hook performance countervails the minor weight increase. In hook making, the inside eye diameter is usually the diameter of the wire used for the particular hook. This means that the smaller the hook and finer the wire, the smaller the eye; and, due to the small eye on some hooks, it is as easy to thread a tippet through a size 22 as to pass a *Hexagenia limbata* through a size 22. The *Big Eye Series* has a size 22 with the eye equivalent of a size 16. This should be a significant boon for fishing in low light or for using the heavier, ultra-strong tippets to master large trout. Again, in diminutive hook sizes, there is no float problem with the minimal weight increase.

Cold Forging. Cold, flat forging has dubious value. The increased metal on the vertical axis is at the expense of the metal on the horizontal axis, metal that would have to be bent anyway. What is gained on one axis is lost on the other. In small hooks, forging may merely produce a more brittle bend without producing a stronger bend.

Bend. The stress concentration of a sneck converges at the top rear of the shank, the point where the wire drops for the gap. The flatter curve of the Limerick spreads the stress concentration over a greater length of wire for increased strength. Slope-shanked or curved hooks distribute the stress concentration over a greater wire-length yet for remarkable strength. Up-sloped shanks, which place the draw line close to the shank line, also have improved resistance to force.

Shank Length. Shank length is an integral part of hook strength. To some extent, hooking a trout depends on the bend, whereas landing a trout depends upon the shank. A longer shank allows greater distribution of stress and, consequently, allows less wire damage. Thus, to some extent, shank length determines the integrity and reliability of a hook. A stressed hook squirms as the longer shank flexes and deforms to accommodate the stress.

Leverage Arm. Ironically, a small hook may be stronger than its larger counterpart. Despite a decrease in wire diameter, a small hook, more compact and with a shorter leverage line (an imaginary right-angle line from the direction of draw to the shank), may resist more gram-force than a larger hook with a longer leverage line. The wider gap width and the resulting longer leverage line has a profound influence on hook performance.

Forging. As noted, various factors determine the strength of a hook: temper, wire diameter, bend, forging, steel composition, and processing. Additions to the steel alloy may decrease brittleness while increasing hardness and elasticity of the wire. However, different wire diameters react to tempering and cooling differently; consequently smaller hooks may require a separate process. To produce a tough and flexible hook, a company may also inject a "protection gas" during tempering to maintain the carbon content of the steel.

THE SMALL DRY-FLY HOOK

A small hook under stress is not dead steel. At every moment, a different design or geometry is brought to bear upon the hook as it seeks to accommodate the stress (the force) and distribute the strain (the result of force). The stress-strain graphs encourage regarding the hook as a dynamic shape-shifter. Unlike large hooks, small, pliant hooks undergo extreme deformation.

Although there is no consummate small hook, there are features that might make one more effective. The graphs suggest those features that produce, theoretically at least, the ideal small hook. The following dry-fly ideal is based on viewing the small hook as a dynamic, shifting shape.

The Small Hook Paradigm

1. A forged, sproat bend with heavier wire in the bend. The heavier bend would lower the center of gravity of the hook and improve its stance on the water.
2. A 10-degree lift on the tapered fore-shank opens the gap for effective hooking. Due to the extended forging (a spear length on the shank), gap spread is limited during stressing.
3. The lifted fore-shank shortens the leverage line, thereby diminishing the force on the hook. The lifted fore-shank cants the wing back in a dun design. The leading edge of most mayfly duns cant back between 50 to 60 degrees. A lifted fore-shank hook appeared in 1934. The I. G. Grahame hook had only a short lift, about one-fourth shank length. *The Hardy Angling Guide Coronation Number* (1937) claims that the Grahame hook, apparently used for North Country patterns, captured trout well. Like many angling oddities, the Grahame hook vanished from the shelf.

4. The lifted fore-shank advances the lower hackle barbs, resulting in a wider stance for better balance.

5. A flat-forged bend transfers the strain to the pliant tapered shank. The tapered shank acts as a "shock absorber" or spring absorbing and spreading the stress over a longer wire length. The same effect could be created by lengthening the fore-shank. But for small hooks, the tapered shank duplicates the flex of an extended shank. Forged, long-shank hooks are more pliable and, consequently, stronger. The brittle forging of the bend passes the stress to the pliable, extended shank that absorbs the stress through round-house bending. Consequently, the forged, extended shank hooks produce steep slope graphs over a wide range of exerted forces, due to their prolonged resistance. Under stress, the fore-shank flexes, extracting stress from the bend.

6. A greater wire length absorbs the stress, thereby decreasing its overall impact. With a short-shanked hook, the mechanical stress is usually concentrated or gathered at a single position on the bend. Such a conclusion argues the advantages for demi-patterns, where long-shanked hooks are used for micropatterns. A small hook with a long shank is a contradiction. Therefore, an annealed and tapered shank produces "the spring" over a shorter distance. Tapered shanks are not new. A tapered fore-shank appeared on the Edgar Sealey S4324, a flat bend hook that appeared at the turn of the century. It was an attractive sproat with a delicately tapered fore-shank.

7. The 10-degree lift would also result in a 10-degree point angle for effective penetration. The point should appear on the lower, outside edge of the hook wire to chisel home quickly. Bending the point out, thereby creating an *out point*, is often done to achieve better penetration.

8. The increased wire diameter along the bend places greater strength in the sector of greatest stress.

9. Although some may argue that a cone point requires greater force for penetration, a dropped-cone point, with the point on the lower rim, would create a strong, penetrating point.

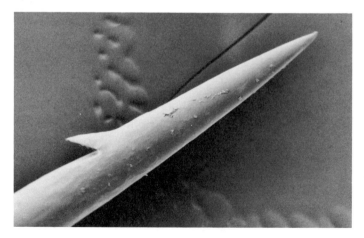

Hook Point

*T*he *Methods*

TYING THE MICROPATTERN

Datus Proper, in *What the Trout Said*, observes that "The most telling criticism of sparse dressing is that they make the hook appear prominent. That is a hard problem to beat in assembling a small fly for a large trout." Sparse dressing, however, is the natural garb of an insect. The tyer can use, however, finer hooks or camouflage the hooks in various ways. In the world of insects, nature dresses her broods in scanty apparel. Many small patterns are not delicate; they do not match the hatch. Proper discovered that the Large Dark Olive (*Baetis rhodani*) weighed .5 grains, whereas a winged imitation on a size 16 hook (3X fine) weighed 1.3 grains. Proper considered this hook too fine for the trout taking the olives. The problem, then, is how to produce a delicate and seductive pattern, a pattern that attracts and entices a take. The following methods, some traditional and some innovative, help master tying small.

Concepts of Micro-Tying

(1) Maintain delicate tying by avoiding over-threading. To minimize bulk, limit the wraps and flatten the thread. Sparse and delicate tying is the key to micropatterns. Thread may be flattened in three ways.

THE COUNTERSPIN

Counterspinning the bobbin unravels the twist and flattens the thread. Most thread is counterspun when the bobbin spins in a counter-clockwise direction (when viewed from shank to bobbin). That is, most tying threads have a *Z* twist: the direction of twist represented by the middle stroke of the letter Z. While the thread whirls, compress and flatten the thread further by stripping it down between the thumbnail and forefinger. Some threads may have interior S twist threads.

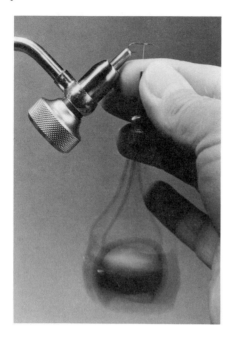

The typical Z twist of tying thread

Spinning the bobbin to flatten the tying thread

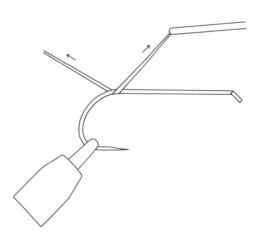

The Thread Glide: Trap the thread in the bend as illustrated and saw back and forth to align and splay the strands. After flattening, slide the thread forward on the shank to mount and begin tying.

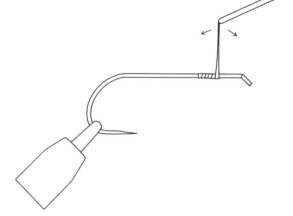

The Thread Rock: To flatten the thread after it has been mounted or during the tying process, press the thread against the shank and rock back and forth. This splays the strands and results in a short length of flat thread.

THE THREAD ROCK

Rocking a twisted, multistrand thread back and forth splays the strands and flattens the thread. First, firmly mount the thread. Then, with thread pressed against the hook shank, rock it back and forth to splay the strands. Wraps with broad thread will hold material better than wraps with tightly corded thread.

THE THREAD GLIDE

The glide, or "sawing" the thread, splays and flattens the strands. Before mounting the thread, extend the thread about three inches and "saw" it back and forth against the hook bend. This produces a flat section of thread excellent for foundation wraps and micropatterns.

(2) Minimize the journey of the thread. For example, when mounting wings, tail and dubbing, mount the thread immediately behind the head space on the hook. This becomes the wing base. Add the wings on the base. Then, select and trim tails to size and mount the butts about one-half way down the shank. The thread travels back to secure them and ends at the hook bend. Finally, add the dubbing and make the journey forward to wing mount point and complete with the hackle. Use 8/0 thread.

(3) In conventional tying, it is common to wrap on material before trimming the excess. Most tyers will find that for small-fly tying it is best to measure, trim material to correct length, and then mount the material. This avoids close trimming on very small patterns. It is often impossible to trim close enough to avoid ragged ends.

(4) The hook heel and point may be camouflaged with an overwing or feather barbs. Chironomid patterns, tied on curved or round hooks, may have bodies wrapped *around the bend to the barb itself.* Anal brushes may even cover the point for complete camouflage.

(5) On small patterns, stiff hackle may prevent hooking. After missing several grayling rises on the Slovene Unec, I noticed how truly bristly the barbs were on my Gray Palmer. The short, stiff barbs prevented point penetration. I pruned the bottom hackle and immediately connected. Vincent Marinaro noted in *In the Ring of the Rise* that ". . . stiff hackles act as a guard in front of the hook point. (This was never very apparent with large flies and large hooks; but with the increasing and desirable use of small hooks and small flies. The stiff hackle guards the point even more efficiently than ever before, because, as the bend narrows and the point gets closer to the shank, the point is guarded by the stiffest portion of the hackle.)" To solve this, Marinaro's thorax tie splayed the hackle fore and aft between the wings to eliminate the guard and expose the point. Marinaro's outrigger tails, mounted at *right angles* to the shank, further supported the hook.

(6) Match the materials to the method and the mission of the pattern. Many problems in micro-tying are solved merely by using minimal amounts of material. Sequencing, proportion and symmetry are especially important when tying micropatterns. Select the proper size, weight and style of hook for a particular pattern. And, like all tying, select the appropriate color (or color harmony) based on tradition or on the natural.

approximately 50°

Touching Wraps

THE TOUCHING WRAPS

To produce a smooth thread bed, angle the tag end of the thread as illustrated. As the working thread wraps back, it will slide down into position for touching wraps. Touching wraps create smooth, single-lap bodies and foundations.

The Mole Microcaddis

Designing The Micropattern

Versions of popular patterns vary significantly. Materials and methods differ. Patterns are often created empirically over time with gradual material substitutes based on popularity and availability. Experimentation makes fly-tying fascinating. Art has no finality. There are, however, some considerations for tying the small pattern.

(1) Due to the diminutive size of the pattern, heavy wire hooks may be used to increase strength.

(2) There are certain materials and methods most appropriate for the small pattern. Various synthetic and natural materials are suitable for small patterns. The softer, shorter dubbings are especially useful: mole, squirrel, silk, and camel down. Certain feathers or feather parts are most appropriate for micropatterns; stripped herl, goose biots, and feather barbs produce segmented bodies that often attract trout. Cul de canard creates emergers and traditional dries.

(3) As in all tying, form, proportion, and color often evolve from tradition, the natural or the fancy of the tyer. Attractor patterns usually sanction greater imagination.

(4) Micropatterns may drift undetected. They sometimes require an element of attraction, some enhancement or overstatement that draws attention: flash, contrast, movement, color, or seductive silhouette. The smaller the pattern, the more tempting it should appear. Something should set the pattern apart from all the surface drift that passes over a trout.

Micropatterns have a double nature: They must attract (usually by emphasis) and deceive (usually by verisimilitude). Once the trout stalks the pattern, the pattern must be natural enough to prompt a take. Tinsels and synthetics create flash; variegated hackles and soft fibers or feathers create movement. Whether the trout that took an Adams would have taken an attractor is a moot point. The mood of the trout, the angling conditions, the particular drift or retrieve all determine and obscure the cause. No matter, a pattern unseen is a pattern refused.

The Micropattern Methods

BLACK'S EXTENDED-BODY METHOD

Bill Black, a thoughtful and imaginative tyer, produces pliant and realistic extended bodies. Reasonably durable, Black's super-glue bodies are realistic and effective. This simple and rapid method allows tying extended bodies for micropatterns.

(1) Place a fine needle (size 5–15) firmly in the vise. Care must be taken when tying on an exposed needle point. Tyers should dull the needle point and wear protective eyewear.

(2) Lock the thread onto the needle, about 2 millimeters back from the point.

(3) Mount one, two, or three appropriately colored Microfibetts on each side so that they traverse the needle.

(4) Wrap the thread down the needle to proper body length.

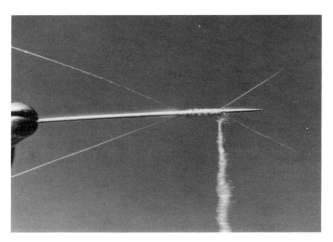

The mounted tails

(5) Wrap the thread back to the butt and figure-eight, once or twice, to divide the tails. This makes the tails emerge from the sides of the extended body.

(6) Mount ultra-fine dubbing, such as Spirit River's Fine & Dry Synthetic Dubbing, to the thread.

(7) Add a drop of Aron Alpha Superglue to the threaded body and quickly dub the body. Caution should be taken with all cyanoacrylate adhesives. Follow all warnings carefully. Time is not as critical if Dave's Flexament is used. However, a few seconds should elapse to tack the glue before the dubbing is overwrapped. Seamstuff, a waterproof, silicone sealer produced by W. L. Gore Associates, works well. This viscous, adhesive silicone requires

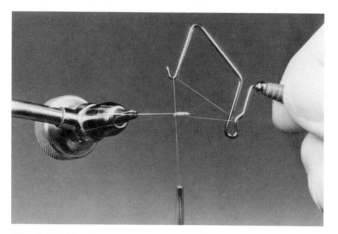

The dubbed body

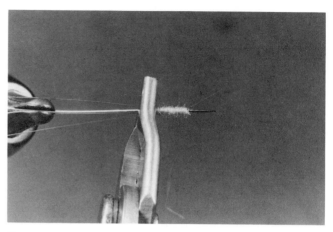

Removing the body with flat-nosed pliers

Rolled body Blue-winged Olive

After mounting the body, add wings and hackle

time to dry. No matter which adhesive is used, it should be applied thinly and thoroughly to the thread underbody.

(8) Finish with a couple of half-hitches at the body base, and trim excess dubbing and thread.

(9) With flat-nosed pliers, remove the body from the needle before the cement hardens. This is best accomplished by gripping the *needle* with the pliers and pushing against the base until the body disengages the needle. Gently shape the body as illustrated.

(10) When mounting the body, wrap over the Microfibett butts, fold them back and lock with several wraps. Trim excess before adding wings or thoracic dubbing.

THE ROLLED BODY

Perhaps the most unusual material for making an extended body is Scotch Removable Poster Tape (Product 109). This sticky membrane easily creates *buoyant*, extended bodies, with or without tails. The tape, sticky on both sides, is a high-tack membrane that, when rolled around tails or on itself, forms a soft and durable body. Other double-sticky membrane tapes or foam mounting tapes may be used for larger extended-body patterns—grasshoppers, adult damselflies, and dragonflies.

There are several significant advantages to the tape patterns. First, the tape creates shaped and soft bodies. Also, the tape membrane is buoyant, never requiring floatants. Although the tape patterns may appear large, they are lightweight and, when properly designed, may be cast with ultra-light fly rods. Furthermore, tails or dubbing may be locked within the rolled body. Fine dubbing may be placed on the tape prior to rolling; when rolled, the dubbing within the translucent tape produces a soft, inner glow of gut. Furthermore, the loosely rolled dubbing traps air for maximum flotation. This technique is excellent for extended Chironomid bodies. Two dubbings, such as red and white Antron, may create the inner gut color and the breathing gills or trailing shuck.

To form a rolled body, apply about two centimeters of tape to an X-Acto Self Healing Cutting Mat or glass sheet. Once applied, remove the tape liner to expose the outer sticky membrane. For a tailed mayfly body, press tails, such as Microfibetts, on the tape parallel to and about two millimeters from the edge. The *overhang* of the tails constitutes their length. Then, with your finger tip, roll the tape edge toward and over the tails. Continue to roll the tape, forming a cylindrical body. For a slender, light body, make few rolls; for larger bodies, roll until the desired width is achieved. With a sharp blade, cut the excess tape against the mat or glass and remove the rolled, tailed body. To make bodies larger than a single tape-width roll, merely mount the tape to another tape section as required. To preserve tack for dubbing, do not touch the rolled body more than necessary.

The rolled body may be mounted on the hook shank and dubbed in the traditional manner; however, the best way to dub the extended body is to roll it in soft, fine dubbing before mounting it on the hook shank. The sticky body will pick up the fine dubbing. After completely cloaking the body with dubbing, roll it firmly between your fingers to adhere and smooth the dubbing. The pearly white membrane will whiten any attached dubbing. For a small, delicate pattern, use mole fur. Some short dubbings, however, may not adhere well to the sticky surface; most dubbing must be long enough to cover and cling. The spongy, supple body must be firmly mounted to the hook shank to prevent movement during tying. Mount the rolled body at mid-shank and complete the tailed mayfly with wings and hackle.

To make the Scotch Bloodworm (*Chironomus*), press in a tuft of white Antron or CDC barbs. For the bright, inner body, roll a tiny, tight rope of blood-red dubbing (Finesse Crimson 17 or Scintilla Vivid Red 32). Press the dubbing robe on the middle of the tape. Roll the tape to capture the anal tuft and inner dubbing. To reveal the dubbing gut, limit the number of body rolls to two or three. Cut the body to length and mount directly above the hook point on the shank. Add dark mole dubbing for the thorax and then mount the wings—a bundle of dun CDC barbs that screen the hook bend and point. Trim and flare the excess CDC barbs to imitate the pupa's cephalic fan. Tied in this manner, the pattern will float flush in the surface film.

A variety of patterns may be produced, incorporating the rolled body. The tape, in the shape of a trapezoid, will produce a taper at each end. Roll the long edge of the trapezoid first, creating a shaped body with mounting taper. Caenis bodies may be rolled *sans* dubbing. For a tidy mount, trim the body to length before mounting.

THE BEAD METHODS

Rather than merely slipping a bead on a small hook, make it an integral part of the architecture. This may be done in various ways. Beads are usually mounted by slipping the bead over the hook point and threading it around the bend to the eye. Often, removing or flattening the barb allows the bead to slip over the hook point. After the bead slips to the eye, tying thread buttresses it in place. The pattern is then tied. Branko Gasparin of Slovenia has a different method for mounting beads. As in Gasparin's Polyfeitus pattern, an emerging caddis, the bead is slipped over a straight pin and slid to the head. The pin is then bent up and the excess cut. A few file licks taper the mounting foot. The beaded pin is then mounted *above* the eye of the hook. The pattern is tied in the conventional manner. The heavy bead turns the pattern upside down to lessen the chance of snagging. Unlike the traditional mount, this method does not restrict the hook gap; consequently, beads may be tied on small hooks with this method.

Another bead method installs the bead as under-thorax. Mount a beaded hook in the vise. This hides half the bead, leaving only a "hint of glint."

Mount the wing case slip (approximately eight barbs for a size 18 hook) securely at head position. Whip off the thread.

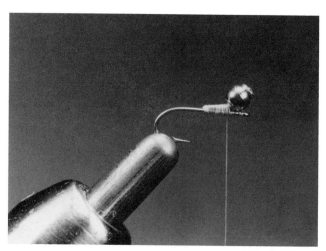

The Pin-Bead Method

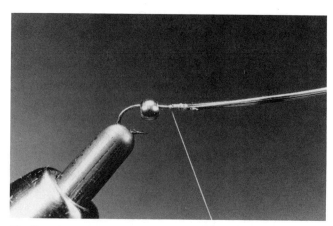

The Bead Methods: Mounting the wing case

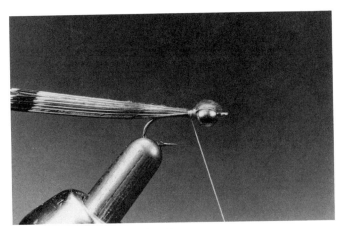

The Bead Methods: Folding the wing case

The Bead Methods: Mounting the tails

Slip the bead over the threaded base of the wing case, and attach the tying thread directly behind the bead. Fold the wing case over and secure. Take thread down to shank rear.

Mount the tails and spiral the body forward directly behind the bead. Secure with several wraps and trim excess. Whipping off a bead pattern is usually done directly behind the bead; this leaves visible thread wraps on the body. Dubbing, however, can cover those thread wraps.

After tying the pattern and before whipping off, apply a high-tack wax to the first quarter inch of the thread extending from the fly. Dust on a fine, short dubbing such as mole. Whip the head so that the dubbed thread is laid down while bare thread snakes beneath it to whip-finish the pattern.

It is also possible to hide the whip finish directly behind the bead. Three or four whips are made, and then the thread is tugged behind the bead and out of sight. Repeat two or three times and then place a drop of cement behind the bead.

THE CDC DUBBING LOOP

Cul de canard barbs may be stripped from the stem and spun in a dubbing loop. This produces a shaggy, bubble-snatching dubbing or a hackle with exceptional flotation. It is one way of producing a standard dry hackle or mock palmer hackle, as the CDC stem is often too fragile. Dry patterns may also be hackled with either the standard or parachute method in this manner. Although the CDC may be mounted like a regular hackle, the thick and thin stem either produces bulk or breaks. If you mount the CDC as a conventional hackle, select those with strong, slender stems. There are, however, many ways to use the barbs *sans* stem. It should be noted that if the barbs are stripped from the stem by hand, then a small foot or "hook" appears (actually, a curlicue of stem) at the base of the barb.

STRIPPED CDC BARBS

I have found that the most efficient method to gather barbs is to stack two or more CDC feathers and pull off, from tip to base, their barbs. Then, while keeping the stripped barbs bundled, turn the feather over, and match the stemmed barbs over the stripped barbs. Hold all barbs firmly and strip the opposite barbs, allowing them to bundle with the first cluster.

First, overlay and match two or more CDC feathers. Grip the lower barbs with the thumb and forefinger of the left hand.

Pull the stem (counter to the barb-growth path) with the right hand to detach the lower barbs.

Next, rotate and align the stemmed CDC barbs with the detached barbs. Grip both the attached and detached barbs.

Again, pull to detach all the barbs.

Trim to crop the feet (the barb curls) and to even the ends. The feet or curls will produce a knobby, coarse dubbing. The feet may also be trimmed after the barbs are mounted, but not spun, in the dubbing loop. Remember too that the freer and longer the CDC barbs are mounted, the more buoyant the pattern.

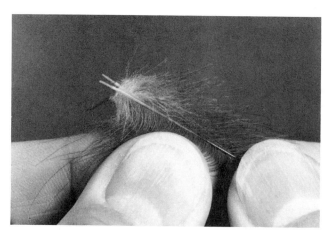

Match the CDC feathers

Detach the lower barbs

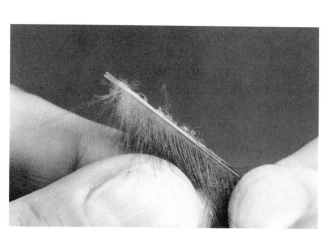

Rotate and align the stemmed barbs with the detached barbs

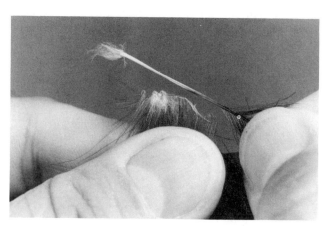

Detach all the barbs

Trim the barb feet

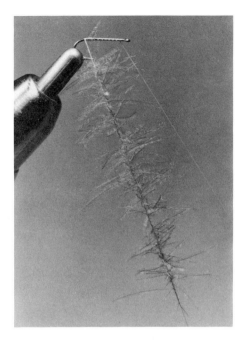

The CDC Dubbing Loop

THE MOCK PALMER

CDC feathers make excellent mock-palmer hackles, as they offer abundant barbs to the water surface for increased flotation. A mock palmer, actually "chenilled" CDC barbs, can be created with a dubbing loop. The mock palmer builds the body of a palmer pattern as well as a forward faux-hackle. Mount the thread and fashion a dubbing loop at least seven times longer than the hook shank. Apply high-tack wax to the thread. Mount stripped barbs in the dubbing loop. Continue to strip and mount until adequate barbs are placed in the spinning loop. For long tendrils, the barbs should be mounted at the barb base. Trim the base that extends beyond the doubled threads. Spin the loop to lock in the barbs, and then, while stroking the barbs to the rear to avoid overwrapping, spiral the palmer forward. This produces a body with extreme flotation due to the numerous trailing tendrils. This is an excellent method for mayfly emergers, mayfly duns and caddis patterns. When combining palmer

The Mock Palmer

and front hackle (faux-hackle) on patterns, it is best to palmer the shank fully. Then, return the working thread to secure the overwing, before wrapping the overwing with the front hackle. The working thread, rather than the spun hackle, should secure the overwing.

THE BOBBIN-LOOP PARACHUTE

With the limited space available, tying off a parachute hackle can be a problem with micropatterns. Wim Alphenaar places a loop of thread at the head with several overwraps. He then wraps the parachute hackle and passes the hackle tip through the loop. When the loop ends are pulled, the hackle tip slides beneath the wraps before the pattern is whip-finished. It is possible, however, to create a loop with *the tying thread itself* that captures and secures the hackle tip. A midge bobbin facilitates passage through the loop.

TYING OFF THE PARACHUTE HACKLE

1. Firmly mount the hackle concave-side down on the shank.
2. Extend and double the tying thread. Loop doubled thread back and overwrap approximately three times. End of doubled thread should extend one inch beyond overwraps. The doubled thread loop, very strong even in 8/0 thread, may be mounted above or beneath the shank for proper parachute placement. For a tight parachute, loop should emerge from shank at a single point.
3. While keeping doubled loop taut with hackle pliers or a single-hook whirl, wrap parachute hackle tightly around the loop base. Each hackle wrap should snug against the hook shank. When completed, pass hackle tip through doubled loop. Draw doubled loop closed by pulling the tag end of doubled loop. Remove Single-Hook Whirl as doubled loop closes and secures parachute hackle. Trim excess hackle stem and thread tag. Stroke hackle barbs back while whip

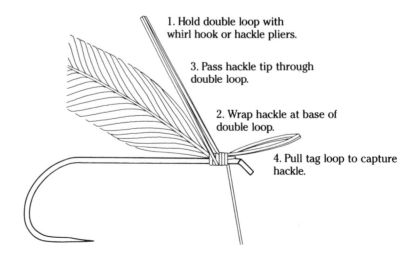

1. Hold double loop with whirl hook or hackle pliers.

3. Pass hackle tip through double loop.

2. Wrap hackle at base of double loop.

4. Pull tag loop to capture hackle.

Tying off the Parachute Hackle

finishing. A cement bead may be placed on the "hub" of the parachute for durability.

CDC WINGS

Marc Petitjean (Switzerland) bundles CDC barbs and mounts them as standard mayfly wings. Spinner wings may also be done in this manner. On patterns smaller than 14, the CDC barbs may be bundled and figure-eighted for either standard dun or spinner wings. One method that creates dun wings pivots a full CDC feather through a CDC barb bundle, thereby dividing and fanning the barbs forward. The soft, gauzy CDC wings are easily erected and positioned.

VEILED WING BUDS

The veiled wing design comes from Andria Urban of Macedonia. After tying in tails and abdomen for an emerger pattern (such as a mayfly), he mounts the tips of two matched CDC feathers at the rear of the thorax, one on each side. After the thorax is dubbed, the wing veils are *loosely* looped, convex side out, above the thorax and tied in at the head. Each CDC feather is mounted slightly off-center in emulation of the twin budding wings during emergence. These puffy, veiled wings offer two broad feathers to the water surface, thereby creating excellent flotation. The pattern hangs in the surface.

To align and adjust both wing loops, fold them over a dubbing needle, wrap two or three at the head, and then adjust the loop length by pulling both stems against the needle. When completed, whip finish the head. A sharp backcast strips water from the looped buds so that the refreshed pattern returns for a long float. Size and color may be changed to match a variety of emerging mayflies or caddis.

CDC Veiled Wings

CDC DUBBING

Marjan Fratnik of Slovenia produces some interesting bodies with CDC barbs. On patterns smaller than 12, a single CDC feather may be mounted by the tip and twisted tightly to form a feather "yarn" that is spiraled forward as body. However, to omit the bulky stem, the barbs may be stripped and the curlicue feet clipped. Mount the soft barbs to the thread just as you would dubbing. Twist the thread slightly to catch the barbs and then wrap the body. Depending on the length of the barbs, a bushy or trim body is produced. A bushy body may be trimmed for neatness. These waterproof barb-bodies are simple and effective for most dry-fly patterns.

Fratnik also makes CDC dubbing by placing the feathers in a small coffee-mill. The high-speed propeller chops the barbs and removes them from their thicker stems. The stems, then, may be removed after milling or discarded while dubbing. To produce finer CDC dubbing, *cut* the barbs free of the stems and mill longer. Longer milling chops the barbs into shorter, more easily dubbed fragments. The longer the mill time, the finer the dubbing.

To mount CDC dubbing, daub high-tack wax on the thread, and blot the dubbing on. Twirl the dubbing between the fingers, in a single direction, to scarf it tightly to the thread. The result is a dense, waterproof body. Finger wax—a *light* wax-smear on the fingers—helps to bind the fibers and produce dense dubbing.

DUBBING HACKLE

Spun in a spinning loop, CDC dubbing may also be used for faux-hackles. Dubbing hackle should be briefly milled to preserve long barbs. After milling, remove all stems and mount a fine haze of CDC dubbing in a spinning loop. Once spun, the CDC flares into a hackle or palmer hackle appropriate for most patterns. *When mounted with protruding barbs, there is nothing that floats a pattern as well as CDC faux-hackles.*

BLACK'S CDC MAY

Bill Black offers other methods for mounting CDC hackles.

1. Mount Microfibetts tails, figure-eight and split. Take two or three dubbed wraps beneath the tails and then dub the body.
2. Stack two or three CDC feathers and mount.
3. Clip excess and restack excess. Cut the stem to form a V and mount over wings with extended barbs forward. Trim extended barbs for hackle.
4. Finish pattern so that the CDC hackle sweeps out to one side.

BLACK'S CDC MIDGE

1. Mount one strip of Crystal Flash as ribbing. Dub tapered body and counterwrap the ribbing.

2. Stack three or four CDC feathers and mount with tips extended over the hook eye.
3. Trim extended barbs approximately one-half body length. Create fanned hackle on each side by figure-eighting the extended barbs. Prune and remove CDC stems.

CDC PATTERN INDICATOR

Dyed CDC barbs make excellent pattern indicators. Two effective patterns that utilize the markers are the small, dark midges and micro-caddis that are most difficult to see on the water. The small (18 or 20) Campyla caddis (Little Sister Sedge) can be tied this way. Wrap in Kelly-green CDC barbs for body; then align and mount two or three CDC dun feathers as overwing and whip off. A tuft of barbs, base-wrapped to bundle them, may be tied in, at the top of the head, and then trimmed to desired length. This produces a small, yet visible pattern marker that will fluff after each cast. The best color that I have found for markers is a bright, pale yellow.

FLARED CDC HACKLE

Angelo Droetto of Italy, a devotee of CDC designs, creates a CDC hackle collar *sans* stem. First, remove and bundle CDC barbs.

The barb bundle is then placed over the hackle placement point on the hook and wrapped on. Because the barbs compress easily, a small head results. A few thread wraps *behind* the hackle will flare it. The barbs may also be mounted forward so that when the body is wrapped on, it covers the base of the barbs. The thread then passes through the barbs to flare them back. In both methods, the result is a flared and dense CDC hackle. After mounting the barbs, it is possible to pull them "flat" forward and trim to length. Droetto's favorite CDC pattern, an olive dun, is tied with a pale green body, cream thread ribbing and a dense CDC hackle. This barb-only technique is reminiscent of the Spanish stacked-barb method for hackling. This is an exquisite method for various small trout patterns.

The Droetto Method: After securing the base of the CDC barbs, mount the tail and body. The body covers the base of the barbs. Pass the thread through the barbs to erect and flare them before whip-finishing the head.

THE MODIFIED DE FEO MOUNT FOR CDC FLANK HACKLE

The late Charles De Feo mounted salmon fly beards by wrapping a single feather beneath the shank, clipping the veed tip and then drawing the feather to splay the barbs and adjust the length. The stem was then trimmed. A modified De Feo mount creates CDC flank hackles. Snip the vee tip from stacked CDC feathers. With the barbs trailing back, straddle the veed barbs over the shank at the hackle point. Hold the barbs down while securing them with several wraps. Then, before the final fastening wraps, gently lift the barbs parallel to the shank. Finally, trim the raised stems and crop the barbs to length.

Black's Emerger with flank hackle

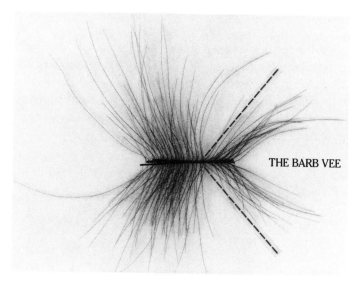

Stacked CDC stems with attached vee tip
For emerger Tircos, Blue-Winged Olives, and Microcaddis, Bill Black stacks the CDC stems as shown and trims the veed tip. The barbed stems are shortened and restacked to match pattern size. He then mounts the stacked stems parallel to the shank so that the barbs extend on either side. Thread wraps between the barbs lock the stems along the shank. A dash of dubbing, which shoves the barbs rearward, covers the CDC stems. He then trims the trailing barbs to length.

THE BLACK GNAT WITH CROSS HACKLE

Stacked and mounted CDC barbs, with or without stems, may be figure-eighted to produce cross hackles, hackles that seem to cross the shank at right-angles. This is a common method for hackling micropatterns, such as Caenis and Trico Spinners and Black Gnats. On micro hooks a bundle of CDC barbs may be figure-eighted for cross hackles. Black's stacked stem method may be used to create extended cross hackles as seen on the Black Gnat. Depending upon barb length and hook size, a bundle of barbs may be merely figure-eighted for cross hackles. Another method for creating cross hackles is to mount a bundle of CDC barbs with tips forward. After trimming the butts, divide and figure-eight the barbs. The barbs on both sides should extend from the shank at right-angles. Figure-eight fine dubbing for a thorax. The extended and fanned barbs offer superior flotation. The Cluster Microcaddis, that appears in this text, improves significantly with fore-and-aft CDC cross hackles.

Black Gnat with cross hackle

THE CDC

1. Mount hackle barbs or Microfibetts for split and spread tails. Then complete the body with stripped herl, synthetic or CDC dubbing.
2. After trimming the thickened stem base of two short, fine-stemmed CDC hackles, mount the butts at the wing-mount position with tips facing rearward.
3. Then, plant a CDC barb bundle at the wing-mount position. After the wing bundle is secure, pull the CDC feathers forward, one on each side of the wing bundle, and tie off at the head. This flattens and fans the wing bundle into a single "panel." The panel wing may be left natural (if mounted to length) or trimmed for size and shape. A hackle may be added on the wing base before the side feathers are folded forward or a hackle may be wrapped over the forward extension of the side feathers. If required, the wing base may be dubbed before the side feathers fold forward and the hackle mounted. To create a sparse, smooth-water profile, figure-eight CDC barbs on the wing base prior to folding the side feathers forward. The CDC Panel-Wing produces the distinctive thoracic swell and splayed flat wing common to many mayfly duns.

The Black Gnat Cross Hackle viewed from beneath

The CDC Panel Wing Dun

THE CDC SHUCK

A bundle of CDC barbs, in a variety of colors, may be tied in to imitate a shuck. The advantage is its delicate scantiness and yet its ability to float a pattern. On smaller patterns, CDC barbs may be sparsely looped for realistic shucks. Due to the fact that the maximum length of a CDC barb is only about 25 millimeters, the larger shucks cannot be imitated with a loop. Shucks may be made with the minute CDC nipple plumes.

THE CDC STRIKE INDICATOR

Finally, here is something for those anglers who wish a functional strike indicator on the tippet or leader. Select two or three matched CDC feathers (pale yellow is highly visible), and loop them in as illustrated.

Trim the excess. The CDC bundle *cushions* the knot, thereby minimizing breakage. If the CDC goes under, a brisk backcast restores its fluff. In addition, the CDC strike indicator can swim small nymphs beneath the surface. And, when the strike indicator is no longer required, you merely grasp the CDC fluff and pull it away from the *line end* to open the loop. This strike indicator is far more effective and natural than others; it is merely a feather floating on the stream.

THE DEMI-PATTERNS

The demi-patterns, shrunk patterns tied on standard hooks, offer the trout a diminutive tie. Sometimes trout distinguish the pattern, not as feathered steel, but as a small insect. When trout willingly accept them, there are several advantages to the demi-patterns.

Although not strictly micropatterns, the demi-pattern is tiny and traditional. Mounting the pattern, or pattern parts, farther back on the shank has historic precedent. "Perhaps the first American writer of record to suggest moving the hackle on a dry fly a long way back from the eye of the hook," writes Paul Schullery, "was Dr. Edgar Burke . . . who wrote a small book called *American Dry Flies and How to Tie Them* (1925)." Later, Vincent Marinaro, "though not the first to advocate moving the hackle back, brought the idea to successful fruition." Certainly J. C. Mottram pushes a pattern back in *Fly-Fishing: Some New Arts and Mysteries* (1915). He describes a reed smut larva pattern that "need not cover the whole length of the shank; it should be tied towards the hook end. . . ."

There are several significant advantages to the dwarfed demi-patterns. The spear and heel of the hook merge with the tail. A larger and longer hook increases the gape and improves hooking. In down-stream presentation, the pattern masks the naked shank. Finally, a greater variety of hook shapes and weights may be used for small patterns.

When tied on the back or bend of the hook, a pattern may imitate an emerging or ascending nymph. Instead of tying cluster patterns, such as two Tricos on a shank, tie a Trico on half a shank. These "rumble-seat" nymphs, emergers, duns, and spinners can be remarkably effective.

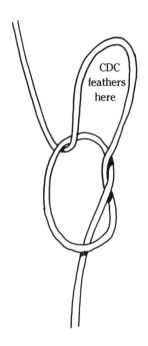

CDC feathers here

CDC Strike Indicator

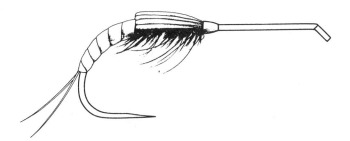

A Demi-Nymph: Various nymphs, pupae, larvae, and dries may be tied short, presenting the illusion of a tiny insect.

DUBBING METHODS

Although the pattern was created in 1900, it was not until 1934, twenty years after his death, that R. S. Austin's secret was revealed. His fur formula was kept a secret so that he, and later his daughter, might have a monopoly in supplying the authentic formula. Austin, a Devonshire fly tyer, concocted the Tup's Indispensable out of urine-stained wool from a ram's scrotum mixed with cream seal fur, lemon spaniel hair, and yellow mohair. G. E. M. Skues, who christened and popularized the pattern, added a pinch of crimson seal's fur in place of the mohair to produce a pink tint. This unique dubbing was first disclosed, according to John Roberts, in Alexander Mackintosh's *The Driffield Angler*. "Take a little fine wool from the ram's testicles," Mackintosh writes, "which is a beautiful dusty yellow."

Dubbing and dubbing methods have long fascinated tyers. Dubbing is basic to tying, whether tying macro or micropatterns. But, selecting the proper dubbing and dubbing methods is crucial for small patterns. Understanding the origin and nature of dubbing makes mastering dubbing rudimentary.

It is impossible to say exactly when dubbing—mounting fur or hair on a thread that is then spiraled along the shank—first appeared. We know much more about winging and hackling than dubbing. The term itself adds to the problem. As far back as 1450, dubbing meant to attach a fly to the line as well as to dress a fly. By 1570, dubbing meant to dress, to array, to adorn or to invest, apparently in any manner, including "dubbing" a knight. The difficulty is that the term refers to any manner of dressing a fly, not necessarily the act of dubbing itself.

Most early tying descriptions suggest that the body material was a short skein tied in at the bend and wrapped forward rather than *attached* to the thread and wound forward. In the second century, Martial writes of "fraudful flies" but does so without description. "Ruby-colored wool" wrapped around hooks took "spotted fish" according to Aelianus' *De Natura Animalium*; but this early third-century work does not tell us how the hook was wrapped. And the *Treatise* (1496) describes a "body of blacke wull & lappid abowte wt yelow threde" without detail. Juan de Bergara's enigmatic Astorga manuscript (1624) refers to the *color* of hare and camel fur, but the bodies were, apparently, strands of silk, linen, and "sieve canvas." And John Donne, the metaphysical seventeenth-century poet, sings of the "curious traitors, sleeve-silk flies." According to John Waller Hills, Thomas Barker gives us, in the middle of the seventeenth century, the first portrait, although a blurred one, of fly tying: wrap in body and ribbing, make the body and over-run the tinsel.

But by the eighteenth century (and very likely much earlier), we encounter current dubbing methods. In Izaak Walton's *The Complete Angler* (the later Hawkins edition of 1766), an extended footnote lists important dubbing materials: bear, camel, badger, camlet (popularly understood as camel hair and silk), Turkish carpet yarn, seal's fur, hog's wool or hog's down "plucked from under the throat and other soft places of the hog," squirrel's tail, fox, otter, yellow fur of the marten "from off the gills or spots under the jaws," hare and foumart (polecat), and barge-sail "under which there is almost a continual smoak [sic] arising from the fire and steam of the beef kettle" which in time "dyes the tilt of a fine brown." Tyers picked out the yarn from the tilts or awnings made from discarded sails. Walton notes that "harsh" calf hair will "never work kindly nor lay handsomely." Like the modern tyer, Walton has a large needle to raise the dubbing "when flatted with working." Surely the short furs—such as the fur from the marten's cheek and the downy tail fur from the fox-cub—must have required mounting directly to the thread.

Although there are other examples to plump the tale of dubbing, the truth must be nigh to 1700. Ted Niemeyer, a scholar of tying history, believes that dubbing methods, as we understand them, date from about 1750 or earlier. He bases his verdict on an antique pattern, resplendent with fiery-brown pig's wool dubbing. We may never know when a tyer first discovered that crewel, silk, or fur, perhaps too short to be lapped along the hook, could be mounted to a waxed thread and then spiraled down the shank.

The term dubbing refers to the material, either natural or synthetic, as well as the method for mounting the material. Dubbing is a popular method to achieve shape, volume, and color while creating texture and translucency. Eric Taverner writes that "The best furs for body-dubbings are those which are naturally luminous and have kick in them, so that the fibers stand out well from the shank and catch the light." A thoughtful tyer looks beyond color and patterns to the basic properties of dubbing: absorbency, dye affinity, durability, and luster. The tyer should select the dubbing with the most desirable qualities—such as diameter, length, and surface structure—for the particular pattern. Each fiber, natural or synthetic, has specific properties. The tyer should understand the purpose of the pattern, possess the necessary skills to create the pattern, and have knowledge of the materials employed. A tyer cannot threaten his materials to make them act appropriately; he must understand what they can and cannot do.

The size, shape, diameter, surface, and physical structure—all determine the characteristics of dubbing. The microscope reveals the surface contours. For example, the scales of wool and its crimpy wave create cohesion and cling. The smooth, "glass rod" surface of silk strands creates luster. Under the microscope, a cross-cut of wool is circular or oval; a cross-cut of silk is triangular. That is why wool "sponges" light while silk reflects it. Millions of chains, with various lengths and shapes, make up the molecular arrangement of fibers. Fibers with long molecular chains are stronger than those with shorter chains. Wool has "a *molecular* crimp" (a spiral helix resembling a coiled spring) not to be confused with the wave crimp of each individual fiber. This molecular crimp creates wool's spring and elasticity. When chains are aligned and oriented lengthwise, then the fiber is very strong, but neither highly elastic nor flexible. If not aligned, the spaces between the chains increase the fiber absorbency to water and dyes. It is not important to study the molecular structure, merely to recognize that the properties of each fiber are already established at the molecular level.

Almost every size of fiber is available from the silk-soft musk ox underfur to the spiky, stiff seal guard hairs. The diameters of fibers are commonly measured in microns: One micron equals one millionth of a meter. Microns are impossible to visualize. Most pelt furs range about 10 to 15 microns and, consequently, are easily dubbed. Coarse hair fibers and guard hairs, such as those found in goat and yak, range from 90 to 140 microns. Wool can range from 18 to 50 microns, from very fine to very coarse. Easily dubbed musk ox underfur is about 17 microns, while fine Bombyx mori silk is only 12 microns. Camel underfur is about 19 microns. If factors such as diameter, length, crinkle, elasticity, resilience, and cohesion are equal, then any dubbing 30 microns or finer will dub readily.

The key to dubbing is the direction of twist on the thread and the direction of twist around the shank. John Veniard, in *Fly Dressing Materials* (1977), observed that "Any material which has a twist given in it, as called for by this method, should be wound in the opposite direction to the twist. In other words, if two silks are twisted together anti-clockwise to embrace the dubbing, they will not untwist when wound clockwise to form the body. This eliminates re-twisting the silks while forming the body." Two parallel strands will twist counter-clockwise when wound in a clockwise (viewed from the hook eye to the hook bend) action toward the hook eye; therefore, it is best, when using a dubbing loop, to twist the dubbing loop in a counterclockwise direction. As the wraps pass down the shank the twist will be reinforced. H. G. McClelland argues that a tyer should "Twist the tying silk the same way . . . which the dubbing was spun." Eric Taverner also noted this when he wrote, "Spin on the tying-silk a pinch of dubbing, twisting the silk from east through south to west; this ensures the spin remaining during the process of winding the silk round the shank." The east-south-west (viewing from shank to hand as indicated in the text illustration) produces a counter-clockwise spin.

To illustrate this, take two contrasting lengths of floss and tie them in at the bend. Hold them parallel and then begin to spiral the floss toward the head. As you wrap toward the head, the two flosses assert a tighter and tighter counter-clockwise twist on both strands (more overlaps per length).

Mastering the twist, masters dubbing. Mount the thread at the bend of a long-shanked hook. Add sparse but adequate dubbing along two inches of thread. Mount the dubbing counterclockwise (viewed down the thread toward the shank) by rolling it hard between the thumb and forefinger. Then, once it is rolled well, drop the fingers back on the exposed thread at the base of the dubbing. Continue to twist the thread counterclockwise on its own axis until the dubbing catches and tightens along the thread. Once the dubbing is tight, keep twist on the thread to prevent unwinding. Then, with the hand on the

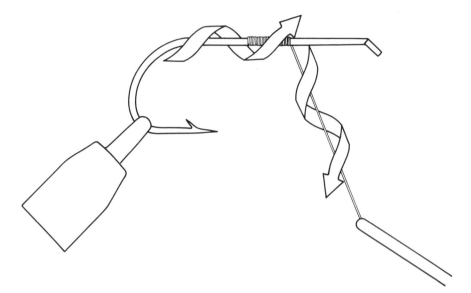

The Thread Twist: While winding along the hook shank, the tying thread accumulates, through momentary counterclockwise wrist-action, a mild Z-twist. To increase thread twist, mount dubbing with a Z-twist. Then, as the dubbed body spirals up the shank, the dubbed thread becomes tighter and denser. If the thread is not thoroughly twisted on its own axis prior to wrapping the body, the first few body wraps may produce fuzzed or loose dubbing. The essence of dubbing micropatterns lies in short, scanty dubbing and tight thread.

thread and not on the bobbin, spiral the dubbing down the shank. If the hand holds the bobbin, the thread will unwind, resulting in slack dubbing.

On some nineteenth-century patterns, the dubbing was so sparse that the thread color showed through and merged with the dubbing to produce a muted blend of thread and dubbing. Now we cover our thread with dubbing and even trim the shagginess. But even trimming dubbing has historic precedent. Halford encouraged tyers to "trim and arrange the body with scissors." We have forgotten the dubbing methods of old. Today, the thread color usually matches the dubbing color rather than serving as a contrast or modification. The singular advantage of matching thread color is that the thread is disguised.

Once I commented on a shaggy, disheveled, dubbed pattern by Robert McHaffie, the renowned Irish fly tyer. McHaffie gently told me, in a puff of pipe smoke, that the scruffiness had purpose. It did two things: It allowed the thread to "breathe," that is, the color to show through, and it produced a translucent body when wet. It was then that I knew that I knew not.

Originally, the dubbing needle fluffed the body or hazed the hair hackle. H. G. McClelland, in *How to Tie Flies for Trout* (1898), notes that "In dressing some flies, the dubbing that has been wrapped on the body should now be picked out with the dubbing needle, so as to soften the outline of the body and give it a woolly effect." This is seldom done today with much frequency.

FLUSHING PHEASANT TAIL BARBS

The soft-tipped pheasant tail barbs zipper together, refusing to be stacked. When you wish to align the tips while preserving a flat barb panel, grip the angled tips between the thumb and forefinger of the left hand. Hold the barb base in the right hand. By gently pulling and rocking or rotating, in the appropriate direction, the base of the barbs with the right hand, the barbs are momentarily separated, realigned, and reattached. Continue to rock and realign the barbs until all the tips are flush. This method "squares" the overwing of the Brambridge Caddis and "flushes" the tail barbs of Sawyer's Pheasant Tail Nymph.

THE HAIR-HACKLE METHOD

As the dry fly evolved from the wet fly, it was only natural that the first *hackle* was dubbing. McClelland calls this "shoulder dubbing" or hackle. "With dubbed flies the dubbing itself, picked out from beneath the shoulder with the needle, is sometimes considered to be sufficient." To this day, the furs of some animals, such as dormouse tail hairs, are used for low-floating patterns in Slovenia. The naturally oily property of dormouse fur makes excellent dry-fly "dubbing hackle." Various hairs and furs—especially short, spiky hairs treated with flotants—furnish hair hackles. Snowshoe pad-hair also creates superior "hackle" for micropatterns. Some long-fibered synthetic dubbings also make excellent hackles. Synthetics absorb significantly less water than natural fibers. As in all hair-hackle patterns, use a minimal amount of synthetic dubbing for the hackle.

In *Floating Flies and How to Dress Them* (1886), Halford notes that "The effect of this [the spun dubbing-loop] will be to twist up the silk and fur between the two ends of it . . . into a rough-looking hackle, which is used exactly like an ordinary one, the silk representing the central quill, and the fur the fibres of the hackle."

When mounting conventional or parachute hair hackles, avoid excessive hackling. Limit the number of wraps. Use one or two turns fore and aft of the wing. Only a modest amount floats a small pattern.

THE DUBBING DUST METHOD

When dubbing, bulk is essentially created by cording. When palm fed, long-fibered dubbing strands drag other strands on the thread. In turn, these strands drag others that increase the dubbing volume. A dubbing needle, with fibers parallel to the thread and wrapped flat against the shank, does not create the translucent halo often sought in tying. By contrast, the dust method avoids cording while creating gauzy dubbing on the smallest of hooks.

First, select dubbing, natural or synthetic, that is extremely fine fibered. Stack the fibers parallel into a dubbing skein. Next, with sharp scissors, dice the dubbing fibers into short, 2-millimeter (or less) lengths.

See page 138 for a photograph and description of the Spin-Dust Method.

Next, twirl the thread back and forth between your left thumb and forefinger while you daub the thread with dubbing. Dust the spinning thread until it is suitably hazed. For a fleecy, translucent haze, merely wrap the dubbing as body. For fine, dense dubbing, twirl and compress the dubbed thread between thumb and forefinger prior to wrapping the body.

Dubbing is durable and can imitate a variety of creatures. It allows light and air to work their wonders. A low-twist with high-luster dubbing creates translucent fibers that trap air prisms that shatter and scatter the light much like the natural emerger shrouded in air. In dry patterns, the captured air increases flotation; in wet patterns, dubbing absorbs water for suitable water entry and sink. Dubbing is one of the oldest, and, with the marriage of natural and synthetic fibers, one of the most modern tying methods.

The Dubbing Brush

The dubbing brush, although essentially a method for larger patterns, is particularly appropriate for micropatterns. The weight of spun wire encourages small patterns, tied on light hooks, to sink. Twisted wire, rather than thread, captures the rich, dense fur, bristling and glistening on a dubbing brush. Thinking wire instead of thread perhaps began with Frank Sawyer's Pheasant-Tail Nymph, one of the first popular wire patterns. In any case, dubbing-brush patterns, with fur spun on a wire core, have exceptional water entry and sink. And, spun on fine wire, fur or feather can even float a pattern.

My first encounter with the Czech "dubbing brush," natural dubbing spun on a double-wire core, was in Europe. Milan Pohunek of Prague, the Republic of Czech, points out that the Iron Curtain was not waterproof. Although it plugged the entry of Western tying products, it only filtered Western tying information. Czech has a short, but rich history of fly fishing. In 1852, Karel Amerling wrote *Fauna: Czech Animals (Fauna ci Zvfrena Ceska)*. It describes taking "salmon trout" in Eastern Bohemia with silk and horse-hair "insects" "at which the trout jump when the sky is cloudy." Other writers like Zdenek Simek and Karel Liska wrote about the "the feathered iron" after World War I. For the most part, Czech tying is eclectic, taking techniques and patterns from throughout the world, but there are some unique ties, including a wooden fly.

With Dr. Milan Pohunek and Milos Zeman, I fished the Ohre, a trail-water fishery south of the Ore mountains and northwest of Prague. Before the Ohre empties into the Elbe, it ribbons through the hop yards below Nechranice dam. A heavy caddis hatch made selecting patterns simple, but made fishing difficult. Our largest trout was Zeman's brightly marked twenty-inch brown. Zeman then showed me an unusual material—long, creamy strips that reminded me of raffia, a palm leaf imported from Madagascar and once popular for tying. But this was not raffia. The fine strips were cambium, the inner layer between the bark and the wood of various trees. Prior to tying, the cambium strip must be soaked in water to soften. When dampened, the pliable cambium strip wraps easily to form a tight, segmented body.

In 1983, the Czechs drew upon their own resourcefulness to create a dubber, a unique tool for spinning wires. In 1986, they demonstrated their electric dubber for the first time at a meeting of the Czechoslovak Fly-Fishermen in Česke Budějovice. After the entry of free enterprise in November 1989, the Bohemia Flyfishing Company was founded, which now markets various colors of the dubbing brush. The dubbing brush and the general concept of spun-wire dubbing may be applied to micropatterns.

There have been a few crank or spinner dubbing machines: notably the Orvis Dubber, a hand-crank spinner that formed dubbing strands, and the traditional wooden dubbing block. At present, dubbing brushes, in various colors, are sold ready-made for tying. But for the tyer who wants to spin his own, a few tools make it simple.

1. Single-edged razor blade or scalpel
2. High-tack wax. To hold the fur or feather strips in place, I use a high-tack wax such as Wapsi Premium Superstick or Loon Tackle's Swax High-Tack. With only minuscule amounts, these waxes have superior hold. Ultra-soft waxes may "lick" or "string," an adhesive trade characteristic called *legginess*, when applied along the thread. Merely stroke the thread smooth with the fingertip.
3. Sharp, serrated, straight-bladed scissors. Serrations trap the fine fur and prevent it from being pushed away.
4. Various diameters of malleable wires
5. Various fur strips
6. A spinner or spinning vise

THE SPINNER

A vise, either crank or spin, that allows a hook to rotate on its own axis may be used to create a dubbing brush. The Renzetti vise with attached Au Sable Speed Crank, the rotating Dyna-king Tube Vise and other rotary vises may be used. Cranking the wires closed can be a slow process, often disturbing the dubbing. In contrast, the inertia of the brass spinner quickly produces dense twists, 18 or more per centimeter, even on thick, .28-millimeter wire. A tight twist is required to lock in each barb or fiber. A heavy spinner twirls the wires with only a few, fast spins, preventing, in the process, any displacement of the

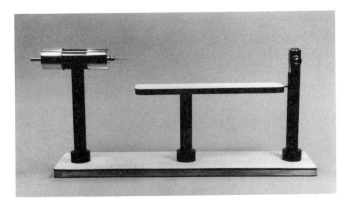

The dubbing-brush spinner

fur or hair. The tighter the spin, the denser the dubbing. The spinner has a table that raises to hold the fur or hair. The table pushes down and rotates out of the way before the fur is spun. A rubber holder grips the two end-wires while the spinner tightens them. As they tighten, the wires becomes shorter and pass through the rubber holder. It is often necessary to hold the end of the wire for a controlled twist while the spinning head is spun rapidly. A small hook on the brass spinner head anchors the soft wire strands that grip the dubbing strip. The vise is then spun or rotated so that the dubbing material is twisted, flared, and locked between the wire strands.

Although the traditional dubbing whirl can accomplish some of these dubbing procedures on fine wires, the Spinner is more efficient in producing a uniform twist.

THE WIRES

Standard ribbing wires, in various diameters, may be used, as well as thicker wires. Spooled wire, void of kinks and twists, should be used. To prevent kinks and twists, remember to remove the wire on line with the coiling, not over the end of the spool. Various wires, electrical and craft, in a variety of colors and diameters can be used. Even fine, soft lead wires can be spun to trap fur for small, weighted nymphs. Spooled lead wires, .015 (.40 millimeter) and finer, twirl best. Micropatterns require the finest diameter lead wire available. When spinning lead wire, slowly and smoothly twirl the wires while holding the ends with moderate tension. Rapid and abrupt whirling will quickly break lead wire. Lead wire may break at the spinner hook. Standard wires are normally looped over the spinner hook. However, to minimize breakage of lead wires, *double* the wire before looping it around the hook. Then, twist the end (the same direction as you will spin) over the standing core prior to spinning. This doubles and strengthens the wire wrapped around the hook. Excellent weighted scuds and nymphs may be created with squirrel, beaver, mole, or muskrat fur spun on a lead core.

THE FURS

Strips of Australian opossum, mole, squirrels, muskrat, and rabbit produce attractive brushes. I use the shorter, softer furs with guard hairs that produce brushes of mixed textures and colors. Chopped furs may be laid between waxed wires and spun. Spiky brushes, however, are made with fur strips mounted between waxed wires. Different colors may be attached to each wire for a spun, variegated brush. *For spiky brushes, cut the fur strips longitudinally across the shoulder or body.*

When cut in this manner, the fur will be at a right angle to the hide and the wire core.

Various materials may be spun, including synthetic dubbing and feather barbs. No matter what material is spun, it is important to spread it out sparsely, without gaps. The length of wire at each end can be used for body material, while the connected fur becomes the body, thorax, or legs. Deer hair

A squirrel strip

may also be spun if the strip is narrow. Although often requiring an extended shank, spun-wire deer hair makes excellent heads or bodies. Spun wire itself can be wrapped for the body, significantly increasing the pattern weight and sink.

Furthermore, intriguing dry fly fur hackles can be produced with this method. The concept is not new. James Ogden, who claimed invention of the floating fly about 1839, tied his Hare's Ear Dun with fur hackle: "The lightest fur from the hare's face spun on pale yellow tying-silk, and worked as a hackle." And Halford's Gold-Ribbed Hare's Ear, the original dry fly, had "hare's fur picked out at the shoulder to form legs." Halford used a dubbing loop with "the silk representing the central quill, and the fur the fibres of the hackle." It was mounted and wrapped like ordinary hackle. But unlike a thread core used by Ogden and Halford, a wire core does not unwind. A spun-thread core produces excellent cul-de-canard hackle, but it requires constant tension to stay together. After removal from the spinner, the thread core must be kept taut by anchoring it on a card and must not unravel while mounting and winding. Glues and silicone sealers can be used to fuse the thread core to limit unraveling, but some tension is still required. Although wire does not have the axial twist of thread, many things that can be done with thread can be done with wire. If fine wire (.10 millimeter or finer) is used, then spun cul-de-canard barbs will float a pattern. This eliminates the thick, fast-tapered CDC stem. As there are numerous barbs per wire-length, weight is usually not a problem. Part of the pleasure with the dubbing brush is experimenting with the many possibilities. Here are two wire-methods that many tyers will want to try.

THE METHODS

(1) *Single-Strand Wire.* Loop the end of a single wire strand over the spinner hook and whirl momentarily to lock in. Trim excess. Slide the opposite end into the rubber glide. Smear the wire with adhesive wax. Twirl the spinner. Using a fine, long-fiber dubbing, merely touch the spinning wire with dubbing. The dubbing immediately catches and winds on tightly. Slowly move the dubbing wad along the wire for even coverage. Long-fibered dubbing pro-

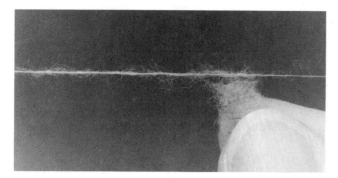

Dusting the spinning, single wire with mole fur

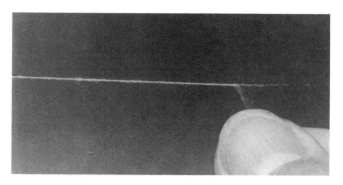

Long-stranded dubbing fed on single wire

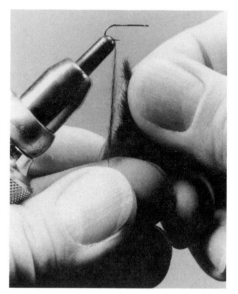

The Spin-Dust Method: After applying a high-tack wax to the thread, lightly touch a finely diced dubbing along the thread. While applying the dubbing, the thumb and forefinger of the left hand swiftly spins the thread back and forth. The result is a fine fur-coated thread. For a tight and dense body, roll the dubbed thread between the fingers before tying a pattern.

duces a corded or segmented body. Short-fibered dubbing, such as mole, creates fine, shaggy strands. The result is an ultra-fine dubbing wire for small nymphs, shrimp and larvae. Wire patterns are often whip-finished with thread or a single half-hitch of the wire.

The dubbed wires may be over-ribbed with a fine wire after spinning. The single strand method is excellent for small patterns. Fine, short dubbing, such as mole or chopped squirrel hazes the wire, creating a halo.

(2) *Double-Strand Wire.* Loop the wire over the spinner hook and press the trailing ends into the glide post.

To securely hold the fur strip, I momentarily whirl the spinner to close and lock the wire at the spinner hook. The wires then press together for a firm hold.

Smear wax on the wire sections that will receive the fur strip. A fine daub of wax should appear along the wire. If there are wax dribbles, smooth with a finger to create a fine film. This helps hold the fur strip in place while the hide is trimmed prior to spinning.

Use a scalpel or straight edge to make miniature "zonker" strips. Holding the hide taut, *cut the fur strips from the hide side*. To avoid cutting the fur or

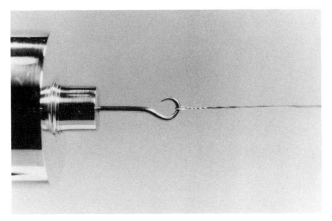

With a brief spin, close the wires at the spinner hook

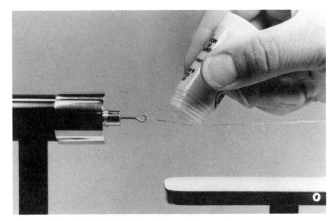

Apply the high-tack wax

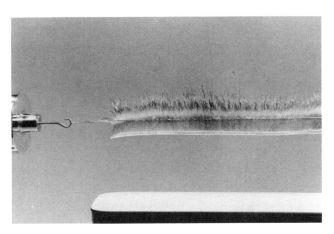

Mount the fur strip

Trim the hide with scissors

hair, do not lay the hide against anything while cutting. I find it best to mark a cut-line to achieve a uniform fur strip; otherwise the finished dubbing brush may have inconsistent density. The wider the fur strip, the denser the dubbing. Spinning works best with narrow fur strips. If the dubbing is too dense, it may prevent a tight wire twist. Most fur and hair strips, depending on the density and stiffness of the fibers, should be from 1.5 millimeters to 3 millimeters wide. For narrow zonkers, pliable hides are more difficult to cut than the thin-skinned dried hides. Micropatterns require soft wires, approximately .10 millimeter to .12 millimeter, for brushes. With minimum tension, hand hold the ends of fine wire to diminish breakage. Allow the wire to shorten while whirling.

To mount most furs, cut a 10 to 12 centimeter fur strip, about 3 millimeters wide. Align the fur strip, with the hide attached, between the strung wires. Carefully trim to remove the hide strip from the trapped fur. The hide backing allows the fur to be mounted and handled while controlling the density of the spun brush. It also allows the furs to be mounted at right angles to the wire.

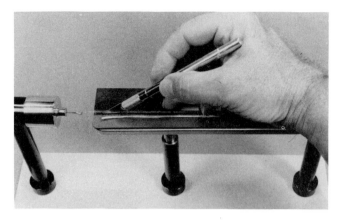

Trim the hide with scalpel and cutting board

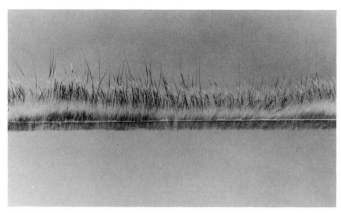

The mounted and trimmed fur strip prepared for spinning

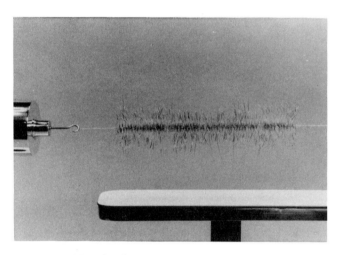

The spun dubbing brush

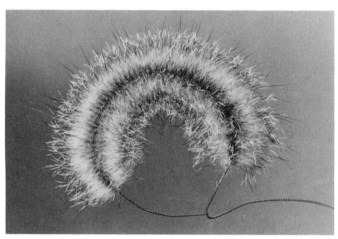

A double-wire squirrel brush

A double-wire mole brush

Sharp scissors help make long, straight cuts to separate the hide from the fur. Fur strips may also be mounted with a wide bulldog clip. After securing the clip to the fur, trim the hide strip and then mount the fur between the waxed wires. It is also possible to trim the hide strip with a scalpel after it is mounted between the wires. If this is done, a self-sealing cutting board, placed on the pivot table, should back the fur strip during trimming. A bulldog clip and a cutting board produce a straight, smooth cut.

The amount of overlap on the "hide-side" is important. The length of the "hide side" becomes the "underfur" in the spun brush. *For micropatterns, trim both sides of the fine-wire dubbing brush to create narrow brushes.*

Twirl the spinner. As the wires tighten, they shorten and pass through the rubber holder. It may be necessary to hold the end of the wire for a controlled twist while the spinning head is spun rapidly. The spinner should produce a densely spun wire with the hairs and fur locked, twisted, and flared between the wire strands.

The length, density, and amount of "underfur," as well as overfur, may be controlled prior to spinning. The length of guard hairs and fur is not critical if the dubbing brush is trimmed. The guard hairs, however, may be easily detached once the hide strip is removed. The guard hairs, held and aligned by the wire core, are easily extracted prior to spinning the brush.

Dubbing brushes may be mounted and wrapped like yarn strands or tied longitudinally for legs or wing cases. Even spun wire *sans* dubbing can make a body or shellback. No matter how it is used, the dubbing brush adds another dimension to tying small patterns.

TURKEY FLAT WINGS

Turkey flats make excellent wings for small patterns. Wing slips from the fine, soft, barbed turkey flats are more easily controlled than traditional quill wings. Due to the symmetry, a single feather produces both wing sections. A single puff of Grumbacher's Tuffilm Fixative (matte) on the back of the turkey flat will maintain the shape and allow removal of the paired wing sections. Place the wing slips back-to-back to form a single wing and mount like traditional quill wings. For parachute patterns, post wrap both wings to consolidate and position.

THE VOLJC WING

Dr. Bozidar Voljc of Slovenia developed durable wings for his Slovenica sedge series. To make this wing, select contour feathers (body feathers) of the appropriate size and color. Any contour feather may be used, especially those from duck, grouse, woodcock, or partridge. Strip the base flue from the contour feathers. A clear, high-tack PVC glue, a polyvinyl chloride resin, is required. Other waterproof, high-tack glues may be used. Before using PVC glue, read the label and take all necessary precautions. Use adequate ventilation and avoid all contact with the glue. Place a swatch of nonelastic (or limited stretch) fine-mesh nylon, such as a lady's stocking, in a small embroidery hoop.

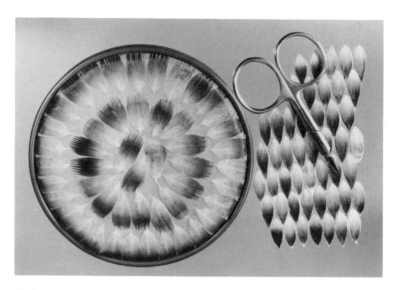

Various contour feathers, glued to a nylon backing, create the durable Voljc wing. After drying, the wings are cut from the sheet, folded along the stem, and trimmed to shape. Voljc wings create a variety of wing profiles for the micropatterns.

First, while using a dauber and rubber gloves, apply a fine film of PVC glue to the stretched nylon. The nylon should be tight but not taut. Excessive stretch will cause the feathers to warp and rumple when released from the embroidery hoop.

Next, blanket the back of each feather with a *fine* film of glue. Then, immediately caress the barbs back toward the feather tip, making them parallel to the feather stem.

Finally, press each feather firmly onto the tacky nylon. After mounting each feather, clip the stem short. Some tyers find that pressure, such as a glass sheet, applied to the feathers during drying, produces an exceptionally flat feather. After drying, the wings are ready to shape. For long-term storage, place the wing "plates" between paper sheets.

To shape a Voljc wing, fold the feather along the stem and trim, using the contour of the thumb "to route" the trailing edge of the caddis wing.

THE WEDGE-WING DUN

In 1932, Roger Woolley, in *Modern Trout Fly Dressing*, considered winging small flies as the "height of attainment in trout-fly dressing" and "the most difficult part of the art." G. R. Pulman, in 1851, advises the tyer not to attempt winging until he has "attained considerable proficiency in all other operations." In 1886, the inevitable error of tying, according to Frederic Halford, was winging.

For decades, tyers have struggled over wings. They are a nuisance, and, sometimes, an absolutely necessary nuisance. *Wings may be, on some waters and at some times, the essential signal that provokes the rise.* From the beginning, tyers were fascinated by the worth of wings. In 1914, George

LaBranche wrote that "I am of the opinion . . . that the colour, or perhaps the transparency, of the wings of the artificial fly is quite as important as the colour of the body; and I am satisfied, so far as my own angling is concerned, that all erect winged flies should be tied with wings made of feathers from the starling's wing." Although LaBranche admired the grace of quill wings, he noted that hackle wings, where the turns of hackle imitate the span and veins of wings, are "a better imitation of the wings of the Ephemeridae than are feathers." He had "a decided preference for winged flies . . . because they look more like living insects . . . when they are on the water than do hackled flies." LaBranche apparently wanted the distinct profile of the quill with the fragile translucency of the hackle wing. He conceded that hackle wings have a great amount of light passing through them, resulting in "a better representation of the transparency and neuration [venation] of the wings of the natural insect than can be had from the use of artificial wings." He wanted to marry the quill wing with the hackle wing.

By 1915, J. C. Mottram fully favored simple hackle wraps as spinner wings. "To my mind, one of the best ways of indicating transparency is to omit the transparent parts altogether. First, make four or five turns of white cock hackle around the shank; afterwards the hackle is cut, leaving only those fibres which project laterally; these will rest flat on the water and keep the fly afloat in a most natural manner; floating hackle, none is used."

About two decades later, Roger Woolley continued the tribute to the hackle wing. "A dozen or more bright, glassy fibres of cock's hackle, representing the shade and possibly the veining of the natural flies' wings, allow light to filter through the fibres, and suggest the transparency of the remaining portion of the wings."

While difficult to create, wings have several significant functions. LaBranche noted that slightly separated wings—that is, divided wings—parachute the pattern more lightly and cock it, with wings erect, more often. Evidently, the "v" wing posture slows the descent of the pattern. Wings help duplicate the natural's general profile and may even imitate the distinctive longitudinal veins with hackle barbs or hair fibers. Wings also make a pattern, especially small patterns, visible during the drift.

In general, winging usually requires special mounting strategies. Wings usually require a thread foundation on the hook shank to prevent movement during mounting. And wings must be firmly held to maintain shape and mounted with a taut thread. Halford mounted wings in the middle of the shank (to avoid the hook eye when cropping the butts) and then forced them (along with the foundation wraps) up the shank close to the eye. Most patterns that require wings usually entail tying them on first.

The problem, of course, is whether or not it is possible to produce a *flat, quill-like wing with individual fibers*. Although not a complete solution to LaBranche's dilemma, one answer is the wedge-wing. Sir Isaac Newton declared that "Nature is pleased with simplicity." So too are tyers and trout. The wedge-wing is flat and *as sparse as wanted, even allowing space between the individual fibers if required*. The wedge-wing—a single or double-wing "panel"—is simple, soft, and realistic. Although hair wings and comparadun wings often prove effective, sometimes trout may demand greater verisimili-

A single, sparse and splayed Wedge-Wing

A black extended-body with Wedge-Wing, size 18 hook

tude. The wedge-wing offers a realistic flat wing made from soft and supple reindeer hair.

The advantages of the wedge-wing are numerous. It has a realisitc silhouette and is simple to tie and trim. It provides a small base for parachute and hair hackles. The reindeer fibers compress with little bulk. The wedge-wing may be cut or left natural and the natural pale-gray reindeer hair matches the color of the mayfly dun wing. A wedge-wing may have dense or sparsely splayed fibers. The dense but thin wings possess a translucence similar to that of a natural mayfly wing. The fibers of a splayed wing may even conceivably imitate the longitudinal venation of a mayfly wing. Unlike quill wings, a sparse and slender wedge-wing has less tendency to twist during the cast or presentation. The manner of mounting—with wing cocked rearward—is lifelike and allows ample tying space during mounting. Wedge-wing patterns accept traditional hackles, parachute hackles, cul-de-canard hackles, and hair hackles. "Wedges" may even be sparse and spent to imitate the spinners. A cul-de-canard or hair hackle—merely CDC barbs or hair spun in a loop and wrapped as a hackle—produces some remarkable patterns. With buoyant body materials, wedge-wing no-hackles are exceptionally effective. Finally, the wedge-wings retain their shape longer than the traditional quill wing.

Although reindeer and caribou pelts often appear distinct, some authorities now consider the North American Barren Ground Caribou *(Rangifer tarandus articus)* to be the same species as the European and Asian reindeer *(Rangifer tarandus tarandus)*. Other authorities classify all species of caribou and reindeer as *R. tarandus*. The North European reindeer evolved into two varieties: wild and domestic pie-bald. The word "reindeer" sometimes refers to the smaller, domesticated caribou. The Woodland Caribou *(Rangifer tarandus caribou)*, the largest *Rangifer*, have mature males to 400 pounds. The differences in pelts—from mahogany brown *(R. tarandus caribou)* to cream white *(R. tarandus articus)*—are apparently due to seasonal and geographical differences. White hairs speckle the pelts of all *Rangifers*. The chambered hairs of their coats bestow great buoyancy; when swimming, nearly a third of the body is above water.

Tying a single wedge-wing is simplicity personified. First, select a bundle of soft reindeer hair. Because the fibers will be flattened, only a few are required, approximately 35 for a dense size 18 wing. A sparse and splayed wedge-wing may require only half that many. The number of fibers, of course, depends upon the diameter of the hairs and how dense or splayed the final wing will be. Other fibers may be used, such as caribou and deer, but reindeer is preferred. These soft, compliant fibers are easily flattened and shaped. Any white hairs, common in reindeer patches, should be extracted. Avoid hair with broken tips unless the wing will be trimmed. When making wedge-wings without trimming, select fibers, no matter what pelt, that taper abruptly at the tips and lack the long, black "thread-tips." After removing the underfur and stacking the fibers, mount them on the hook shank. If the fibers are mounted butt-forward, the natural hair tips delineate the trailing contour of a dun wing. To produce a smaller and nearly invisible wing base, often necessary for small parachute patterns, mount the hair bundle by the fine tips. After mounting the bundle, place a small, single drop of Dave's Flexament on the wing base. Allow the cement to penetrate and partially dry. Before the cement is set, flatten the wing (along the hook-shank axis) with flat-nosed pliers or fingernail and forefinger. If the wing is flattened after the cement dries, it will not produce the required flat panel. The completed wing may be left natural or trimmed for greater realism or a particular profile.

A double wedge-wing is made by dividing and splaying the wing bundle into two wing panels. Apply a drop of cement near the base of each wing panel. Allow the cement to soak in and, while still tacky, flatten each wing. Once dried, double wings may be cut merely by folding them together, matching, and trimming. Thus, both wings are easily shaped together. Various wing profiles, such as the narrow oval wing of the *Baetis* dun or the dwarfed circular wing of the *Caenis* dun, are easily cut to shape. Wing marks, such as the dark wing-edge of the *Callibaetis*, may be duplicated with a waterproof

Each wing panel of the Double Wedge-Wing is flat and slender.

marker. After drying and shaping (if required), the pattern is then completed. Wing marks, such as the blotched leading edge of the *Callibaetis*, may be dappled with waterproof markers. If the wing size and shape are critical to the take, the "wedge" makes winging simple.

It's unfortunate that I cannot demonstrate the "wedge" to LaBranche and Woolley. I would like to believe that LaBranche would have appreciated the wedge-wing. It does offer some compromise to his impasse—a flat wing made from separate fibers. The following drawings depict the basic wing profiles for *Baetis* and *Caenis* duns.

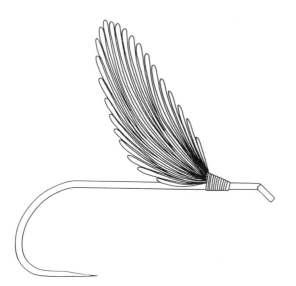

Wedge-Wing: The elongated oval wing profile of the Baetis.

Wedge-Wing: The circular wing profile of the Caenis.

The Wedge Wing Baetis *profile*

*A Blue-Winged Olive Wedge-Wing (*Baetis *profile), size 18 hook*

6

$\mathcal{T}$he Micropatterns

The following micropatterns are especially designed for small hooks and difficult trout. An effective small pattern uses a modicum of materials and the simplest of methods. William of Occam, a fourteenth-century philosopher, created a rational "razor" that cut away intellectual complexity: *"Entities should not be multiplied more than necessary."* So too in tying micropatterns. Materials and methods must not be multiplied more than necessary. Tying the small fly should be based on the principle of parsimony: tying economy, such as a simple thread body or a suggestive daub of dubbing, often creates the most effective micropattern.

Suggestions as to hook model and size, material and color are only recommendations. A tyer should match the hatch of the particular water. Insects will vary somewhat in color, size, and even habits because of temperature, food, light, and water chemistry. All complex or unique tying methods are illustrated in the text. These historic and modern micropatterns, from various countries and times, have proven their worth. Although a few of the following patterns appear complex, most tying procedures are remarkably simple. Some procedures are simple enough for a size-28 hook. The Smidgen pattern, for example, has a small "footprint" on the shank. It is mounted in two millimeters of shank space—and thus it is as easily tied on a size-28 as on a size-18 hook.

The Antunez Caddis (Luis Antunez)

Luis Antunez, a skilled Spanish angler, created this pattern for slow, clear streams. *No matter what the pattern, an inverted hook may not significantly produce more takes. Furthermore, hooking a trout on an inverted pattern may be more exacting.* The inverted spear, however, may produce a nigh-weedless pattern.

A hook spear that hangs beneath the surface may be a refusal factor for difficult trout. A pattern lacking a hanging spear may offer the trout only scant discrimination between the artificial and the natural. Inverted patterns only print the surface with the body and hackle. However, large, inverted hooks

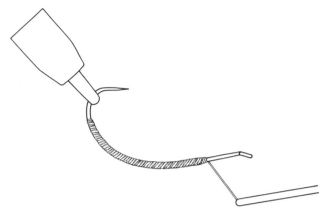

Inverted hook orientation for tying the Antunez Caddis

tend to catch trout in the upper mouth, where damage to sensitive organs may occur. This caddis requires a fine wire curved hook with a short spear and adequate gap. An up-eyed hook facilitates tying.

Hook: Tiemco 2487 or Daiichi 1140

Thread: Body color or body dubbing color

Body: Tying thread or ultra-fine polypropylene dubbing or similar

Overwing: Stacked deer body hair or bundled CDC barbs

Hackle: Cree or Grizzly

Antennae: Two coq de Leon barbs or pheasant tail barbs curved, either fore or aft, with the fingernail

A CDC variant of the Antunez Caddis uses CDC barbs, much like the Unec Midge, for overwing and hackle. A stripped peacock herl forms the body. On smaller patterns, tying thread creates the body. Coq de Leon barbs for antennae add realism. Tying the caddis is done with an inverted vise head and an inverted hook. The jaws should grip the lower heel of the hook, just beyond the body wraps.

The key to tying the Antunez caddis is to measure and trim the overwing *prior* to mounting. This avoids the difficulty of trimming close in a narrow space once the overwing is mounted. After cropping the overwing to length, hang it across the inverted shank and secure with two locking wraps. Then align the overwing and anchor it with further wraps. The tips of the overwing should obscure the hook point. Trim the lateral hackle for proper profile and float. With an inverted bend and point, the pattern is especially appropriate for weeded spring creeks.

The Blue-Winged Olive (Tatsuhiro Saido)

Saido's tiny "threaded" Blue-Winged Olive has a bent foreshank that imitates the body profile of a drifting dun. Saido notes that "A floating mayfly dun has a distinctive body shape. Six legs and a part of the abdomen support its body

The Blue-Winged Olive (tied by Tatsuhiro Saido)

and lift its head from the surface of the water. The tails and the end of the abdomen sometimes touch the surface and sometimes touch on and off. This characteristic body shape is very important to imitating a floating mayfly dun . . ." I have also used the shank lift to cock the wings back, dun fashion, to open the gap and to improve hooking. Although long-shanked, the Tiemco 947 BL has a raised fore-shank. Take care when bending the fore-shank to minimize hook damage. The shank, while the most plastic portion of a hook, should not be bent abruptly. This sparse pattern, especially appropriate for slow, smooth waters, achieves a realistic silhouette with cut and matched hen-feather wings. To achieve an accurate profile, apply head cement to the stemmed feather slips to stiffen them prior to trimming.

Hook: Mustad AC 80000 BR, 94840; Tiemco 100; Daiichi 1190, 1180, size 20–24

Thread: Yellow olive, 6/0 or 8/0

Tail: Ginger hackle barbs

Body: Tying thread

Hackle: Ginger, cropped on bottom and top

Wing: Blue dun hen contour feather, cut to shape

TYING SAIDO'S BLUE-WINGED OLIVE

1. Prior to tying the pattern, lift the forward ⅖ of the hook shank approximately 30%.
2. Apply a thread foundation and mount the divided tails.
3. Create, with tying thread, the body and thorax.
4. After mounting and wrapping the hackle, trim the top hackle barbs.
5. Apply a thin coat of Dave's Flexament to both wing slips and trim. The wings should be narrow, approximately 2 millimeters wide for a size 22 hook.

6. Mount the wings stem-forward directly on top of the thorax. Secure with wraps and trim excess stems. Whip-finish and clip the under-hackle.

The Brambridge Caddis

The Itchen at Brambridge is low, slow and clear. Small, realistic patterns, like the Brambridge Caddis, are often required to take the late-summer browns. For long drifts, the pattern, which utilizes pheasant tail barbs instead of the more buoyant deer hair, should be soaked with a liquid floatant and dried prior to fishing. The Pheasant Tail Caddis, a similar and simpler pattern tied by John Mingus, merely bundles stacked pheasant tail barbs for the overwing. A dubbed body and somewhat flattened overwing enhances flotation.

Hook: Orvis 4641, Daiichi 1180, size 18–22

Thread: Unithread 8/0, brown, gray, or black

Body: Finely diced mole fur, brown, burnt orange, or black

Thorax: Folded pheasant tail barbs and mole fur

Overwing: Pheasant tail barbs, dyed or natural

TYING THE BRAMBRIDGE CADDIS

1. Align the natural tips of a panel of pheasant tail barbs. This is done by "rocking" the panel and stroking the barbs into new alignment. Continue to do this until all barb tips are flush. Then mount the base of the barbs at the head so that the tips extend above and beyond the hook eye. When folded back, the overwing should extend about one-half shank length beyond the hook bend.

2. Wrap the barb base and spiral the thread to the rear. Add mole dubbing and dub the body and the barb base. Return the dubbed thread to the rear thorax point.

3. Fold the overwing back. Splay the barbs moderately for flotation. Finally, lap and whip-finish to secure overwing. Dubbing should cover whip-finish.

The Brush-Bug: The Mayfly Nymph

An excellent introduction to dubbing-brush tying is the Brush Bug Series. This generic pattern may be tied and trimmed to imitate a variety of small (or large) insects. *With only two materials—a tail and dubbing brush—a tyer can create a complete, weighted nymph with tail, abdomen, ribbing, wingcase, and legs.* The dubbing brush becomes the abdomen, legs, and wingcase. The core wire, silver or gold, creates the ribbing when exposed by trimming. Due to the broad, flat profile and weight, this technique effectively imitates various small mayfly nymphs. It also creates a realistic shrimp pattern; wrap and trim the dubbing brush (with heavy core-wire) for body and legs. Then cement and fold back the top hairs for the shellback. I prefer to create the flat wingcase with a smear of high-tack wax. If the pattern is momentarily held to a warm tying lamp, the wax penetrates the hairs. Then the hairs are caressed back and trimmed to length.

Hook: Orvis 4641, Mustad 94845, Tiemco 101 and 5262, other standard or extended-shank hooks, size 18

Wire: Gold or silver, .10-millimeter diameter or finer

Tail: Microfibetts or nutria guard hairs

Body: Clipped dubbing-brush abdomen

Overwing: Cemented, folded, and trimmed hair

Hackle: Dubbing-brush fibers

TYING THE BRUSH-BUG MAYFLY NYMPH

1. Mount tail.
2. Mount wire tag of dubbing brush 3/4 shank length.
3. Wind dubbing brush forward to head. While wrapping, stroke the fibers back to avoid trapping them beneath the ensuing wraps. At head, secure dubbing-brush tag and whip-finish.
4. Clip the abdomen so that the wire core shows through the dubbing for ribbing. Trim the hair beneath the thorax to expose the gap.
5. Place a smear of wax or drop or two of cement on the top, thoracic hair. Caress the wet fur back and flatten for the wingcase. When dry, trim the wingcase for length and shape. A horizontal flare of hair should project from each side for legs.

The Budding Midge

The budding or shucking midge, a remarkably effective pattern, imitates the red-phase emergence of the *Chironomus*. The stripped herl body (or the various other bodies including the sparkle synthetics) suggests the discarded, trailing shuck. The low, horizontal float and emerging body marks the moment of emergence. J. R. Harris, in *An Angler's Entomology* (1973), describes insect emergence: "When a nymph starts to hatch, the abdomen of the dun is partially withdrawn, so that a space appears between the tail end of the dun's body and the tail end of the nymphal shuck, and this space is filled with gas. The tail end of the hatching nymph then immediately assumes a much greater lustre, and in fact it strongly resembles a section of glass tube which has been filled with mercury. *This effect is even more noticeable in the pupae of those long-legged midges, the chironomids,* when they are hatching at the surface of the open water of lakes, and I think that it explains the added attraction which a flat tag of gold or silver gives to many artificial flies." The stripped peacock herl and the sparkle synthetic bodies prove more effective at times than dull dubbings. Another pattern that takes advantage of a dominant shuck is the Shucking Midge, a variant of Michael Martin's Antron Midge. In this simple pattern, fine Antron extends rearward. Half of the extended Antron forms the shuck, while the other half folds forward as wings, veiling a dubbed mole body. A dry hackle completes the Shucking Midge.

> *Hook:* Tiemco 947 BL or 101; Partridge K14ST; this fine-wire "nymerger" hook has a silver finish that "reflects the colours of the sub-surface world of the trout and grayling," sizes 18–20
>
> *Thread:* Dun, 8/0
>
> *Optional Breathing Fan:* Short, white CDC barbs, optional
>
> *Shuck:* Stripped peacock herl, feather stem, feather barb, CDC dubbing, or sparkle synthetics such as Lite Brite or Antron
>
> *Body and Wings:* Furled and looped red or orange-red fine-stemmed or stemless CDC feather
>
> *Legs:* CDC barbs figure-eighted or tied parachute (spinning loop method) at base of emerging body

Mount and figure-eight the CDC barb legs immediately behind the hook eye.

Add a furled orange or red CDC feather for the emerging midge. Short, stemless CDC feathers offer appropriate emerging midge's bodies for size 20 and 22 hooks. Furl the feather by tightly spinning it and then folding it in the middle.

Wrap the stripped peacock herl for the shuck and whip-finish the pattern at the base of the budding body. For increased buoyancy add a tuft of CDC at the end of the shank prior to wrapping the shuck.

Another budding midge, the Smidgen or Micromidge, has a furled shuck of fine Antron, a crimson CDC torso, and either figure-eighted CDC legs or a parachute hackle. This simple pattern may be tied on size 22–26 hooks. The base of the shuck, torso, and hackle require approximately 1 millimeter of shank space for mounting.

The Bubble Smut

This pattern imitates an emerging *Simulid*. Tied in larger sizes, it may also simulate a variety of insects that emerge with a bubble shroud. The CDC barbs trap air and fold over the bead. A touch of black dubbing mimics the black fly body shrouded in air as it emerges to the surface. An optional bubble tail, a strand of Krystal Flash, may draw attention to this diminutive pattern. As Doug Swisher and Carl Richards noted in *Emergers*, the black fly is one of the five major taxa participating in "behavioral drift," usually with peak periods occurring shortly before sunrise and immediately after sunset. Black flies "emerge from the pupal case on the bottom and ride to the surface enclosed in a bubble of air that clings to each insect. The bubble is produced between the inner pupal case and the outer body by cutaneous respiration." The gas keeps the insect dry and buoyant. The extent to which the glistening sheath can be seen varies with the light and angle. At some angles, it is nearly invisible. At other angles, it refracts so much light that the encased insect is nearly invisible.

Hook: Mustad AC 80250 BR; Daiichi 1640; Tiemco 2487 and 101; size 20–24

Thread: White 8/0

Bubble Tail: Optional, one strand Krystal Flash, two or more inches long

Body: Silver wire body and swollen thorax

Encapsuled Body: A dubbed dot of black mole fur immediately behind the thorax to imitate the body shrouded by the bubble. Larger hooks may imitate the thorax with a silver or glass bead.

Wings: None

Hackle: White CDC collar, barbs equal total hook length

Tying The Bubble Smut

1. Mount the Krystal Flash strand.
2. Secure fine silver wire and wrap the abdomen.
3. Form the swollen thorax and add a dot of dubbing (black, orange, or yellow) between the abdomen and thorax. The dubbing may be added either to the waxed wire or thread.
4. Load white CDC barbs in a spinning loop and wrap twice at the head.
5. Whip finish the pattern.

The CDC Magic (Gerhard Laible)

The CDC Magic, when momentarily pulled under, traps air. After a brief pause, the pattern pops to the surface, imitating, perchance, the emergence of a mayfly. Nearly every CDC pattern will do that, but the CDC Magic is designed to capitalize on that momentary emergence. The simple design, which appears in Gerhard Laible's *CDC Flies* (1993), has a hackle barb tail and dubbed body. Its simplicity recommends it for micropatterns. In the original tying sequence,

The CDC Magic (a modified tie)

after a full CDC wing and hackle barb tail are mounted, the body spirals forward to cover the wingbase. The tyer then crops the rear half of the wings to create a bubble trap. I have found that a fuller, simple pattern may be tied differently.

Mount the tail and body. A body may be made from CDC dubbing or stripped peacock herl. Then, measure and trim a bundle of CDC barbs. Next, fold the CDC bundle (base of barbs pointing toward the tail) over the thorax and secure with two or three thread wraps.

Post both wing sections together and dub in front of the wings to erect them. This yields a slender body and full wing. The rear half of the wing folds up to create the cropped post. Take fine-nosed pliers and pull off the barb tips to produce the correct length of forward wing. Make certain the front barbs are long enough. When pulled under, the front CDC barbs must fold back to trap air.

The CDC Olive Emerger (Andrija Urban)

Before using polycelon for flotation, Urban used dried mushroom. The polycelon pattern was an improvement that solved several problems. 1. The polyacrylics, Creslan and Orlon, imitated the bubble sheen beneath the integument. 2. The posture of the pattern (sinking abdomen and floating thorax) improved while obscuring the polycelon with the fly body. 3. The veiled CDC represents the budding wings of the emerger. 4. The crinkly Antron mimics the trailing shuck.

Hook: Mustad AC 80050 BR, Tiemco 2487, sloped or curved shank hooks; size 18

Thread: Brown 8/0

Tail: Partridge spade barbs

Ribbing: Stripped Peacock Quill

Abdomen: Creslan, Rayon, and rabbit fur fibers applied with a dubbing loop

Wing pod: Narrow, olive polycelon panel tied as wing pod

Overwing: Two CDC feathers veiling wing pod

Thorax: Olive and orange Antron applied with dubbing loop

Tying The CDC Olive Emerger

1. Mount tails and ribbing.
2. Dub body forward. Spiral ribbing forward and secure. Trim excess.
3. Mount tip of two CDC feathers and polycelon panel.
4. Dub thorax. Fold polycelon forward, secure, and trim excess.
5. Veil CDC feathers forward above polycelon, secure, and trim excess. Finally, whip-finish the head.

The CDC Pupa

This simple pupa may be tied on the smallest of hooks, sizes 20 to 26. The clumped and folded CDC floats the pupa in the surface film. As for many CDC patterns, simplicity of tie can produce an effective pattern. For a variety of patterns, use different colored threads and CDC barbs. Contrasting or radiant colors help to draw attention to this petite pattern. Other body variations, such as white Antron or stripped peacock herl, may be used.

> *Hook:* Circular or curved hooks, Mustad AC80250, Mustad AC80050, Mustad AC80100; Tiemco TMC2487; Tiemco TMC200; Daiichi 1140, sizes 18–26.
>
> *Thread:* Pale yellow, orange, or red, 8/0
>
> *Body, Wingcase and Thorax:* Bundled CDC barbs

1. Wrap a thread body from thorax to mid-bend and back.
2. Clump CDC barbs and mount at thorax with ends extending fore and aft beyond the thorax. Trim the aft-ends for budding wings. Fold the fore-ends back and lap with thread. Return thread to head. Fold CDC wingcase barbs forward. Prune the fore-ends, overlap with thread, and fold under for legs. Whip-finish the pattern. Leg barbs should be broken to length.

The CDC Snowshoe Emerger (Tom Rosenbauer)

The unique properties of the snowshoe pad hair and CDC allow this pattern to swim in the surface film. Rosenbauer's CDC Snowshoe Emerger is based on a Galen Mercer design and the Adirondack pattern, The Usual, created by Francis Betters and popularized by Bill Phillips. Credit should also go to Craig Mathews for the synthetic trailing shuck. Like The Usual, this pattern is fished drag-free until, after drawn under, it is retrieved as an emerging may or caddis.

The CDC Snowshoe Emerger (tied by Rosenbauer)

Hook: Mustad AC 80250 BR and AC 80100 BR; Tiemco 2487; Partridge K4A, light-wire curved-shanked hooks, size 18

Thread: Unithread, 6/0 to match dubbing

Shuck: Sparkle Yarn or Z-lon

Body: Beaver or rabbit; smaller patterns may require mole. Dubbing color matches the hatch

Wings: Short, clump-wing of snowshoe pad hairs

Hackle: Teased head dubbing

TYING THE CDC SNOWSHOE EMERGER

1. Mount Sparkle Yarn or Z-lon trailing shuck, ¾ shank length.
2. Dub abdomen, ¾ shank length, with fine dubbing.
3. Mount a clump of snowshoe pad hair for wing pod.
4. Mount CDC barb collar with a distribution wrap, beard style.
5. Complete pattern with a head of hare's ear dubbing. Whip-finish.

The Female Adams

This somber lady, a traditional Adams with a small yellow-fur egg sack, is an elegant pattern, especially effective for spring creek and chalk stream trout. Matty Vinceguerra's egg-sack Adams, described in Richard Talleur's *Mastering the Art of Fly-tying*, incorporates a small loop of polypropylene yarn beneath the shank for an egg sack; the egg sack actually increases buoyancy. It is this touch of color that makes this lady such an effective pattern. According to Harold Smedley's *Fly Patterns and Their Origins* (1950), the first Adams was tied about 1922 by Leonard Halladay of Michigan and used by C. E. Adams on a local stream to imitate, of all things, the flying ant. The ubiquitous Adams pattern, and its variations, has the neutral color of a caddis and the silhouette of a mayfly. It is one of North America's favorite patterns. It imitates caddis, stoneflies, mayflies, mosquitoes, and a wealth of nature's creatures. The true value of the pattern lies in its variegated, but neutral, colors. Even the gravid female is dressed in somber gray. The wound hackle produces a mottled gray brown mix that effectively suggests a variety of insects, including the Spotted Winged Quill *(Callibaetis)*, the Spotted Sedge *(Hydropsychidae)*, and even midges *(Chironomidae)* and Reed Smuts *(Simuliidae)*. The banded grizzly-point wings may suggest the vibrant fluttering of an insect attempting to fly. It is an excellent pattern, not only for rainbows and browns, but also for grayling. The Adams has been praised on the English chalk streams as an excellent pattern for shy, selective trout. Halladay's original dressing is enhanced by the availability of quality genetic capes. But perhaps nothing improves on this pregnant lady who has a touch of color and class.

Hook: Mustad 94840 or AC 800000; sizes 18–24

Thread: Unithread, black or gray, size 6/0 or 8/0

Body: Natural gray muskrat or medium gray synthetic

Wings: Paired and divided grizzly points (hackle tips)

Tail: Mixed grizzly and brown, or ginger hackle barbs

Egg Sack: Fine, pale yellow dubbing, natural or synthetic

Hackle: Mixed grizzly and brown, ginger, or cree

TYING THE ADAMS

1. First, lay down a thread foundation for the wings. Measure and match two grizzly hackle tips so that when mounted their length equals the shank length, excluding the head. Select wide hackle points that have dense, bold barring and rounded tips. Slender hackle tips can become lost in the hackling. If the tips are matched and mounted "convex to convex," then the dry-fly wing curve appears. However, the bold barring is hidden between the wings. Straight hackle points, matched "concave to concave," place the darker barring on the outside, where it is preferred. Mount the hackle wings, tips pointing to the right, with authority; they should neither move nor rotate during mounting. Wings mounted in this manner resist wind pressure and maintain posture. A thread bead in front of the wings correctly cocks them. Some tyers prefer to mount the hackle-tip wings pointing to the rear; this discourages wing twisting because the wings are channeled in the lateral pressure of the thumb and forefinger. Sometimes the wings are stripped to length, over-wrapped and the stems drawn down to position the wings. This method, however, encourages the wings to twist when pulled into place.

2. Next, wrap thread to the rear of the body, directly above the rear of the barb, for tail placement. Combine several stiff hackle barbs from the grizzly and the brown hackle. Cut off any soft webbing at barb base and align the tips with a hair stacker. Proportion the tails and securely wrap them in.

3. To mount the egg sack, add a pale yellow bead of dubbing, slightly larger than the diameter of the body, to the rear shank.

4. Add muskrat or medium gray rabbit fur for dubbing. Do not over-dub the body. Mount the dubbing on a single thread and twist clockwise to attach the fibers to the thread. As you wrap on the body, continue to keep the dubbing taut. Complete body dubbing about 1 millimeter behind wing-mount point.

5. Mount and wrap in the hackle—one cree saddle hackle. The hackle stem is usually tied along the foreside of the hook shank with the dull side of the hackle pointing toward the tyer. The hackle is then bent sharply so the dull side faces toward the hook eye. Wind the hackle forward. Secure the hackle stem with the thread and whip-finish.

The Foam Emerger

In Wim Alphenaar's *Vliegbinden & Vliegvissen* (1991), the Midge Emerger, the Green Hatch, the Pond Olive Emerger, and the Foam Emerger all utilize foam strips for flotation. Foam readily compresses, making micro-emergers possible. In each pattern, dubbing or feathers creates the budding wings. However, CDC budding wings and coq de Leon tails produce exceptional realism and buoyancy.

> *Hook:* Partridge K14ST or similar; size 18
>
> *Thread:* Unithread, pale yellow, 6/0
>
> *Abdomen and Thorax:* Match the hatch foam strip
>
> *Budding Wing:* CDC hackle tips
>
> *Thoracic Dubbing:* CDC dubbing

TYING THE FOAM EMERGER

1. Mount coq de Leon tails.
2. Use fine-stripped foam, such as Larva-Lace or Orvis fly tying foam panels, and trim as illustrated.
3. Mount the end of the foam, spiral the thread forward. The thread should appear intermittently to segment the foam body.
4. At the thorax, mount a tailing tuft or loop of CDC barbs to suggest the emerging wings. Dub forward with CDC to complete the thorax.
5. Pull foam taut and whip-finish the pattern.

The Hackle Wing

Datus Proper, in *What the Trout Said* (1982), revived and improved Roger Woolley's antique hackle-wing design. Although the design is not often encountered, its simplicity recommends it. As a design and not a pattern, the hackle wing may imitate various duns. With slight modification, the design also imitates sundry spinners. Using 8/0 or 12/0 thread, the size of the pattern is only limited by the size of the hackle.

> *Hook:* Mustad AC 80000 BR and 94840; Tiemco 101; sizes 18–24.
>
> *Thread:* Unithread, 6/0 or 8/0. Color should match the hatch.
>
> *Tail:* Hackle barbs
>
> *Body:* Tying thread or fine dubbing, synthetic or natural. Dubbing color matches the hatch.
>
> *Wings:* Several hackle turns

TYING THE HACKLE WING

1. Woolley offers complete directions. "To tie this wing, take the tip of a bright cock's hackle of suitable colour and size for the fly being tied, and tie it in by the stem with two or three turns of the tying silk at the shoulder, just as if you were commencing to make a plain hackled fly."

2. "Take one, two or more turns of the hackle around the shank of the hook and fasten off with one turn and a half hitch of the tying silk round the tip of the hackle. Cut away the tip of the hackle."

3. "We now have a bare hook with a hackle wound on it, a hackle fly with no body."

4. "Next, evenly divide the fibres of the hackle and stroke them into the position of the wings of a Spent Gnat, at right angles with the hook shank. Pressure between the thumb and the forefinger will cause the fibres to remain in this position until they are fixed so by the figure of eight tying, and for the upright-winged fly the fibres need tying down *on top* of the hook only, just to divide them into two wings." Woolley forms spinners by tying down the top and bottom barbs.

5. To make duns, Proper adds split tails and body, either dubbing or thread, and figure-eights *beneath* the hackle to lift and align the barbs with the shank. Rather than clipping the lower barbs, this clusters them for improved flotation.

The Humpy

It is often said that the generic Humpy is all insects because it is none. There are, however, few flies in the wallet that match the mottled caddis or some emergers as well as a Humpy. In minuscule it imitates small terrestrials and caddis. When a Z-lon trailing shuck is added, the Humpy mimics the emergers. Needless to say, the micro-Humpy proves effective on most hyperselective waters. Despite conventional wisdom, a small Humpy, sizes 18–24, is not particularly difficult to tie. It does, however, have some unique requirements of hook, thread, and materials. Because of body bulk, the hook should have a moderate gap. The body hair—from reindeer—must be fine and soft to produce the smaller patterns.

The origin of the Humpy, sometimes called "Goofus," has been ascribed to several people and several proto-patterns. However, in a discussion of origins, the argument usually leads to a tyer from San Francisco. The late Jack Horner, a member of the Golden Gate Angling and Casting Club, tied the Horner's Deer Fly, which had a folded-deer-hair body ribbed with thread, while the natural tips of the hair formed the wings. According to Jack Dennis, the term "Humpy," which comes from the pattern's distinctly humped body, may have originated near Jackson Hole, Wyoming. The term Goofus, popularized by Dan Bailey of Montana, sometimes refers to a Humpy with mixed brown and grizzly hackles. Today, however, Humpy and Goofus are synonymous for their myriad variations.

Perhaps the best qualities of the Humpy are its buoyancy and imitative capacity. Although typical Humpy water is quick, heavy, and nervous, the micro-Humpy is realistic enough for spring creeks, chalk streams, and still waters. Perhaps, as Westerners say, the Humpy is effective because it imitates anything that the trout wants. This popular pattern can constitute over thirty percent of the total patterns sold during a Western season.

The Humpy presents interesting tying problems in proportions and material manipulation. If the Humpy proportions are wrong, the pattern becomes awkward and gauche. Even a small error in proportion distorts its demeanor. A few tying tricks make the micro-Humpy easier to tie.

Proportions: The length of the body hair must account for the underbody, overbody, and wings. Having long, soft fibers for tying makes this pattern much easier to tie. The number of body fibers will determine, to some extent, the body length; the more body fibers, the wider the body bends will be. Hence, more length will be required for the bends at the rear and wing base. Fewer fibers, of course, bend more abruptly. The body hair will constitute the underbody, the overbody, and the wings; therefore, correct length is critical.

Material Manipulation The final problem is the separation of the body hairs from the tail fibers. With a tying thread underbelly, the problem of mounting dubbing while maintaining separation is eliminated.

Hook: Tiemco 101 and 102, Orvis 4641; sizes 18–24

Thread: Unithread, 6/0, pale yellow. Counter-spin thread to produce a flat, multi-strand wrap that does not cut the soft body hairs.

Tail: Fine coq de Leon barbs or *Z-lon trailing shuck*.

Overbody: Soft reindeer or caribou body hair. For patterns under size 20, the body hair of mule deer, whitetail and blacktail is too coarse.

Underbelly: Pale yellow tying thread, the most common and effective color

Wings: The natural ends of the body hair

Hackle: Cree hackle

TYING THE HUMPY

1. Using a hair stacker, align the natural tips of several coq de Leon barbs. Smaller hooks require fewer fibers. Measure the tail fibers according to the shank length (which is the "known length") and firmly wrap the tail fibers on the shank immediately above the rear of the barb. Some tyers advocate that the tail mount space should occupy half the shank length. This increases the diameter of the "humped" body. The final, rear wraps around the tail should be "slack wraps" to prevent tail flare. After mounting the tail, wrap the thread to mid-shank.

2. Next, take a small sheaf of caribou or reindeer body hair. Remove all short fibers and underfur by hand and stack to even the natural tips. Select body hair that does not have long thread points. Like most tying, the tyer should strive for a delicate body—undertie rather than overtie.

    Measure the length of the hair bundle from the eye of the hook to the tip of the tail; *this is the correct length if the butt of the bundle is mounted at mid-shank on a standard hook.*

3. Mount the hair butts firmly at mid-shank; do not allow the material to twist during wrapping. To avoid fiber twist, use firm wraps and finger pressure on the body bundle. It is important to keep the tail fibers from mixing with the body fibers. To accomplish this, hold the body

bundle slightly above the tail fibers throughout the tying process. A little practice makes this natural.

4. Wrap a smooth thread underbelly. If a dubbed underbelly is required, then add dubbing with the right hand only. Such a method is not as awkward as it sounds. Twist the dubbing on firmly with the right thumb and index finger. Dub the underbelly forward, slightly beyond the mounted underbody.

5. Next, fold the overbody forward, making certain that the body fibers are aligned, tight, and directly over the underbody. Wrap the thread over the overbody from mid-shank to the three-fourth shank point. This thread platform forms the foundation for the hackle. Be certain to leave adequate space for hackle and head.

6. On small patterns, it is not necessary to figure-eight or post the wings.

7. Mount a cree hackle and wrap, concave side forward. Tie off the hackle and whip-finish.

Knotted Patterns

A knotted or cluster pattern is two or more patterns on a single hook. Halford wondered, as early as 1886, whether or not a small 00 Black Ant pattern might imitate two mating gnats. These mating micropatterns permit the use of stronger tippets and stronger hooks with wider gaps. Two midges mounted on a size 20 hook can make each midge an incredible 2.5 millimeters long, equivalent to some size 26 to 28 hooks. Knotted patterns are usually simple— a finely dubbed body enclosed by wings or hackle at each end. The following patterns, essentially as simple, are more effective. The Cluster Microcaddis and Cluster Chironomid have several advantages: an authentic silhouette,

The Cluster Microcaddis

color contrast, color attraction, and hackled hook, the flared barbs obscuring the bend and point of the hook. The buoyant Knotted Trico, a copulating spinner pattern, uniquely mounts double tails and wears a realistic, dark quill body. As with all knotted patterns, avoid overdressing.

The Cluster Microcaddis

Hook: Orvis 4641, Tiemco 900 BL; size 20

Thread: Unithread, orange, Light Cahill or Rusty Dun, 8/0

Tail: None

Body: Tying thread

Overwing: Dun CDC barbs

Hackle: Badger or Grizzly

TYING THE CLUSTER CADDIS

1. Wrap complete shank with thread underbody.
2. At shank rear mount CDC overwing.
3. Wrap and secure aft-hackle on CDC base.
4. Wrap thread on body to mid-shank.
5. Take one wrap around overwing, then continue thread travel around body to head. Position overwing directly on top of shank.
6. Tie down front of CDC overwing.
7. Mount and secure fore-hackle; then whip-finish head.

The Cluster Chironomid

Hook: Orvis 4641, Tiemco 800 BL; size 20

Thread: Unithread, orange, Light Cahill, Rusty Dun or black, 8/0

Tail: None

Body: Tying thread

Wings: Turkey flat or hen panel; white CDC barbs

Hackle: Dun or black

TYING THE CLUSTER CHIRONOMID

1. Wrap complete shank with thread underbody.
2. At shank rear, mount overwing panel.
3. Wrap and secure aft-hackle on panel.
4. Spiral thread around body to mid-shank.
5. Take one wrap around overwing, then continue thread travel down body to head. Position overwing directly on top of shank.
6. Tie down front of CDC overwing.
7. Mount and secure fore-hackle, then whip-finish head.

The Knotted Trico

The Knotted Trico

Hook: Orvis 4641, Tiemco 800 BL; sizes 20–22

Thread: Unithread, black

Tail: Fine Microfibetts or coq de Leon barbs

Body: Black thread or stripped peacock sword herl

Wings: White CDC barbs or Z-lon, Antron, or Sparkle Yarn

Hackle: None

TYING THE KNOTTED TRICO

1. Wrap shank and figure-eight CDC wings at shank rear. Use minimal barbs for wings. Trim wings to length.
2. Add stripped peacock sword herl and wrap body to mid-shank.
3. Place two wraps over herl at mid-point to secure. Add at mid-point two coq de Leon barbs as tails. Match ends and position proper length to the rear. Trim forward length to match rear length, thereby creating two pair of tails. Continue herl body to head and wrap off. Trim excess herl. Add fore-hackle and whip-finish pattern.

The Comparadun (Al Caucci and Bob Nastasi)

Introduced in *Comparahatch* (1972) and explored further in *Hatches* (1975), the Comparadun is more a design than a pattern. It imitates all mayfly duns, and has proven its worth on spring creeks. Its companion, the hackled Comparadun, has received less attention than the sparse version. Selecting the correct hairs solves much of the tying problem. The hairs should be soft and void of the extended black thread tip found on some hairs. Size, proportion, and color of the pattern should match the hatch.

TYING THE COMPARADUN

1. Stack and bundle deer body hair. Caucci and Nastasi recommend a ⅛″ diameter bundle when rolled and compressed.
2. With natural tips over the hook eye, mount the bundle with increasing thread pressure to compress.
3. Angle-cut the excess deer hair and wind thread in front of wings. Tight thread wraps against the base erect the wings. Wind thread to end of shank.
4. Add a button of dubbing at the rear of the shank and divide 4 to 6 stiff feather barbs or Microfibetts for tails.
5. With the proper color of dubbing, wrap a tapered body to the wings. Pass the dubbing beneath the wings and reduce the taper toward the eye. Whip-finish the pattern.

The Deems' Mayfly (Deems Okamoto)

The Deems' design lends itself to small mayflies, such as the Trico and the Blue-Winged Olive. This sparse, Spartan tie unites an extended body and long tail for stability. The extended, splayed, and cocked tail encourages the pattern to land and float properly. The single wing decreases erratic flight, whereas its drag promotes a body-first descent. According to Okamoto, wingless flies require more air time to cock themselves and may tilt prior to water contact during windy conditions or low presentations. Okamoto discovered this during a *wall test*, where the fly is thrown a distance of two or three feet before striking a wall; then you observe its ability, after impact, to land upright.

Tying the Deems Mayfly begins with mounting the tails a short distance down the bend, tilting the tails down about 20 degrees. Three wraps are placed *under* the tails, cocking them up. Additional wraps, with a gentle but firm pull around the central tail, splay the outer tails. The thread travels forward to the wing mount point, approximately two eye-lengths behind the hook eye, to mount the wing. Three flat wraps secure the turkey flat wings. To erect them, bead the wings in front and then post.

Deem's Mayfly (tied by Okamoto)

Next, mount the hackle and "post" the stem against the wing posting, creating a vertical hackle. Apply thinned cement to the body and the base of the wings and hackle. After the cement is nearly dry, the thorax is dubbed and the hackle wound, concave side down. Each ensuing hackle wrap should be *below* the preceding wrap. The final hackle wrap brings the hackle stem over the head, where it is secured with flat wraps.

Hook: Tiemco 100, 921, 2487; for the ultra-small patterns, Tiemco 501 and 901B; Daiichi 1480; sizes 18–22

Thread: Unithread, color matches dubbing and natural, 8/0

Tails: Short, broad polar bear guard hairs or substitutes

Wings: Turkey flat panels

Body: Tying thread

Hackle: Dun or cream

Thorax: Ultra-fine polypropylene or dyed beaver

The Drifting Midge Pupa

This drifting midge pattern obscures the hook point and attracts with a segmented body and a pinch of color. It is an excellent slow-water pattern for visible, selective feeders. Variations of this pattern, with dry hackle in place of the CDC barb legs, may also prove effective.

Hook: Tiemco 947 BL or Daiichi 1190

Thread: 8/0 gray

Drifting Midge Pupa: Fold the pupal case forward and tie down. For enticing contrast, a narrow collar of bright, blood-red CDC dubbing may be added between the thorax and abdomen.

The Drifting Midge Pupa, or DMP, is tied backward with the head-thorax over the hook gap. First, mount a strip of pheasant tail for the pupal case. Next, mount a few barbs of cream or salmon-colored CDC barbs in a dubbing loop. Spin and wrap in. The CDC barbs should extend slightly beyond the hook gap.

Drifting Midge Pupa: Finally, mount and spiral forward a stripped peacock hurl for body. Whip-finish at the eye. The singular merit of the DMP lies in the concealment of the hook bend and spear.

Body: Stripped peacock herl

Collar: Bright, blood-red CDC dubbing

Pupal Case: Pheasant tail barbs

Pupal Body: Stripped peacock herl

Breathing Plume and Anal Brush: Short, white CDC breathing plume may be added prior to mounting the pupal case. The anal brush is attached before wrapping the body. Both the plumes and brush assist in suspending the pattern in the surface film.

The pattern is tied backward, with the head-thorax over the hook gap. First, mount a strip of pheasant tail for the pupal case. Next, mount cream or salmon-colored CDC barbs in a dubbing loop. Only a few barbs are required. Spin and wrap in. CDC barbs should extend slightly beyond the hook gap. Fold the pupal case forward and tie down. Add a band of bright, blood-red CDC dubbing for a narrow collar. Finally, mount and spiral forward a stripped peacock herl for body. Whip-finish at the eye.

The Emerging Pond Olive (Charles Jardine)

Artist and author Charles Jardine created this effective pattern for the emerging olive nymph, especially the bantam *Baetis* nymph. The wing pads of a senior nymph, upon approaching eclosion, darken, hence the black wing pads. The black wing buds contrast with the general pale olive, perhaps drawing attention to the petite pattern.

Hook: Mustad 94840, 94845; Tiemco 5210, or 900 BL; Daiichi 1190, sizes 18–20

Thread: Pale olive-yellow or olive thread

Tail: Wood duck or three pale yellow-olive feather barbs

Body: Pale olive dubbing (rabbit and Antron blend)

Wing Case Buds: Two black biots or black feather strip trimmed short.

Wing Case Overwing: Slip of olive cosset feather (the short, fringed and slightly rounded goose shoulder feather)

Thorax: Pale olive dubbing

The F Fly (Marijan Fratnik)

Hook: Mustad 94840, 94845; Tiemco 101 or 900 BL, Partridge CS20; sizes 18–22

Thread: Pale yellow, orange, or gray

Tail: None

Ribbing: None

Body: Furled CDC feather, twisted and wrapped; pale yellow tying thread

Wings: Clumped CDC barbs, mounted as overwing, sedge style

Hackle: None

My first encounter with CDC patterns occurred over seven years ago while fishing in Slovenia. Although the Moustique flies, which use wrapped CDC feathers as hackle, are excellent floaters, they are fragile. A Slovene tyer, Marjan Fratnik, developed the F Fly, a popular and durable CDC pattern. At first, I rejected it as a wisp of fluff that no trout would take. Wrong. Not only does it take trout, it often takes selective trout under difficult conditions. The pattern, as effective as it is simple, imitates, perhaps, a variety of downwings, caddis, and midge. Its simplicity offers an excellent introduction to CDC patterns.

TYING THE F FLY

1. Select a fine-stemmed, long-barbed CDC feather. Mount the tip of the barbs at the rear of the hook shank. Twist the feather to create a tight cord. Wrap this furled or spun feather forward as body. Whip-finish and trim excess. Smaller bodies are often wrapped with tying thread; however, a furled CDC feather or CDC dubbing increases flotation.
2. Overlap and align the stems of two or more (depending on hook size) CDC feathers. Mount the aligned barbs, tips to the rear, over the shank and whip-finish the head. Fratnik strokes the wing forward about 60° and places a single small drop of cement—such as Dave's Flexament—on the wing base. This will plump the wings forward for a high float. On smaller patterns, I use a thread body and stripped CDC barbs for the overwing. Omitting the CDC stems produces a buoyant, symmetrical pattern. A yellow CDC marker tied in at the head increases visibility.

The Gold-Ribbed Hare's Ear dun (traditional)

Gold-Ribbed Hare's Ear (Traditional Dry)

Seldom listed as a dry, the Gold Ribbed Hare's Ear, in the smaller sizes, is an exceptional pattern when fished in the surface film as a still-born olive. F. M. Halford describes the GRHE dry: "This is probably the most killing pattern of the present day in the Test and other chalk streams; in fact, one of the most skillful and successful anglers in the county of Hants scarcely ever uses any other dun, from the opening of the season in March until the closing of the river. It is equally efficacious for trout and grayling." Apparently, the original *gold-ribbed* pattern was wingless. According to John Roberts, "F. M. Halford was later responsible for the addition of wings." Yet, Ogden's original Hare's Ear pattern presented in Halford's *Floating Flies and How to Dress Them* (1886), listed pale starling wings. Thomas Christopher Hofland, author of *British Angler's Manual* (1839), refers to a Hare's Ear Dun, making a similar pattern, perhaps, rooted in the traditional even before Halford's time. Despite its effectiveness as emerger and dun, Halford would eventually reject the generic GRHE in favor of more species-specific patterns.

Hook: Mustad AC 80000 BR, 94845, 94840; Tiemco 102 (size 17), 100, 5210; Daiichi 1190; sizes 18–20.

Thread: Pale primrose, 8/0. Halford does not list a thread color for the GRHE; this is the color used in Ogden's Hare's Ear.

Tail: Whisk of "Red cock's beard hackle" (Halford)

Body and Legs: "The body is formed of dark fur from the hare's face, ribbed with fine flat gold, and the hare's fur picked out at the shoulder to form legs" (Halford). For micropatterns, use fine gold wire. Apparently, the dubbing from a leveret—a young, first-year hare—was sometimes used for body dubbing and, consequently, for the hackle. The pale, short leveret hair had reduced guard hairs. Pulman refers to the "flax from the leveret's head and neck." Hare *fleck* evidently was dubbing "from the outside the shoulder of the hare."

Hackle: Thoracic hare fibers teased out.

Wing: "Medium or pale starling" (Halford)

SOME SMALL-FLY WATERS

Excellent *Trico* and *Caenis* waters of a western spring creek. The intruding weed mass offers important shelter for the trout.

The mute currents of the River Itchen at Twyford, where micropatterns can be the only effective flies.

A nymphing trout taking *Baetis* emergers. Note that the trout's continuous movements have scoured the lie. (The River Itchen at Brambridge)

A good trout high in the water and "on the fin."

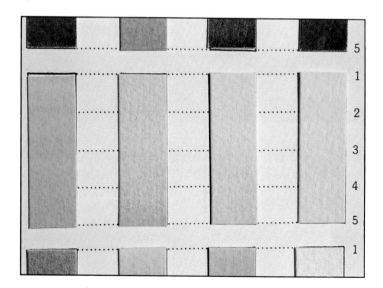

The color code

The Micropatterns

The Antunez's Caddis

The Blue-Winged Olive (Saido)

The Brambridge Caddis

The Brush Bug: RFC Scud

The Bubble Smut

The Budding Midge

The CDC Olive Emerger (Urban)

CDC Particular

The CDC Pupa

The Cluster Microcaddis

Deem's Mayfly (tied by Okamoto)

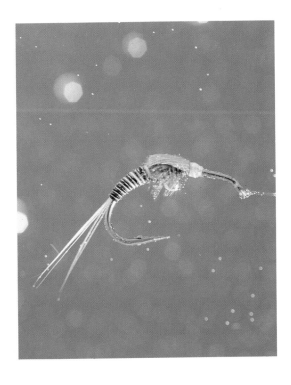

The Demi-Nymph

The Drifting Midge Pupa

The Emerging Pond Olive (Jardine)

The Emerging Sedge

An Extended Body Mayfly (the Black Method)

Extended-Body Wedge-Wing

The F Fly (Fratnik)

The Foam Emerger

The Gray Goose (Sawyer)

The Gray Palmer

The Greenwell's Glory

Greenwell's Spider
(soft-hackle—tied by Edwards)

The Hackle Wing

The Hardoon Caddis (Hardoon)

The Humpy (size 22)

The Itchen Chalkie (Downs)

The Moustique Fly

The Nymerger

Partridge and Orange
(soft-hackle—tied by Edwards)

The Patkova Krem Pupa (Urban)

The Pazur Sedge (Pazur)

The Pheasant-Tail Caddis

The Pheasant-Tail Nymph (Sawyer)

The RFC Hackle Fly—Dun

The RFC Hackle Fly—Spinner

The Rhyacophila (Edwards)

The Riffle Sedge (Price)

The Smidgen (size 22)

The Snowshoe PMD Dun (tied by Grobert)

Spanish Smut

The Suspender Midge Pupa (Goddard)

The Taff's Cased Caddis (Price)

The Timsbury Dun (Hardoon)

The Timsbury Emerger (Hardoon)

The Tricolore

The Unec Midge

Waterhen Bloa (soft-hackle—tied by Edwards)

The Gray Goose Nymph (Sawyer)

Sawyer's Gray Goose may be considered the nymphal stage of the Adams. Like the Adams, which sometimes serves as a *Callibaetis* dun, the Gray Goose may serve as the *Callibaetis* nymph. In fact, the Gray Goose Nymph serves for any small, pale mayfly nymph, especially the translucent olive nymphs. Sawyer, however, tied the Gray Goose to imitate the pale wateries, the spurwing, and the cloeon. The Gray Goose Nymph is tied in the same manner as the Pheasant Tail Nymph. "Take out four herls from the wing feather, tie these in so that the tips can form setae for the nymph, then dress in the same manner as with the PT. At the butt end of the herls the colouring is darker, as with the pheasant tail fibres and this, lapped backwards and forwards, can bring about a well defined thorax and wing case." The fine gold wire, a prominent part of the pattern, should show through the dressing.

Hook: Mustad 3906 B, 94833, 94838, 94840; Partridge E3AY; Tiemco 3761, 5210; Daiichi 1180; size 18.

Thread: Fine gold wire.

Tail: Gray goose wing-feather barbs—". . . only the parts of these which have a lightish grey, green, yellowish appearance."

Body: Gray goose barbs spun on gold wire

Rib: None; the goose fibers twist around the gold wire as in the Pheasant Tail Nymph.

Legs: None

Thorax: Thorax base built with wire wraps. Wrapped and lapped gray goose barbs form thorax.

The Gray Palmer (Traditional)

Variants of this simple pattern, also known as Griffith's Gnat, may be wrapped with a brown or black palmer, but they are more difficult to track on the drift. The original George Griffith dressing was a peacock herl body and a palmered grizzly hackle. The pattern is similar to the Witch patterns that date from the beginning of the twentieth century, such as the Grayling Witch. First mentioned in H. A. Rolt's *Grayling Fishing in South Country Streams* (1901), the Witches have sundry variations. The Gray Palmer lacks a red tag or ribbing. According to John Roberts, Rolt was the first to weight patterns with lead strips for deep-lying fish. *For hooks size 20 and smaller, use the fine long herls from the base of the peacock sword.* These herls, below the "spatter herls" at the tip, are under 1 millimeter wide and over 20 centimeters long. For small patterns, sword herls are superior. Mount and wrap the palmer concave forward, resulting in a forward cupping of barbs for better flotation.

Hook: Mustad AC 80000 BR, Orvis 4641, Tiemco 101 and 900 BL; sizes 18 and 24

Thread: Danville 6/0 black or gray

Tail: None

Ribbing: None

Body: Bronze green peacock herl, note comments

Wings: None

Hackle: Grizzly, Cree, brown, or dun palmer hackle

Greenwell's Glory (James Wright)

Devised by Canon William Greenwell and tied by James Wright, Greenwell's Glory imitates, depending on hook size and hue, the ubiquitous olives. The Canon, after a fishless day, brought the desired dun to James Wright of Sprouston. Wright tied an imitation that proved productive. Harold Smedley describes the celebration the next day. "There were present the famous Kerss brothers—James and Charles; Brown, the angling schoolmaster of the village, and members of the Wright family. Mr. Wright suggested the name Greenwell's Glory and it was so christened in Kelso whiskey." Other writers, including John Roberts and Frank Elder, believe that the original pattern was wet. In any case, the tailless dry carries the tradition.

Hook: Mustad 94840, 94845; Daiichi 1180; Tiemco 5210; size 18

Thread: Primrose (light yellow), 8/0

Tail: Traditionally none, though, a tail may be added for increased flotation.

Body: Primrose tying silk, waxed to produce a pale olive

Rib: Fine gold wire

Hackle: Light furnace, the so-called Greenwell hackle. Determining the original hackle has been a tying conundrum. Frank Elder, in *The Book of the Hackle* (1979), claims that "although the original tie was written as a coch-y-bonddu hackle, what was certainly used was what we now call furnace. If, as we presume, the hackle was a hen hackle, then not only must it have been without black tips, but it was almost certainly a pale furnace, for while a furnace with a bright red outer is common in a cock hackle, it is very rare in a hen."

Wing: Starling, an ersatz for the original blackbird slips

Hardoon Caddis (David Hardoon)

This small skating caddis uses three badger hackles. The dark center of the hackle creates the illusion of a central body. Hardoon mounts three badger hackles of various lengths, concluding with the smallest hackle in front. An optional method is to mount the base of a saddle hackle and wrap forward, finishing with smaller barbs at the hackle tip. When drawn, the cone shape facilitates the skating action of the pattern. Golden badger saddle hackle makes excellent body and wings for the Hardoon Cinnamon Caddis.

Hook: Mustad AC 80000 BR or AC 80050 BR, Tiemco 101; sizes 18–20

Thread: Black, 8/0

Tail: None

Body: Three badger hackles—The butt-hackle barbs slightly longer than the hook gap, the middle hackle barbs slightly shorter than the gap, and the front hackle barbs three-fourths hook gap.

Wing: None

Antennae: Two fine stripped hackle stems

The Itchen Chalkie (Donald Downs)

This pattern, which imitates a cased caddis, is uniquely suited to miniature imitations. Although originally tied to mimic the white snail shells incorporated into the caddis case, the knots, when inked with various colors, can also duplicate the variety of pebbles and sands used in case building. For a sinking variant, fine wire knots, gold or silver, spiral on to imitate the smaller saddle, purse, and tube-cased caddis. Cast in the riffles on slack line, the Itchen Chalkie tumbles and founders like a dislodged caddis case.

Hook: Select straight or curved shank hooks with adequate gap to accommodate the method, Daiichi 1190 and 1100; Tiemco 101, 3769 and 2487; Mustad AC 80050 BR and AC 80250 BR.

Thread: 6/0 black or gray

Tail: None

Body: Fine dubbing, synthetic or natural, especially mole and beaver

Overbody: Knotted thread, cord, or wire

Wings: None

Hackle: Sparse black barb legs

Gills: None

TYING THE ITCHEN CHALKIE

1. Tie several closely spaced knots on a length of thread, cord or wire. To vary the bulk of the knots, tie single and double overhand knots. The thread or cord diameter should vary according to the shank length of the hook. If a white thread or cord is used, marking pens can variously color the knots to imitate an array of case materials. For a sinking pattern, knots may be tied in fine wire. Close the wire knots, but do not tighten them.
2. Tie in the end of the knotted strand.
3. Dub, with coarse or fine dubbing depending on the desired effect, a uniform, narrow body. On size 20 and smaller hooks, use mole dubbing, mixed with finely chopped Antron.
4. Spiral the knotted strand along the shank to form the clumps of debris on the case. Tie off.
5. Add a few hackle barbs for legs and lacquer the head for realism. A peeping caddis is created by an exposed body segment. Downs' original pattern had a length of white fluorescent silk tied to form "the

white shoulders peeping out of the top of the ball gown" and a doubled, pale red hackle for legs.

Lunn's Particular (William Lunn)

According to John Waller Hills, William James Lunn was fishing with Gilbey, the Gilbey of London Gin fame, on Park Stream, the 26th of April, 1917. Fishing was poor. Gilbey eventually complained to Lunn, "The trout are too particular today." Lunn gave him a new pattern that immediately caught three fish. "Why, what's this fly?" Gilbey queried. "It's a Lunn's Particular," was the reply.

Evidently, according to Harold Hinsdill Smedley, the term "particular" was English slang for "particular favorite," a reference to one's accustomed or favorite drink. So, as Smedley concludes, ". . . Lunn was really making a little joke when he told Gilbey, a liquor distiller, that this fly was his *particular*." It has been the particular of trout ever since.

William Lunn was river keeper of the Houghton Club waters for forty-five years. Today, the water still remains under the stewardship of the Lunn family. In *River Keeper* (1934), J. W. Hills praises Lunn's Particular, an olive spinner imitation. "Therein lies its excellence: it kills well when fish are taking olives, and is marvelously good when they are shy or are taking spinners. It succeeds whether sunk or floating. If I had to be limited to one fly, I should choose it." Lunn created several popular patterns, including the Houghton Ruby and Sherry Spinner, but it is the Particular, a classic tie, that seems to take impossible trout.

Hook: Mustad 94840, 94845; Partridge L3A; Tiemco 5230; Daiichi 1180, size 18

Thread: Crimson, the original dressing called for Pearsall's gossamer, shade 13, the same color used in the Houghton Ruby

Wing: Two medium-blue cock hackle points, put on flat (tied spent). Lunn used lighter hackle tips later in the season.

Lunn's Particular (traditional)

Tail: Four barbs from the Rhode Island large hackle

Body: Undyed hackle stem of Rhode Island cock

Hackle: Medium Rhode Island cock hackle tied sparse

TYING LUNN'S PARTICULAR

1. Mount tails and attach body.
2. With touching spirals, wrap body forward to the wing base point. Secure and trim excess.
3. Select two hackle points with parallel edges and rounded tips. Figure-eight, spinner style, the two hackle points. Trim excess. A drop of Superglue may be added at the wing crossing.
4. Mount and wrap sparse hackle. Secure hackle, trim excess, and whip-finish head.

The Micrognat

A furled CDC body, an Antron overwing, a mole-fur thorax, and CDC barb legs produce an excellent micrognat. To form the tightly furled CDC body, clip hackle pliers on the CDC barbs and spin. Use fine, crinkled Antron for the sparse overwing. This is a hatching midge.

The Moustique Fly (Traditional)

This archetypal CDC pattern, used for over one hundred years, originated in the Swiss Jura Mountains, bordering on France. Dr. Jean-Paul Pequegnot traces the pattern to Vallorbe within the Swiss Jura. In *French Fishing Flies* (1987), he describes the French connection. "In Franche-Comte, where it is well known and widely used, it is sometimes called the Mouche de Vallorbe or, more often, the Cul de Canard. Aime Devaux made excellent ones with a body of yellow tying silk in the Franche-Comte manner with a gray supporting hackle just behind the duck down collar, which greatly improved the posture of the fly." Devaux's method, called a *reverse* or *umbrella* dressing, cocked the rear hackle barbs forward to prevent the soft fore-hackle from lying back. The double-hackle (cock and cul de canard) improves flotation.

The Moustique appears in a variety of floss colors—especially yellow, red, and green. Taff Price of England finds this pattern representative of the tiny mayflies, especially the pale watery (*Baetis fuscatus*) and small spurwing (*Centroptilum luteolum*). For the hackle, select CDC feathers with long, fine stems. Some patterns add two blue-dun hackle tips for wings.

Hook: Mustad AC 80000 BR, Orvis 4641, Tiemco 101, Daiichi 1180 and 1190, sizes 18–22

Thread: Danville, 6/0 or 8/0 pale yellow, orange, or other

Tail: Traditionally none or hackle barbs

Ribbing: None

Body: Tying thread or floss

Wings: None, consult following note

Hackle: Cul-de-canard feather tied in as hackle collar and trimmed to length

The Muha Reka

Kindred to Fratnik's F Fly is the palmered *Muha Reka*, "the river fly." For fast water, the trailing barbs of the palmered CDC hackle possess superior flotation. The Muha Reka, tied with a single CDC feather, is an appropriate method for small patterns. When tied with a natural CDC feather, the pattern has a lower, cream body and a dark dun overwing. The cream body ensues from the pale cream barbs and stem at the base of the CDC feather. Due to the length of the CDC feather, the pattern should be tied in sizes 18 and smaller. The Muha Reka, floating low in the surface film, best imitates an emerging caddis.

TYING THE MUHA REKA

1. Select a fine-stemmed CDC feather appropriate for the shank length. For a tighter, smoother body, use flat-nosed pliers to flatten the stem before wrapping. For distinct abdominal segments, select a dark CDC feather with a cream or white stem. A CDC feather is usually paler on the concave side. In any event, mount and wrap the feather to expose the pale stem.

2. Mount the *stem base* (the proximal point) of the CDC feather at the tail mount position. It may be necessary to crop the thick, distended

The Muha Reka: The CDC stem creates distinct abdominal bands.

stem bulb before mounting. The stem should extend 3/4 body length, creating a smooth underbody. Wrap the CDC feather forward, allowing the barbs to flare along the shank. I space the wraps *one-stem width* apart to liberate the barbs. *I have also found that the spaced spirals expose the thread foundation color, increasing the attraction of this pattern.*

3. At the head position, overwrap the CDC stem and allow the feather tip to extend aft, creating an overwing. Crop the wing and trailing barbs approximately 1/2 shank length beyond the hook bend.

The Nymerger

These simple CDC "nymph-emergers" may be tied on the smallest of hooks. They imitate the "emergence drift" of small mayflies. Some nymphs make preliminary ascents to the surface prior to hatching. They often drift a few feet on the surface and then sink, only to surface downstream. They drift on or just beneath the surface. Patterns tied without the dubbed thorax tend to swim just beneath the surface.

Hook: Tiemco 900 BL; sizes 18–24

Thread: Unithread, 6/0 underbody color

Tail: CDC barb tips

Ribbing: None or tying thread

Overbody: CDC barbs

Thorax: CDC barbs or finely minced CDC dubbing beneath CDC wing case

Wing Pads: Splayed CDC barbs

Legs: None

TYING THE NYMERGER

1. First, lay down a thread base for underbody. Then, mount stripped and stacked CDC barbs so that the natural ends extend beyond the hook bend for tails. Tail length should equal shank length. For a realistic tail, prune and break the barbs to length.

2. Wrap thread forward to mid-shank. Fold CDC overbody forward and over-thread from mid-shank to head.

3. Add finely diced CDC dubbing and dub back to mid-shank.

4. Fold wing case back and whip-finish at mid-shank.

5. Trim and flare the extended wing case buds.

Patkova Krem Pupa (Andrija Urban)

Andrija Urban of Skoplje developed the Patkova Krem Pupa, the "Cream Pupae with CDC." The Krem Pupa, imitating the emerging caddis, drifts in the surface film. The light-wire hook, veiled CDC wing, and CDC dubbing produce buoyancy.

Hook: Mustad 94833, Kamatsu B 830, Tiemco 2487, size 18

Thread: Dark brown, 8/0

Body: Cream Antron and chopped CDC (4 to 1 ratio)

Wings: Two, fine-stemmed CDC feathers

Hackle: Single wrap of partridge spade feather

Thorax: Fine rabbit hair and dark brown Antron

TYING THE PATKOVA KREM PUPA

1. Dub abdomen to mid-shank.
2. Mount two dun CDC feathers by tips at mid-shank. When folded forward, their concave sides should face outward.
3. Dub thorax and add a single wrap of partridge body feather for legs.
4. Fold CDC feathers forward, crossing stems at head.
5. Whip-finish.

Pazur Sedge (Dr. Kreso Pazur)

Hook: Daiichi 1180, Mustad AC 80000, Tiemco 101, sizes 20–26

Thread: Danville, 6/0 black

Tail: Two or three brown hackle barbs

Ribbing: None

Body: Brown feather barb overbody, pale yellow-green dubbed body

Wings: Gray quill sections tied on caddis style

Hackle: Brown dry hackle

This diminutive Croatian sedge, created by Dr. Kreso Pazur of Zagreb, is an extremely effective clear, slow-water pattern.

The Petitjean Dun (Marc Petitjean)

Marc Petitjean of Switzerland bundles CDC barbs and mounts them as mayfly dun wings. On the smallest patterns, CDC barbs may be bundled and figure-eighted for dun or spinner wings. One method of tying the MP dun is by mounting a complete CDC feather behind the wing bundles. Pulling the CDC feather through the middle of the wing bundle erects and fans the wings forward. The wings are then trimmed to shape. The downy CDC wings are easily positioned and erected, resulting in soft, gauzy wings. Sometimes Petitjean wraps a few turns of wire around the top of the hook bend so that the tail sinks, emulating the posture of an emerging insect.

Hook: Mustad AC 80000 BR, 94840 and 94845; Tiemco 101 and 102; sizes 18–20.

Thread: Match dubbing color

Tail: Coq de Leon barbs

Body: Finely minced CDC dubbing

The Petitjean Dun (tied by Petitjean)

Thorax: One complete CDC feather

Wings: CDC barb bundle

Hackle: None

TYING THE PETITJEAN DUN

1. Stack and mount coq de Leon barbs for tails.
2. Dub finely minced CDC barbs three-fourths the shank length.
3. Mount the tip of one CDC feather (the thoracic feather) at the front of the dubbed abdomen.
4. Position a bundle of dun CDC barbs against the front of the abdomen, tie down, and then dub the thorax.
5. Pull the thoracic feather forward through the middle of the wing bundle to erect and splay the wings.
6. Tie off the thoracic feather at the head and whip finish.
7. Press the wings together and shape them with scissors.

This method creates CDC fan wings similar to Marc Petitjean's method.

The Pheasant Tail Nymph (Frank Sawyer)

Developed for the upstream "induced-take," Frank Sawyer's Pheasant Tail Nymph is a modern classic. Designed to imitate the swimming olive nymphs, the pattern is pitched upstream of the trout. After the pattern sinks below and ahead of the trout, the rod raises the ascending nymph in front of the trout. Such a method may provoke or "induce" the trout to take. Sometimes Sawyer would anoint the tippet and nymph with trout body slime to increase the sink and taste.

Frank Sawyer, a keeper of the Wiltshire Avon, spent a life observing the fish and fly life of his river. The spartan silhouette, feathered tails and spindle profile effectively imitate the *Baetis* nymph. The pattern is tied so that the pheasant-tail fibers constitute the tail, the body and the oval thorax. The reddish brown body, when wet, closely matches the deep brown of some *Baetis* nymphs. Sawyer felt that the natural pheasant tail color was more effective than a dyed color. "The red of the pheasant tail body and wire tying that I use could not possibly be mistaken by us for an olive, or greenish yellow coloring. Yet fish take it readily when creatures with this latter coloring are hatching. It is not an exact copy of coloring, as we know it, but fish are deceived by it." The black pheasant-fiber base creates the dark wing pads typical of the nymph. The correct fiber length is critical to achieve the dark wing pad. Even if the color was not a match for the natural, Sawyer made certain that the profile and action emulated the nymph it represented. The pattern is legless, due to the fact that the nymphs relax their legs beneath the body when swimming to achieve a torpedo taper. The hook, muffled neither by hackles nor dressing, requires only moderate pressure to home the point during a take.

> *Hook:* Mustad 3906 B, 94833, 94838, 94840; Partridge E3AY; Tiemco 3761, 5210; Daiichi 1180; sizes 18–20.
>
> *Thread:* None; Sawyer's unique tying method uses the fine reddish-brown transformer wire with an .005-inch diameter instead of thread.
>
> *Tail:* "Four centre fibres of a browny-red cock pheasant tail" (Sawyer)
>
> *Body:* Pheasant tail fibers spun on wire and wound forward.
>
> *Wing Case:* The lapped base of the pheasant tail fibers.

Tying the Pheasant Tail Nymph

1. After covering the shank with wrap of fine wire, build an oval thorax on the front third of the shank. When completed, wrap the wire to the rear. Do not overdress the nymph with excessive wraps of ballast.

2. Take four pheasant-tail barbs and wrap in at the rear of the hook so that they extend about 1/8 inch beyond the bend. Some *Baetis* nymphs have long and prominent tails; thus, imitations should match this conspicuous feature. Next, spin the four feather barbs onto the wire. Spinning combines the colors and improves body strength. To reduce bulk, some small hooks may require only three pheasant-tail barbs.

3. Next, wrap the body firmly and evenly to the hook eye. At the head, separate the fibers from the wire and wrap the wire back immediately behind the thorax.

4. Now, bend the fibers back over the top and sides of the thorax. Lap the wire over the thorax to secure the wing case.

5. Finally, wrap the wire to the head position. Bend the wing case fibers forward and finish with six turns of wire at the head. Although Sawyer tied no knot, a few tyers finish with two half-hitches of wire. Trim excess.

The RFC Trico, size 22 hook

The RFC Hackle Fly

This pattern imitates the various stages—nymph, dun, and spinner—of the mayfly. Depending upon hackle size, color, and pattern shape a variety of insects may be imitated, including the dry caddis and stonefly. The pattern is excellent for small imitations when using the extremely slender, fine-stemmed Hoffman saddle hackles. Similar to the brush bug method, only the tail and palmer are mounted. The pattern is then shaped by trimming.

TYING THE RFC HACKLE FLY

To create this quick and simple pattern, tie in the tail and palmer hackle. The proper silhouette is then created completely by cropping. It is also possible to strip the barbs, prior to palmering, to produce a smooth "quill" abdomen. Depending upon the stem diameter, strip a length of barbs, approximately four times the shank length, to fashion a half-shank abdomen. A silver badger saddle hackle makes excellent body and wings for Tricos.

Nymph

1. Tie in sparse feather barbs for tail. When mounting thin barbs for tails, a single barb on each side may prove too sparse. If two or three are mounted on each side they will seldom align. This, in fact, may improve flotation. One method, I have found, to produce a stiff, distinct tail is to mount two or three barbs on each side. Then, touch each tail set with a drop of cement and caress each set into a single, fused fiber.
2. Select the appropriate size (barb length equals leg length) and colored saddle hackle.
3. Mount the hackle tip and palmer the hook.
4. Trim the body, leaving a few barbs on the top and sides. Cement or wax the top barbs down and trim to length, creating a wing case. The side barbs become legs.

Dun

1. Mount two to four feather barbs for tails. Splay the tails with thread wraps between them. The tails should occupy the same horizontal plane as the hook shank.
2. Select the appropriately colored saddle hackle and palmer the hook.
3. Prune the abdomen and underside of the thorax. This leaves a semi-circular hackle collar for legs and wings.

Spinner

1. Mount two to four feather barbs for tails. Splay the tails with thread wraps between them. The tails should occupy the same horizontal plane as the hook shank.
2. Select the appropriately colored saddle hackle and palmer the hook.
3. Trim the abdomen and the top and bottom of the thorax. The extended barbs on each side form the spent spinner wings.

The Brush Bug: RFC Scud

This simple scud pattern has excellent entry and sink. The whirled wire gives weight and metallic flash to the pattern. All scud-shrimp patterns should be tied on straight shanks for adequate gap and natural profile.

Hook: Orvis 4641, Mustad AC 80000 BR, Tiemco 101; sizes 18–20

Thread: Unithread, Light Cahill

Underbody: Tag end of dubbing brush, 3/4 shank length.

Body: Short-fibered, sparse dubbing brush: cream or pink underfur blended with Antron or Z-lon.

TYING THE RFC SCUD

1. Lay wire down for 3/4 shank length. Wrap securely.
2. Spiral dubbing brush forward and whip-finish at head.
3. Extract top fibers and fold all fibers beneath hook shank.

The Brush Bug RFC Scud

The Rhyacophila (Oliver Edwards)

The *Rhyacophila*, or Green Rockworm, is the largest genus of the Trichoptera, with more than 100 species known in North America. Regardless of the fact that a mature larva may range over 30 millimeters, immature larvae may be imitated with size 18 hooks. Corded dubbing and ribbing create the deep, abdominal constrictions. This tying technique may be effective for other patterns requiring distinct abdominal segments.

TYING THE RHYACOPHILA

1. Mount the fine ribbing at the rear of the shank.
2. Fashion a spindle of dubbing, tapered at both ends. The long, fine parallel fibers must be matted and shaped.
3. Next, attach one end of the dubbing spindle to the rear of the shank. Carefully align the dubbing spindle with the tying thread and press together. Then, smoothly twist the thread and the spindle together. Continue to spin until a smooth, tapered cord results.
4. Now, while sustaining twisting tension, wrap the spindle forward, leaving a small space between the segments. If the length was properly calculated, the end taper should fall near the head. Wrap the spindle off two eye lengths behind the eye. Secure the dubbing (actually corded fibers twisted together) with several thread wraps.
5. To create the conspicuous segments, spiral the ribbing up the seam or crevice created by the corded body. Force the ribbing deep into the crevice with the thumbnail. When completed, secure the ribbing and trim excess.
6. Mount the partridge barbs, beard fashion, for the short legs. Fan the legs laterally and forward. Trim the excess butts.
7. Finally, taper a distinct head. Lacquer the head after whip-finishing the pattern.

Hook: Partridge K4A; Tiemco 2487, 947 BL; size 18.

Thread: Unithread, black, 6/0.

Abdomen: Fine, long-fibered polypropylene, bright green. The long fibers cord quickly, thereby creating the body segments.

Ribbing: Fine, pale yellow monofilament for small patterns. The original pattern used fine, creamy-translucent Swannundaze to create the distinct seam between the body segments.

Legs: Hungarian partridge barbs.

Head: Tapered and lacquered black tying thread.

The Riffle Sedge (Taff Price)

Taff Price, the caddis master, uses CDC feathers in place of stacked hair to produce an effective, fast-water pattern. The original pattern utilized whole, stemmed CDC feathers, rabbit dubbing, and hackle-stem antennae. The following variant, especially suited to small patterns, uses stripped CDC barbs

After wrapping the underbody of the Riffle Sedge, flare each CDC bundle directly on top of the shank. Trim the densely flared bundles for a caddis profile.

for the wings. The pattern is fished either *waked* or dragless on the surface. It dances down heavy riffles, yet is realistic enough for spring creeks.

Hook: Tiemco 101 or Orvis 4641; sizes 18–22.

Thread: Dun, gray, or black threads may be used for the body.

Tail: None

Body: Various dubbings may be used, especially pale yellow CDC dubbing. On smaller patterns, various colors of tying thread may be used.

Wings: Natural or dyed CDC barb bundles. When completed, the flared wing is trimmed to shape.

Hackle: Badger, cree, or grizzly or extended CDC barbs

Antennae: Coq de Leon barbs or substitutes

TYING THE THREAD-BODY RIFFLE SEDGE

1. Wrap a pale yellow thread body.
2. Mount, with one or two wraps, a CDC barb bundle directly on top of the hook shank. Wrap thread in front of the CDC bundle.
3. Mount another CDC bundle immediately in front of the previous bundle. Again, wrap thread in front of the CDC bundle.
4. Continue to mount wing bundles until the body is completed. The final front CDC bundle may be spun around the shank for legs.
5. Trim the body to create a caddis profile. The Riffle Sedge may have a conventional forward hackle, spun CDC barbs or several CDC barbs, pulled away from the thorax, as forward hackle.

The Smidgen

The smidgen imitates a shucking midge, especially the crimson species of *Chironomini,* and has proven effective for smutting spring-creek trout. Although trout cannot spell, many find a midge within the smidgen. After

Smidgen: Prepare shuck by spinning a fine noodle of dubbing with hackle pliers. Fold the furled noodle, allowing the strands to twist together. Mount the furled shuck, which extends slightly beyond the hook bend, at mid-shank. Next, mount and post a tuft of blood-red CDC barbs, approximately ¾ shank length, for the budding body. When waxing the thread, spin the thread back and forth between the fingers while revolving the wax tube. This leaves tiny licks of wax along the thread. After waxing, dust the thread with dark brown mole fur and wrap the thorax on the shuck base.

Smidgen: Mount a parachute hackle and wrap dull side down. Notice that the hackle wraps pass between the hook shank and the shuck. After a few wraps, secure the hackle at the head and whip-finish. The pattern also performs without hackle. The Smidgen is usually tied on a circular or curved-shank hook.

Smidgen: Because the pattern is secured to the shank at one point (in approximately two millimeters), it may be tied on the smallest of hooks. Further, the enticing color contrast makes this an excellent micropattern for spring creeks.

The Smidgen, size 22 hook: The constricted "footprint" of the Smidgen makes it appropriate for the smallest of hooks.

ecdysis (the actual shedding of the larval integument), the midge pupa remains dormant and hidden until it swims to the surface, where *eclosion* (adult emergence) occurs. The Smidgen simulates the moment of eclosion, the most vulnerable period. There is seldom a time on any water when midges are not hatching. Spring, summer, fall, and winter all have midge hatches. Trout water makes midge water. Year-round waters can produce phenomenal winter midge hatches. The Smidgen should be tied with restricted wraps and minimal bulk. *Although not commonly available, small silver hooks might be more obscure. Chameleon-like, the silver hook may reflect the surroundings of watery reflections and bubbles, thereby hiding the hook.*

Hook: Orvis 4641; Tiemco 101; sizes 22–26

Thread: Unithread, orange or dun, 8/0 or 12/0

Shuck: Long, fine dubbing fibers (white or cream Antron or Z-lon) furled or looped for shuck

Budding midge: Blood-red CDC barbs, trimmed

Legs: Dun CDC barbs, parachute hackle, or none

Body: Finely hashed mole fur, brown, or black

TYING THE SMIDGEN

1. Shuck strands may be furled or looped, folded back, and then secured at mid-shank. Prepare shuck by spinning a fine noodle of dubbing with hackle pliers, allowing it to furl together. Shuck should extend slightly beyond the hook bend. Shuck may also encircle hook shank to cloak the hook.
2. Spiral thread forward and figure-eight CDC legs at head. Trim legs within body length. If a parachute hackle replaces the CDC legs, mount the hackle after dubbing the thorax. The pattern also performs without legs or hackle.
3. Next, mount blood-red CDC barbs at thorax. CDC barbs may be lapped once and posted to erect. The budding body should be about 3/4 shank length.
4. Wax thread and dust on brown mole fur for thorax. Dub thorax and whip-finish.

For simplicity of tie, the hackle can be wound around the shank itself, immediately in front of the mole body.

The Soft-Hackled Fly (Traditional)

According to Sylvester Nemes, the soft-hackle fly is the quintessence latent in all insects: nymph, larva, emerger, dun, and dry. A pattern without top or bottom. A pattern without an insect, because it is all insects. The soft hackle, pushed away from the body by the swelled thorax, squirms and writhes with the undulating current. The size of the soft-hackle, one of the smallest of all possible patterns, is limited only by the size of hackle—the length of the barbs and the diameter of the stem. Scalp hackles, such as those found on the starling, provide micro soft-hackles. Thread may used to build the body and form the thorax. Tying a size 22 soft-hackle pattern with thread body, mole thorax, and scalp feather is easy. Even on a size 24 hook, thread easily builds the body and forms the thorax. The crux of tying the soft-hackle lies in minimal hackle wraps. One or two wraps with a "half-hackle" enable the body to show through. To make a half-hackle, place the feather on the tying table, tip toward you and convex side up. Carefully strip the barbs from the right side of the hackle. Trim the tip back so that the first barb equals either shank length or hook length. Mount the hackle by the tip and wrap in. The barbs may be either "concave" over the shank, enveloping the pattern or "stand-off" to represent dry wings. The latter design, when "greased," is fished as a dry or emerger—upstream, dead-drift to a specific, raising fish.

According to Oliver Edwards of England, a North Country spider is tied with Pearsall's *Gossamer* tying thread, not silk floss. Finish the body on the shank opposite the hook point or no longer than midway between hook point and rear of barb. Dubbed bodies should show the thread through with only a sparse, fine haze of fur. Ribbing wire should be the finest available. The "umbrella" hackle should be sparse also, two turns. When wrapped, hackle barbs should extend to the end of the scant body, to the end of the hook bend, or to points between. When tails are called for, they should match the design—sparse and somewhat long.

The Dark Watchet for the Iron Blue Dun, the Poult Bloa for the Blue-Winged Olive and the Starling Bloa for the Pale Watery are, according to Edwards, *confidence* flies.

Dark Watchet

Hook: Partridge L3A; sizes 18–22.

Hackle: Blue dun from jackdaw's throat. Possible substitute, California quail (*Lophortyx californicus*).

Body: Pearsall's Gossamer, orange and purple twisted together and dusted with mole's fur.

Head: Pearsall's Gossamer, orange

Poult Bloa

Hook: Partridge L3A; sizes 18–22.

Hackle: "Hackled with a light blue feather from the under-coverts of a young grouse wing, taken before the bird is strong on the wing, the lighter side of the feather toward the head of the fly. This feather darkens rapidly on the live bird from August onwards" (Edwards).
Possible substitute, California quail (*Lophortyx californicus*).

Body: Primrose yellow, number 3

Head: Primrose yellow, number 3

Starling Bloa

Hook: Partridge L3A; sizes 18–22.

Hackle: The palest, under-covert feather from a young starling's wing. "This under-covert feather is a beautiful silvery beige colour. Sometimes it seems to have a faint, pinkish cast" (Edwards).

Body: Straw or white tying thread

The Soft-Hackle Trico (Sylvester Nemes)

Hook: Tiemco 102Y (size 19), 101; Partridge A (1X short, size 16), sizes 19–22.

Thread: Black or dark olive, 8/0

Body: Short wrap of peacock, slightly longer than half shank length

Syl's Midge, size 22 hook (Nemes)

Hackle: Light grizzly hen

Head: Two turns of peacock herl

Tail: Three or four strands of clear, sparkle poly or Z-lon, shank length. The tightly crinkled strands of Z-lon produce "visual volume" without physical mass on micropatterns.

Syl's Midge (Sylvester Nemes)

Hook: Tiemco 102Y (size 19), 101; Partridge A (1X short, size 16), sizes 19–22. Nemes advocates matching the midges, even the size 22s, with a size 16 sproat, light wire hook.

Thread: Danville, olive, 8/0

Body: Plump peacock herl, mounted between point and barb

Hackle: Two turns of gray hackle found just behind the orange scalp of the Hungarian partridge

The Spanish Smut

This diminutive smut imitation is effective for short-range, feeding trout. It duplicates the distinctive "bowling pin" profile of a drifting *Simulium* larvae. The typical smut or black fly larva is about 6 millimeters long, approximately the shank length of a size 18 hook. Some are as small as 3 millimeters and a rare few are over 12 millimeters long. The naturals attach themselves to rocks and vegetation by a posterior ring of hooks and prolegs, and travel by "rappelling" downstream on silk "ropes." An upstream presentation of a drifting, sunken smut on a delicate tippet imitates this act.

Although patterns are not common, the insects are. Their slipper-shaped cocoons can carpet some river beds. The larval imitations, like the naturals, are cream, olive, gray, and black, with a cylindrical body and a swelled posterior. Any smut pattern should have enough weight for fast-water entry, yet be light enough for natural current drift.

Wide-gaped hooks or curved hooks are required because the swelled body eliminates some gap. A Spanish pattern has a lacquered body with a tuft of dubbing for the head. It drifts on a light tippet just beneath the surface. The following pattern incorporates CDC barbs for buoyancy. It should drift in, or just beneath, the surface film. The sink and drift of the pattern may be further established by the weight of the hook and the density of the CDC gill cluster.

Hook: Circular or wide-gap hooks, Mustad AC 80250 BR, AC 80100 BR, AC 80000 BR, Tiemco 2487, 101; Daiichi 1180, 1640, Orvis JA 8988, select wire diameter for drift depth; sizes 20–28

Thread: Pale yellow, 6/0 or 8/0 thread. Other colors, such as tan, brown, and pale green may be used.

Tail: None

Body: Tying thread

Wings: None

Hackle: None

Gills: Short, pale yellow, or white CDC barbs

1. To achieve a smooth body, pull out a length of tying thread. Counter-spin the bobbin. While the bobbin spins, flatten the thread between the thumbnail and the index finger by stripping the thread down.
2. Form the lower body, allowing adequate gap, to the middle of the hook bend. Maintain flat thread during body building.
3. After forming the lower body, add a CDC fan at the head
4. Complete the thoracic section by forming, as illustrated, the bowling-pin profile. Whip-finish the pattern.
5. Apply a light coat of fast-drying nail polish or nail hardener to the pattern.
6. After drying, invert the pattern, belly down, for final coats of nail lacquer. The inversion allows the lacquer to form a bulbous body on the outside of the upper bend.

The Sparkle Dun (Craig Mathews and John Juracek)

Craig Mathews and John Juracek developed a simple, durable, inexpensive, and effective fly design, the Sparkle Duns and Sparkle Spinners. The Sparkle Dun has become, in a remarkably brief time, a standard tie. The Sparkle Yarn shuck performs two functions: the shimmer attracts trout and the crinkle traps bubbles.

Make certain, Mathews and Juracek caution, that the wing is forced upright by pulling it up and beading in front of the wing base. "Do not wait to force the wing up with dubbing as it will only creep forward over the hook eye as it lies in the fly box." When tying the pattern, first mount the wing, then the trailing shuck and finally the body. Continue the body in front of the wing.

The Sparkle Dun (tied by Mathews)

Hook: Mustad 94840, AC 80000 BL; Tiemco 101; Daiichi 1180; sizes 18–22

Thread: Unithread, matches dubbing color, 6/0

Shuck: Olive-brown Sparkle Yarn or Z-lon, one-half to full shank length

Body: Yellowish orange, synthetic or dyed mole

Wing: Dun deer body hair, dyed

The Super Grizzly Emerger (John Goddard)

In mid-season on the Kennet, John Goddard encountered trout that ignored the congregations in his fly boxes until he found one of Mathews' Sparkle Duns. A wild Kennet brown accepted that offering on the first drift. After further experimentation, Goddard found that the Super Grizzly Emerger matched the emerging olives. Needless to say, throughout the summer Goddard found that the pattern took rainbows, browns, and graylings willingly. This attractive pattern, akin to what might be called an Adams Emerger, proves productive when any of the small summer olives appear.

Hook: Mustad 94840, 94845; Daiichi 1180; Tiemco 5210; sizes 18–20.

Thread: Brown or purple, 8/0. I prefer Unithread orange, the thread used for Goddard's Super Grizzly pattern.

Shuck: Pale yellow or gold Krystal Flash (original recommendation), Z-lon, or Sparkle Yarn

Body: Gray goose wing barb

Hackle: One red and one grizzly tied together. A single cree may also be used.

Wings: None

The Super Grizzly Emerger (Goddard)

The Suspender Midge Pupa (John Goddard)

The earliest discussion of midge larva and pupa patterns appears in J. C. Mottram's *Fly Fishing: Some New Arts and Mysteries* (1915). Small cork wedges suspend the patterns vertically beneath the surface. Mottram concludes that "They are intended to be cast before rising fish, just like a dry fly, and must not be worked." The vertical drift can be achieved with a small cork bead "threaded on the gut above the first knot of the fly." Various attempts have been made to suspend drifting midge and pupa patterns; perhaps the most celebrated is Goddard's Suspender Midge Pupa, which incorporates a small ball of Ethafoam enmeshed in nylon.

Inspired by Charles Brooks' Natant Nylon Nymph, Neil Patterson and John Goddard sought material with better buoyancy than nylon or polypropylene yarn. Patterson discovered Plastazoat, a packing material. Later, closed-cell Ethafoam proved effective. Not only did it suspend the pattern, but the bright white Ethafoam suggested the breathing fan of the pupa. Goddard found that "the Suspender Midge Pupa dressed with dark green or brown bodies and tied on small size 16 or better still 18 hooks proved to be amazingly successful for any trout lying close to the surface including those that were apparently smutting, and even when dragging in an adverse current, would often still be taken by trout which would turn and follow them and yet still take in a confident manner."

> *Hook:* Mustad AC 80000 BL; Partridge L2A; Tiemco 100, 102 (size 17), 2487, size 18
>
> *Thread:* Unithread, brown, 8/0
>
> *Body:* Originally, brown or green seal fur. Micropatterns usually require mole or an ultra-fine, nonabsorbent synthetic dubbing.
>
> *Rib:* Fine, silver Lurex or any fine, reflective synthetic strip. Avoid the weight of wire.
>
> *Tail:* White nylon or Z-lon
>
> *Thorax:* Brown turkey feather barb
>
> *Float Ball:* White Ethafoam or similar enclosed in fine, white nylon mesh, a lady's nylon stocking. The ball is mounted first over the hook shank and eye. Size the ball to float the pattern.

Taff's Cased Caddis (Taff Price)

Taff's Cased Caddis, a variant of an Oliver Edwards tie, uses a trimmed palmer case, burnt acrylic head and body and partridge barb legs. The pattern may be weighted or a brass bead may be slipped on the tippet for weight. Tie the legs slightly down the hook bend with dubbing to imitate the thickened forelegs; the extended legs merge and mask the hook. The case should use hackle that contains webbing for absorbency and sink. The pattern imitates those cased caddis that are torn from rocks and sent adrift.

> *Hook:* Orvis 4641, Tiemco 101 and 947 BL, size 18
>
> *Thread:* Black or gray

Tail: None

Case: Trimmed palmered hackle. Mix hackles—cree, grizzly, and badger—produce a variegated case.

Body: Short length of pale yellow or orange acrylic or nylon yarn burnt at the end to imitate the head capsule

Legs: Several mottled partridge hackles tied slightly down the hook bend

Timsbury Dun (David Hardoon)

This realistic burnt-wing dun has a quill body and coq de Leon tail. Some skill is required in construction, but the result is an exceptionally effective pattern.

Hook: Mustad 94840, 94845, AC 80000 BR; Tiemco 101, Orvis 4641, sizes 18–20.

Thread: 6/0 or 8/0 dun

Tail: Coq de Leon barbs

Body: Quill body

Wings: Burnt, dun hen body wings

Hackle: Medium dun hackle

Timsbury Emerger (David Hardoon)

The Timsbury water of the Test runs flat and slow. The river sometimes requires small, effective patterns for the trout and grayling. David Hardoon of Hong Kong fishes the Timsbury section and has developed several simple, effective patterns for selective trout. The Timsbury Emerger incorporates a

The Timsbury Dun (tied by Hardoon)

realistic quill body and crinkled Crystal Hair, Antron, Sparkle Yarn, or Z-lon strands for the shuck. The pattern imitates a variety of small quill insects such as the Iron Blue Quill. The tiny duns are difficult to detect on the water and often drift unnoticed by the angler, just another phantom hatch.

Hook: Mustad 94840, 94845, AC 80000 BR; Tiemco 900 BL or 101; Daiichi 1180 and 1190; sizes 18–20.

Thread: Dun, 8/0

Shuck: Crinkled Crystal Hair or Z-lon fibers, shank length

Body: Stripped peacock herl

Wings: None

Hackle: Medium dun hackle

The Tricolore

According to Jean-Paul Pequegnot, "Around 1910 a former tax collector of Guingamp created a very full fly of three different colored hackles: badger at head, reddish brown in middle, light ash gray at rear. These were wound, one after the other, along almost all of the hook shank. It was almost the reappearance, in a more elaborate form, of the old Chenille of Charles de Massas. But, giving in to the taste of modern anglers, it had a little body in black silk, without hackle at that point, and a reddish brown tail.

"Andre Ragot recognized the advantages of this fly which were, to be sure, a good float and visibility superior to that of the classic flies. He gave the fly its present name and added two more variants to make up the following trio."

Badger head hackle
Black head hackle
Yellow head hackle

Resembling the French flag transformed into a fly pattern, the tricolore is universally recognized. This "trivisible" has various color combinations. French patterns usually have the palest hackle at the rear. American tyers often place the palest hackle at the head for visibility. The most common combination, perhaps, is badger or black, red or ginger, and dun, in mounting order. Pequegnot further comments on the tricolore's companion on the other bank, Edward Hewitt's Bivisible. "The two flies were created in the same period. When a good idea is in the air, it flies over all the continents."

TYING THE TRICOLORE

The key to tying the tricolore is the selection and mounting of hackles. Each hackle should have barbs slightly longer than the hook gap. The hackle barbs should not vary much in length for the wraps required. Caress the barbs of the preceding wrap back to avoid trapping them. Do not allow the palmering wraps to trap barbs already wound in.

The Tular

The Tular

Beyond the Slovenian border flows the Croatian Kupica—a small, clear, and nervous stream. Mladen Markas Goranin, artist and writer, copies in feather and fur as well as in paint, the various caddis that dance above its riffles. One pattern, Merkas's high-floating MMG Tular, is simplicity personified.

Hook: Mustad 94840, AC80000; Tiemco TMC101; Daiichi 1180, size 18–26.

Thread: Dun, 8/0. (Note following comment.)

Body: Badger palmer

Overwing: CDC feather

Antennae: Pheasant-tail barbs, optional

First, tie in, at the tail position, the tip of a single CDC feather. Gather and secure most of the trailing barbs with the tip. Then, palmer the pattern with a dry hackle. Next, the CDC feather *loosely* loops over the palmered body to form the overwing. Secure the stem at the head and trim excess. Two pheasant-tail barbs may be added for antennae.

If a dark-centered hackle, such as badger, is palmered, then the dark center of the feather will create a distinct body. The reversed and splayed barbs of the overwing suggest, perhaps, the distinct venation of a caddis wing. The term *Trichoptera*, the scientific order of the caddis, means "hair wing"; thus it is only appropriate that the fuzzy CDC feather forms the wing. The Tular, or "caddis," floats well, even when the underbarbs are trimmed for a low float. If tied small enough, the Tular makes an effective midge pattern. By threading the shank and spacing the wrapped palmer, various underbody colors appear.

The Unec Midge

The Unec Midge, named after the enchanting and enigmatic Slovene chalk stream, is simple and productive. For sizes 22 and smaller, pale yellow tying thread forms the body; for sizes 20 and larger, a stripped peacock-herl. Wind the body before mounting the overwing. Mount the overwing, a CDC barb bundle, with the feather base to the rear and the tips extending beyond the hook eye. Divide and figure-eight the extended front CDC barbs to form the lateral, hackle legs that support the pattern. Whip-finish the pattern. Trim the splayed legs. A pale yellow marker may be added on top of the "hackle legs" for visibility. Trim the rear of the overwing to extend slightly beyond the hook bend. *In the smaller sizes, the Unec Midge is an excellent microcaddis imitation.*

Hook: Orvis 4641, Tiemco 101, Daiichi 1180 and 1190; Partridge L3A; sizes 18–24

Thread: Gray 6/0 or 8/0.

Body: Pale, yellow tying thread or stripped peacock herl

Overwing: Stripped and bundled CDC barbs

Hackle: Splayed CDC barbs

The Voljc Sedge (Dr. Bozidar Voljc)

Hook: Mustad 94840, 94845, AC 80000 BR; Tiemco 101; Daiichi 1180 or 1100; sizes 18–20

Thread: Danville black or gray, 6/0

Tail: None

Ribbing: None

Body: Palmered ginger, grizzly, dun, or badger

Wings: The Voljc wing, a prepared contour feather glued to nonelastic nylon and trimmed to shape. Consult description of Voljc wing preparation in the text.

Fore-Hackle: Same as palmer hackle

Antennae: Optional, coq de Leon or pheasant tail barbs

The Voljc Sedge, size 18 hook

After a decade of sedge study in Slovenian streams, Dr. Bozidar Voljc developed the Slovenica Series, a society of sedges with a durable overwing. Although simple patterns to tie, the wings require time and care. The pattern consists of a palmered hackle, an overwing and a fore-hackle.

TYING THE VOLJC SEDGE

1. Wind thread from wing base to hook bend
2. Mount dry hackle, concave side toward eye, and palmer to approximately 3 millimeters behind hook eye. The barb length should slightly exceed the hook gap.
3. Rough cut the wing from nylon sheeting. Fold the wing along the stem and trim to length and shape. If the wing is held between the thumb and forefinger, the curve of the thumb traces the trailing curve of the wing.
4. Apply a glue smear to the top of the palmered hackle barbs. On small patterns, Dave's Flexament works well.
5. Measure the wing length, then trim excess. Mount the wing over the shank with several thread wraps. The barbs, glued to the roof of the overwing, trap air and lock the overwing in position.
6. Mount and wrap the fore-hackle, concave side toward the eye. If desired, add antennae.

A CDC palmer and fore-hackle creates an effective mutation of the traditional Voljc sedge.

TYING THE EMERGING SEDGE

1. Mount the thread and fashion a spinning loop at least seven times longer than the hook shank. The mock-palmer creates the palmer hackle as well as the forward faux-hackle.
2. Mount stripped CDC barbs in the dubbing loop. Continue to strip and mount CDC barbs until approximately six times shank length is mounted. For long barbs, mount the spinning loop at the base of the barbs. For a sparse palmer and fore-hackle, mount fewer barbs and trim the barb base that extends beyond the spinning loop.
3. Spin the loop to lock and to create a dense, flared palmer hackle. While stroking the barbs to the rear (avoid overlapping), spiral the palmer forward three-quarters along the shank toward the eye. For spring creek angling, each palmer wrap may be slightly spaced—approximately the space of a double wrap of the CDC spinning loop—so that the barbs extend freely for flotation.
4. While retaining the twist in the CDC mock-palmer, cross the working thread over the palmer and mount a trimmed Voljc wing. After securing the wing with the working thread, wrap the remainder of the spun CDC palmer as a dry fore-hackle.
5. The working thread then returns to tie off the hackle and complete the head. For realism, antennae—two coq de Leon or pheasant-tail barbs curled with the thumbnail—may be added to complete the pattern.

*T*he *Tackle*

The Fly Rod

In *In the Ring of the Rise*, Vincent Marinaro wrote, "I have designed all my trout rods to carry only one weight of line, a 5 weight. A 6-weight system would probably work just as well on the theory that these two weights are the most efficient of all sizes: they will return greater dividends to the caster in terms of delicacy of delivery, wind-bucking qualities, length of cast, and the use of lighter rods. All my trout rods from six to nine feet handle only one reel and line size. It has been an entirely satisfactory system."

Improved technology now makes a 3-weight rod comparable to Marinaro's 1976 5-weight cane. Light lines make light casts. That is why we use light-line rods for micropatterns. Some slow waters are terrifyingly smooth— tippets land like cables and trout explode like fragments. Complex micro-currents tug tippet and fly in a fantastic *danse macabre*. I want the supplest and softest line possible, a line that swims with the currents. Although drifts may not be long on such waters, they should be delicate and natural.

Light rods now range from 1 and 2 (the ultra-lights), to 3 (the extra-light) and 4 and 5 (the lights). Today, rod sales indicate that the standard, popular light rod is the 3-weight. According to Don Green of Sage, the 3-weight rod is perhaps the lightest weight with adequate efficiency for wind and distance. There are some superb light-line rods available today. Certainly 1- and 2-weights, the ultra-lights, cast well and capture powerful fish. But for some anglers, the 1-weight rods may not generate sufficient line speed for efficient distance. Expansive Western spring creeks and their frequent deleterious winds (not to mention their powerful fish) may require heavier line weights, such as the 4 or the 5.

The stiff rod is used not only for distance, but more importantly for controlling trout better. A light, stiff rod allows the angler to feel and control fish, while a "soft" tip grants a reprieve to strained tippets. A tip is made "soft" in two ways: by flex and by mass. Reduced mass in the rod tip allows the tip to respond quickly, requiring only minor energy for acceleration. A low-mass tip may be exceptionally stiff, allowing the angler control over powerful fish. Thus a narrow and stiff tip permits speed during the cast and control during the battle.

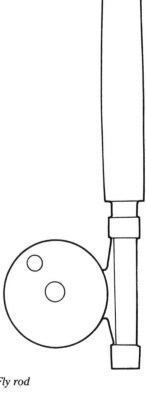

Fly rod

On the other hand, a rod tip made "soft" by flex may not control trout. Such a rod tip allows the trout to work its will. A fast plunge into weeds would be difficult to control. Of course, the tippet strength has importance here also. The trout can pull no harder than the tippet allows before breaking. But sudden action, such as strikes and surges, are best controlled with a stiff rod and low-mass tip. Such rods control powerful fish yet yield for heavy takes and tugs. Perhaps the perfect rod has a progressive taper that slowly stiffens into strength. A rod should not bottom out; an angler should not run out of rod when landing large trout. A rod should have a high "breaking point" (the lowest point of notable rod flex), about two feet above the handle. These progressive rod tapers and stiffer blanks shift the action toward the tip; the flex should not pass into the lower butt or handle. This increases tip speed and generates tight line loops. Tight loops push less air.

The modern ultra-light rod delivers more line speed than the 5- or 6-weight rods of the past. Line speed translates into greater distance, more wind penetration, and tighter trajectory. Line speed is achieved by stiff, light, high-modulus blanks with slender diameters. Light, stiff rods "rifle" long line. Other elements affect rod stiffness: the aerodynamic drag of rod guides, the ferrule design and the directionality of fiber wrap. Lower, reserve butt strength pushes a long line when required and controls heavy fish. Also, fibers wrapped laterally or helically (interwoven spirals) along the blank provide hoop strength. Hoop strength, the resistance offered by a tube to crushing, prevents rods from collapsing at some point along the compression side during the extreme strain of casting. Each angler will accommodate the strengths and weaknesses of individual rods, but I have come to believe that most micropattern anglers favor a stiff rod with a low-mass tip.

The Reel

The special requirements of micropattern fishing make unusual demands on a reel. Not all reels work optimally for small patterns and surely a reel is more than merely a storage container for line. Here are some factors that are important for small-pattern angling.

A smooth reel with adjustable drag may be the most important tool for landing large fish on small hooks. An adjustable drag prevents backlash while allowing regulated resistance. To protect thin tippets, select a large diameter reel with an adjustable, smooth drag. Also, charge the reel with maximum backing to create a sizable diameter core that freely feeds line during the strike. For micropattern fishing, beware of wide reels with modest diameters. Such reels promote small central cores and rough drags.

When line is pulled out, a coarse click drag must first overcome the initial resistance or friction of the pawl. A click drag reel may create a series of grating tugs on the outgoing line. It also may require an initial burst to "break" the pawl loose. *This initial resistance can, at times, snap a fine tippet.* Some reels, such as Loop reel's conical suspension roller system, work on a pressure system that feeds line out *without* the initial required tug. First designed in 1986 by Kurt Danielsson of Sweden, the Loop reel is rather unorthodox. The smaller Loop reels, models 1 and 1.5, have *some* features appropriate for

The loop reel

The Orvis bar-stock CFO reel

small-fly angling: a low starting resistance and a large spool diameter for swift line recovery. Other reels may prove as efficient, even those with a click drag. Clickless reels, without the tug of the pawl, require little or no inertia to overcome static line. To encourage uniform rotation, spools should be counter-balanced for smooth spin.

Some wide-sided reels with arbors or spindles running on roller bearings are remarkably smooth—line flows with a constant caress, protecting tender tippets. Furthermore, a wide-sided reel produces less drag when line is pulled out and allows rapid retrieves for an advancing trout. Such reels have a quick pickup and negligible increase of drag during unspooling. As line escapes with a running fish, a narrow arbor or spindle significantly increases drag. Narrow, wide diameter reels allow line to escape quickly without a significant increase in breaking drag. Wide spindles also increase the retrieve ratio. To test spindle drag, slowly strip out about fifty feet of line while noting the increase in drag. Drag profoundly increases with line length. No wonder, then, that power trout snap tippets.

If a click reel is used, it may be best to minimize the drag, allowing only enough resistance to prevent over-spin when the line is swiftly stripped from the reel. *To decrease drag when a trout runs, drop the rod tip to allow a smooth release of line from the reel.* The click is to prevent overrun, not to produce drag. An exposed rim or flange permits palming to increase drag while fighting a fish. Now available with disk drag, the Orvis CFO, a smooth click reel, is a standard for micropattern angling.

All line and leader connections should be smooth to prevent guide grabbing while traveling. Fewer knots also decrease the possibility of snagging during casts or shoots.

Reel Drag

More force is required to pull line from a narrow spindle than from a wide spindle. With fly line fully spooled, a typical 3- to 5-weight fly reel will have a 3.5-centimeter radius of line. The formula to compute the resistance ratio between a full reel (3.5 centimeters at Radius B) and a nearly empty reel (.5 centimeters at Radius A) is:

$$\text{Force A} = \frac{\text{Force B} \times \text{Radius B}}{\text{Radius A}}$$

or

$$\text{Force A} = \text{Force B} \times \frac{3.5 \text{ cm}}{.5 \text{ cm}} = \text{Force B} \times 7$$

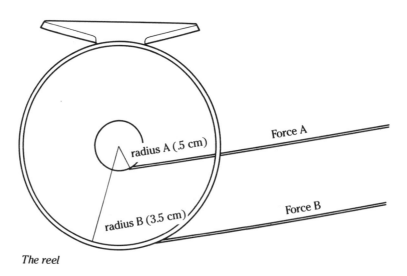

The reel

For example, if Force B at full reel is 100 grams, then Force A at the arbor will be 700 grams. Consequently, the force required to drag out line at the arbor, the smaller radius (A), is *seven times greater* than that required to drag line at full reel (B). This, of course, assumes that the torque created by drag (any mechanical resistance) is constant for all rotational speeds. It also assumes that there is no rod or water resistance. When we add the further resistance of rod guides, rod angle, and water, tremendous resistance is placed on the hook and tippet. Finally, when a trout circles, pulling line sideways through heavy water, tremendous stress is placed on the hook and tippet. A reel that permits smooth drag and rapid line flow decreases breakage.

The Leader Match

It is remarkable that some knowledgeable and experienced fly fishers ignore leader matching, especially with micropatterns. The traditional problem with a straight tapered leader (with or without a self-tippet) is its lack of rigidity in the butt section. The butt section should be about .018 for 3 to 5-weight lines. The line flex (stiffness) should be matched to the leader flex for a smooth, continuous transfer of energy. It is possible, though, to have the butt section so stiff on light lines that the line tip and butt section slap water. A good section-to-section match allows energy transfer, avoids hinging, and pushes the fly forward without excessive energy. A diameter change in leader or tippet sections of .002 (two-thousands) will have little or no adverse effect. But a diameter differential of .004 between sections will hinge and hinder some energy transfer. It is best to keep sections within .002 of each other.

Poor Example: .006 tied to .0010

Better Example: .006 tied to .008 tied to .0010

Herein lies the problem: the fly fisher must travel from the butt section to the tippet with few knots. Knots are not the angler's friend; they add odd weight, mate with each other, collect debris, and grab rod guides. The best system is a knotless leader with a long, level butt section for turnover and a long tippet section for presentation. The traditional two-knot leader is a compromise. A straight butt section is tied between the line and the leader. This reduces the diameter and, consequently, eliminates some knots in the traditional multi-sectioned leader.

J. C. Mottram gave the definitive description of the perfect leader for shy trout. The leader should "decrease evenly, but slowly, until within a yard of the fly, when suddenly it becomes quite thin and remains so right up to the fly. For very shy fish this cast has points in its favor; it causes the fly always to fall very softly, and, because a good length of it near the fly is of fine gut, it will not, as it falls, disturb the surface of the water near the fish, but it does not lend itself to great accuracy." Today, the long-tapered and long-tippeted leaders, ranging from thirteen to sixteen feet, attempt to accomplish as much. If presentation is the most important element in fly fishing, then leaders that sacrifice straight-line accuracy for an appreciable gain in soft presentation are not only acceptable but essential.

There are other factors that effect leader and tippet. For example, the longer the section, the less stiffness it will have for a given diameter. It is possible to achieve a near 5X performance merely by shortening significantly a 6X tippet. Obviously, this does not decrease the diameter; it only affects the relative rigidity of the section. It is impossible to lengthen a 3X tippet to achieve the presentation and natural drift of a 6X. Nonetheless, a long 5X tippet will duplicate and perhaps even surpass some of the characteristics of a shorter 6X.

Modern nylon is much stronger per diameter than the historic horsehair or gut. The fine diameters make fishing the smaller flies possible. In the late 1970s, monofilament manufacturers offered cofilaments (one nylon type sheathed over another nylon type) and copolymers (nylons chemically bonded to form larger polymers). Depending upon the polymer makeup, nylon does absorb water. All quality tippet materials are now copolymers. What is required in a leader or a tippet is (1) tensile strength, (2) abrasion resistance, (3) minimal water absorption, (4) wet knotstrength, (5) controled stretch, and (6) suppleness. Some of the characteristics are contradictory. For example, the elasticity and suppleness, which prevents the fly from being pushed to the trout, fosters a natural float upon the water.

The X Designation

Due to the uniform material (nylon) used in the manufacture of leaders and tippets, various formulas have evolved. With modern developments, the breaking strength of the X designation has increased. The dimensions, however, have not. At present, the breaking strength of 8X (slightly under 2 pounds) is 1.75 pounds, that of 1X (slightly over 13 pounds), 13.5 pounds. Invariably, tests demonstrate that the breaking strength is slightly less than indicated. Storage, age, and knots all affect the breaking strength. Usually the selectivity of trout determine pattern size and pattern size determines tippet size, or X rating. Therein, of course, lies the challenge: large, muscular trout on tender tippets.

The Rule of Four

According to the rule of four, all the fly fisher does is multiply the X designation by four to determine correct hook *balance*—balance means that the tippet will have the power, the rigidity, to push the pattern out, yet be soft enough for a natural float.

Example: 5X tippet times 4 equals size 20 hook.

It is possible to select a hook size smaller or larger than indicated. A sparsely dressed size 18 or a fully dressed size 22 will match the impedance (the resistance) of a balanced pattern. The smaller the hooks become, the less critical impedance matching becomes: the critical difference between a size 26 and size 28 is negligible.

To determine tippet size, the procedure is reversed; divide the fly size by the tippet size.

Example: Size 20 hook divided by 4 equals a 5X tippet. Therefore, a size 20 hook balances best with a 5X tippet.

The Rule of Eleven

To determine the X designation of a tippet, the fly fisher applies the rule of eleven. Subtract the tippet decimal designation (fractions of an inch) from the number eleven. First, convert the thousands designation to a single number. A six-thousands tippet (.006) becomes 6. To find the X-rating, subtract 6 from 11. The answer, for most practical purposes, is the X designation. In this example, the X designation is 5X.

Example: .005 tippet diameter converts to 5. Eleven minus 5 is 6. The tippet is 6X.

If tippets ever become metric, then a new formula will have to be developed. Remember that these formulas should never be construed as divine decree. As Emerson wrote, "A foolish consistency is the hobgoblin of little minds."

The Line

The American Fishing Tackle Manufacturers Association (AFTMA) established a code for fly lines based upon the first 30 feet of line in grains. The measure unit derives from the average weight of a single grain of wheat reckoned at 7,000 grains per pound. The AFTMA weights for fly lines 1 through 5 have a 20-grain differential with a 12-grain tolerance. Note too that the line ranges fail to overlap. A 90-grain line would be as much a 2- as a 3-weight.

AFTMA FLY LINE CHART

Based on the grain weight of the first 30 feet of fly line, excluding any level tip:

Line	Grain Weight	Range
1	60	54 to 66
2	80	74 to 86
3	100	94 to 106
4	120	114 to 126
5	150	134 to 146

Under the AFTMA system, tolerances are fairly wide. In most cases the balance of line and rod is a matter of preference. The AFTMA rating assumes that the average caster will aerialize approximately 30 feet of line beyond the rod tip. It also assumes that if the rod balances with 30 feet of line, then that balance will persist for customary longer and shorter casts. According to Don Green of Sage Rods, the modern rod is designed to aerialize 35 or 36 feet of line, not just the AFTMA 30 feet.

When casting distances shorter than 30 feet, a heavier line may match rod flex better. When casting beyond 30 feet, a lighter line may match. Although lines vary, there is some truth to the statement that *for every 5 feet of line beyond the taper the line weight increases by one weight.* For example, a 5-weight line (at 4.9 grains per foot) would require about 4 feet to accumulate 20 grains, the AFTMA line range. A 3-weight (at 3.5 grains per foot) would require about 5.5 feet to accumulate 20 grains. As line extends or recovers during casting, it virtually becomes many different lines. A good caster accommodates the various lines within a line.

Suppleness may be the most significant quality when selecting lines for spring-creek angling. The Cortland 444 and Scientific Anglers XPS lines are perhaps the standard choices for slow water and selective trout. Both line models have long front tapers for presentation and long rear tapers for mending. These lines are smooth and supple, presenting the fly with minimal disturbance and maximum freedom. A rapid front taper on DT lines would assure loading the rod at short casting distances. Distance is seldom a factor; suppleness is always a factor. The suppleness, when rifled by a modern fast rod, produces distance with tight loops. Throwing *"deltas,"* those sharp, running wedges at the front of a fast cast, result from flat line trajectory, extreme rod speed, and suppleness of line. A fine-line diameter would also foster penetration and distance when required.

Notice that while fly line weights are scientifically calculated, rod weight is still an art. Furthermore, light-line angling is often done at short, "spring-creek distances." A 15-foot cast with a 3-weight rod would require, according to the AFTMA chart, an 8-weight line. A 15-foot cast with a 4-weight rod would require an 11-weight line. The point is simple; the appropriate but short line may not load the rod. The graphs indicate that for DT or WF lines at 30 feet, performance will differ little. For some lines there will be no difference even at 40 feet, the end of the belly. But longer casts, casts beyond the belly, will reveal differences. A heavy line may collapse the rod, leaving little energy left to throw the line. A short-line rod should have appropriate line weight to load and power the rod. As Ted Leeson noted, "A 5-weight line is only a 5-weight at 30 feet. At shorter distances, it weighs the same as a 3- or 4-weight; at greater distances, the same as a 6- or 7-weight." Quantifying a fly line, i.e., profiling the variance of weight per unit length, can increase our understanding. Some rods tolerate changes in line lengths and weights better than others. Some rods communicate the cast to the caster. Other rods are remarkably silent. Casting a line is one thing; aerializing and mending make different demands upon a rod. Although a rod may not distinguish any difference in loading 30 feet of an 8-weight line or 70 feet of a 3-weight line, casting and aerializing 70 feet of 3-weight line is different.

Furthermore, fly lines vary within the upper or lower range limits established by the AFTMA. The *Cortland 444 Lazer Line 3-Weight* graph profiles both the DT and WF lines. Both are AFTMA 3-weights. The DT, however, enters at 105.63 grains, while the WF enters at 93.26 grains. The average 3-weight is 100 grains, ranging from 94 to 106 grains. As the ranges do not overlap, the light WF is considered a 3-weight. Depending on the rod, casting these two lines may be significantly different. The heavier DT might prove superior for short casts, while the lighter WF, for delicate, longer casts. The behavior of lines, even within the same AFTMA rating, may vary. Most manufacturers recognize that line tapers or profiles should vary with the particular line weight.

Anglers who regularly cast lines shorter than 30 feet may improve rod performance by increasing the line weight. Spring creeks may restrict casts. Casts of 20 feet may not be unusual. Assuming that a 10-foot leader-tippet is used, the fisherman is casting only about 10 feet of line, *less* than one-third the established AFTMA rod rating. The under-loaded rod may fail to turn over the leader. The first eight feet of a fly line, whether a 3-weight or 8-weight, weigh very much the same. Line weights only increase substantially when the heavier belly is included.

The Line Match

Ted Leeson developed an insightful method for *tuning* a rod for maximum efficiency. First, you must determine the *window of optimum casting distances* for a rod. Begin casting, *sans* leader, gradually working line out until you identify the distance at which the rod loads with a smooth, comfortable cast. Note the line length. Continue extending line until the rod overloads, until the casting becomes labored and inefficient. Again note the distance. These minimum and maximum distances define the optimum range of the rod.

Suppose, for example, that you have a 4-weight rod that casts best between 25 and 45 feet with a DT-4-F line. This distance may be translated into an optimum weight range, in this case, 100 to 180 grains. If the typical cast made is about 30 feet, then a DT-6 line will match the principal casting properties at that particular distance. Leeson, of course, does not recommend a line change for every change in distance. However, casting will improve within the established window, and the rod will still comply to the occasional cast outside that range.

The Line Taper

In the 1970s, Vincent Marinaro encouraged the widespread use of the weight-forward line. "I am a firm believer in weight-forward lines, particularly the kind designated as rocket tapers. I do not know why anyone would want to use double tapers and deny himself the blessings of the weight-forward line. The alleged advantages of the double taper are illusory." For Marinaro, a double-taper (DT) line required a bulkier and heavier reel. He rejected the notion that double-tapered lines mend or roll cast more efficiently than weight-forward (WF) lines. When mending long lines, however, a DT may perform better than a WF, especially if the caster attempts to roll the heavy WF belly with the light running line. Yet, what makes a rod delicate and efficient is often more the caster than the casting tools.

For moderate casting distances, the graphs show that the modern, long-belly WF line is remarkably similar to the DT line. Thirty feet of WF roll and mend like 30 feet of DT. In fact, some WF lines have longer, more delicate forward tapers than their DT companions. A rod never *feels* the taper of a line: It *feels* only the distributed line mass.

Six-weight rods may be used, but it does require smooth, controlled casting, especially exhausting all line energy before the line touches the water. Any errors in excess energy may spook fish for yards. A rod works only when given energy. In the complex interplay among caster, rod, and line, a rod can only pass some of its stored energy to the line. Even in a simple overhead cast, the energy transfer is intricate. First, energy is given to the rod to pick up the line. The rod consumes some energy while transferring energy to the line. The heavy line loads the rod, returning energy back to the rod. During this time, the caster has accelerated the loaded rod to the vertical. The rod then stops dead as energy throws line into the backcast. The extending line loads the bending rod. The caster now drifts the rod forward, increasing rod energy. At maximum acceleration, the rod stops, passing energy into the extending, forward cast. Ideally, the line extends straight and smoothly, exhausting all energy prior to touching the water.

The *Fly Line Mass Distribution* graphs (in the appendices) illustrate the mass profile for some standard and popular micropattern fly lines. Each graph marker (a block or a cross) indicates a foot unit of fly line. All the fly lines profiled may be regarded as standard and serviceable. To a practical degree, the mass profile, representative of line diameter, portrays the taper of the particular fly line. Most fluctuations in mass are minor, having little or no effect upon the cast, particularly if the "soft point" is spread throughout several inches. Nevertheless, some nonuniformity in mass-foot units may produce discontinuity in the flexural strength and, consequently, the performance of the fly line. Any point of significant diminished flexural strength may be a serious flaw in a fly line. At that point, a fly line may hinge, failing to pass its energy down the extending line. The flexural strength and uniformity of the line determine line flow. Discontinuities such as hinging destroy the free flow of energy through the line during casting, resulting in some loss of power. When shooting line, the line streams from the rod tip. Each guide buffets the line as the rod relaxes in a series of dampening (or damping) oscillations. Dampening is effected by the degree of deflection, the stiffness of the rod tip, the inertia of the rod tip, and the aerodynamic drag. Hinging will impede line flow, retarding travel through the guides.

The Furled Leader

The high, dry mountains of central Spain were dust and rock in August. A bright, heavy heat hung in the windless canyons. When we arrived at the Tajo, a few trout rose to cinnamon caddis, but we knew it would be difficult. I mentioned to Luis Antunez, friend and ardent angler, that I must replace my leader. He promptly handed me one. I told him I didn't use braided leaders on light lines: They often thwacked the water. For these conditions, I wanted the softest presentation possible. He smiled and replied, "You must use it then." He insisted. Luis had given me *a furled thread leader*. To humor him and to wade the cool Tajo, I quickly connected the soft, supple leader to my line. After all, I could always tactfully change it later behind the bend. I waded into the shallows and made a preliminary cast. My line drove out, but the leader drifted down with scarcely a surface smear. Revelations can occur even when casting. With my next cast, I tried to slap the water. The line rifled out, but again the

The furled leader

leader parachuted softly. Needless to say, a few shy trout were taken and released that day under a heavy Spanish sun. But, more important, an angler learned something about furled leaders. Furled leaders land and pick up with little water disturbance and, when properly designed, excel even in wind. *Although the furled leader may not take the place of all leaders in all angling situations, it is uniquely effective for small flies and selective trout in clear, slow water.* Carrying a few furled leaders can sometimes solve the difficulties encountered with exacting waters and timid trout.

The leader is an extension of the fly line. It must transfer the energy of the line to a light tippet and a small fly. The ancients had their leaders built into the line. Originally, leaders were merely a continuation of the "plaited" fly line. In the John Hawkins' edition of *The Complete Angler* (1766), a fly line must be "very strong" and, "for the greater facility of throwing, should be eighteen or twenty [horse] hairs at the top, and so diminishing insensibly [imperceptibly] to the hook." The complete angler made his own furled line-leaders with horse hairs and a hand winder, "an engine lately invented, which is now to be had at almost any fishing shop in London."

"Walton's engine" consisted of "a large horizontal wheel and three small ones, inclosed in a brass box about a quarter of an inch in diameter; the axis of each of the small wheels is continued through the underside of the box, and is formed into a hook . . . and is set in motion by a small winch in the center of the box."

To make the line-leader, an angler connected three strands to the hooks and cranked the handle to spin them. When taken off the winder, the three spun strands furled together to make a tapered line. ". . . take as many hairs as you intend each shall consist of, and, dividing them into three parts, tie each parcel to a bit of fine twine, about six inches long, doubled, and put through the aforesaid hooks; then take a piece of lead, and a conical figure, two inches high, and two in diameter at the base, with the hook at the apex, or point; tie your three parcels of hair into one knot, and to this, by the hook, hang the weight.

"Lastly, take a common bottle-cork, and cut into the sides, at equal distances three grooves; and placing it so as to receive each division of hair, begin to twist: you will find the link begin to twist with great evenness at the lead; as it grows tighter, shift the cork a little upwards; and when the whole is sufficiently twisted, take out the cork, and tie the link into a knot; and so proceed until you have twisted links sufficient for your line, observing to lessen the number of hairs in each link in such proportion as that the line may be taper."

This charming description is a practical introduction to furled leaders. "Walton's engine" produced a three-runner, furled line-leader. A more delicate and supple leader may be made with two furled runners. The furling or spinning can be done with a crank furler or brass leader whirls. The advantage of the crank furler, beyond the fact that it produces more uniform and smoother leaders, is the fact that the number of spins can be computed for a particular leader. If the furler is "geared" at one revolution for ten spins, then computation is simple. This allows replication of leaders.

The advantages of a furled leader outweigh the disadvantages.

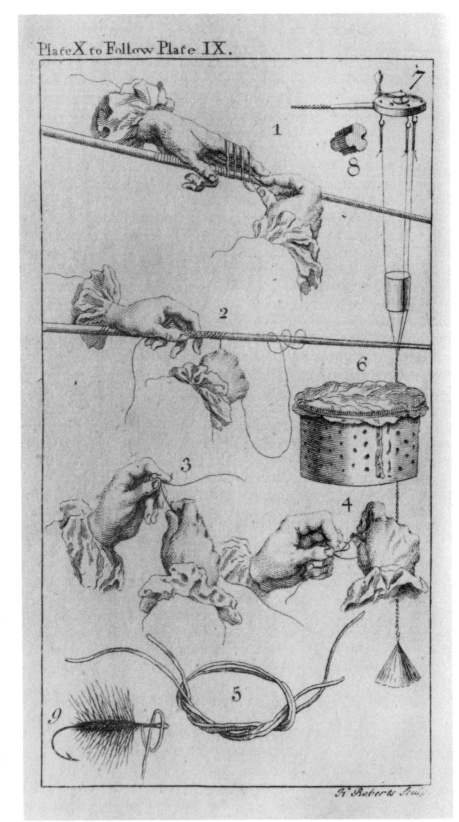

Plate X to Follow Plate IX.

Walton's engine (figure 7) shown furling a line hung on a conical lead weight. The shaped "nut" (figure 8) separates the strands of horse hair during furling. Note also the illustration of the "Water-knot" or Surgeon's Knot (figure 5). "To tye a Waterknot, lay the end of one of your hairs about five inches or less, over that of the other, and through the loop which you would make to tye them in the common way, pass the long and short end of the hairs, which will lie to the right of the loop, twice, and wetting the Knot with your tongue, draw it close, and cut off the spare hair." The Complete Angler, Izaak Walton and Charles Cotton. Copper plate engraving by Ryland. John Hawkins (Second Edition), 1766.

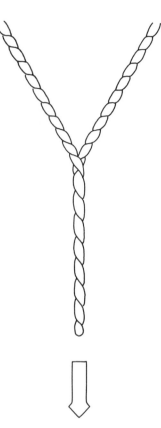

ADVANTAGES OF THE FURLED LEADER

1. *Drag reduction.* The soft and supple leaders swim well on the surface.
2. *Natural turnover.* Even for short distances, the weight of a furled leader allows it to extend effortlessly.
3. *Cracks and crannies.* The cracks and crannies, the twisted interstices created by furling, hold sink and float creams. However, the neutral density of a naked leader produces a slow sink and a natural drift for small nymphs.
4. *Limited shine.* Unlike monofilament leader, a furled leader has no casting flash.
5. *Tight loops.* The extreme suppleness achieves tight casting loops even at close ranges.
6. *Elasticity.* Depending upon material and twist, a furled leader may stretch 15% or more of the total length. This elasticity absorbs the shock of the strike and the struggle.
7. *Variable designs.* Part of the pleasure of furling lies in exploring new leader designs. The dressing and the degree of twist determine whether a leader floats or sinks. Wire or sink paste add accelerated sink. Leaders may be modified in various ways to redefine their character and function.

DISADVANTAGES OF THE FURLED LEADER

1. *Soft and supple.* The remarkable suppleness permits dragless drifts and promotes, if care is not taken, snarls and tangles. The best method for extracting tangles and unraveling twists is to gently pull the end of the fold. Afterward, sharp tugs will straighten and relax the leader.
2. *Dressing.* A furled leader may require dressing or periodic redressing.
3. *Casting.* Furled leaders require smooth, controlled casting.

Drawing the furled leader to unravel

The Long-Leader Heresy

The long leader, 15 feet or more, is often looked upon as the solution for shy, selective trout. Despite the energy required to straighten it, the ability of the wind to return it, and the remarkable macrame possible, many experienced anglers believe that the longer the leader, the more productive the leader. The singular advantage of a long leader is that it minimizes the effects of line slap and line shadow by separating the fly from the line. Traditionally, clear, slow water requires a long leader—a nine-and-a-half-foot leader plus a three-foot tippet or a nine-foot leader lengthened by a four-foot tippet. I prefer, if possible, to shorten my leader and lengthen my tippet. A heavy wind can blow back an extended tippet. But, in terms of trouting, a long tippet is more effective than a long leader. Furled leaders allow casting longer tippets. Short, furled leaders have the mass to straighten out long tippets, tippets over three feet. The longer tippet keeps the leader away from the fish and increases the shock-cord absorption of the take. A five-foot furled leader and a three-foot tippet (total eight feet) allow for accurate, delicate presentation and few casting problems. When trout are tucked into banks or slotted between weed beds, a short, furled leader delivers the pattern with accuracy. A standard nylon leader pushes the fly with mass and stiffness. The furled leader does it with suppleness and mass. A furled leader produces a tighter loop for greater accuracy. In shallow water, the trout window is smaller; therefore greater accuracy is required. Of course, with a smaller window, there is less chance of disturbing the surface during presentation. Line drop should be outside the window. Line slap compels a trout to slam his window shut. Furthermore, smaller patterns, with less weight, wind resistance, and deflection, normally fly more accurately than larger patterns.

I took the first furled leader I made into the backyard for a dry cast. I hoped it would extend with a slow, soft cast. My cast pushed the leader out thirty feet. The line landed, but the leader, paralyzed in midcast, hung four feet off the ground. I did not understand. I laid the rod down and walked to the leader. The leader, tippetless, was held in mid-cast by a single strand of spider's web strung across the yard. Evidently, a tender web caught and held the delicate, drifting leader. Surely this was a soft descent. Like mountain climbing, it's the descent that counts. Leader slap may spook wary trout, and calm, clear water can make a midge land like a muddler. The furled leader makes a difference. A supple thread leader can pitch the pattern softly into the trout's strike zone.

The Theory of Furling

If the ends of a cord are counter-spun and then folded together, it is apparent that the spin directions coincide. With adequate spin, the cord will furl upon itself. A furled leader, with a built-in taper, is made in this manner.

Furled leaders are not only influenced by the material used, such as thread, nylon, or wire, but also by the number of laps and the amount of twist. The direction of twist, either to the left or right, is described as the "Z" or "S" twist. When the thread or cord hangs vertically, the spiral of the twist conforms to the *center* section of either letter. For example, a clockwise spin (when viewing the top of the hanging cord) produces an "S" twist. When using spun strands, furling should continue the original twist direction of the thread.

The degree of furling affects the final product. Even soft threads can become hard and wiry. A tight furl makes the leader harder, stronger, heavier, stiffer, and shorter. A tight leader is less absorbent, more abrasive-resistant and prone to kink. Conversely, a loose furl creates a softer, lighter, more absorbent and more supple leader.

How does the furled leader compare to a braided or woven leader? Furled leaders, like braided leaders, appear in a variety of lengths and densities from floating to fast sinking. They make it possible to match the density of the line to the density of the leader. There is a tendency of a sink line to belly down first, leaving the pattern in a shallower plane. As a consequence, there is a sag in the line with a resulting lack of contact when a trout takes. With a sink leader, the plane is more level. If a sink furled leader is used with an intermediate line, the sink angle straightens as the leader sinks faster than the line. Consequently, takes are telegraphed more quickly to the rod and angler, and it is easier to control the depth at which a pattern swims.

Braided leaders trap water that flushes on the cast. They are generally heavier than furled leaders. Furled leaders lack the air core and have finer diameters. The tip may be a simple thread loop. Consequently, they are excellent for small flies and finer angling. Like a braided leader, a furled leader is usually connected with a loop-to-loop system. Although secure, it requires no knot or glue and is quickly accomplished on the stream. By varying the following elements of furling, an assortment of leaders may be made.

THE ELEMENTS OF FURLING

1. The material (thread, monofilament, wire)
2. The length of laps and runners
3. The number of laps and runners
4. The diameter of the material
5. The stiffness of the material
6. The degree of twist
7. The temporary dressing (flotants, sinks)
8. The permanent dressing (silicones, waterproof seals, stiffeners)
9. The length of dressing or fixative
10. The taper
11. Various combinations of the above

MAKING THE FURLED LEADER

Equipment. With adequate directions, making a furled leader is simple. It requires a double-hook furler (or two leader whirlers), a traveling anchor hook, a furling nut, two small whirlers, and two or more moveable pylons. The double-hook furler has a central crank that rotates a large drive wheel that in turn spins two small hooks that connect to each runner butt. A high "gear" ratio allows the furler to spin each runner quickly. Knowing the crank ratio and the number of turns allows duplication of any given leader. Brass leader whirls, although they may also be used for spinning and forming a leader, do not allow accurate replication. The revolutions of the whirling spinners, which hang from the butt of the runners, cannot be counted. Furled leaders may also be made with mechanical or electric spinners—hooks attached to wire-wrappers, electric Dremels, or variable speed drills. If the duration of spinning is timed, the degree of twist may be duplicated with some accuracy.

The pylons, which form a *V* with the furler hooks and the anchor hook, frame the leader. They establish the length and laps of each section. Pylons may be as simple as two nails in a board. The anchor hook maintains tension on the runners and prevents their coiling together. As the runners furl, they shorten, thereby pulling the weighted anchor hook toward the furlers. A leader will shorten approximately 10% or more of the layout length. A 10-foot leader layout, for example, may create an 8-foot finished leader.

Matarelli brass leader whirls

The double-hook furler has a high-gear ratio that quickly spins each runner.

Leaders may be made from various threads (polyester, Dacron, Kevlar, or nylon) as well as nylon monofilament or tippet material. A three-strand nylon thread (with a 10-pound breaking strength at .25 millimeter diameter) is excellent for many tied leaders. Use the larger spools, those that hold 300 yards or more. Due to doubling and furling, the leader is significantly stronger than a single thread. Although gauged atypically, Climax's Duramax 8X tippet has a breaking strength of 5 pounds, about twice the breaking strength of nylon. Duramax's nylon strands, compressed and entwined in a graphite base,

The weighted, traveling anchor hook maintains tension and separation of the runners during furling. As the runners furl, they shorten, thereby pulling the anchor hook toward the furler head.

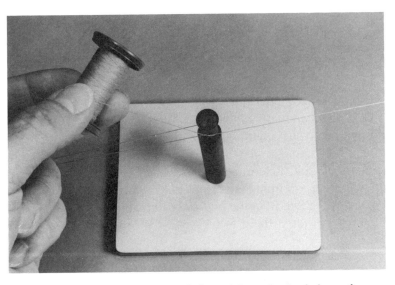

The moveable pylons, along with the furler and the anchor hook, frame the leader, establishing the lengths and laps of each section.

are remarkably supple and abrasion-resistant. The finer Duramax tippet material creates strong, furled leaders with excellent mass and turnover. Dai-Riki's Diver tippet material, a fluorocarbon monofilament, has an approximate specific gravity of 1.75. Standard monofilaments range from 1.06 to 1.14 specific gravity. Once subsurface, Diver descends about one-third faster than standard monofilament. Part of the pleasure of designing furled leaders is exploring the various threads and monofilaments available.

Select the visible colors—cream, yellow, orange, pale blue and rose—for floating leaders. From below, they merge into the light and, from the surface, are easier to trace during the drift. The neutral colors—gray, green,

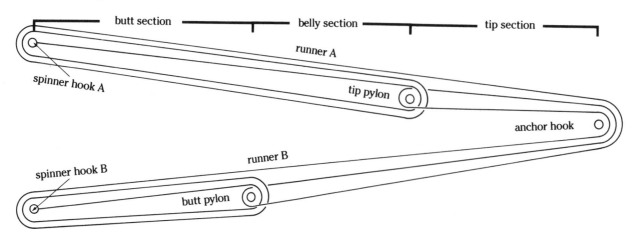

The traditional furled leader pattern

and brown—are reserved for the sink leaders. I often combine colors for codes that indicate various characteristics such as purpose (wet or dry), line weights (light or heavy), or action (supple or stiff).

THE TRADITIONAL FURLED LEADER

As illustrated, the traditional furled leader is a *continuous* strand of thread that forms the runners and laps of the taper. The expanded view illustrates the terminology and layout of a traditional furled leader.

The pylons should be placed in alignment with their respective furler hooks and the Anchor Hook. To form a standard, fine-thread, floating leader, place the *butt pylon* four feet from Furler Hook A (creating the butt section); place the *tip pylon* three feet from the *butt pylon* (creating the mid-section); and place the *anchor hook*, three feet beyond the *tip pylon* (creating the tip section).

THE TRADITIONAL STRINGING PATTERN

In the following photographs, the distances between the furlers (the spinners) and pylons and between the pylons and anchor are greatly contracted to illustrate the stringing pattern. The lengths and laps of each section are variable. The staggered pylons, which may be positioned to fabricate various tapers, determine the taper and the taper lengths. When furled (uniting both runners), the traditional leader has a 10-strand butt (between the spinner hooks and the butt pylon), an 8-strand mid-section (between the butt pylon and the tip pylon) and a 6-strand tip (between the tip pylon and the anchor).

FURLING

Now, spin the furling hooks and compute the revolutions. Remember that the leader will be tighter where it is finer, at the anchor hook. A high spin count

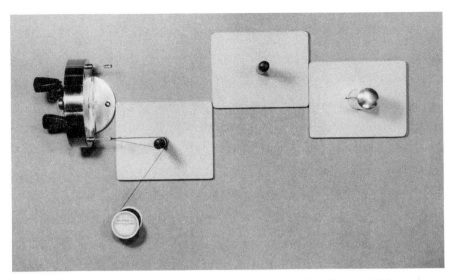

The traditional stringing pattern. Tie the thread to furler hook B as illustrated. Wrap twice around the butt pylon.

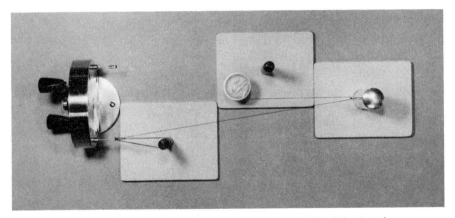

Extend the thread back to furler hook B, then to the anchor hook and the tip pylon.

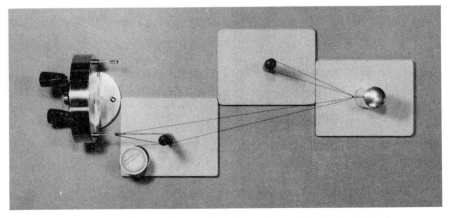

Wrap the thread around the tip pylon, back to the anchor and then to the butt pylon.

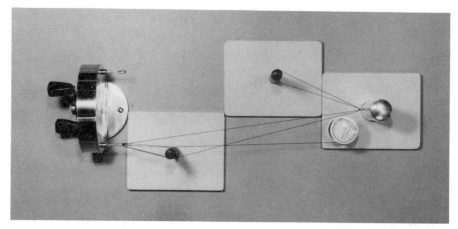

Pass the thread through the loop made by the butt pylon; then extend the thread back to the anchor hook.

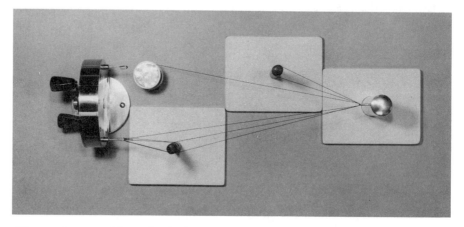

After passing around the anchor hook, the thread travels to furler hook A.

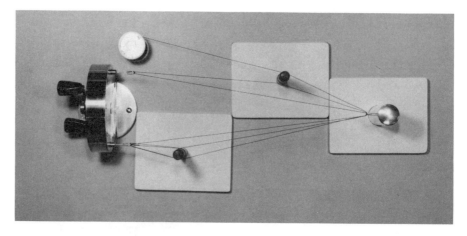

The thread journeys around furler hook A, through the loop made at the tip pylon, then back to furler hook A.

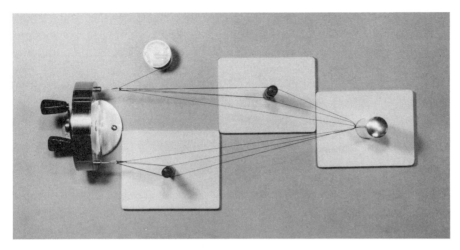

The thread, after looping around furler hook A, laps again to the tip pylon, passing through the loop at the tip pylon and then home to furler B, where it is tied off. Make certain to capture the loops with the thread.

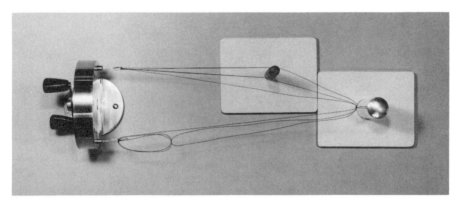

After removing the pylons, the thread strands should loop together at each pylon point as depicted. The distance and thread laps between the furlers and pylons, between the pylons and anchor determine the taper and weight of the particular leader.

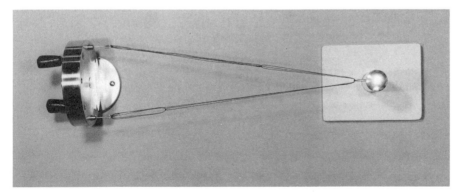

Remove the pylons and the excessive slack in both runners before spinning. When spun, runner A and runner B furl together, creating a single, tapered leader.

creates a stiffer leader. During furling, the anchor hook travels as the leader shortens. Fine threads may require more butt laps, perhaps 2,000 revolutions or more. Depending upon thread diameter and leader length, the number of spins will vary from approximately 1,500 (heavy thread) to 2,500 or more (fine thread). Usually, about 100 or more twists per foot of layout leader will be required. The finished leader may have anywhere from 3 twists to 6 twists per centimeter at the butt and 12 or more twists per centimeter at the tip.

FORMING

After furling, the leader requires forming. Forming creates—by allowing the two, separate runners to coil together—a single, tapered leader. While both runners are still mounted on the furling hooks, hook a leader whirl into the anchor loop of the leader. With the whirl attached, remove the leader from the anchor hook. Hold the end of the leader so that it does not furl together at this time. Although the whirl holds the leader tip, place a furling nut between the two runners about ten inches from the hanging whirl. Keeping the nut between the runners, allow the whirl to spin and furl both runners into a single cord. As the spinner twirls, the double runners furl together, forming the leader.

    The furling nut creates a smooth, even furl throughout the leader. As the forming continues, slowly move the nut, about ten inches at a time, farther down the leader toward the butt. The whirl spins as the runners furl together. In this manner, the complete leader is formed and aligned.

    Furling will be tighter or denser at the thinner tip. To avoid a densely furled tip and a slack butt section, furl and form the leader in two steps. First, furl the *complete* leader to acquire the requisite spin for the tip and mid-sections. Then, form the forward half of the leader, keeping both butt runners separate and connected to the furler hooks. After forming the forward half, secure the previously formed portion to prevent twisting. Then, continue to furl the butt section with added revolutions of the furling hooks. Finally, form the butt section with the furling nut and allow the complete leader to relax and straighten. For example, a complete fine-thread leader may be furled 1500 times to produce a densely spun tip and mid-section. After forming the tip and mid-sections, another 500 spins may be added to the butt section. This is the best method for producing smooth, densely furled leaders. In this manner, the degree of furling can be regulated for each leader section.

    After forming the leader, remove the furling nut and disconnect the two runners from both furling hooks. While maintaining the twist in the leader, tie the two runners together with a single or double overhand knot. Trim the excess. Jacket the knot with waterproof cyanoacrylate glue. Remove the whirl and gently allow the leader to "unravel" and relax. I use lightweight whirls on each end to calm and straighten the leader. Finally, label and package the completed leader.

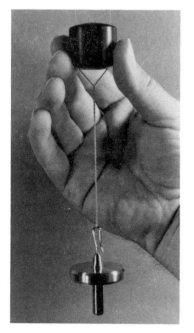

Forming the leader: As both runners spin together, the furling nut slowly travels toward the butt, creating a dense, evenly spun or furled leader.

FURLING HINTS

1. Keep the runners approximately equal in the number of laps. A heavy runner will dominate a fine runner when furling. To produce a symmetrical furl, the laps should be alternated and staggered on the runners.

2. Furl the same direction as the thread twist.

3. Finer threads may require more laps.

4. Remove the slack from the runners before spinning. This diminishes the loops and slack in the completed leader. This is especially critical when furling monofilament. Maintain equal and mild tension on both runners when forming and furling. During furling, slack runners may catch and twist together. Don't allow the runners to twist together until they are completely spun. Excessively taut runners, however, may resist spinning.

5. Experiment with a monofilament butt and a polyester tip. Try also leaders made with 5X and 6X tippet materials and with core threads heavier or lighter than the lap threads. Experiment with weight forward and double tapered leaders as well as progressive leader tapers. Vary the thread weights. Also vary the length ratios in the butt, middle, and tip sections: light leader—40% butt, 30% middle, 30% tip; heavy leader—50% butt, 30% middle, and 20% tip.

6. Use a weighted spinner and furling nut to achieve a smooth, uniform furl.

7. After the leader is furled and the butt knotted, use two light spinners, one at each end, to straighten and relax the leader.

8. It may be necessary, during forming, to tighten a strand. With the thumbnail and forefinger, milk any loose strands down to the butt. Retie the butt knot to eliminate the slack in the runners. Modest practice should eliminates all loose strands.

9. A silver ring or loop on the leader accepts a tippet. Dismount one runner from its furler hook and slip the silver ring over the runner. I use fine wire to thread the runner through the silver loop. Next, slide the ring down to the anchor hook. Make certain that the ring is located at the anchor hook and at the extreme end of the leader before spinning the runners. After the runners are spun and before they are furled together, hang a whirl on the ring so that the silver ring remains at the extreme end of the leader. The breaking strength of the silver ring is approximately ten pounds.

To make a leader loop, merely open the tip with a pin and saturate the loop with waterproof glue. This forms an open, rigid loop for tippets. A tippet may be built into the leader itself. After forming the taper and before furling, tie in a tippet about 10 or more inches from the anchor hook. The excess tippet should extend beyond the anchor hook. Lock the tippet under the anchor hook and curl the excess near the leader tip. When the leader is furled, the tippet will extend from the extreme end of the leader.

10. To prevent thread twist during leader layout, remove the thread from the spool in the manner in which it is wound. Do not pull the thread over the end of the spool. Remember that the thread should spin the same direction as the twist in the thread.

11. The finished runners will, due to spinning, be shorter than the layout runners. Allow for approximately 1/10 total length reduction or more.

12. Apply liquid or paste flotants to floating leaders and paste sinks to sink leaders. To stiffen and waterproof a leader, use a silicone seal. Hard waxes may also be used to waterproof a leader.

13. A convenient code for a leader is the number of feet per ply section. For example, a traditional furled leader (a 6-8-10 ply leader), might be designated as a *235*, that is, 2 feet of 6 ply, 3 feet of 8 ply and 5 feet of 10 ply. The sum of the notation equals the total leader length.

The Knotted, Furled Leader

Perhaps the simplest introduction to the furled leaders is the knotted method. There are two significant advantages to the knotted leader: exceptional control of the taper and a single end-loop for lightness. Knotted leaders easily produce weight forward, double taper, and ultra-light leaders. Single overhand knots keep the strands in position during furling. The knots, waterproofed with cyanoacrylate glue, do not hold the leader together: Furling locks the knots and the strands within the runners. The knots receive negligible strain during angling.

LEADER LAYOUT

Mount the core thread (the thread foundation upon which the leader hangs) on furler hook A with a knot, and extend the thread and loop over the anchor hook and back to furler hook B. Then extend the thread 3/4 down runner B. Tie off with a single overhand knot. Trim the excess thread while leaving a two-inch tag to mark the location of the knot. This forms the longest tapered section. Next, after mounting the thread to hook A, lap one-half the distance on runner A. Again, leave a two-inch thread tag. By alternating the laps on the runners, develop the desired taper.

When the taper is formed, place a drop of penetrating, waterproof cyanoacrylate gel on each knot. Let dry. Then, while taking care not to cut the standing threads, trim the knot as close as possible. *The knot does not hold the leader together*; it merely holds the laps in place while the leader is furled. Only minor pressure will be placed on the knots locked within the runners. After removing the pylons and tightening both runners, spin the furler hooks.

Be careful that any knots do not capture excessive twists behind them. Milk the twist over the knots. Use the thumbnail to milk or caress any excess slack to the butt. Merely retie the butt knot to eliminate the slack, and cut off the excess.

With furling nut and hanging whirls, form the knotted leader in the same manner as the traditional furled leader. Brief practice and moderate care eliminate most problems.

Leader Layouts. The following leader layouts offer the micropattern angler a variety of specific leader designs. As in all furled leaders, the number of laps may be varied to produce heavier tips or butts or mid-sections. Mid-laps can create double-tapered or weight-forward leaders. Vary the designs to meet your particular requirements.

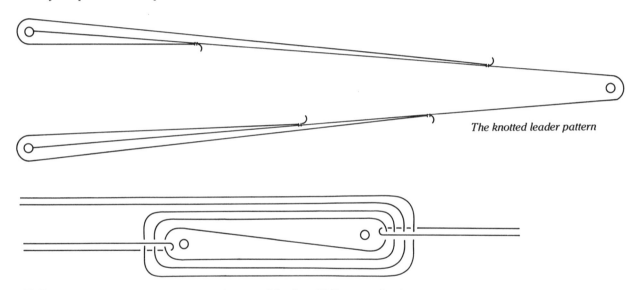

The knotted leader pattern

Midlaps create weight-forward and double-tapered leaders. Midlaps may be strung, as illustrated, with any number of laps and lengths to achieve a variety of weighted sections.

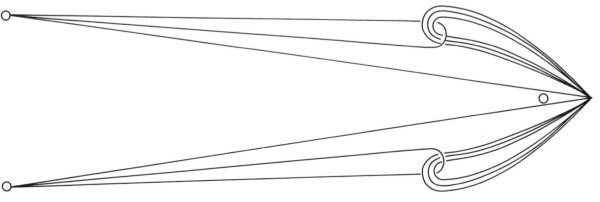

The weight-forward leader pattern

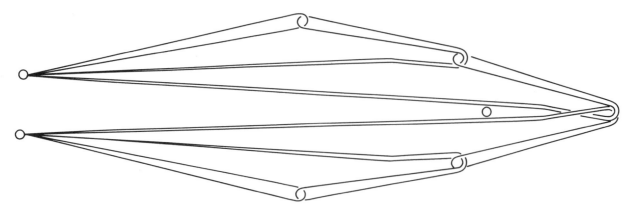

The eight-twelve leader pattern

The Knots

A tapered fly line, a matched leader, a fine tippet, and a small hook—all are connected with knots, knots that increase drag, knots that grab guides, knots that mate. And sometimes, knots that break.

The accepted breaking strength of any given knot is often misleading. Breaking strength may be reckoned by wet or dry tests and by slow or fast tests. All will yield different results. Breaking strength is also determined by how the knot is tied. A reliable knot tied abruptly and sharply becomes unreliable. In fact, the way a knot is tied may be just as relevant, at times, as what knot is tied. This is especially true for the fine and tender tippets required for micropatterns. Only slight differences in knot formation may produce significant differences in breaking strength. A well-formed knot—one that is smoothly and methodically tied—is an investment in angling.

Proper knots assist the layout of leader and tippet with minimal casting energy. There should be limited hinging or flexure differential between the sections. All connections should "carry the arc" when hooped. This permits progressive energy transfer from section to section to produce extension and layout of the thrown leader.

When hooped, an efficient knot "Carries the Arc."

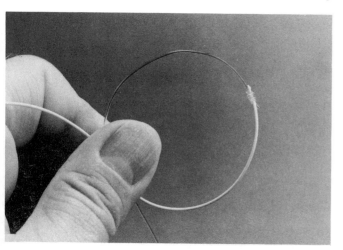

A leader-line connection that "carries the arc"

ASPECTS OF THE KNOT

1. Each knot should be perfectly formed and correctly balanced. An excessively large knot may hinge and catch. Small knots risk breakage. The diameter of the material and number of wraps determine the bulk and weight of a knot.
2. Take extra care when using artificial aids; they can produce deceptive confidence. When using a knot tool, make certain that it produces a superior knot. Sharp edges and abrupt forming against the tool may produce a frayed or inferior knot.

3. Make certain that the particular knot matches the material and the purpose.

4. Gently form and close a knot. Abrupt closure can cause friction and skewed or strangled wraps.

5. Lubricate the knot with water prior to closure.

6. Never tolerate uncertainty. If not pleased with the formation of a knot, retie it.

7. Use clippers to trim the excess tags. Store the trimmed tags in the vest, not in nature. Long tags may catch guides, mate together, or capture weed pennants. Under pressure, some knots with short tags may release. For safety, tags should extend about 1 or 2 millimeters.

8. Retie knots on long-standing tackle.

9. Practice knot tying. Tie knots smoothly, deliberately, and firmly.

10. Some argue that after landing a heavy fish, knots should be retied. Others claim that such knots are firmed and tested, far less likely to break than a fresh knot.

11. Avoid burning or curling a tippet with excessive friction and abrasion.

12. Avoid prolonged, direct sunlight on reserve tippets and leaders. Keep heat and sunlight off tippet and leader material whenever possible. Store all leaders and tippets in a cool, dark and dry place. Some manufacturers recommend that after one year all fine tippets and leaders should be replaced.

Fine tippets are susceptible to strangulation. For example, a single Overhand Knot, such as a "wind knot," may significantly weaken a tippet. The same is true for any knot design that applies pressure to a single strand. When tying fine tippets, remember that, although they are easily seated, they may require extra wraps or loops for security. For the standard tippet-to-fly knot, I use the Spinning Knot illustrated in *Fly Tying Methods*. To increase the knot strength, the tippet loops twice through the hook eye before forming the knot. *The extra loop through the eye significantly expands the contact point and, consequently, increases the knot strength.*

THE JAM-HITCH TO LOOP (LEADER KNOT)

The Jam-Hitch, a simple Spanish knot, connects furled leaders to line loops. The Overhand End Knot on the furled leader should be coated with a waterproof glue to maintain formation. Although the Stopper Knot lodges tightly against the loop when pulled taut, leaders are easily changed. The Jam-Hitch resembles a careless connection, but when properly tightened, there is minimal hinging and maximum strength.

FIGURE-EIGHT LEADER KNOT TO LOOP (LEADER KNOT)

The following knot, first illustrated in *Hardy Angler's Guide* (1937), is a secure connection for leaders, especially furled leaders, to line-loops.

Jam-hitch to loop

THE PERFECTION LOOP (LEADER LOOP)

The Perfection Loop is not recommended for fine tippets. Fine tippets may break at this knot. The Perfection Knot, which creates an in-line loop, is excellent for a leader-to-line loop. Make the counterclockwise loops in the following order:

1. Form the *first loop* behind the standing line. Hold the loop between the left thumb and forefinger.
2. Make a *second loop* in front of the standing line.
3. Add a *third loop* between the two previous loops.
4. Pass the *second loop* over the *third loop* and under the *first loop* to form the leader loop.

THE WATER KNOT (LEADER LOOP)

The Water Knot is one of the oldest knots used in angling. Peter Owen, in *The Book of Outdoor Knots*, noted that the Water Knot first appeared in print as early as 1496. The Water Knot, sometimes erroneously called the Surgeon's Knot, is only vaguely similar to the original Surgeon's Knot illustrated in the Owen text. Although more awkward to tie, the original Surgeon's Knot, with extra wraps, is also an effective knot for fine tippets.

An illustration of the Water Knot appeared in Hawkins' edition of Izaak Walton's *The Compleat Angler* (1766) and later in Frederic Halford's *The Dry Fly Man's Handbook* (1913). Halford noted that "it has been adversely criticized by modern authorities" yet he found "no practical disadvantage from its use." In Halford's day, the Water Knot was a *gut knot*. Although neither as aesthetic nor as symmetrical as the Blood Knot, it is strong and simple. When using fine tippet material, five or more wraps may be required. The Doubled Water Knot—especially appropriate for connecting an ultra-fine tippet to a heavier leader—is tied exactly like the standard Water Knot; however, the terminal portion is first doubled, then treated like a single line section.

1. With the ends pointing in opposite directions, overlap the two sections to be joined about four inches.
2. Form a loop in the middle of the doubled sections.
3. Pass *both ends* of the tail section through the loop.
4. Continue to pass both ends of the tail section through the loop *five or more times*. Remember that both sections—the tail and the tag end along the tail—pass through the loop.
5. Moisten the knot and close it by pulling all four strands. Trim the tag ends.

THE PITZENKNOT (FLY KNOT)

Edgar Pitzenbauer of Bavaria created this simple, small, and strong knot.

1. Pass the tippet through the eye and slide the fly about eight inches down the tippet out of the way.

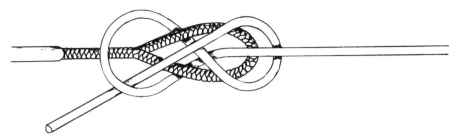

Figure-eight knot to loop

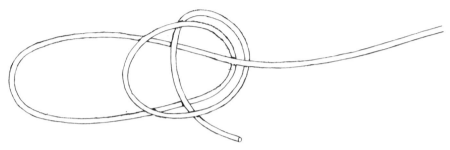

Perfection loop

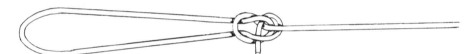

Perfection loop

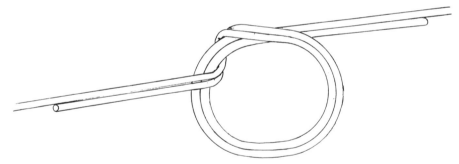

Water knot

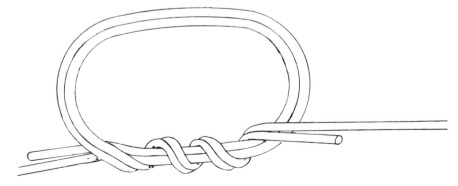

Water knot

Pitzenknot

2. Fold the tippet back and allow the fly to dangle. This keeps the fly away from your hands while tying the knot.

3. Wrap the tippet *three times only* back toward the fly.

4. Pass the tippet tail through the loop as illustrated.

5. Pull the standing end away from the fly so that the knot slides and snugs against the eye. Then, *pull again until you feel a knot-set, a turnover of the knot against the eye.* If you fail to feel the knot-set, retie the knot. Trim the tag.

THE DOUBLE PITZENKNOT (FLY KNOT)

The Double Pitzenknot, a Clinch Knot, may be improved with three or four wraps, then closed with a lubricant. The disadvantage of the Double Pitzenknot is that the finer and more flexible the tippet material, the more difficult it is to form.

1. Pass tippet through hook eye.

2. Wrap end twice around tippet.

3. Fold tip back and pass twice around eye loop.

4. Pull firmly to close.

THE SHOCK GUM KNOT (LEADER TO SHOCK GUM)

The elasticity of shock gum, or paragum, protects fine tippets from the strike shock and struggle of large trout. Furthermore, with elasticity to 100%, it maintains hook tension during the struggle. Spooled shock gum as well as prepared looped sections are available. For far and fine angling, use the smaller diameter shock gum, either the 11 pound (.55 mm diameter) or the 10 pound (.45 mm diameter). When attaching shock gum to a leader, avoid bulky knots. Matt leaders grip shock gum better than slick leaders. If the leader is slick, lightly roughen the connecting end with a fine-grit sandpaper, 400 or 600 fine grit. Using a traditional 9½-foot straight-taper leader, cut off a two-foot butt section, and insert an 8- to 10-inch shock gum section. Due to the thick diameter of the shock gum, use a *double-wrap* Surgeon's Knot to secure it. Make certain that the knot is carefully formed and fully closed. A drop of waterproof Superglue may be added to each knot. Finally, attach a tippet to create a standard 12-foot leader.

John Goddard of England uses the following formula to create light-line leaders with shock gum:

1. A 3-foot leader butt section (20-pound test)

2. A 10-inch mid-section of shock gum

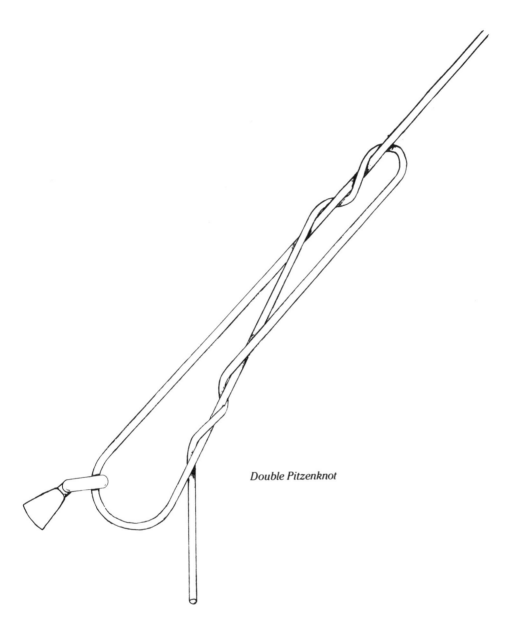

Double Pitzenknot

3. A 12-inch leader section (10-pound test)

4. A 12-inch leader section (6-pound test)

5. A 2-foot or longer tippet section

Cut the shock gum three or more inches longer than necessary; when tightening, the gum will slip until it finally catches. Goddard uses the four-wrap Blood Knot to connect the leader to the gum.

THE IMPROVED BLOOD KNOT (LEADER AND TIPPET KNOT)

Doubling the finer tippet increases the strength and reduces the diameter differential between the connected sections, resulting in better turnover. The Improved Blood Knot is tied in the same manner as the standard Blood Knot.

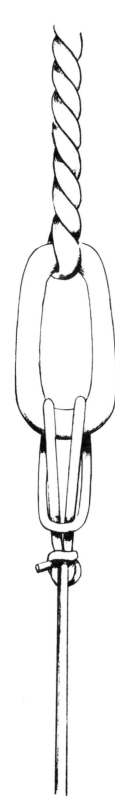

Tippet to ring

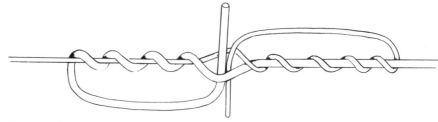

Four-wrap Shock-Gum Blood Knot

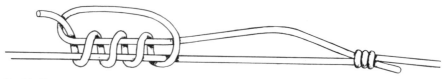

Double Uni-knot Shock-Gum connection

The doubled end merely acts as a single strand. When connecting two sections of differing diameter use twice the turns (or more) on the finer section. Make certain that the wraps of both sections tighten smoothly and simultaneously to form a firm knot. Trim the tag ends one or two millimeters. Consult the illustration of the four-wrap shock gum Blood Knot.

THE DOUBLE UNI-KNOT SHOCK GUM CONNECTION (LEADER TO SHOCK GUM)

Mark Sosin and Lefty Kreh, in *Practical Fishing Knots II*, connect the leader to the shock gum with Double Uni-Knots. Again the leader material should be "matted" with fine sandpaper before tying. The number of wraps will determine the bulk. For a small knot, two to four wraps should be appropriate. If only two wraps are used, add a drop of waterproof Superglue to each knot.

Placement of the heavy, supple shock gum section is critical for an effective turnover. If the shock gum appears close to the line tip (such as between the line and the leader), then hinging may occur. If the shock gum section appears too close to the fly, then the heavier gum will slap the water. Generally speaking, the shock gum should be placed about one-fourth to one-third down the leader, depending on the diameter and stiffness of the leader. This position allows a degree of impedance matching, "carrying the arc," to avoid hinge and slap.

TIPPET TO RING (TIPPET TO LEADER)

When connecting a tippet to a ringed leader, make certain that the tippet forms as illustrated. The miniature silver ring adds negligible weight and permits quick tippet replacements. Avoid Perfection Loops on ultra-fine tippets; use other knots, such as the Surgeon's Loop.

THE SURGEON'S LOOP

The extra wraps of the Surgeon's Loop, actually a fetal Water Knot, protect tender tippets. It is a simple and quick loop.

1. Double the tag end and form two loops.
2. Pass the *loop end* through the double loops.
3. Moisten and tighten.

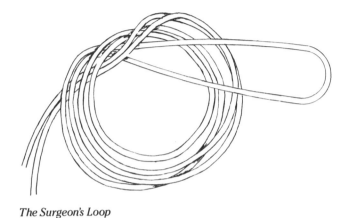

The Surgeon's Loop

THE NOOSE-KNOT

Though the Perfection Knot is not recommended for fine tippet loops, the Noose-Knot, or *der Schaufenknoten*, makes a strong and simple tippet loop. The numerous wraps conserve the strength and distribute the strain placed on a fine tippet.

1. Create a double loop as illustrated. Place your left forefinger in the bend loop while holding the end loop and standing part with your right hand.
2. Crank your left forefinger to produce four or more wraps in the section held between your hands. Then pass the end loop through the bend loop, moisten, and slowly close the knot. Trim excess.

The Micropattern Vest

Stuffed with brave new patterns, tippets, spools (and the thousand other items that fish and flesh are heir to), the fly fishing vest celebrates our sport. It is the badge of the fly fisher. It is also intimate apparel, seldom exposed to casual eyes. In it we hide the things that take trout. Our properly charged vest promises independence and success. Yet, the vest was not always part of fly fishing. It is, in fact, a rather recent invention.

Lee Wulff, credited with the creation of the first fly vest in 1931, observed that the vest did not become immediately popular— anglers rejected the idea of wearing equipment outside their clothing until about 1946. Perhaps World War II, with all the harness of combat, turned anglers toward the vest.

Pass lower loop through top double loop. Close knot.

The Noose-Knot

One vest cannot serve all masters. A boat vest, a bone-flat vest, and a spring creek vest all differ in design and purpose. With the variety of fish and fishing conditions, several vests may no longer be a mere luxury—if we select rods for particular applications, perhaps we should select vests in a simlar fashion. All anglers, and particularly small-pattern anglers, have a "vested" interest in design. Many anglers argue whether or not a vest should have many, smaller pockets or fewer, larger pockets. Experienced anglers often conclude that it is better to seek a particular pattern in a few, large boxes than to pursue a pattern in numerous, smaller boxes. Yet, those same experienced anglers often require specialized pockets for pliers, thermometer, and glasses. Although some select the ultra-light mesh vests, others will bear their fardels under a heavy fabric. The popularity of deep wading (especially in spring creeks, chalk streams, and lakes) and float tubing has increased the popularity of the short vest. Owing to the fecundity of slow, deep waters, the short, deep-wading vest is often preferred for micropattern fishing. But a short vest may be a mixed blessing; it tempts deep water and wet fly boxes. Even short vests do not promise dry fly boxes while float tubing. For deep or difficult wading, the rod-butt loop can serve as a wading staff tie-down.

Although selecting a vest for micropattern fishing is a personal decision, there are basic considerations when choosing any vest. There should be no exposed, or "marrowed," seams. Exposed seams, which avoid labor-intensive workmanship, *may* indicate other cost-cutting measures. All stitch locks should be tight and uniform and should follow the proper lines. Puckering or irregular stitching will probably not affect the durability of a vest, but it may generally indicate sloppy detailing. Bar-tacking should appear at all stress points, including the mount corners of pockets. Although there are other acceptable brands, Talon and YKK zippers are recognized, in the trade, as the best brands. Vest fabrics vary from the very light cotton shirting to Supplex to heavy polyester and cotton blends. Whatever the fabric, it should be strong enough to carry equipment, yet light enough for drape and ventilation. I usually spray a new vest with Scotchguard for water and stain repellency.

Although fabric content may be identical in different vests, there may be a significant difference in water repellency, fabric weight, weave type, and tightness and finish. And there may be a significant difference in design, fit, and cost. When selecting a vest, stuff it with your fly boxes and check the casting fit. A final consideration is how the vest utilizes space. There should be none wasted. Top and bottom of both front panels should have zippered access.

Small-fly fishing, often associated with the heat of high summer, favors the light, ventilated mesh vests. Earlier mesh vests often hung up or tore on brush. But the new generation of mesh vests is remarkably durable. The advantages of the mesh are ventilation, light weight, and compaction for travel. Furthermore, while they are quick drying, they do not absorb or hold water. The resin-treated poly mesh (for body) is a significant improvement over early meshes. Tippet material, which should be replaced each year, should never be exposed to extended sunlight if possible. Keep tippet spools covered.

All vests, whether mesh or fabric, should be comfortable. Cut, especially of the neckline and armholes, is just about as important to fit and casting ease as is size. Keep in mind what you will habitually wear under a vest. Some manufacturers consider the fly vest an over-garment and size it accordingly, making their vests one-half to one full size larger to accommodate under-clothing. To reduce the weight carried on the neck, vest should be cut wide around the collar and broad across the shoulders to distribute weight evenly. Some manufacturers do not consider the knit collars to be load-bearing. They claim that a knit collar, which may be decorative at best, can place pressure on the neck if not cut full enough.

Nearly every vest has an attached or detachable fly holder. A natural wool patch, nonelectrified, should have long, tightly curled hair to secure barbed hooks. Micropatterns seem to burrow into a wool patch. And larger dry flies left on a wool patch usually have deformed hakcles. Some synthetic patches may be washed and may even hold better than inferior wool patches. Small, barbless patterns do not secure in wool patches; all micropatterns, whether barbed or barbless, should be carried in spacious fly boxes. Cramming patterns into compartments deforms delicate wing, hackles, and tails.

There are other sundry details to consider when selecting a vest for micropattern angling. Size and placement of Velcro tabs are important, especially when carrying small fly boxes. For proper closure, both rug and hook Velcro patches should be larger than one square inch. Some manufacturers now "T-mount" their Velcro, placing the strips at right angles; whether the pocket is flat or full the patches catch and close. The open-sided cargo pocket—based on the game pouch of shooting jackets—is good for extra clothing, a rain jacket or, when moving in heavy brush, a trout net; but there are perhaps as many things lost from a cargo pocket as are carried in them. A stitched-face pocket, which stays open when empty, provides easy entry and exit for fly boxes. Soft fabrics such as a lightweight Supplex do not have three-dimensional pockets for easy entry and exit. A stiffer material holds the "architecture" of the pocket for easy entry and exit. The sunglasses pocket should be large, with a secure closure. Some vests have no closure. When you bend over to release a trout you release your glasses and fly boxes as well.

Other considerations include those small items that are easily lost in the viscera of a vest. Such small items are safely stored in heavy ziplock bags. A good test is to fill the vest, turn it upside down, and shake it. Nothing should fall out. Like some anglers, I often add Velcro strips to "sleeve" pockets or wherever else required. Remember to mount the Velcro beneath the pocket lip for easy opening. Velcro may also be used for lamb's wool patches that can then be removed for washing. Retrievers and their dangling accessories—such as clipper and flotant—should be mounted either *inside* a vest or *inside* a pocket. While still convenient to hand, the tools are less likely to entangle lines or brush, and, if mounted inside a pocket, they may avoid total loss if broken or detached. Some of the "appendages," such as pliers, can be expensive.

A few modern vests have vertically stacked pockets. Stacked pockets avoid the bulk of rib pockets that often get in the way of the upper arm and the casting stroke, especially when float tubing and deep wading. Natural and unrestricted arm movement lessens casting fatigue.

Pocket sizes among manufacturers are not standard, but they should accommodate your fly boxes with minimal space loss. The rib pockets, the lower front fly pockets, are the most used; their importance was evident when Gary Borger had Stream Designs create a custom vest for him, with rib pockets of near steamer-trunk capacity. Make certain that the vest will accommodate the larger boxes used for micropatterns.

Not many countries take the fly vest as seriously as we. Modern vests turn inside out to carry themselves. They multiply to produce more vests. They range in color from the traditional British tan and forest green to olive, gray, raspberry, and camouflage. Even the vibrant "high-tech" colors are available. Even red, espoused as a complement to photography, has entered the waters, joining the earthy slates and browns. However, because of the technical nature of micropattern angling, less obtrusive colors are recommended. Colors should be nonreflective and should conform to the environment.

While the marketplace and manufacturers struggle to create the perfect vest, here are recommendations for a technical micropattern vest. These recommendations are based on the functional analysis of small-pattern angling:

1. The vest should be short—not to exceed 18 inches along center back from collar top to bottom seam—for deep wading and float tubing.

2. The vest should have few but spacious pockets that accommodate the largest fly boxes.

3. The vest should be a neutral color, especially browns, olives, olive-browns, or grays when bank fishing and paler tans, blues, or slate grays while float tubing or wading.

4. There should be specialized pockets for extra spools, pliers, file, forceps, thermometer, and Polaroids without possible loss, the tools of technical fishing.

5. All pockets should be face sewn for shape with T-mounted Velcro closures. Some pockets may be size changeable, with removable partitions for specialized fly boxes and gear.

6. The back pocket should be lightly cushioned and waterproof.

7. The vest fabric should be high-tech, resistant to wear and grime.

8. If more than one outside top back zipper is used, then they should open and close in opposite directions. This will avoid confusion as to which pocket something may be in.

9. The vest should have wide shoulder panels to distribute the load evenly over the shoulders, rather than on the neck.

10. The vest should have vertically stacked pockets and no lower side pockets to get in the way of casting.

11. The vest fabric should dry quickly and, perhaps, have a completely waterproof pocket or two.

Modern chest vests, excellent for the humid weather of river meadows, also offer many features for the micropattern angler. When thoughtfully designed, the chest vest holds an inordinate amount of tackle for its size. A chest vest may hold less than the traditional vest, but an adequate amount, when well selected. Its minimalism may even encourage an intelligent abridgment of tools and tackle. The harness should distribute the weight comfortably and restrain the vest. Saddle-bag chest vests, with packs fore and aft, carry more and balance the load; the design, however, may interfere with high-back float-tubes. For access to the rear pack, merely release the chest belt and rotate the vest. Those chest vests that convert to waist packs make walking spring creeks more enjoyable; heavy chest vests wax lighter when worn at the waist. In all cases, care should be taken to prevent dumping tackle in the stream. For this reason too, the front, fold-down panel should not droop. When not used, the vest should be closed. A quality chest vest should include:

1. Adjustable straps to position the vest firmly for deep wading.
2. Strap panels that hold extra reels or spools
3. A Velcroed panel for pliers, forceps, thermometer, pencil, and other tools
4. A tippet dispenser that holds a minimum of four spools (4X, 5X, 6X, and 7X)
5. Velcroed fly boxes that attach to a front, fold-down shelf
6. Permanent retractors that hold frequently used tools
7. Conversion to a waist-pack for overland travel

In all vests, whether traditional or not, form should follow function. Vests should accommodate and make accessible the trim and tackle of angling. A quality vest is expensive. After the rod, reel and waders, the vest is perhaps the most important piece of equipment. A good vest should be familiar and friendly. It holds our hopes. It may pilfer tools and secrete them away for weeks in labyrinthine chambers. It may be bloated with useless essentials. And the pockets, invariably too small and too few, may hide the proper fly until the last pocket. A vest may even viciously trap a single barbless pattern while parachuting barbed battalions into tall grass. But beyond the frustrations, there is a sense of completeness as we wade the waters "in full harness." And vests offer themselves up to fondling, a rite of spring. There is pleasure, if not promise, in filling the bowels with trappings and trifles, the mere bagatelles of trouting. The worst that can happen to a vest, apart from loss, is to be new.

The Trout and The Water

And now for Water, the Element that I trade in.

—SIR IZAAK WALTON

A natural stream may vary significantly over a short distance. The following "stream sections" are important components of moving water. In our proto-typical stream, insects might appear in specific sections, depending on their requirements. Some "cosmopolitan" insects are adaptable to a variety of habitats, dwelling in deep and shallow waters, in swift and slow waters, in marl and stone substrata. However, most insects are more selective in their habitat requirements, often dependent upon current speed, depth, plant life, and substrata.

Roderick Haig-Brown was right: A river never sleeps. Streams often mingle turbulence with tranquility. Turbulence, the disruption of the contin-uous directional (the laminar) flow, occurs where adjoining velocities fluctu-ate, where flow direction changes abruptly and frequently. Turbulence results in surface disturbance, irregular surface levels and, due to trapped bubbles, obscured underwater zones. Bubble lines often trap small, hapless insects. Flow is retarded by objects or accelerated by incline. It is pushed to banks and deflected. Sunken weed patches spawn twisted skeins of currents that unravel in the flow. Currents fold when a stronger flow dominates a weaker one. Water boils or wells when pushed to the surface by subsurface obstructions like plant mass or undulations of the streambed. I have cast to such boils believing they were smut rises. Needless to say, the plants did not rise to my fly. When two currents couple, they create seams. When one drift collides and lifts another, there are rips or undulations. And between and among the drifts are

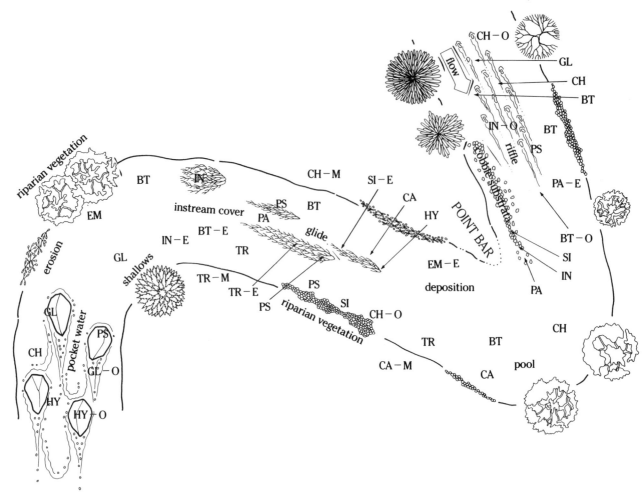

The prototypical stream and the natural dispensation of small insects

The Small Insects:
BT = *Baetis* (Blue-winged Olive, Little Olive)
CA = *Caenis* (Caenis, Angler's Curse)
CH = *Chironomids* (Midge)
EM = *Empidids* (Dance Fly)
PA = *Paraleptophebia* (Mahogony Dun)
HY = *Hydroptila* (Micro-caddis)
OC = *Ochrotrichia* (Bivalve or Tortoise caddis)
LE = *Leucotrichia* (Ring-horn caddis)
OX = *Oxyethira* (Mottled Micro-caddis)
IN = *Inermis* (Pale Morning Dun)
SI = *Simulid* (Reed Smut)
GL = *Glossosoma* (Saddle-case caddis)
AG = *Agapetus* (Saddle-case caddis)
PS = *Pseudocloeon* (Tiny Blue-winged Olive)
TR = *Tricorythodes* (Trico)

Insect Behavior
E = Emergence
M = Mating flights
O = Ovipositing

miniature, more delicate microcurrents pulling and pushing the flow. And it is upon such a traveling table that the tippet and fly must trace the perfect drift. The shallower the water or the faster the flow, the greater the translation of the topography of the streambed by the surface. The slow, silent flow of a spring creek or chalk stream, braided with microcurrents, obscures the streambed. The clarity of such streams permits observation of trout by the angler as well as observation of the angler by the trout. Understanding the stream sections and the "natural dispensation" of insects allows the angler to select an appropriate imitation.

1. *Pools.* Pools are characterized by relatively deep, slow-moving, or reduced flow. Pools are frequently used by fish for cover and rest. They usually have a pronounced scouring section resulting from obstruction or constrictions. Pools may have minor surface disturbances, but always have some flow restriction at the pool tail crest. Pools, generally deeper than sounding areas, are often located immediately downstream from the axis of a bend. Due to deposition, the pool bed is usually composed of sand or silt.

2. *Riffle.* A riffle, either deep or shallow, gathers divergent flow at high discharge. Bed material is concentrated rocks or gravel. The water gradient is steep and the cross-section is usually symmetrical. Exposed cobble and boulders are usually present. Flow lacks notable restrictions. The shallower and faster the flow, the more the surface expresses a coarse and cobbled streambed. In fast, thin water, the surface interprets the topography of the bed. The choppy, dancing surface expresses the cobbles and stones on the streambed. Thin riffles may not hold trout, but they do usually nurture profuse hatches. If deep enough, riffles may hold foraging trout. Rocks shelter trout from the flow and from each other. Trout often move into deep riffles to feed upon the prolific insects.

3. *Point Bar.* A point bar may occur on the inside of a bend, an area of deposition in contrast to the erosion of the outer bend. Accumulation often forms a point bar adjacent to a pool, resulting in an asymmetrical cross-section.

4. *Riparian Vegetation.* Bank vegetation (sedges, rushes, grasses, forbs, and deciduous and coniferous trees) provides shade, bank stability, and protective cover for trout and insects, minimizes light and abates water temperature. When bank vegetation is restricted or eliminated, then so are the trout. Riparian cover provides food, rest, concealment, escape, and protection from predators. Cover cools and protects the water as well as ameliorating erosion.

5. *Glide.* A glide is a section of stream that flows smoothly and slowly with moderate velocity (10 to 20 centimeters per second). There is little or no surface turbulence, and no hydraulic control—an obstruction or restriction that the flow must pass over or around. The profile is level or moderately sloped downstream. Glides usually slide over uniform channel bottoms. In a manner of speaking, a spring creek or chalk stream is a glide with microcurrents, minor surface turbulence

created by plant mass and plant channels. A glide is a riffle without significant surface turbulence. A wide, shallow pool with low turbulence and the tailwater of a pool with low turbulence are also called glides. In a spring creek, the smaller, easier trout will often lie near rapids or riffles. Glide trout are often more challenging than the indulgent riffle trout. The faster the water, the more aggressive the rise.

6. *Instream Cover.* Instream cover, such as surface turbulence, logs, and plant mass, offers trout sanctuary.

7. *Pocket Water.* Pocket water, a small pause of water in an otherwise turbulent flow, offers the trout sanctuary and sustenance. Pockets provide rest, cover, and food for trout. A steep gradient accelerates the flow, while obstructions, like rocks and boulders, eddy and rest the water before it tumbles away. Large, deep pockets may hold good trout. Turbulent, oxygen-rich waters may deliver drifting nymphs and larvae to the pocket, and insects may emerge in the relative calm of the eddy.

RISE REFLECTIONS

To the observant angler, the rise is a cryptograph for deciphering the message of pattern selection. It is, however, not a perfect code. Different rise forms may indicate the same insect; much depends on water speed, trout trajectory, hatch density, and insect movement. And particular waters, like particular trout, may have individual rise characteristics. Nevertheless, since the last century, rise forms have been an index to the insect. Observation and reason are the most important trouting tools. It is only by intense and creative observation that rise analysis approaches some precision. In this respect, fly fishing becomes an act of reasoning from the rise (the effect) to the insect (the cause). To decode some of this mystery requires understanding of the rise. The generic title of rise includes any form of fish-feeding movement or water disturbance. A trout does not have to ascend to rise.

Writers often recommend that the angler should present the fly upstream and centered on the rise. However, for highly selective trout, it is often more effective to cast upstream and off the near side of the trout. The fly will then fall in the monocular field of the trout's vision and will allow, consequently, less precise scrutiny of the pattern. In order for the trout to bring the pattern into binocular vision (trout do not have extensive eye movement), the trout may have to move; and this movement, once begun, can initiate an instinctive rise and take—a rise and take that would not overwise have begun. In short, the trout, caught off balance, may be committed to a rise that he would not have originally initiated. In this manner, the angler provokes the rise and defeats the trout. Obviously, some trout may only rise to examine the pattern without a take. Such a rise may be termed the perusal or investigative drift. A trout may drift nearly vertically for some distance before a refusal or take. Nonetheless, a pattern placed beyond the critical visual acuity can activate more complete rises by selective trout.

Nonselective trout may be taken with casts directly upstream of what may be called (for want of a better phrase) the *arc of absolute perception*. Diagrammatically, the fly is presented upstream of the trout. In this case, the fly will drift through the arc and into the binocular and triangular field of vision. Remember that this does not mean that the trout only sees in and around the arc. The trout can, under certain conditions, see beneath and beyond the arc. The 160° sight cone of the trout becomes compressed by refraction into a 97° cone through which the trout views the world. Yet, the trout does have difficulty seeing beyond the surface mirror. It can see the dimpling of hackle feet in the surface, but color and detail are "through a glass darkly." And the window, that ring of bright water, is backlighted so that again little color and detail is evident. Because of the structure of the trout eye, some authorities assert that the trout's eye admits about four times more light than the human eye. And the trout eye, which relies more upon the optical rods than upon the cones, is more sensitive to contrast and movement than to color and detail.

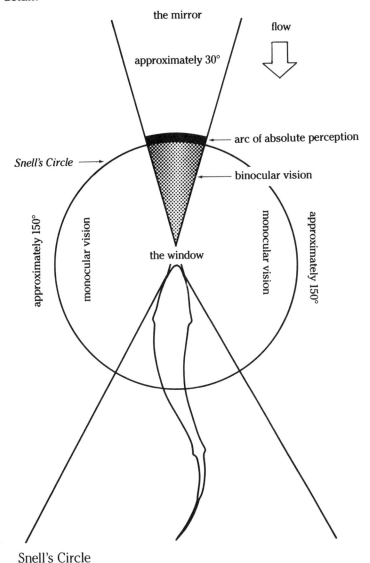

the mirror

flow

approximately 30°

arc of absolute perception

Snell's Circle

binocular vision

approximately 150°

monocular vision

monocular vision

approximately 150°

the window

Snell's Circle

Vincent Marinaro's *In the Ring of the Rise* (1976) was one of the first modern books to draw attention to the fact that the trout places the fly at the edge of the window for the purpose of observation and taking. More recently, Brian Clarke and John Goddard's *The Trout and the Fly* (1980) makes reference to Snell's circle, the circular boundary between the mirror and window. They argue most convincingly that it is at the ledge of the optical window that the trout first views the full fly.

The arc of absolute perception is merely the surface arc of Snell's Circle that is overlapped by the trout's binocular vision. This arc, and it is a suggestive theory only, may be the perceptual band at which the trout sees the complete fly with color and detail and decides the fly's authenticity. The distance of the arc—from the surface point directly above the trout's eye—is approximately equal to the depth at which the trout lies. Note also that the deeper a trout lies, the farther away the arc will be and the larger the vision cone will be.

Fright, sexual behavior and the territorial imperative may cause activities similar to feeding. But generally speaking, the following behavior patterns usually indicate actively feeding trout.

1. Trout that rise
2. Trout that hang high in the water
3. Trout that hang above or behind plant mass
4. Trout that appear stationary in lakes
5. Trout that lie in open channels
6. Trout that inhabit shallow and exposed lake margins
7. Trout that move across or downstream
8. Trout that actively graze in the plant mass
9. Trout that chase other trout
10. Trout that lie at the side or in front of stream rocks
11. Trout that occupy a lie in a stream
12. Trout that cruise open water
13. Trout that lie at the edge of a rip, two contrasting water speeds

There are traditional observations that form some of our understanding of the rise. Young trout are showy; mature trout, staid. Large flies are swirled, and smaller flies are sipped. Slash rises indicate a fluttering fly. During heavy hatching, trout may establish a rhythmic rise pattern. When this happens, the angler should time the cast so as to deliver the fly on schedule. Bubbles indicate a dry take. If a trout takes a dry fly, the air sucked in with the fly will be discharged from the gills as bubbles that will form part of the rise form. This is a classic indication of a dry take.

MOUTH TIME

It is generally understood that a trout in fast water has faster mouth time than a trout in still water. Trout often drift with the insect, tilt up and take, then dive down with a shut mouth that prevents drag. In slow water, the mouth need not close until the trout begins the dive. A mouth held open after the take may offer too much resistance; however, water can escape through the gills. In slow water the trout need not close his mouth so quickly, thereby encouraging the angler to miss the strike. "Trout that have lived for tens of thousands of years in lakes where the main food source has been zooplankton, such as the cutthroat trout in Yellowstone Lake, Wyoming, have evolved long, fine gill rakers that increase the efficiency in feeding on these small organisms." Like tiny whales, trout may drift and engulf zooplankton and water, then close their mouths and expel the water past the gills and gill rakers, which trap the zooplankton. According to author and angler Nick Lyons, any downstream drift should take into account the tapered shape of the trout's head. This makes it difficult to hook downstream trout. An angled drift or a drift that moves the trout from position and a slight increase in strike time may improve the possibility of catching the trout. Small patterns in smooth water are often taken on the nib or snout. The narrow mouth may offer a reason why it is so difficult to catch trout on a downstream drift.

According to *Trout*, "The most striking feature of these results is the vast array of organisms that trout eat. Although at certain times trout may eat primarily one species of prey, especially when a large aquatic insect is emerging so that adults drifting on the water surface are easily captured, most of the time they eat at least some of lots of different organisms and frequently eat about equal proportions of three or four main groups." Thus, "trout are relatively opportunistic and they eat primarily those organisms that are most abundant and available." Furthermore, ". . . trout appear to have some degree of individuality in their feeding habits, which also plays a role in producing the variety of diet usually observed among trout in streams."

The following rises are usually considered basic rise forms. And there are variants on the theme. This brief knowledge should enrich an understanding of the rise.

THE BULGING RISE

Bulging is a common expression of feeding trout. The trout tilts above the surface and then slides under. When a trout links bulges together, it is called *porpoising*. A melting V-wave may trail from the bulge; this usually denotes a heavy trout or shallow water. If a trout is too deep to rip the surface, only a water hump may appear. The bulge rise often leaves a fading dappled disk of water behind. The direction of the trout sometimes can be ascertained by the raised lip—the higher or fuller ring edge—of the resulting rise. Remember that if the trout does not break the surface with its head, then it is probably taking active emergers or subsurface suspenders.

The presence of gas beneath the nymphal sleeve during emergence of some insects imparts a rapid ascent. They are buoyed to the surface by the air trapped beneath their integument. Chironomids, Reed Smuts (*Simulium spp.*), and some mayflies emerge quickly in a cloak of gas. The gas film keeps the insect dry and ready for emergence. During the migration of damsels when the hatch struggles toward shore, trout may carouse and bulge with abandon. The bulging rises may be swirly and showy and are often audible because of

POLAROID SUNGLASSES
The compensation for bright summer days is the evening rise. Fall and late summer angling, such as evening sedge rises and spinner falls, is often in the low light of dusk. According to Trout, "feeding intensity is greatest at lower light intensities typical of early morning and late afternoon. Many fish species feed most actively during these so-called crepuscular (twilight) periods." An amber lens, acting much like the orange and yellow filter in black and white photography, will filter the blue and the grays to give higher contrast and sharper detail. Many polaroid lenses, whether amber or gray, are often too dark for these twilight periods. Select the lightest color polarizing lens available. An amber or pale-yellow polarized lens that sharpens details in low light is the best choice. Available too are light tan polarizing lenses designed specifically for low-light conditions. These have a silicon coating that repels grease and smudges; due to the hydrophobic film, water also beads and runs off.

the enthusiasm with which it is executed and the active insect it usually pursues.

THE DORSALING RISE

In this rise form, trout cruise with dorsal exposed just beneath the surface, selecting, *en passant*, insects adrift or emerging. It may be that trout with mouth agape engulf and filter the insects in a seining sweep, pumping the excess water through the gills. Such a rise form requires an *en masse* presence of food: pharate caddis, suspended smuts, midge pupae, or emerging mays. It may be questioned just how much a surface-drifting trout actually sees; however, if such a trout is actually feeding, then deception usually is not too difficult. Dorsaling trout often arrow beneath the surface with consistent direction and speed. It is only necessary to intercept the trout with an appropriate pattern. Dorsaling trout may intermittently gulp surface life. Trout that take dries and periodically expose their dorsals are called gulpers.

Gulpers are common on the expansive western waters. A gulping trout leaves a series of surface sips, and will carouse through heavy hatches. Like dorsaling trout, this aggressive feeding is usually directional and only tangent to the established feeding line when pursuing more food. Both the dorsaling and gulping trout take a wide range of emergent and nymphal life.

THE SMUTTING RISE

This rise form is common on slow or static waters. The term smut, in trouting use since 1889, usually refers to any number of small insects, the *res minutiae* of the insect world that forms a significant part of the trout diet. This rise form bespeaks of reed smuts and midges as well as minute mayflies, microcaddis, and tiny terrestrials. It is a slowly, silently exploding dimple. With a near-vertical attitude, the smutting trout may either penetrate the surface with a nose tip or merely suck the insect down from beneath. The former is indicated by bubbles; the latter, by sound. Smutting trout often rise to chironomids whirling on the surface. The English term "buzzer" describes its circular dance. The smutting rise is either a surface kiss with air that ends in small beaded bubbles blinking on the rim, or it is a suction sip that tears the surface tension and draws the insect down. Water molecules exert an omnidirectional attraction—they weave an elastic and cohesive fabric, a membrane that the trout must snap. But such a rise is done with minimal disturbance; it is a deliberate, yet delicate wink that dissolves rapidly. This rise indicates insects that are small, stillborn, or spent. In the leeward flank of lakes, where the wind has swept sheets of spent insects, this rise form may declare the presence of mayflies. In the deep or profundal sections of silt-bottomed lakes, such rises usually indicate hatching chironomids.

THE TAILING RISE

In the shallow, littoral strips of lakes and the static, back pools of slow streams, trout, feeding in a near-vertical pose, may break the surface with their caudal or tail fin. This stationary rise usually indicates food trapped in the plant mass—shrimp, caddis, and other various creatures both great and small. Trout may actually harvest the dense vegetation in this manner. A hanging trout is a difficult trout. Once, on the river Kennet, I confronted a large trout nose done in ranunculus. I could approach within rod-length, but I could not draw attention to my nymph drifting nearby. Even a touch on the tail with the rod tip failed to disturb the feeding fish. The intense concentration of a tailing trout is not broken easily except by rout. They often ignore any surface fare, and it is usually difficult to penetrate the plant mass with a pattern without getting hung up. In shallow streams, tailing trout have been observed dislodging nymphs and larvae and then, after dropping downstream, reaping the harvest. The tailing rise is an index to food forms that are either trapped in the plant mass or incapable of rapid retreat.

DIFFICULT TROUT

There is no simple, single answer for selective trout. Although previously used, the term *selective* was popularized by Doug Swisher and Carl Richards' *Selective Trout* (1971). Perhaps *demanding trout* is the better phrase. Few trout, even selective ones, key upon a single species or stage of natural even during a hatch. But all demanding trout are extraordinarily capable of detecting aberrations in the presentation or the pattern. That makes them difficult. Some selective trout tolerate stalking; others flee in terror. Even those that tolerate the angler can be remarkably critical in the selection. Part of the problem lies in determining what makes them selective and demanding.

1. Traditionally, selectivity means that trout deliberately select a particular species (or family) of insect. Such species selection may also be keyed to a particular stage—nymph, emerger, or spinner.
2. Selection may also include a particular pattern. *Pattern selectivity* is often encountered on spring creeks and chalk streams. A pattern is presented and the trout seem to take the pattern readily. It is as though the pattern has a counterpart in nature unknown to the angler. However, when the angler returns later, the next day or the next week, the trout may faithfully ignore the same offerings.
3. Selection may also be *size*. This is especially true when the smaller insects—such as midges, smuts, and microcaddis—appear. Color and silhouette seem far less significant than size alone.
4. Selection may be a predilection for a *particular presentation*. If a downstream, dead drift, or a "waked riffle" drag is the only enticement, then trout are selective to a specific presentation.

When trout are selective and demanding, the angler has several options. *Use Smaller Flies:* There are days when smuts look like stoneflies. Hook size deceives not only the trout but also the angler. A size 18 may be equal to or twice the length of a size 24. A fundamental rationale for this book is the contention that selective trout appear less intimidated by smaller patterns. Trout may take large insects, but the small insects often constitute the principal diet of selective trout.

Change Patterns: A trout, rhythmically rising, may require several drifts and several pattern changes. A day on Idaho's Silver Creek exhausted 32 different pattern changes. Numerous pattern changes does not indicate success. At least, not for the angler. If presentation is proper and the trout continues to rise, then pattern change may be required. Some trout, merely by their aggression, seem destined to take. Others, at times, seem to know all the subtle faults of an imitation. G. P. R. Pulman, in *The Vade-Mecum of Fly-Fishing for Trout* (1851), contends that selective exaggeration may be the philosopher's stone to tying. . . . it is impossible to dress it sufficiently delicate to equal nature, it becomes necessary to exaggerate some parts, so as to produce a proper harmony and proportion in the general form." The critical elements of a pattern include:

1. *Size.* This includes dimensions as well as mass.
2. *Color.* Color is more meaningful near the surface than at depths where turbidity and restricted light limit color.
3. *Silhouette.* Silhouette may be significant for dry flies that are backlit by the sun.
4. *Materials.* Tying materials and tying methods determine, to a significant extent, how a pattern will behave on or in the water.
5. *Stance and imprint.* The dry fly's imprint upon the water and the resulting light pattern may produce a particular signal that provokes rises.
6. *Visibility.* It is more important that the fish rather than the angler see the pattern. A pattern unseen is a pattern rejected. Flash, color or movement increase the chance of a trout take.
7. *Camouflaging hook and tippet.* Cloaking the bend and spear of the hook with an overwing or hackle may increase takes.
8. *Drift or Movement.*

Which critical element is most important may be a moot point. Perhaps, at times, one or several may be part of the selective process. George La Branche, in *The Dry Fly and Fast Water*, believes that position, action, size, form, and color constitute the correct order. An experienced micropattern angler might list (in descending order) the critical elements as presentation, size, silhouette, and color.

Sometimes, a single element may override any errors of color, size, or silhouette. But the better patterns combine elements that appeal to the predation of fish. Various experiments can be done to qualify the selective nature of trout. Tie patterns of various colors but the same size and silhouette to see if they are critical in particular waters. Break off the "bend and barb" to determine whether there are more takes. Do they take the upstream cast as readily as the downstream cast? Same patterns but heavier tippets? Different angles of presentation? Such experiments, of course, are highly limited. No angler can repeatedly present, under the same conditions, the same fly in the same manner to the same trout with the same disposition. But such field tactics do seem to define the issues better and clarify some obscurities at times. We sometimes encounter problematic water in which a certain pattern produces exceptionally well. The next day or the next week, the pattern may be emphatically rejected. It was the time and the condition and the trout that made the pattern. Nothing can replicate that success except the same time, the same condition, and the same trout.

Trout may also quickly pass through the hatch cycle from nymph to emerger to dry and on to another insect. Sometimes an effective pattern dies on the water, ignored by actively feeding trout. And, conversely, it is not unusual for a trout to take a pattern that has been consistently ignored. Other times, an exotic change—to a different size or a different pattern—provokes takes.

Change Presentation: More often than not, the problem is presentation. Search for the proper cast and drift for that fastidious trout. Toss more slack or change the angle of the drift. Novel drifts may produce trout that otherwise would not take. G. P. R. Pulman encourages the angler to "humour one's fly" with a light delivery and let it swim or flutter upon the surface.

Change Fly Stage: Often, well-educated trout appear to be feeding on dries when in fact they are taking emergers, stillborns, or spinners trapped in the surface film. One brown trout on the Anton refused nearly a winter's worth of tying, until offered a small dead-drift midge pupa. He wanted emergers, not dries. Although Ronalds, quoted in Pulman, declares that "the duns form the sheet-anchor" of fly fishing, not all trout take duns during a hatch. Many take emergers.

Change Pattern Profile: Subtract from the pattern; trim the hackle, wings, or body to create a sparse profile. Insects are fragile and delicate. Often our patterns are too full or float too high for selective trout.

Change Tippet Size: Difficult trout often begin with a 6X tippet. Try lengthening the tippet for a "softer" drift. The problem may be with the behavior of the pattern on the water, rather than with the trout detecting and shying from the tippet, as it is tugged countless ways by the microcurrents. The modern tippet is remarkably tough. With care, even large, powerful fish may be landed on small hooks and fine tippets.

Conserve the Cast: Every angling confrontation is different. If possible, select aggressive trout that appear to want a pattern. Make each cast a complete act. Take time to capture insects on the drift, beneath the rocks or on the bank. Fewer casts often make better casts. What flutters across the stream or lies beneath the rocks may be more important than a single cast.

Vary the Retrieve of Drift: Generally, small creatures are incapable of the faster movements of larger creatures. Change the retrieve or the speed of the retrieve. Increase slack for a dry drift. A longer, stronger tippet may be used if the angle of presentation is changed. If possible, present the fly in such a manner that the pattern is *between* the tippet and the trout. Experiment with the angle of presentation.

The Presentation

DRIFT AND DRAG

Frederic M. Halford, in *The Dry-Fly Man's Handbook* (1913), defines drag. "Any deviation from the natural course governed by the flow of the stream, and any acceleration or diminution of the pace of the living insect on the part of the artificial fly, is designated drag." The cause of drag is simple: the pattern is connected. "The line is on the water, and the varying speed of the current acting on the different parts of it will tend to retard or accelerate the pace of the artificial fly, or even pull it out of the normal course." Drag not only pulls the pattern from the natural drift line, it may also pull the pattern under. Drag is usually identified by the resulting wake; however, even a natural, dragged along by a breeze, may produce a wake. Drag is more than a drift with wake; it is the total unnatural swim of the imitation. Drag, though never entirely eliminated, is limited by several factors:

1. By selecting the most appropriate drift line. Choose the line of approach with the least change in current speed. This is usually directly above or directly below the rise. Lateral presentations usually extend over several varied water speeds. Use forethought in anticipation of drag.

2. By line manipulation as drag occurs. An angler can throw slack or reach cast to readjust the drift as currents create drag. In heavy, fast water, line manipulation may begin as soon as the line lands and may continue throughout the drift.

3. By short-line casting. Less line on the water means less drag and more accurate casts. The traditional upstream presentation, from the blind end of the trout, usually allows the nearest approach. If longer floats mean more drag, then the pattern should alight above and outside the trout's window. This position may be calculated as one foot upstream (actually 13.5 inches) for each foot of trout depth. This will place the pattern outside the trout's window. The difficulty, of course, lies in an accurate estimate of trout depth.

4. By using supple lines and leaders. Despite the current rage for stiff fly lines that rifle through the guides, a soft, supple line and leader may, at times, be advantageous. Such lines and leaders have "current response"; they reply quickly to the complex currents and "go with the flow." Hybrid lines (long belly weight forwards) offer some of the properties of a double taper and the forward thrust of a weight forward. A long belly line, whether a double taper or weight forward, offers improved line control and mending. A long-belly, fine-diameter 3-weight line follows the flow better than a 6-weight line. Matched to a long rod, it will roll cast efficiently and will drape with less water contact. Supple leaders and tippets conform to the current more completely and foster natural floats.

5. By presentational casting. Halford confirms the advice given by dry-fly anglers: Never throw a straight, taut line. Presentational casts, aerialized mends, land on the surface with the proper configuration for the particular drift, allowing the pattern to approach the rise without excessive drag. Presentational casts include loops, hooks, ripples, and serpentine casts.

6. By reading the currents. Spring creeks and other slow waters present complex currents—undulating weed beds produce microcurrents that push and pull the pattern in a distorted dance on the surface, a dance that selective trout often reject. Water is retarded or accelerated by objects and slope. It is deflected by banks and rocks. Weed patches produce twisted skeins of currents that coil and unravel in the flow. Complex currents fold (where a stronger flow dominates a weaker flow) and boil (where plant mass or undulations of the streambed push water patches to the surface). They produce seams (where two drifts zipper together) and rips (where equal currents collide and lift). The shallower the water and the faster the flow, the more the topography of the riverbed is transmitted to the surface.

The Downstream Drift

In *The Practical Angler* (1857), W. C. Stewart, of spider fame, enumerates four advantages for fishing upstream. The first is that the angler approaches the fish from the blind side, the tail. The second is that the angler strikes against the fish, whereas in downstream fishing, the fly may be pulled away from the fish. The third advantage is that the angler disturbs the water below the trout, rather than above. And last, Stewart wrote that the angler presents the fly more naturally, that is, without drag. Stewart, a borderer, lived when wet-fly downstream was the accepted technique. Upstream angling is older than Stewart—the first mention of upstream angling, according to John Waller Hills, appears in Robert Venables' the *Experienced Angler*, published in 1662, "a year after the third edition of the Compleat Angler."

Hills assesses the value of the downstream drift. "Downstream fishing, here and now, in this twentieth century, is better for certain persons and certain occasions. You avoid many difficulties. Wading is easier, and casting less incessant. Your line is taut and you are more likely to hook a fish. Also, as it is always taut, you know where your fly is and know where to look for rises. This is the great difficulty of upstream fishing, especially in quick and broken water." Although, according to Hills, "there is a certain reticence to-day about downstream fishing," the downstream drift is used to a greater extent than supposed. The downstream drift has historical precedence.

It is true that a fairly long line must be thrown downstream, simply to reach fish before they are disturbed. This is what Hills calls a long line downstream and a short line upstream. But if the angler wades slowly with care, then fish will rise to a hatch within short time and distance. Due to the fact that the current straightens the line, downstream fishing is often considered a novice method. Downstream fishing can be, however, an art unto itself. The first mend should be made before the line hits the water. Do not wait until the fly acquires drag. Then it is too late. If a downstream, slack drift encounters a rising trout, then the chances of a take increase. The slack, downstream drift eliminates drag and obscures the tippet.

Frederic Halford, in *The Dry-Fly Man's Handbook* (1913), states that when wind and occasional places demand a downstream float, "Then it is possible to fish downstream or partly across and partly down even with a floating fly." The downstream float, which Halford called "drifting," "requires that the angler should let out a length of line far greater than that required to cover the fish rising below him. As the line descends in the forward position of the cast it is checked not only by tightening the grip, but also by bringing the rod-hand back towards the body." This allows the fly to land above the rise with slack line. As the fly floats down, the angler's rod lowers and the fly proceeds over and below the rise. It is recovered slowly either by retrieving line gradually with the left hand or "by returning the fly laterally over the bank below the fish." To Halford the downstream drift was "a manoeuvre of desperation" that seldom led to a second cast.

Where waters are wadeable and fish difficult, the downstream drift may prove productive. Edgar Pitzenbauer of Bavaria has fished, for over twenty-five years, the exacting waters of Slovenia. His quarry, the grayling, have prominent dorsal fins, forked tails and underslung mouths. They also have a reputation: they challenge both the angler and the pattern. There is a mid-European legend that grayling, more a gourmet than a gourmand, feed upon gold nuggets. Some of these "nuggets," these small patterns, work well for selective trout. Large, shy grayling require small flies, accurate casts and soft presentations. Any threat detected by the gregarious grayling may alarm the entire shoal. Pitzenbauer wears olive clothing and wades silently to avoid spooking fish. Unlike trout, who often grab a passing fly, grayling slowly and softly suck. Such a take requires accurate strike-timing. And grayling often follow the fly extended distances before taking, thus the necessity for a drag-free float. Consequently, selective grayling are often considered far more difficult than selective trout.

The Pitzenbauer's presentation is a study in the downstream drift. First, Pitzenbauer wades very slowly downstream. He faces or quarters downstream so that the rise or rises are below and to one side. The angler should be to the side of the delivery; the fly should not float down the wading turbulence. Then, he casts a concise length of line relatively high and parallel to the water. He bounces the line back, allowing the fly to land directly above the rise. Next, he drops the rod tip. In so doing, the line creates a loop, approximately twenty inches in diameter, on the water near him. The rod tip must halt high in the cast, drop and then slowly extend (a downstream reach cast) during the drift. As the water extends the slightly serpentined line, the loop dissolves and the line lengthens into an eight-meter or longer float. The extended, relatively straight line allows quick hooking. Over the years, the Pitzenbauer downstream drift has seduced some sage grayling and trout.

According to Bill Willers' *Trout Biology*, the territory of a trout depends upon the degree of visual isolation. There may be border zones between territories that are occupied, periodically, by occupants of each territory. Vegetation, rocks, turbidity and other components screen trout from one another, allowing greater trout density and, consequently, smaller trout territories. When an angler enters a trout territory the inhabitant flees to another, thereby dislodging trout from their territories up and down the stream. An angler may be completely unaware of this hidden alarm system that disrupts the trout territories and hierarchies for meters around. Trout are attentive to each other; to scare one trout is to scare several. Most salmonid studies support the view that trout refrain from making extensive movements, except when spawning, beyond their territories. Because all members of a hierarchy will defend a particular stream section, any intrusion will cause disruption. An exception to the territorial imperative is the errant trout; large trout may prefer to cruise and forage rather than to establish a territory. In any case, entry and wading should be made with care and, if possible, cover. Placing a plant mat or rocks between you and the rise may allow that rise to continue.

Line Tactics

A small fly, camouflaged by size, may drift unnoticed. Line tactics, executed by hand and rod, imitate various insect activities that draw attention. As with all imitative actions, vary the speed and frequency. Insects move in diverse ways: rowing (*corixidae*), curling (*chironomidae*), undulating (*baetidae*), winging (*hymenoptera*) and jetting (*anisoptera*). The nonswimming legs are usually folded against the body. Remember that most insect movement is slower and more subtle than that often imparted to an imitation. Even large dragonfly nymphs, propelled by anal expulsion, attain speeds of only 50 centimeters per second for short bursts.

Rod action and position play significant parts in how the movement is transmitted to the pattern. If the rod tip points toward the pattern, use a lengthened tippet as a shock cord. Angling the rod to the left or right of the retrieve direction may also offer some yield to a hard take. A soft-tipped rod, held high, may merely absorb the quick, staccato strips so that the pattern runs smoothly rather than expressing the desired pulses.

Line tactics also diminish drag, either by line mending during the drift or by throwing a running loop during the cast. Here, then, are some essential line tactics for the small fly, a fly that may either be unnoticed or unnatural.

The Short Strip: The short strip, which imitates scuds and *Baetis*, is a brisk retrieve of five or six inches of line through the index finger, the trigger finger, on the rod. Keep the rod low so that the staccato pulses are transferred to the fly. Strip immediately behind the index finger.

The Damp Scrape: Heavily hackled patterns are scraped two or three feet across the water surface. Small, sparse patterns may move, to use Leonard Wright's phrase, only "the sudden inch." This disturbance, mimicking the struggling or skating caddis, leaves a seductive wake that attracts trout. Vary the "suddenness" imparted to "damp" patterns. With small patterns, the movement may be accomplished with the rod tip alone. Merely flick or lift the tip so that the pattern "imprints" itself on the surface.

The Dip: The dip, an "attraction action," imitates emerging insects, such as midges, seeking a fragile meniscus for hatching. This action is used on pupa or suspender patterns floating just beneath the water surface. The rod tip is lifted gently, but quickly, so that the pattern bobs in or to the surface briefly before settling or sinking. This gentle gesture is used to attract trout to small, imitative patterns hung in the surface.

The Errant Run: The errant run imitates the movement of erratic swimmers such as scuds, corixae, and hatching caddis. With a combination of short-strip and rod-tip movement, make the pattern run erratically with twitching, sporadic speed. Use a loop retrieve to impart the motion.

The Leisenring Lift: The Leisenring Lift, primarily a stream tactic, allows the angler to present a pattern realistically to a visible trout. Cast the pattern above the trout, allowing it to sink before addressing the trout. When the pattern drifts within range, lift the rod tip to "emerge" the pattern directly in front of the trout. This is an excellent tactic for the various bubble emergers.

A somewhat similar phenomenon occurs in lake fishing, where a natural, such as a chironomid pupa, emerges from the depths. As the bubble-jacket insect rises, the bubble expands, increasing the buoyancy and acceleration. A deep-retrieve tactic includes increasing the acceleration of the retrieve and applying a sudden stop. Somewhat akin to Wright's "sudden inch," the *sudden stop* encourages a following or trailing trout to intercept and capture the pattern. Due to a natural feeding response, the trout may take—a take perhaps never committed to originally. The sudden stop can sometimes seduce trailing trout. Obviously, some trout may turn away without a take.

The Swimming Nymph: Cast with a fairly straight line, and use a drop retrieve, a figure-eight retrieve with falling loops, to maintain constant contact with the pattern. This generic retrieve imitates a variety of aquatic insects. Due to the continuous tension, the strike must be quick, but gentle. The rod tip may be angled away from the retrieve line to absorb the shock of a take. Some anglers allow the line to slip during the strike, preventing breakoffs produced by taut, straight lines.

The Deferred Strip: Cruising trout, particularly in shallow sections of spring creeks, may be startled by line movement or pattern entry. To prevent this, cast softly beyond a cruise lane or across a pool, and allow the pattern to settle. Wait. When a cruising trout nears, gently lift and swim the pattern. Even the gentlest motion may attract attention. On one small spring creek, I cast and tucked myself behind a tree. I waited. When a cruising trout neared, I merely "touched" the pattern on the bottom. The movement produced a puff of silt that attracted the trout. He came, he saw, he took. This ambush technique may be combined with a variety of retrieves.

The Draw Cast: On tightly rising trout, cast above and beyond the drift line. Draw or scrape the pattern along the surface to align the drift to the rise. The tactic may be used for either upstream or downstream drifts. Once aligned, it may be necessary to toss slack line, with a ripple cast into the drift, especially if the drift angles away.

The Anchor Cast: Sometimes it is necessary to cast over and on a weedbed or bank. Spring creek wading often places a weed mat between the angler and the trout. The weeds, although screening the angler, present a problem. The mat will immediately arrest or anchor any line or leader that touches down. To produce a natural float beyond the anchoring weeds, overcast and bounce (or ripple) the line back to produce slack, thus offering extra leader and tippet for the drift. This tactic is best for short casts, close to rising trout.

Eric Taverner, in *Trout Fishing From All Angles,* describes this "Cross-weed Cast."

"After many attempts I stumbled upon the solution: to cast a slack line over the weeds a little above the fish, so that the line and the top of the cast rested on top of the weeds and the remainder pivoted round and went down to the fish at the pace of the current." Taverner's Crosscountry Cast, where an angler casts over land to a close-lying bank trout, also entails the pivot. The most difficult part of the anchor cast is in determining where to place the anchor or pivot point on the weed patch or bank.

The Loop Retrieve: The loop retrieve, also known as the palm retrieve, recovers line smoothly and continuously. Holding the line between the thumb and the index finger (the forefinger), twist the hand to the left and then grasp the line with the last three fingers. Next, release only the thumb and forefinger while twisting the hand to the right. Take an advanced grip on the line with the thumb and forefinger. Rocking the hand back and forth pulls line with the thumb and forefinger, then with the last three fingers. While rocking the hand and retrieving line, allow the excess loops to fall from the palm. Release the palm loops after one or several rocking twists. The loop retrieve creates a continuous, steady travel that may be varied in speed. It is an excellent method for small caddis and chironomid emergers in deep water.

The Ripple Cast: The ripple cast, a *vertical* wave cast, throws slack line by driving a subsequent second cast into an already extending and descending cast. First, execute an overhead cast and line layout. During the forward stroke, stop the rod hand in a near-vertical position. Immediately after line layout, drive a tight, short stroke on the same rod-tip trajectory. The second cast should ripple line *above* the rod tip and, consequently, ripple the first cast back. The ripple cast is a more powerful slack-line cast than the conventional tip wag used to create "snakes" on the water. With supple leaders, it has a further advantage of producing more leader slack than line slack. The ripple cast also allows the angler to toss slack into fast flow for an improved drift. This cast, which occurs inside an already descending cast, works only for short distances.

The Presentational Cast: Presentational casting, casting a *shaped* or mended line, should be as common as mending a drift. It minimizes drag, and counteracts currents and loops around rocks. The presentational cast, combined with line mending during the drift, eliminates most drag problems.

A forward wrist roll is the traditional method of casting a running loop, a loop that travels down the extending line. On the forward stroke, the rod should stop slightly beyond the perpendicular. Immediately after the application of the forward power, cast a circling loop down the line before the initial forward cast is exhausted. Apply enough power to orbit the rod tip out of its axis. A wrist roll launches a loop, a cast within a cast, that travels down the descending layout line. An effective wrist roll will propel the loop down the line with straight trajectory. A wrist roll to the right produces a right hand loop; a wrist roll to the left, a left line-loop. An early wrist roll will place the loop near the fly, and a late wrist roll will place the loop near the rod tip.

For right-handed loops, the double cast method may be more efficient. Like the running loop, it is a cast within a cast. After the overhead cast is made, and while the first cast is being realized, a second cast is made that produces a horizontal running loop. On the initial cast, make certain that the rod does not float forward. This creates a cocked rod, ready for the second cast. To make the second cast, merely draw the rod sharply back and then forward again as you would a normal horizontal cast. This sends a traveling horizontal loop down the line. And, as the line is normally to the right of the hand position, the second cast will produce a right horizontal loop on the water. The line energy of the first cast should dissipate before the running loop reaches line position. Excessive energy in the initial cast may straighten out the second, slower cast. The running loop to the left may be made either with the traditional wrist roll or a backhand double cast. With brief practice it is possible to cast right and left loops around objects or to cast loops in the faster current to allow drag-free floats. When correctly executed, the line extends straight, loops, and then continues the straight extension. Timing and energy will determine the loop location when the line lands.

A faster rod, i.e., a stiff rod with a high flexure modulus, facilitates casting a running loop. The softer the rod, the more time differential exists between the caster and the cast, and between each cast. A high flexure modulus rod applies power rapidly and more efficiently. The enemies of casting, atmospheric pressure and gravity, are overcome by timing and energy. Casting is a slow-fast action both in the pickup and the forward cast. This allows the rod to flex before the line accelerates. If the rod accelerates before it possesses maximum load, the energy is merely absorbed by the rod and not passed on to the line.

Unlike double taper or long belly lines, a steep weight-forward line may straighten the running loop before the line touches water. In a double-taper line (and to some extent a long-belly, weight-forward line), the wave travels down the line from a heavier, relatively high-impedance (resistance to disturbance) section to a lighter, low-impedance section. Waves are turned back or reflected if they encounter an abrupt change in the medium in which they are traveling. This means that, at least theoretically, the running loop that is sent down the line wants to return to the caster. If the wave or pulse energy of the loop could arrive at the end, the line would allow unrestricted displacement in the plane of the wave and the wave would return. Of course, this cannot happen unless the line is short and the energy excessive. Also, the resistance to air and line and the brief flight prevents a counter-wave. And the wave energy, as it travels farther from the source, is reduced and dissipated by damping, the progressive reduction of the loop energy. Stiffer lines impart greater energy and speed. They are easier to mend in the air than on the water. In any case, an angler should remember that a running loop is a traverse pulse traveling through the line with all the properties of a wave. If the pulse energy reached the fly, then unrestricted and erratic displacement would take place. The angler would produce an exotic tippet maze upon the water. As long as there is neither excess energy nor hinging (especially between line and leader), the energy transfer should be smooth. This is why impedance matching, matching the approximate resistance to flexure, is so necessary between line and leader, and between leader and tippet. For a simple impedance test, hold the line section in a circle. If the connection smoothly continues the natural curve, then the impedance is matched.

The Tailing Loop

Tossing micropatterns requires control and care. Long leaders, fine tippets and light lines promote casting problems, especially the so-called tailing or trailing loop. The tailing loop encourages the fly to snag the line or results in so-called "wind-knots," knots that profoundly weaken fine tippets. To avoid the tailing loop, which is an erratic displacement of line and fly, follow these hints:

1. Allow the line more time to straighten in the backcast before initiating the forward cast.
2. When initiating the forward cast, drag the line *slowly* forward before applying power. This straightens the line and loads the rod prior to power application.
3. Do not give maximum power, the so-called "power snap" or "power stroke," to the line until the rod hand has passed in front of the ear.
4. Finally, straight rod-tip trajectory is important. Avoid looping or drooping the rod tip down and up during the forward casting stroke. Casting is pushing and pulling a flexible beam through the air. Theoretically, when the rod tip draws an imaginary straight line in the air it achieves efficient, flat trajectory.

LANDING TROUT

Trout should be landed promptly, rather than *played*. Playing a trout suggests indulgence, rather than quickly capturing and releasing an animal; trout are living creatures that deserve respect. They should be landed quickly to avert fatiguing or harming them. It is better to lose a trout than to exhaust it. Sometimes, landing a trout has more to do with the angler than the trout. Often the rods used for close casts and micropatterns are the softer rods, rods not designed to quickly control and land trout. Stiffer, quick-tipped rods that lay out long lines over heavy currents control trout quickly, but these are often not the rods used in micropattern angling.

Clearly, those methods that land trout quickly and avoid handling a trout are best. Here are some considerations when battling and landing trout.

The Battle and the Truce

(1) Several factors make landing trout on small hooks a problem: small gaps, tender tippets and strike time. Moderate and steady pressure solves most problems. Small hooks and fine tippets usually hold well if sudden trout tugs are absorbed by the rod, leader and tippet. For this reason, keep the tip high and apply side pressure only to a moving fish. Furthermore, small hooks can be ingested deeper; consequently, greater responsibility lies with the angler to make the strike on time. Only quick, but minor pressure is really necessary "to home" a hook. With small patterns, the strike should be swift, but soft. This is not a contradiction.

(2) Be swift but gentle to minimize stress and shock to the fish. Small fish may be landed quickly by hand. Consider breaking a fish off if it cannot be landed quickly. Unduly tiring a trout, especially one that is well-hooked and bound for release, is not necessary. An angler often telegraphs his excitement to the trout, which only prolongs the battle. Trout should be landed with moderate attention and released without breaking water. Whenever possible, trout should be landed and released before they know what has happened. For those trout, landing is only a brief interlude.

(3) Use proper "tools" to avoid exhausting the trout. If possible, use a rod and tippet with sufficient strength to hustle a fish in. When possible, use tippets that are *twice* the weight of the taking trout.

(4) Remember that a dynamic trout may exert more force than its own weight on a tippet. A static weight increases its "weight" or force when dynamic and moving.

(5) Keep the struggling fish near the top of the water column to avoid weeds and decrease line resistance. The deep trout has increased line drag. Put side pressure on trout to glide them in. Do not, however, allow the fish's head or body out of the water. Without water resistance, a trout's struggle is more violent and destructive.

(6) To decrease line drag (especially in heavy current), combat trout with as short a line as possible. Long line and swift current release fish. G. P. R. Pulman observed that "The resistance of a swift current is alone sufficient to tear a small hook from the firmest hold in the tender mouth of a trout." Keep the fly in the trout's mouth by positioning the rod to create either lateral or downstream tension on the trout. Upstream tension can extract a small hook. Never grab a taut line or tippet unless the trout has surrendered, ready for release.

(7) Perhaps the only value of a *barbed* hook is with aerialized trout on a slack line. Remember to drop the rod tip when a trout jumps to prevent it from falling on a taut leader and tippet.

(8) Keep the rod tip angled to offer the trout as much rod flex as possible. This usually means that the rod should be held at a right angle to the stressed line. Sudden tugs and runs may break fine tippets. To increase rod resistance when mastering large fish, Taff Price of England places the supple section of the rod (from the tip to the upper butt) under water. The reel is still checked or worked above the water. The trout must then labor against the rod flex as well as the water resistance or drag that dampens and cushions the flex. The water viscosity muffles any sudden tugs or runs. By analogy, this is comparable to pounding a nail under water. This is especially effective during the initial battle, when the trout has speed and power. Essentially, water viscosity creates a retarding force that is the function of the velocity of the moving rod; the greater the rod velocity, the greater the effect of the retarding force. A similar effect is created by placing the hand outside the window of a moving automobile. The greater the speed, the greater the resistance.

(9) Trout that become "weeded," by burrowing into the plant mass and hanging up, are torment for trouters. One method of extracting trout from plant mass is by line thumping or, as Dermot Wilson expresses it, by "line plucking." When a trout becomes caught in the plant mass, Wilson places the rod down and picks up the line between the rod tip and trout. He tightens the line and then plucks it a few times to loosen the trout. Taut-line plucking encourages a trout to "kick" free. Once the trout is free, the rod must pick up the slack line and put the trout on the reel. Large trout should be contested from the reel if possible. There is an empty feeling when a heavy trout bores into weed and you come away with a weed pennant on the hook. Another method to de-weed trout is to place the rod downstream and work the line through the plant ends. Extract the trout by lowering the rod tip to the water while pulling steadily but moderately. It may even be effective, when the trout is well hooked, to offer slack line at times.

The Capture and Release

(1) Use a single, barbless hook for trout that will be released. It is best to file the barb flat on top rather than to pinch the barb down. A pinched barb may fracture the hook or leave a hump.

(2) Use bronzed steel hooks, rather than nickel, stainless steel, or gold. When stolen by trout, bronze hooks corrode more quickly than nickel, stainless steel, or gold.

(3) Take care that the fish does not flop against rocks or other objects. Avoid removing trout from the water. Water cushions the trout's writhings.

(4) When fishing from a high bank, in fast water or with large fish, use a proper net to decrease fight time. When wading, it may be less stressful to the trout to bring it in by hand and quickly release it. Many anglers are proud that they do not use a net; however, this may be affectation if, in the process of landing a fish, they must handle it longer and harder than with a net. However, a net can encourage keeping trout out of water and can cause severe abrasion to the outer mucus "skin" that protects a trout from disease. On the other hand, nets can decrease fight time and bring the trout quickly under control. In some waters, where there is no wading and the banks are high and current stiff, a net may help to reach out to capture the trout. Net movement, and perhaps even net color, can cause panicked runs and broken tippets. If a net is used, it should be large enough for quick capture. When using a net, remember to bring the trout over the net and then lift. Never sweep a net toward a trout. Sink the net, pass the trout over the net, then swiftly lift the net to capture the trout. Once the trout is caught, keep the net in the water to cushion any struggle. An extendable net with a rigid bow is popular in Europe. It may be extended to capture a trout beyond the reeds or to probe the weeds to extract a buried trout.

Nets can be an annoyance to carry, tangling in brush or disrupting a cast. Some nets are carried, hoop up and handle down, on the back of the vest clipped to a pull release. Some "catch and release" nets have a shallow basket depth that reduces trout tangles and speeds trout release. The net should be a soft cord, such as cotton, although some nylon fibers now possess significant softness to avoid abrasion of the trout. Large, coarse knots may scuff and scrape a trout. All nets should be small meshed, with holes perhaps one-quarter of an inch to prevent fins becoming tangled or split. A few nets have knotless, soft nylon.

(5) To lift a large trout, cradle it horizontally with one hand beneath the body and with the other hold it immediately in front of the tail fin on the peduncle.

(6) Anglers catch trout on film as well as on flies. Even in catch-and-release waters, we want memories of a particularly gallant fish. For photography, have the camera ready and try shots with the fish in a natural position in the water. Although this restricts photographs to top and angled views, the best method is to keep the trout in the water. A net in the water can cradle the trout for the camera. Do not exhaust the trout in the process of photography. Always minimize the time out of water for a game fish. To establish size (which is very difficult to determine when there is only trout and water) place a rod or the net near the trout in the water. A macro lens can give a dramatic closeup of fly and trout, briefly held out of the water. A macro lens may also function as a standard lens.

It is best to have someone help handle equipment and speed the waterless time. Autofocus cameras, which permit single-hand work, speed the photographic process, and built-in flashes can quickly capture dawn or dusk trout.

(7) Never touch the eyes or the gill system. Do not squeeze trout; this may damage vital organs, including the swim bladder.

(8) Avoid stomach pumps and spoons. Even with training, the use of a stomach pump may injure fish. Gently spooning the upper throat is superior to a stomach pump. However, it is best to spoon only those fish killed and kept.

(9) Lead the fish to moderate or slow water for revival. Let the trout regain its strength by gently holding its head upstream in the current. The gills should work normally and the trout should gain strength and stability. Never *throw* a fish back. Gently release trout in slow, moderately shallow water. Usually, after the trout regains strength, it will dart away. If it fails to recover when released, recapture and repeat the process.

(10) Trout can be exhausted, even drowned, if kept "on a leash" when facing or running downstream. There is truth in the adage that only dead fish go with the flow. Trout have a negative rheotropism; they must face upstream.

Exhausted trout should be placed upstream in slow flow to receive adequate oxygen. Trout also avoid contact with objects, a negative thigmotropism. If possible, land trout without touching them. One method for reviving a trout is to place it near the surface, pointing upstream. The angler then vigorously paddles water in front of the exhausted trout to increase oxygen. The effectiveness of the paddle method is disputed.

A Micropattern Coda

**"The fisherman sets the highest
value on those fish which have made
the highest demand on his personal
prowess, his knowledge of nature,
his watercraft and his skill."**

—ARTHUR RANSOME, *Rod and Line* (1929)

There are two streams in this book. One stream examines tradition and accepts, modifies, or rejects as need be. Total rejection of tradition, though, would be a denial of much thoughtful writing. Sometimes tradition sires new solutions. We should use the past as admission to the present. The other stream, an intensely creative one, devises modern solutions. All that drifts through these pages, whether from the past or the present, is an attempt to understand that first Heracletian flow. The next bend may offer different insects, different currents, and different problems. This constant change makes fly fishing fascinating.

The East Lodge "mirror" trout that I lost taught me more, eventually, than all the trout taken that season. That trout sent me on a journey of discovery that became, for me, the essence of fly fishing. I wanted to understand more and to perform more proficiently than I had. The journey was not without difficulties. What could I have done to land that Itchen trout? I could have selected a more appropriate hook. I could have used shock gum to absorb sudden tugs or twists. Perhaps I could have landed the trout with improved technique. Yet, despite all this, I still could have lost that trout as I did. Although recent advances in hook construction and leader strength will radically increase our chances of landing large trout on small patterns, there is more that is capricious than certain in angling. And it was exactly the *capricious* that I wanted to understand. I hope that this book has encouraged a closer and more critical analysis of equipment, presentation, methods, and patterns directed toward this end.

To some extent, all angling books are merely elaborate accounts of seduction, made from time to time. Such books offer, as this one has dared, some strategies for that seduction—productive patterns, effective methods, and greater knowledge. I fully recognize that all these solutions are but passing currents too. There are better ways yet.

In the creative intensity of tying, in the trials of presentation, in the battles lost and won, in the very search for solutions live our best memories. While all the anglers, all the rivers, and all the patterns that I have shared with you have become part of the solution, there is never a total solution for the curious fly fisher. "For the everlasting pleasure of those who follow," the changing waters will never allow that.

Bibliography

Alphenaar, Wim. *Vliegbinden & Vliegvissen*. B. V. Het Goede Boek: Postbus 122,1270 AC Huizen, 1991.

Anderson, Norman H. *The Distribution and Biology of Oregon Trichoptera*. Corvalis: Oregon State University, (Technical Bulletin 134) 1976.

Arbona, Fred. *Mayflies, the Angler, and the Trout*. Tulsa, Oklahoma: Winchester Press, 1980.

Bainbridge, W. G. *The Fly-Fisher's Guide to Aquatic Flies and Their Imitations*. London: A. & C. Black, Ltd., 1936.

Borger, Gary. *Designing Trout Flies*. Wausau: Tomorrow River Press, 1991.

Borger, Gary. *Naturals: A Guide to Food Organisms of the Trout*. Harrisburg, Pennsylvania: Stackpole Books, 1980.

Brookes, Andrew. *Channelized Rivers: Perspectives for Environmental Management*. New York: John Wiley & Sons, 1988.

Caucci, Al and Bob Nastasi. *Hatches II*. New York: Lyons & Burford, (revised edition) 1986.

Clark, Brian and John Goddard. *The Trout and the Fly*. London: Ernest Benn, Limited, 1980; New York: Nick Lyons Books, 1981.

Darbee, Harry, with Mac Francis. *Catskill Flytier*. Philadelphia: J. B. Lippincott Company, 1977.

Dieter, George E. *Mechanical Metallurgy*. New York: McGraw-Hill, Inc., 1961.

Edmunds Jr., George F., Steven L. Jensen, and Lewis Berner. *The Mayflies of North and Central America*. Minneapolis: University of Minnesota Press, 1967.

Elder, Frank. *The Book of the Hackle*. Edinburgh: Scottish Academic Press, 1979.

Goddard, John and Brian Clarke. *The Trout and The Fly*. London: Ernest Benn, Limited, 1980.

Goddard, John. *Trout Flies of Britain and Europe*. London: A. & C. Black, 1991.

Goddard, John. *Waterside Guide*. London: Unwin Hyman Limited, 1988.

Hafele, Rick and Dave Hughes. *The Complete Book of Western Hatches*. Portland, Oregon: Frank Amato Publications, 1981.

Hafele, Rick and Scott Roederer. *Aquatic Insects and Their Imitations*. Boulder, Colorado: Johnson Publishing Company, 1987.

Halford, Frederic M. *The Dry-Fly Man's Handbook*. London: George Routledge & Sons, Limited, 1913.

Halford, Frederic M. *Floating Flies and How to Dress Them*. London: Sampson Low, et al., 1886.

Henn, T. R. *Practical Fly-Tying*. London: Adams & Charles Black, 1950.

Hills, John W. *A History of Fly Fishing for Trout*. New York: Freshet Press, 1971.

Hills, John W. *River Keeper: The Life of William James Lunn*. London: Geoffrey Bles, 1934.

Hughes, Dave. *Reading the Water*. Harrisburg, Pennsylvania: Stackpole Books, 1988.

Hynes, H. B. N. *The Ecology of Running Waters*. Toronto: The University of Toronto Press, 1970.

Koch, Ed. *Fishing the Midge*. New York: Freshet Press, Incorporated, 1972.

LaBranche, George M. L. *The Dry Fly and Fast Water*. New York: Charles Scribner's Sons, 1922.

LaFontaine, Gary. *Caddisflies*. New York: Lyons & Burford, 1981.

LaFontaine, Gary. *The Dry Fly: New Angles*. Helena, Montana: Greycliff Publishing Company, 1990.

Laible, Gerhard. *CDC Flies*. Nuremberg: Verlegt bei Traun River Products, 1993.

Leighton, Michael. *Trout Flies of Shropshire and the Welsh-Borderlands*. Shrewsbury: Redverse Limited, 1987.

Leiser, Eric. *The Book of Fly Patterns*. New York: Alfred A. Knopf, Inc., 1987.

Macan, T. T. and E. B. Worthington. *Life in Lakes and Rivers*. London: Bloomsbury Books, 1974.

Marinaro, Vincent C. *A Modern Dry-Fly Code*. New York: Nick Lyons Books, 1970.

Marinaro, Vincent C. *In the Ring of the Rise*. New York: Lyons & Burford, Publishers, 1987.

Mathews, Craig and John Juracek. *Fly Patterns of Yellowstone*. West Yellowstone, Montana: Blue Ribbon Flies, 1987.

McCafferty, W. Patrick. *Aquatic Entomology*. Boston, Massachusetts: Science Books International, 1981.

McClelland, H. G. *The Trout Fly Dresser's Cabinet of Devices or How to Tie Flies for Trout and Grayling Fishing*. London: The Fishing Gazette, (ninth edition) 1939.

Merritt, R. W. and K. W. Cummins, editors. *An Introduction to the Aquatic Insects of North America*. Dubuque, Iowa: Kendall/Hunt Publishing Company, 1978.

Moyle, Peter B. and Joseph J. Cech, Jr. *Fishes: An Introduction to Ichthyology*. Englewood Cliffs, New Jersey: Prentice-Hall, Inc., 1988.

Nemes, Sylvester. *Soft-Hackled Fly Imitations*. Bozeman: Published by the Author, 1991.

Pennak, Robert W. *Fresh-Water Invertebrates of the United States*. (second edition). New York: John Wiley & Sons, Inc., 1978.

Pequegnot, Jean-Paul. *French Fishing Flies*. New York: Nick Lyons Books, 1987.

Price, Taff. *Fly Patterns: An International Guide*. London: Ward Lock Limited, 1986.

Price, Taff. *The Angler's Sedge*. London: Blandford Press, 1989.

Proper, Datus. *What the Trout Said*. New York: Alfred A. Knopf, Inc., 1982.

Pulman, G. P. R. *The Vade-Mecum of Fly-Fishing for Trout*. London: Longman, Brown, Green and Longmans, (third edition) 1851.

Roberts, John. *The New Illustrated Dictionary of Trout Flies*. London: George Allen & Unwin, 1986.

Ronalds, Alfred. *The Fly-Fisher's Entomology*. London: Longman, Brown, Green, and Longmans, 1844.

Rosenbauer, Tom. *Reading Trout Streams*. New York: Lyons & Burford, Publishers, 1988.

Sawyer, Frank. *Nymphs and the Trout*. New York: Crown Publishers, Inc., 1973.

Schullery, Paul. *American Fly Fishing: A History*. New York: Nick Lyons Books, 1987.

Schwiebert, Ernest. *Trout*. New York: E. P. Dutton, Volumes I and II, 1978.

Skues, G. E. M. *Minor Tactics of the Chalk Stream and Kindred Studies*. London: A. & C. Black, 1910.

Skues, G. E. M. *Nymph Fishing for Chalk Stream Trout & Minor Tactics of the Chalk Stream*. London: Adam and Charles Black, 1974.

Smedley, Harold H. *Fly Patterns and Their Origins*. Muskegon, Michigan: Westshore Publications, 1950.

Solomon, Larry and Eric Leiser. *The Caddis and the Angler*. New York: Lyons & Burford, (revised edition) 1990.

Sosin, Mark and Lefty Kreh. *Practical Fishing Knots II*. New York: Lyons & Burford, 1991.

Stewart, W. C. *The Practical Angler*. London: A. & C. Black, Ltd., 1919.

Stolz, Judith and Judith Schnell, editors. *Trout*. Harrisburg, Pennsylvania: Stackpole Books, 1991.

Swisher, Doug and Carl Richards. *Emergers*. New York: Lyons & Burford, 1991.

Swisher, Doug and Carl Richards. *Selective Trout*. New York: Crown Publishers, Inc., 1971; New York: Nick Lyons Books, 1983.

Talleur, Dick. *The Versatile Fly Tyer*. New York: Lyons & Burford, 1990.

Taverner, Eric. *Fly-Tying For Salmon*. London: Seeley & Co. Ltd., 1942.

Thompson, Gerald, Jennifer Coldrez, and George Bernard. *The Pond*. London: William Collins Sons & Company Ltd., 1984.

Veniard, John. *Fly-dressing Materials*. Illustrated by Donald Downs. London: Adam and Charles Black, 1977.

Walton, Izaak. *The Complete Angler*. London: John Hawkins of Twickenham (second edition), 1766.

Ward, J. V. *Aquatic Insect Ecology: Biology and Habitat*. New York: John Wiley & Sons, Inc., 1992.

Wiggins, Glenn B. *Larvae of North American Caddisfly Genera (Trichoptera)*. Toronto: University of Toronto Press, 1978.

Wigglesworth, V. B. *Insect Physiology*. London: Chapman and Hall, Limited, (seventh edition) 1974.

Willers, W. B. *Trout Biology: An Angler's Guide*. Madison, Wisconsin: The University of Wisconsin Press, 1981; reprinted by Lyons & Burford, 1988.

Wilson, Dermot. *Fishing the Dry Fly*. London: A. & C. Black, Limited, 1970.

Woolley, Roger. *Modern Trout Fly Dressing*. London: The Fishing Gazette, 1932.

Wright, Leonard M., Jr. *Fishing the Dry Fly as a Living Insect*. New York: Nick Lyons Books, 1988.

Wright, Leonard M., Jr. *The Ways of Trout*. New York: Nick Lyons Books/Winchester Press, 1985.

$\mathcal{H}$ook Test Graphs

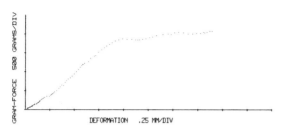 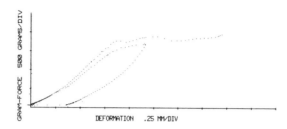

DAIICHI (ORVIS) 1100 SIZE 18: Traditional Dry Fly, Wide gap, Oversized Down Eye, Perfect Bend, 1X fine, Mini-Barb, Bronzed, Orvis Big Eye

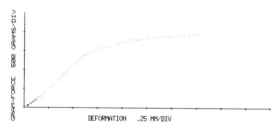 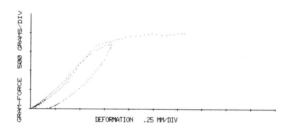

DAIICHI (ORVIS) 1100 SIZE 20: Traditional Dry Fly, Wide gap, Oversized Down Eye, Perfect Bend, 1X fine, Mini-Barb, Bronzed, Orvis Big Eye

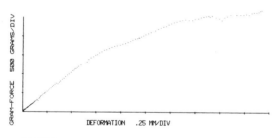 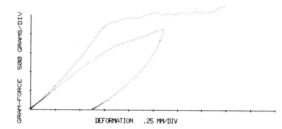

DAIICHI 1140   SIZE 18: Wets & Dries, Scuds, Midge Pupae & Micro-Caddis, 1X Fine, Continuous Bend 20°, Up Eye, 1X Short Shank, Forged, Reversed

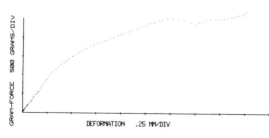 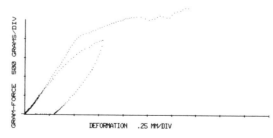

DAIICHI 1140   SIZE 20: Wets & Dries, Scuds, Midge Pupae & Micro-Caddis, 1X Fine, Continuous Bend 20°, Up Eye, 1X Short Shank, Forged, Reversed

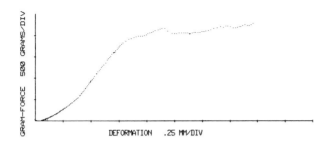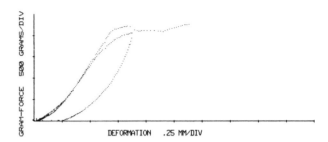

DAIICHI 1180 SIZE 18: Traditional Dry Fly, Round Bend, Down Eye, Standard Shank, Mini-Barb, Bronzed

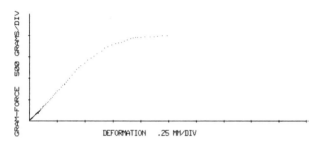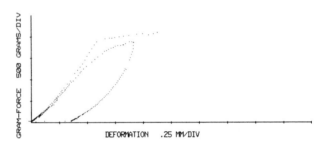

DAIICHI 1180 SIZE 20: Traditional Dry Fly, Round Bend, Down Eye, Standard Shank, Mini-Barb, Bronzed

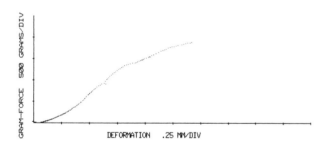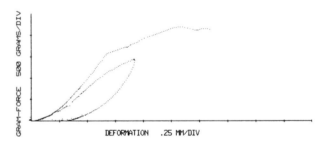

DAIICHI 1190 SIZE 18: Dry Fly, Catch & Release Barbless, Round Bend, Down Eye, Standard Shank

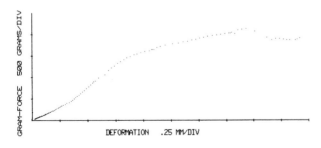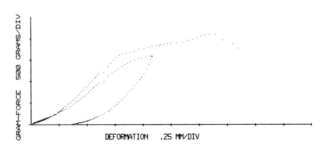

DAIICHI 1310 SIZE 18: Traditional Dry Fly & Caddis, Round Bend, Turned-Down Eye, 1X Long Shank, Forged, Bronzed

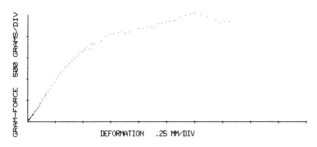 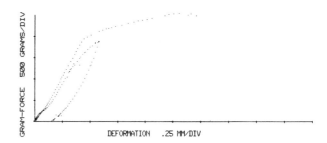

DAIICHI 1330   SIZE 18: Dries, Tricos & Midges, 1X Short Shank, Up Eye, Round Bend, Bronzed

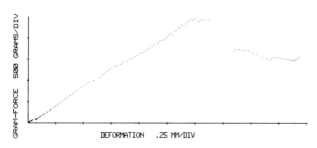 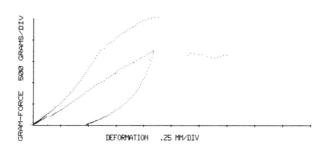

DAIICHI 1480   SIZE 18: Dries, Midges, Spiders & Variants, Limerick Bend, Straight Eye, 1X Fine, 2X Short, Bronzed, Mini-Barb

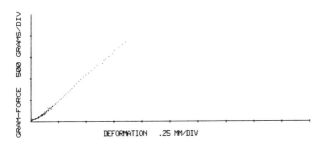 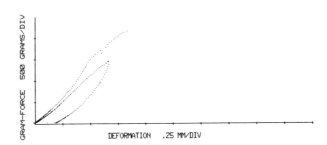

DAIICHI 1480   SIZE 20: Dries, Midges, Spiders & Variants, Limerick Bend, Straight Eye, 1X Fine, 2X Short, Bronzed, Mini-Barb

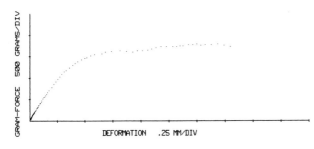 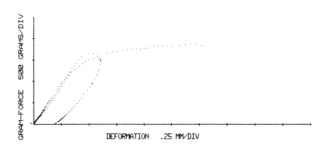

DAIICHI 1640   SIZE 20: Dries, Caddis, Spiders, Tricos & Extended-Bodies, Round Bend, Straight Eye, Reversed, Forged, 1X Short Shank

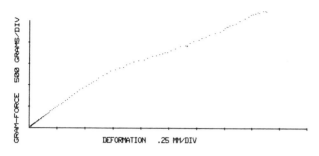
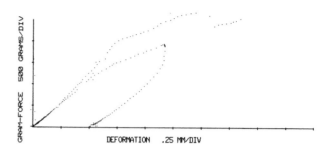

DAIICHI J220 SIZE 20: Emergers, Shrimp & Nymphs, Wide Gap, Offset Bend, Contoured Down Eye, Medium Weight

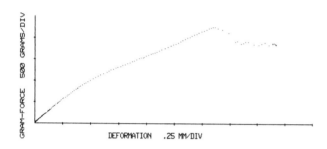
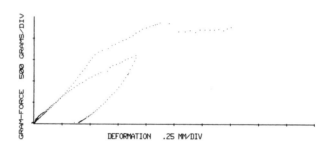

DAIICHI J220 SIZE 24: Emergers, Shrimp & Nymphs, Wide Gap, Offset Bend, Contoured Down Eye, Medium Weight, Bronzed

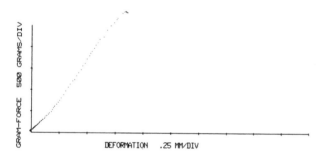
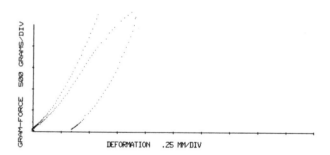

MUSTAD 7957B SIZE 18: Nymphs & Caddis, Hollow Point Viking, Forged, Tapered Down Eye, Bronzed, Long Shank, Moderately Heavier Version of 94840

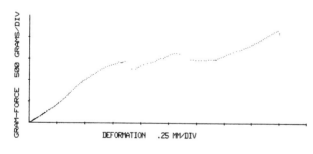
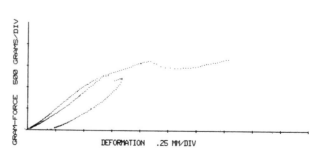

MUSTAD 94833 SIZE 18: Dries, Hollow-Point Viking, Straight, Forged, Tapered Down Eye, 3X Fine Wire, Bronzed

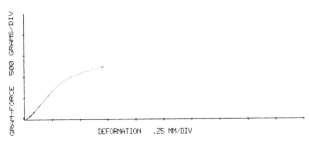
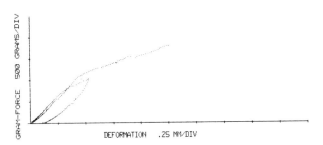

MUSTAD 94833 SIZE 20: Dries, Hollow-Point Viking, Straight, Forged, Tapered Down Eye, 3X Fine Wire, Bronzed

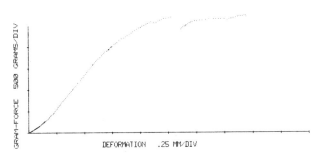
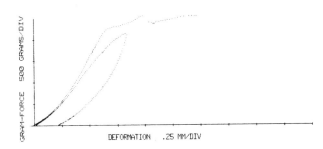

MUSTAD 94840 SIZE 18: Dries, Hollow-Point Viking, Perfect Bend, X-Fine Wire, Forged, Straight, Tapered Down Eye, Bronzed

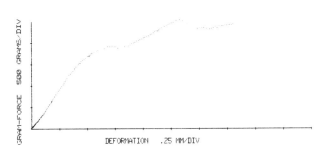
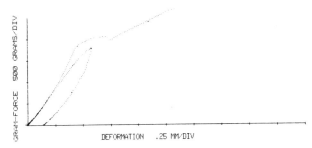

MUSTAD 94840 SIZE 20: Dries, Hollow-point Viking, Perfect bend, X-Fine Wire, Forged, Straight, Tapered Down Eye, Bronzed

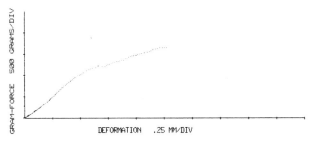
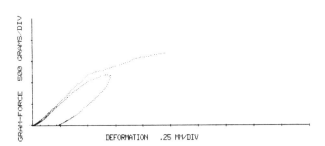

MUSTAD 94840 SIZE 22: Dries, Hollow-Point Viking, Perfect Bend, X-Fine Wire, Forged, Straight, Tapered Down Eye, Bronzed

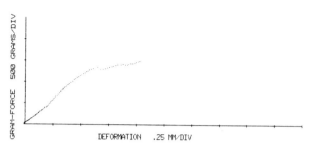
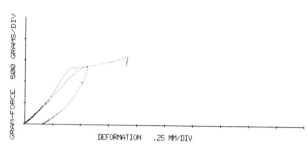

MUSTAD 94840 SIZE 24: Dries, Hollow-Point Viking, Perfect Bend, X-Fine Wire, Forged, Straight, Tapered Down Eye, Bronzed

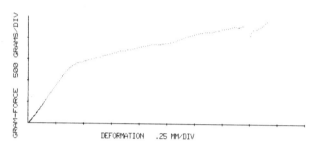
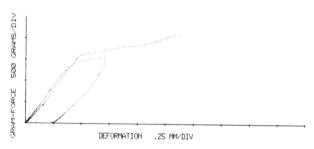

MUSTAD 94842 SIZE 18: Dries, Hollow-Point Viking, Straight, Forged, Tapered Up Eye, X-Fine Wire, Bronzed, Up Eye Version of 94840

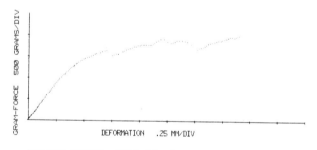
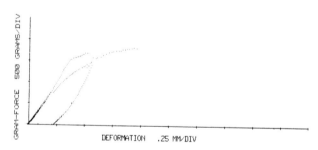

MUSTAD 94842 SIZE 20: Dries, Hollow-Point Viking, Straight, Forged, Tapered Up Eye, X-Fine Wire, Bronzed, Up Eye Version of 94840

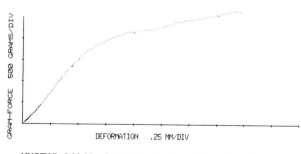
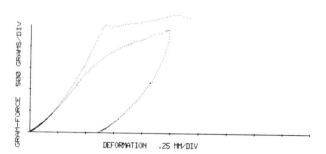

MUSTAD 94845 SIZE 18: Dries & Nymphs, Barbless, Forged, Round, Tapered Down Eye, Regular Wire, Bronzed, Barbless Version of 94840

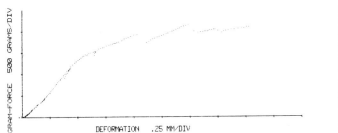
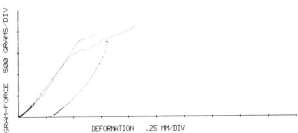

MUSTAD 94859 SIZE 18: Dries & Midge Pupae, Forged, Round, Straight Eye, X-Fine Wire, Bronzed

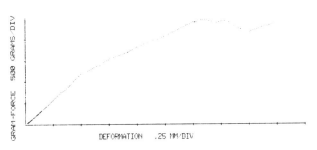
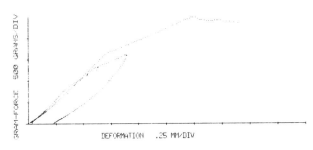

MUSTAD AC80000BR SIZE 18: Dries, Straight, Forged, Small Barb, Turned Down 30° Small Ball Eye, Bronzed

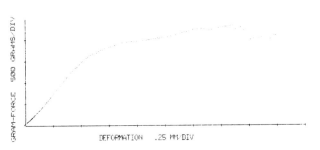
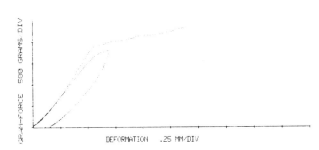

MUSTAD AC80000BR SIZE 20: Dries, Straight, Forged, Small Barb, Turned Down 30° Small Ball Eye, Bronzed

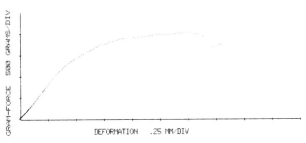
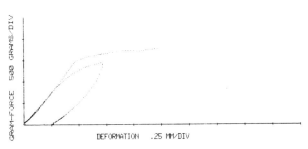

MUSTAD AC80000BR SIZE 22: Dries, Straight, Forged, Small Barb, Turned Down 30° Small Ball Eye, Bronzed

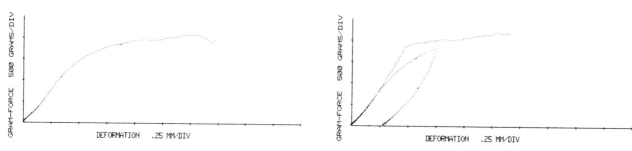

MUSTAD AC80000BR   SIZE 24: Dries, Straight, Forged, Small Barb, Turned Down 30° Small Ball Eye, Bronzed

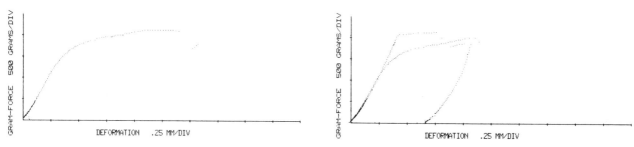

MUSTAD AC80000BR   SIZE 26: Dries, Straight, Forged, Small Barb, Turned Down 30° Small Ball Eye, Bronzed

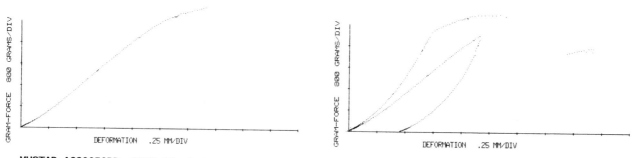

MUSTAD AC80050BR   SIZE 18: Dries, Straight, Forged, Small Barb, Small Ball Eye

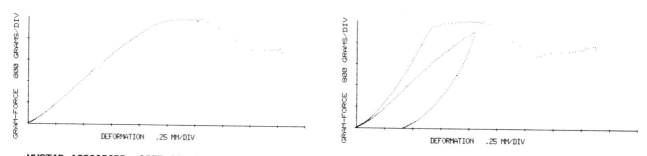

MUSTAD AC80050BR   SIZE 20: Dries, Straight, Forged, Small Barb, Small Ball Eye

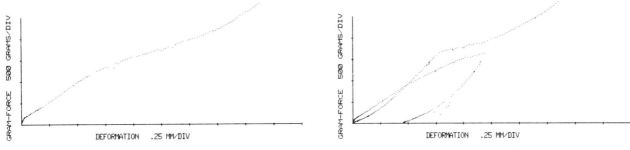

MUSTAD AC80100BR SIZE 20: Dries, Reversed 10°, Forged, Turned Down 30°, Small Ball Eye, Bronzed, Small Barb

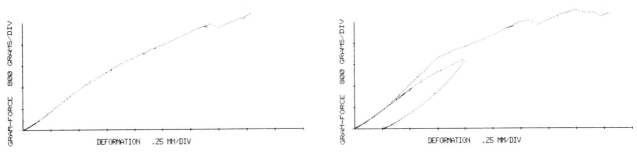

MUSTAD AC80200BR SIZE 18: Shrimp & Caddis Pupae, Reversed 15°, Turned Down 30°, Small Ball Eye, Bronzed, 2X Strong, Small Barb

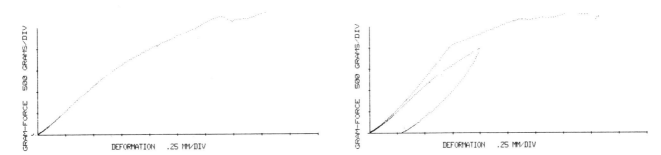

MUSTAD AC80250BR SIZE 18: Shrimp & Caddis Pupae, Forged, Reversed 15°, Turned Down 30°, Small Ball Eye, Bronzed, Small Barb

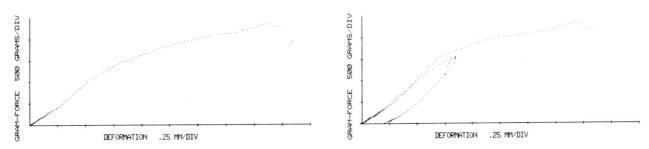

ORVIS JA4641 SIZE 18: Dries, Big Eye, 50% Increased Eye Diameter, Ring Eye, Perfect Bend, Wide Gap, Needle Point, Whisker Barb, Bronzed

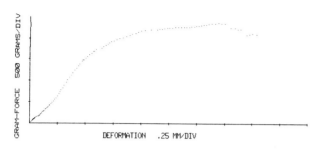
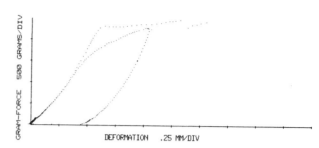

ORVIS JA4641 SIZE 20: Dries, Big Eye, 50% Increased Eye Diameter, Ring Eye, Perfect Bend, Wide Gap, Needle Point, Whisker Barb, Bronzed

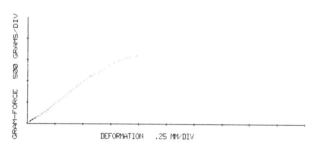
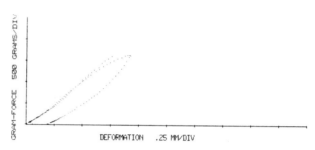

PARTRIDGE E1AY SIZE 18: Dries, Long Shank, 4X Fine Wire, Redditch Sproat Bend, Bronzed

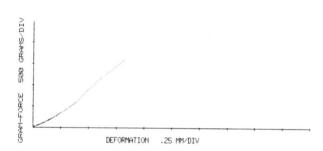
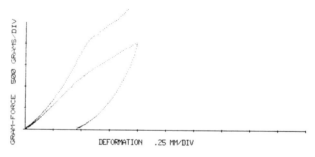

PARTRIDGE J1A SIZE 18: Wets, Limerick Bend, Standard Weight, Down Eye, Medium Barb, Bronzed

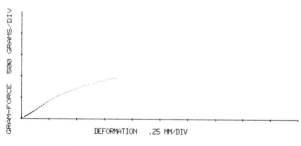
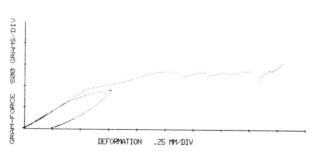

PARTRIDGE K1A SIZE 24: Marinaro Midge, Dries & Nymphs, 4X Fine Wire, Captain Hamilton Bend, Offset, Down Eye, Small Barb, Wide Gap, Bronzed

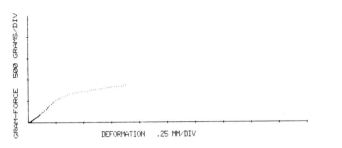
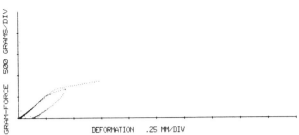

PARTRIDGE K1A SIZE 28: Marinaro Midge, Dries & Nymphs, 4X fine wire, Captain Hamilton Bend, Offset, Down Eye, Bronzed, Small Barb, Wide Gap

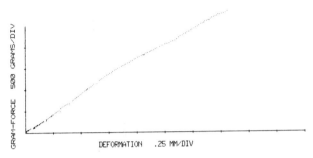
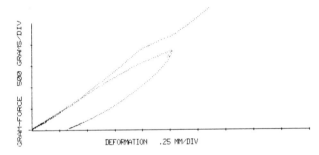

PARTRIDGE K4A SIZE 18: Veniard Shrimp & Larvae, Medium Weight Wire, Round Shank, Down Eye, Offset Bend

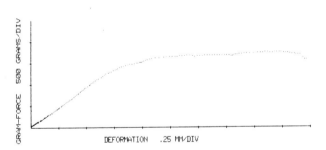
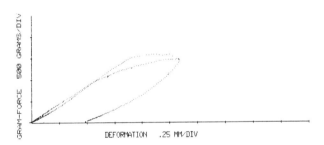

PARTRIDGE L3A   SIZE 18: Dries, Captain Hamilton Perfect Bend, Light Wire, Wide Gap, Bronzed, Short Spear; This model has four weights: heavy (L1A), medium (L2A), light (L3A) and feather (L4A)

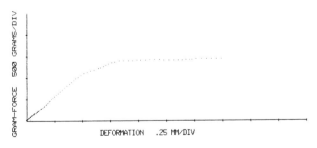
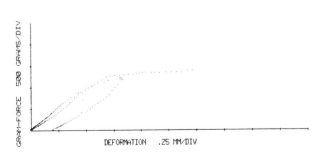

PARTRIDGE L3A   SIZE 20: Dries, Captain Hamilton Perfect Bend, Light Wire, Wide Gap, Bronzed, Short Spear; This model has four weights: heavy (L1A), medium (L2A), light (L3A) and feather (L4A)

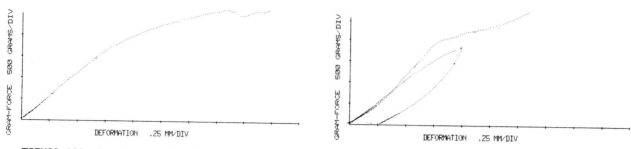

TIEMCO 100   SIZE 18: Dries, Down Eye, 1X Fine, Wide Gap, Forged, Bronzed

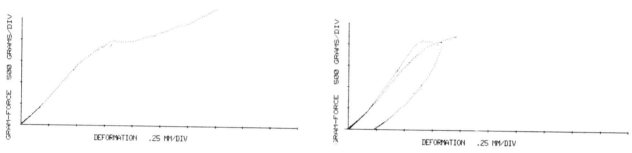

TIEMCO 100   SIZE 20: Dries, Down Eye, 1X Fine, Wide Gap, Forged, Bronzed

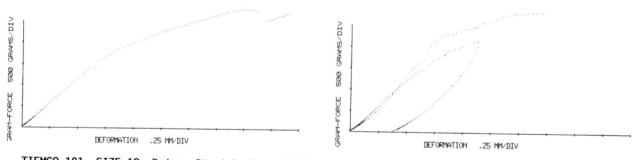

TIEMCO 101   SIZE 18: Dries, Straight Eye, 1X Fine, Wide Gap, Forged, Bronzed

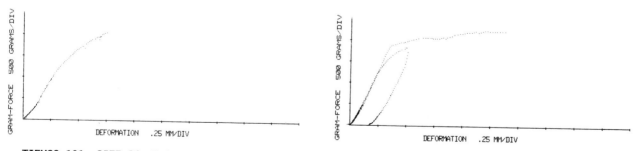

TIEMCO 101   SIZE 26: Dries, Straight Eye, 1X Fine, Wide Gap, Forged, Bronzed

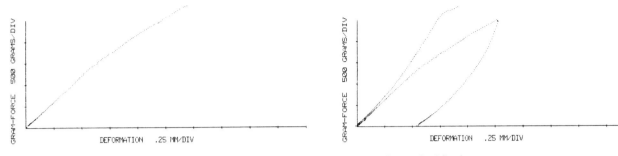

TIEMCO 102Y SIZE 19: Dries, Down Eye, 1X Fine, Wide Gap, Forged, Black

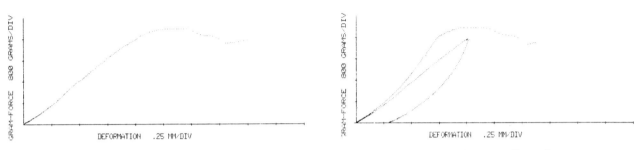

TIEMCO 200R SIZE 18: Dries & Nymphs, Straight Eye, 3X Long, Standard Wire, Forged, Bronzed

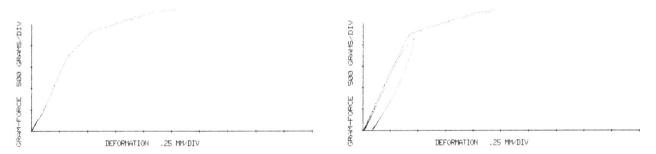

TIEMCO 500U SIZE 18: Tricos & Midges, Up Eye, 2X Short, Standard Wire, Straight Point, Forged, Bronzed

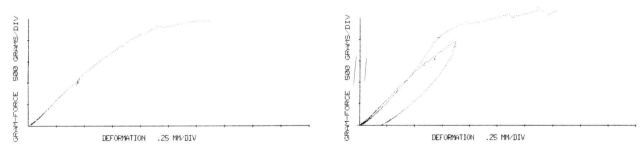

TIEMCO 900BL SIZE 18: Dries, Down Eye, 1X Wide, Semi-Dropped Point, 1X Fine, Barbless, Forged, Black

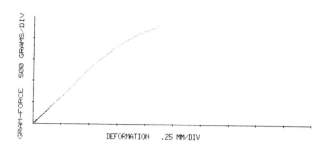
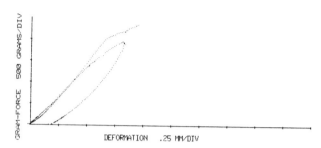

TIEMCO 921 SIZE 18: Dries, Down Eye, 2X Short, Sproat Bend, 1X Fine, Forged

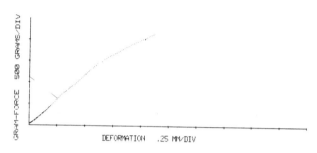
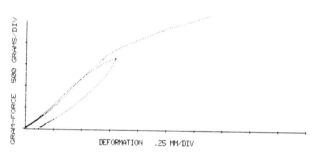

TIEMCO 947BL SIZE 18: Nymphs, Down Eye, Barbless, Variable Long Shank, Turned-Up Shank, Forged, Bronzed

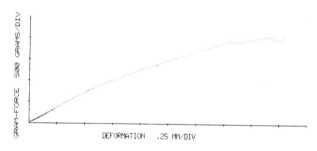
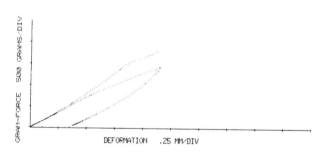

TIEMCO 2487 SIZE 18: Scuds, Pupae & Floating Nymphs, 2X Wide, 2X Short, Down Eye, Fine Wire, Reversed, Forged, Bronzed

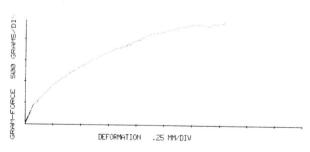
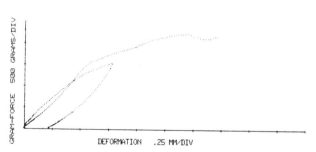

TIEMCO 2487 SIZE 22: Scuds, Pupae & Floating Nymphs, 2X Wide, 2X Short, Down Eye, Fine Wire, Reversed, Forged, Bronzed

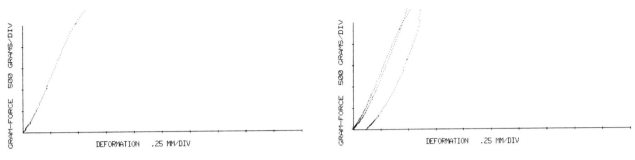

TIEMCO 3761 SIZE 18: Wets & Nymphs, 1X Long, 1X Heavy

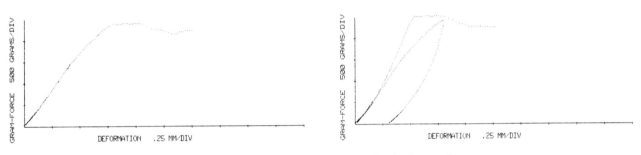

TIEMCO 5210 SIZE 18: Dries, 1X Fine, Down Eye, Perfect Bend, Bronzed

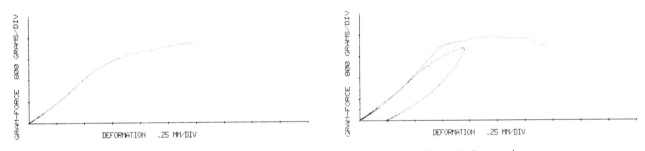

TIEMCO 5262 SIZE 18: Nymphs, Down Eye, 2X Heavy, Perfect Bend, Forged, Bronzed

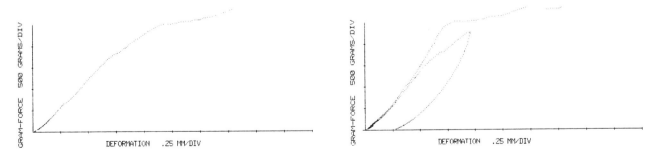

TIEMCO 9300 SIZE 18: Wets & Dries, Down Eye, 1X Heavy Wire, Forged, O'Shaughnessy Point

*F*ly Line Mass Graphs

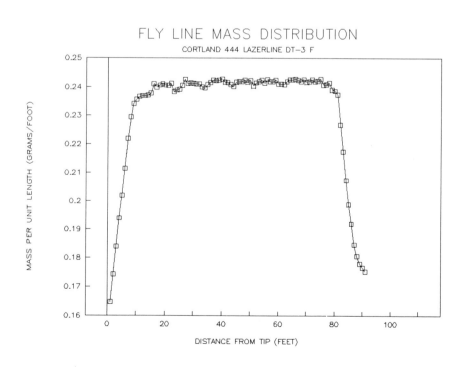

FLY LINE MASS DISTRIBUTION
CORTLAND 444 LAZERLINE

DT—3 F   + ° WF—3 F

FLY LINE MASS DISTRIBUTION
CORTLAND 444 LAZERLINE DT—3 F

FLY LINE MASS DISTRIBUTION

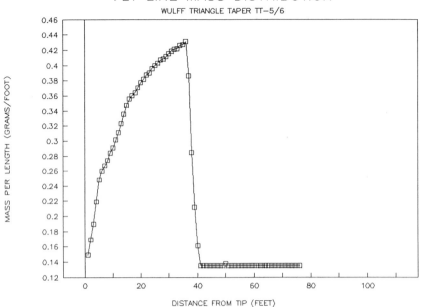

FLY LINE MASS DISTRIBUTION

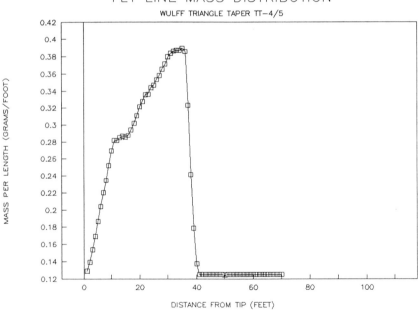

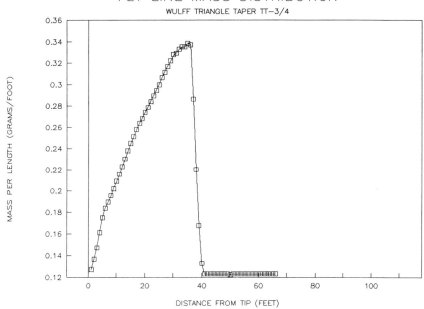

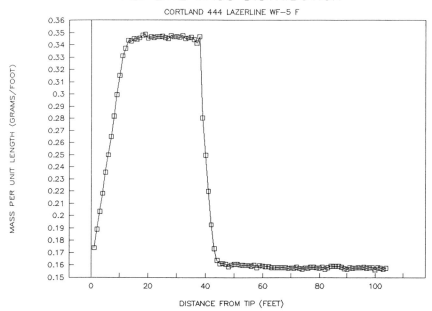

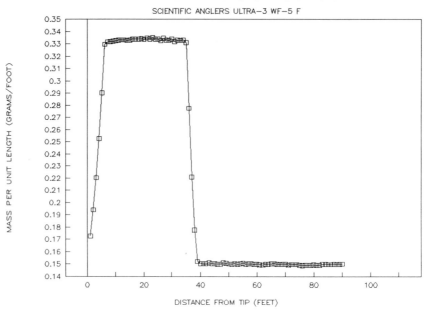

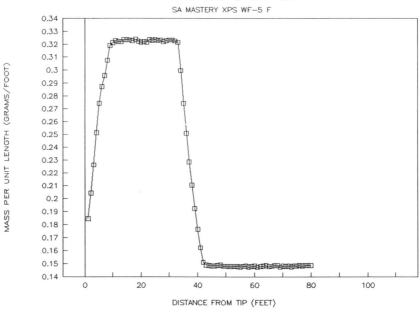

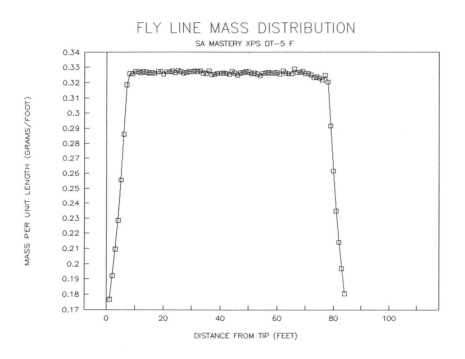

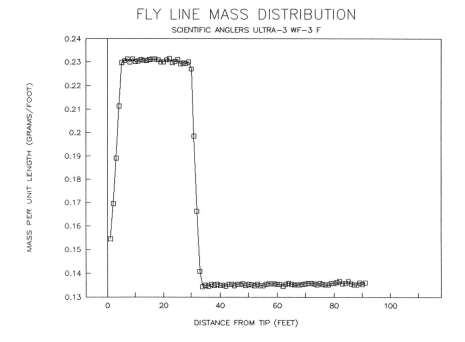

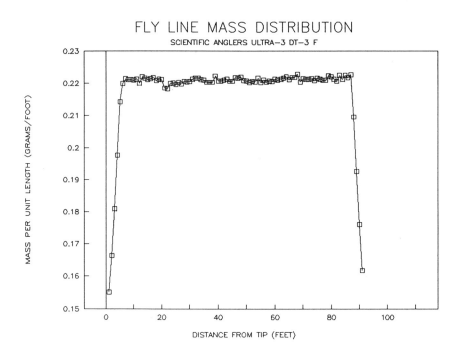

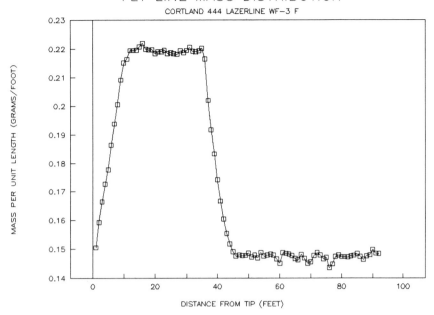

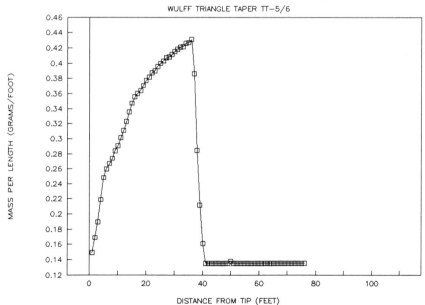

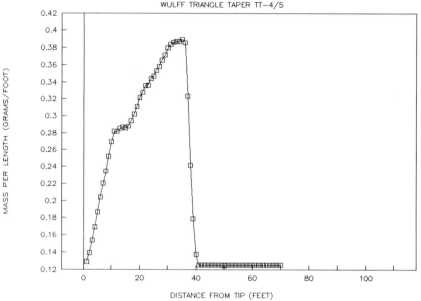

FLY LINE MASS DISTRIBUTION

WULFF TRIANGLE TAPER TT-4/5

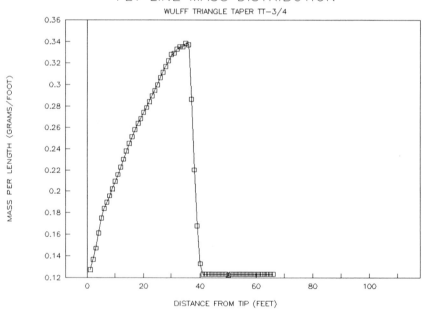

FLY LINE MASS DISTRIBUTION

WULFF TRIANGLE TAPER TT-3/4

FLY LINE MASS DISTRIBUTION

CORTLAND 444 LAZERLINE WF–5 F

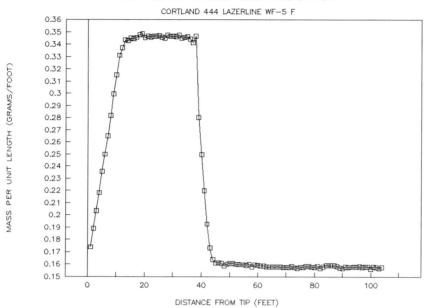

FLY LINE MASS DISTRIBUTION

SCIENTIFIC ANGLERS ULTRA–3 WF–5 F

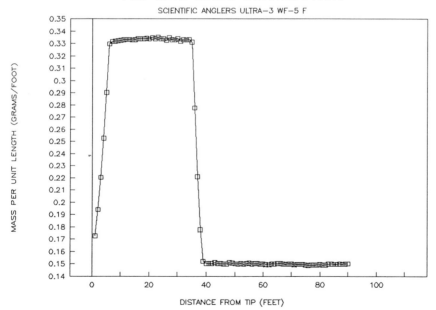

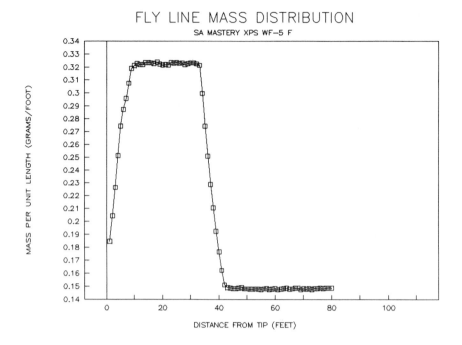

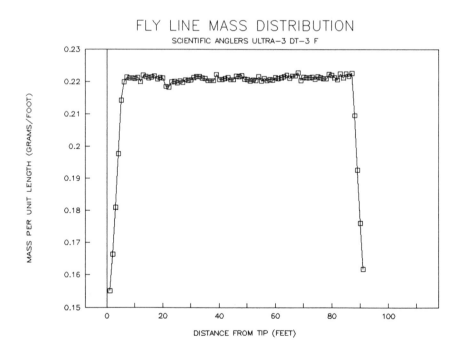

FLY LINE MASS DISTRIBUTION

SA MASTERY XPS DT—5 F

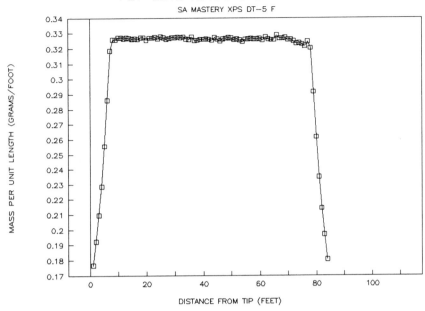

FLY LINE MASS DISTRIBUTION

SCIENTIFIC ANGLERS ULTRA—3 WF—3 F

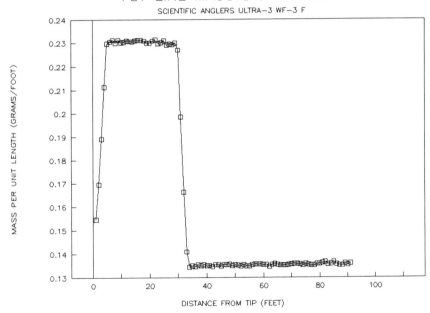

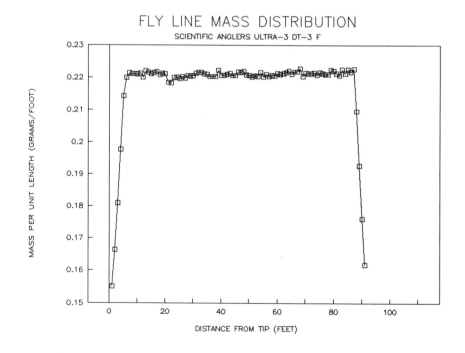

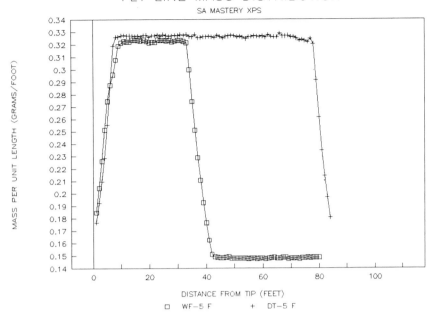

FLY LINE MASS DISTRIBUTION
SA MASTERY XPS

A P P E N D I X

C

Hook Dimension and Test Tables

HOOK DIMENSION TABLE

HOOK CODE–SIZE	MASS	LENGTH	GAP	SHANK LENGTH	WIRE DIAMETER
DAIICHI–1100–18	13.82	8.92	3	6.51	0.413
DAIICHI–1100–20	11.07	7.93	2.49	5.95	0.375
DAIICHI–1100–22	9.29	6.82	2.11	5.16	0.38
DAIICHI–1100–24	6.62	6.09	1.94	4.46	0.329
DAIICHI–1140–18	9.49	6.95	2.9	4.56	0.381
DAIICHI–1140–20	7.68	5.75	2.35	3	0.355
DAIICHI–1140–22	4.38	4.9	1.9	2.6	0.283
DAIICHI–1180–18	12.26	8.64	2.3	6.66	0.39
DAIICHI–1180–20	9	7.2	2.11	5.1	0.354
DAIICHI–1180–22	6.85	6.75	1.75	5	0.326
DAIICHI–1190–18	11.23	8.6	2.62	6.2	0.372
DAIICHI–1310–18	9.06	7.45	2.12	4.6	0.353
DAIICHI–1310–20	9	7.4	2.4	5.24	0.325
DAIICHI–1310–22	7.22	6	1.6	4.52	0.344
DAIICHI–1330–18	10.11	7.6	2.33	5.4	0.345
DAIICHI–1330–20	7.86	6.6	1.95	4.7	0.334
DAIICHI–1330–22	6.09	6.13	1.55	4.3	0.322
DAIICHI–1330–24	5.37	5.32	1.14	3.4	0.321
DAIICHI–1480–18	7.37	7.3	2.1	4.8	0.33
DAIICHI–1480–20	6.03	6.5	1.9	4.08	0.309
DAIICHI–1480–22	5.03	6	1.66	3.65	0.291
DAIICHI–1480–24	4.59	5.45	1.46	3.75	0.294
DAIICHI–1640–18	9.04	7.22	2.54	5	0.357
DAIICHI–1640–20	7.72	5.9	1.94	3.9	0.377
DAIICHI–1710–18	16.39	9.8	2.36	6.75	0.408
DAIICHI–J220–20	9.94	6.2	2.92	4.48	0.372
DAIICHI–J220–22	7.97	5.5	2.35	3.44	0.361
DAIICHI–J220–24	5.59	5.1	2	2.75	0.335
MUSTAD–3906B–18	15.46	8.54	2.31	6.09	0.432
MUSTAD–3906B–20	13.38	7.2	2	3.5	0.33
MUSTAD–7957B–18	13.87	7.95	2.42	5	0.407
MUSTAD–7957B–20	8.72	6.54	1.92	4.4	0.358
MUSTAD–37160–18	37.75	12.25	4.07	8.7	0.534
MUSTAD–37160–20	28.12	10.46	3.46	7.5	0.508
MUSTAD–79580–18	16.5	11.55	2.43	8.54	0.407
MUSTAD–79703BR–18	11.3	8.77	2.42	6.43	0.357
MUSTAD–79703BR–20	6.81	7.12	2.06	4.88	0.32
MUSTAD–79709BR–18	10.54	8.6	2.2	6.32	0.38
MUSTAD–79709BR–20	9.33	7.05	2.03	5.03	0.35
MUSTAD–79718BR–18	8	8.86	2.4	6.6	0.314
MUSTAD–94833–18	9.21	8.56	2.34	6	0.33

All measurements are in milligrams of millimeters.

HOOK DIMENSION TABLE

HOOK CODE-SIZE	MASS	LENGTH	GAP	SHANK LENGTH	WIRE DIAMETER
MUSTAD-94833-20	8.4	7.1	2.01	5.33	0.319
MUSTAD-94833-22	6.16	6.35	1.6	4.54	0.294
MUSTAD-94840-18	11.44	8.7	2.17	6.08	0.383
MUSTAD-94840-20	8.64	7.32	1.86	5.6	0.36
MUSTAD-94840-22	6.71	6.35	1.65	4.6	0.304
MUSTAD-94840-24	5.62	5.78	1.6	4.33	0.29
MUSTAD-94842-18	10.4	8.75	2.18	6.08	0.355
MUSTAD-94842-20	7.61	7.22	2.1	5.06	0.323
MUSTAD-94842-24	5.56	5.87	1.6	4.12	0.3
MUSTAD-94845-18	11.01	8.88	2.02	6.57	0.3
MUSTAD-94845-20	7.49	7.08	1.8	5.48	0.325
MUSTAD-94845-22	6.9	6.48	1.68	4.65	0.333
MUSTAD-94859-18	10.52	8.9	2.22	6.45	0.357
MUSTAD-94859-22	6.34	6.36	1.7	4.45	0.315
MUSTAD-94860-24	5.62	5.6	2	4	0.32
MUSTAD-94863-20	8.64	7.4	2	5	0.33
MUSTAD-AC80000BR-18	13.64	9.1	3.13	6.39	0.434
MUSTAD-AC80000BR-20	10.97	7.97	2.42	5.45	0.364
MUSTAD-AC80000BR-22	8.4	7.12	2.16	5.1	0.316
MUSTAD-AC80000BR-24	8.24	6.42	2.1	4.9	0.353
MUSTAD-AC80000BR-26	6.6	5.65	1.64	4.2	0.34
MUSTAD-AC80050BR-18	19.04	10.86	2.84	8.08	0.437
MUSTAD-AC80050BR-20	15.33	8.86	2.7	6.6	0.398
MUSTAD-AC80050BR-22	11.36	7.56	1.97	5.4	0.435
MUSTAD-AC80100BR-20	10.32	5.92	2.92	4.3	0.389
MUSTAD-AC80100BR-22	8.51	5.58	2.44	3.93	0.367
MUSTAD-AC80100BR-24	6.2	5.25	2.05	3.51	0.336
MUSTAD-AC80100BR-26	5	4.91	1.86	3.39	0.305
MUSTAD-AC80200BR-18	18.52	7.12	3.01	4.92	0.506
MUSTAD-AC80250BR-18	13.49	6.6	3.11	5	0.425
MUSTAD-AC80250BR-20	12.25	6.02	2.49	4.66	0.431
MUSTAD-AC80250BR-22	8.52	5.6	2.4	3.68	0.374
ORVIS-4641-18	13.71	8.55	2.8	6.3	0.397
ORVIS-4641-20	10.33	7.36	2.4	4.9	0.378
ORVIS-4641-22	8.59	6.6	2.15	4.6	0.4
ORVIS-8988-18	9.73	6.87	2.68	5.11	0.367
PARTRIDGE-B-18	25.66	9.5	4.25	5	0.512
PARTRIDGE-B-20	9.38	5.93	2.91	2.8	0.393
PARTRIDGE-CS21-18	16.29	9.8	3.5	7.06	0.413
PARTRIDGE-CS21-20	12.03	7.8	2.94	6.15	0.384
PARTRIDGE-CS20-18	12.23	8.5	3	6.45	0.356

HOOK DIMENSION TABLE

HOOK CODE–SIZE	MASS	LENGTH	GAP	SHANK LENGTH	WIRE DIAMETER
PARTRIDGE–E1AY–18	13.25	9.95	2.8	7.15	0.388
PARTRIDGE–E6AY–20	8.61	7.71	2.7	5.08	0.338
PARTRIDGE–GRS7MMB–20	20.96	12	3.9	9	0.437
PARTRIDGE–J1A–18	8.96	7.09	2.34	5	0.357
PARTRIDGE–K1A–20	7.7	6.92	2.33	5	0.33
PARTRIDGE–K1A–22	6.02	6.35	2.33	4	0.31
PARTRIDGE–K1A–24	5.68	5.55	2.19	3.5	0.31
PARTRIDGE–K1A–26	5.1	5.17	2.15	3	0.306
PARTRIDGE–K1A–28	3.79	4.4	1.64	3.25	0.289
PARTRIDGE–K2B–18	21.04	10.2	3.64	6.6	0.463
PARTRIDGE–K3A–18	22.68	12.05	3.6	8.6	0.424
PARTRIDGE–K4A–18	14.77	7.34	3.55	5.4	0.434
PARTRIDGE–K12ST–18	29.48	15.6	4.32	11.8	0.466
PARTRIDGE–K12ST–20	23.83	14.5	3.75	11.58	0.441
PARTRIDGE–K12ST–22	17.39	13.38	3.64	10.6	0.382
PARTRIDGE–L2A–20	11.1	7	2.75	4.5	0.38
PARTRIDGE–L3A–18	12.98	8.5	3.3	6	0.337
PARTRIDGE–L3A–20	8.44	7.16	2.75	5.12	0.329
PARTRIDGE–L3A–22	5.81	6.1	2.8	5	0.316
PARTRIDGE–L3AY–18	9.73	8.5	3	6	0.337
PARTRIDGE–L4A–18	14	8.8	3.4	6	0.329
TIEMCO–100–18	14.54	9.34	3.02	6.66	0.4
TIEMCO–100–20	11.62	8	2.52	5.56	0.38
TIEMCO–100–22	8.98	7.1	2	4.53	0.367
TIEMCO–100–24	6.42	6.24	1.87	4	0.32
TIEMCO–100–26	5.66	5.74	1.47	3.63	0.32
TIEMCO–101–18	14.64	9.6	2.77	6.73	0.403
TIEMCO–101–20	11.3	8.3	2.33	5.55	0.385
TIEMCO–101–22	9.06	7.54	2.12	5.15	0.36
TIEMCO–101–24	6.41	6.6	2	4.85	0.315
TIEMCO–101–26	5.02	6	1.64	4.46	0.31
TIEMCO–102Y–17	17.88	9.96	3.8	6.71	0.426
TIEMCO–102Y–19	13.34	8.32	2.82	5.7	0.41
TIEMCO–200–18	17.9	10.88	2.64	8.01	0.395
TIEMCO–200–20	13.95	8.97	2.4	6.4	0.381
TIEMCO–200–22	10.1	7.2	2.15	5	0.374
TIEMCO–205BL–18	26.64	12.1	3.8	9.15	0.451
TIEMCO–205BL–20	19.51	10.25	3.1	7.75	0.401
TIEMCO–500U–18	12.05	7.2	2.5	4.9	0.401
TIEMCO–500U–20	8.38	6.12	2	4	0.36
TIEMCO–500U–22	7.85	5.87	1.78	3.96	0.365
TIEMCO–501–20	9.36	6.6	2.1	4.4	0.386

HOOK DIMENSION TABLE

HOOK CODE-SIZE	MASS	LENGTH	GAP	SHANK LENGTH	WIRE DIAMETER
TIEMCO-501-22	7.79	5.8	1.89	3.6	0.363
TIEMCO-501-24	5.42	5.64	1.64	3.7	0.312
TIEMCO-900BL-18	12.04	8.43	2.5	5.85	0.384
TIEMCO-900BL-20	9.13	7.07	2.25	4.75	0.358
TIEMCO-900BL-22	6.55	6.23	1.9	4.48	0.323
TIEMCO-900BL-24	5.66	5.69	1.73	4.29	0.319
TIEMCO-921-18	11.03	7.27	2.45	5.01	0.387
TIEMCO-921-20	8.3	6.36	2.14	4.6	0.353
TIEMCO-947BL-18	15.68	10.53	3.03	7.05	0.4
TIEMCO-947BL-20	11.46	8.63	2.33	6.32	0.372
TIEMCO-2457-18	16.06	7.14	2.87	4.93	0.454
TIEMCO-2487-18	12.02	6.75	2.92	4.75	0.38
TIEMCO-2487-20	9.85	6.3	2.48	4.36	0.37
TIEMCO-2487-22	8.27	5.52	2.2	3.95	0.364
TIEMCO-3761-18	15.16	9.03	2.2	6.34	0.43
TIEMCO-3761-20	12.61	8.18	2.07	5.67	0.403
TIEMCO-3769-18	12.53	6.9	2.19	4.75	0.43
TIEMCO-5210-18	9.99	8.07	2.26	6.24	0.365
TIEMCO-5210-20	6.59	6.9	1.56	5.07	0.32
TIEMCO-5230-18	7.98	8.12	2.3	6.5	0.32
TIEMCO-5262-18	16.74	9.95	2.5	7.55	0.43
TIEMCO-5263-18	16.06	10.87	2.5	8.06	0.43
TIEMCO-9300-18	13.13	8.4	2.5	5.63	0.4
TIEMCO-9300-20	10.42	7.21	2.15	5	0.38

HOOK TEST TABLE

HOOK CODE-SIZE	FORGED	G-FORCE SCALE	ELASTIC LIMIT	PLASTIC FLOW PERCENT	FORCE AT 45 DEGREES	LIMIT OF LINEAR PERFORMANCE	STIFFNESS COEFFICIENT	OPERATIVE FAILURE
DAIICHI–1100–18	N	500	500	9.6	1900	1250	20	1850
DAIICHI–1100–20	N	500			1750	1250	23	1700
DAIICHI–1140–18	F	500	500	22	1320	1320	18	1650
DAIICHI–1140–20	F	500	700	14	1500	1185	26	1600
DAIICHI–1140–22	F	500	500	(b) 23	1100	700	19	1000
DAIICHI–1180–18	N	500			2000	1650	24	1825
DAIICHI–1180–20	N	500	450	13	1400	1100	16	1350
DAIICHI–1190–18	N	500	200	(b) 15	1700	1150	16	1350
DAIICHI–1310–18	F	500	350	17	1750	1300	17	1600
DAIICHI–1330–18	N	500	250	15	2100	1200	39	1900
DAIICHI–1480–18	N	500	100	42	1300	2500	18	2500
DAIICHI–1480–20	N	500	100	(b) 28	1500	1700	29	1800
DAIICHI–1480–24	N	500	250	43	1610	1000	33	1050
DAIICHI–1640–20	F	500	(a) 300	(c) 17	1500	610	17	1250
DAIICHI–J220–20	N	500	700	21	1700	1000	19	1500
DAIICHI–J220–24	N	500	650	39	1500	890	20	
MUSTAD–3906B–18	N	500	500	20	1870	2300	20	2400
MUSTAD–7957B–18	F	500	500	17	2500	2500	33	>2500
MUSTAD–79703BR–18	F	500	400	14	1870	1660	27	1900
MUSTAD–79703BR–20	F	500	(a) 1300	(c) 12	1800	1450	34	1700
MUSTAD–79718BR–18	F	500			1250	1100	15	1125
MUSTAD–94833–18	F	500	100		1500	1000	20	1400
MUSTAD–94833–20	F	500			1200	750	16	1000
MUSTAD–94840–18	F	500	500	11	2000	1800	27	2500
MUSTAD–94840–20	F	500	1000	17	1910	1310	30	1700
MUSTAD–94840–22	F	500	500	(b) 12	1250	700	21	1200
MUSTAD–94840–24	F	500	500	(b) 13	1300	850	25	1340

HOOK TEST TABLE

HOOK CODE-SIZE	FORGED	G-FORCE SCALE	ELASTIC LIMIT	PLASTIC FLOW PERCENT	FORCE AT 45 DEGREES	LIMIT OF LINEAR PERFORMANCE	STIFFNESS COEFFICIENT	OPERATIVE FAILURE
MUSTAD-94842-18	F	500			1750	1150	36	1370
MUSTAD-94842-20	F	500	800	12	1500	1000	31	1325
MUSTAD-94845-18	F	500	660	12	2200	1360	32	1900
MUSTAD-94859-18	F	500			1810	1300	30	1500
MUSTAD-AC80000BR-18	F	500	1200	16	1800	1300	50	2450
MUSTAD-AC80000BR-20	F	500	875	9	1950	1500	28	1700
MUSTAD-AC80000BR-22	F	500	950	(b) 6.8	1880	1000	32	1450
MUSTAD-AC80000BR-24	F	500	950	21	1800	1110	14	1300
MUSTAD-AC80000BR-26	F	500	1300	13	1920	1100	44	1500
MUSTAD-AC80050BR-18	F	800	320	21	3600	3480	32	4000
MUSTAD-AC80050BR-20	F	800	320	20	3470	2730	34	3728
MUSTAD-AC80050BR-22	F	500	300	19	3200	2250	42	>2500
MUSTAD-AC80100BR-20	F	500		(c) 25	1900	1160	19	1500
MUSTAD-AC80200BR-18	N	800	960	21	3200	1650	31	3200
MUSTAD-AC80250BR-18	F	500	250	9	2330	1560	20	2000
MUSTAD-AC80250BR-20	F	500	300	16	2825	1800	31	2400
ORVIS-4641-18	N	500	650	(b) 12	1500	1000	20	1500
ORVIS-4641-20	N	500	1315	7	2310	1400	31	1600
ORVIS-4641-22	N	500			1660	1500	33	1660
PARTRIDGE-CS21-20	N	500			950	770	14	825
PARTRIDGE-E1AY-18	N	500	1000	10	1660	1200	19	1500
PARTRIDGE-J1A-18	N	500	200	36	1200	1500	19	1600
PARTRIDGE-K1A-24	N	500	600		900	500	20	800
PARTRIDGE-K1A-26	N	500	500	(b) 36	1160	800	16	1000
PARTRIDGE-K1A-28	N	500	600		700	500	20	610
PARTRIDGE-K4A-18	N	500	890	12	2100	2000	16	2000

HOOK TEST TABLE

HOOK CODE-SIZE	FORGED	G-FORCE SCALE	ELASTIC LIMIT	PLASTIC FLOW PERCENT	FORCE AT 45 DEGREES	LIMIT OF LINEAR PERFORMANCE	STIFFNESS COEFFICIENT	OPERATIVE FAILURE
PARTRIDGE-L3A-18	N	500		(c) 19	1700	1300	19	1500
PARTRIDGE-L3A-20	N	500			1310	1000	22	1170
PARTRIDGE-L3AY-18	N	500			900	600	12	750
TIEMCO-100-18	F	500		17	2200	1700	22	2100
TIEMCO-100-20	F	500	600	9	1950	1420	27	1950
TIEMCO-100-26	F	500	500	21	1910	1310	37	1750
TIEMCO-101-18	F	500		15	2250	1410	24	2000
TIEMCO-101-20	F	500			2400	1700	30	2100
TIEMCO-101-26	F	500	1300	10	1700	1315	47	1500
TIEMCO-102Y-17	F	500		16	1750	1300	16	1750
TIEMCO-102Y-19	F	500	500	24	2200	1410	25	>2000
TIEMCO-200-18	F	800	400	14	3200	2650	32	3440
TIEMCO-200-20	F	800	400	28	3360	2650	38	3200
TIEMCO-200-22	F	800	800	31	2720	1315	41	2400
TIEMCO-500U-18	F	500			2500	1650	53	2250
TIEMCO-501-20	F	500			2500	1660	54	2000
TIEMCO-900BL-18	F	500		(c) 10	2160	1250	25	2000
TIEMCO-900BL-20	F	500	1000	15	2000	1250	29	2000
TIEMCO-921-18	F	500	1170	8	1900	1320	26	2000
TIEMCO-921-20	F	500			2160	1400	36	2000
TIEMCO-947BL-18	F	500	1400	5	2110	1500	24	1700
TIEMCO-947BL-20	F	500	1500	4	2250	1750	35	2000
TIEMCO-2487-18	F	500	400	(b) 17	1600	800	14	1800
TIEMCO-2487-20	F	500	250	22	1810	1360	22	1700
TIEMCO-2487-22	F	500			1800	500	42	1500
TIEMCO-3761-18	N	500			2500	2410	55	2500
TIEMCO-3761-20	N	700	1400	6	3320	2632	51	2800

HOOK TEST TABLE

HOOK CODE-SIZE	FORGED	G-FORCE SCALE	ELASTIC LIMIT	PLASTIC FLOW PERCENT	FORCE AT 45 DEGREES	LIMIT OF LINEAR PERFORMANCE	STIFFNESS COEFFICIENT	OPERATIVE FAILURE
TIEMCO-5210-18	N	500	880	15	2300	1500	43	2300
TIEMCO-5210-20	N	500	200	(b) 11	1500	1000	29	1260
TIEMCO-5262-18	F	800	1600	14	2640	2080	34	2400
TIEMCO-9300-18	F	500	1110	8	2500	1750	25	1800
TIEMCO-9300-20	F	500			2310	1450	34	2000

NOTATIONS:
a INDICATES THAT THE CURVES CROSS, THEREFORE ELASTIC LIMIT CANNOT BE CALCULATED
b INDICATES THAT PLASTIC FLOW WAS CALCULATED AT 1000 GRAMS-FORCE
c INDICATES THAT CURVES CROSSED DUE TO STRESS FRACTURES OR GEOMETRY CHANGES
F = FORGED
N = NOT FORGED

*I*ndex